U.S. Fish & Wildlife Serv

Synopsis of the Biological Data on the Leatherback Sea Turtle (*Dermochelys coriacea*)

Biological Technical Publication
BTP-R4015-2012

U.S. Fish & Wildlife Service

Synopsis of the Biological Data on the Leatherback Sea Turtle (*Dermochelys coriacea*)

Biological Technical Publication
BTP-R4015-2012

Karen L. Eckert[1]
Bryan P. Wallace[2]
John G. Frazier[3]
Scott A. Eckert[4]
Peter C.H. Pritchard[5]

[1] Wider Caribbean Sea Turtle Conservation Network, Ballwin, MO
[2] Conservation International, Arlington, VA
[3] Smithsonian Institution, Front Royal, VA
[4] Principia College, Elsah, IL
[5] Chelonian Research Institute, Oviedo, FL

Author Contact Information:

Karen L. Eckert, Ph.D.
Wider Caribbean Sea Turtle Conservation Network (WIDECAST)
1348 Rusticview Drive
Ballwin, Missouri 63011
Phone: (314) 954-8571
E-mail: keckert@widecast.org

Bryan P. Wallace, Ph.D.
Sea Turtle Flagship Program
Conservation International
2011 Crystal Drive
Suite 500
Arlington, Virginia 22202
Phone: (703) 341-2663
E-mail: b.wallace@conservation.org

John (Jack) G. Frazier, Ph.D.
Smithsonian Conservation Biology Institute
1500 Remount Road
Front Royal, Virginia 22630
Phone: (540) 635-6564
E-mail: kurma@shentel.net, frazierja@si.edu

Scott A. Eckert, Ph.D.
Wider Caribbean Sea Turtle Conservation Network (WIDECAST)
Department of Biology and Natural Resources
Principia College
Elsah, Illinois 62028
Phone: (314) 566-6301
E-mail: seckert@widecast.org

Peter C.H. Pritchard, Ph.D.
Chelonian Research Institute
401 South Central Avenue
Oviedo, Florida 32765
Phone: (407) 365-6347
E-mail: chelonianRI@aol.com

Editor:
Sandra L. MacPherson
National Sea Turtle Coordinator
U.S. Fish and Wildlife Service
7915 Baymeadows Way, Ste 200
Jacksonville, Florida 32256
Phone: (904) 731-3336
E-mail: Sandy_MacPherson@fws.gov

Recommended citation:
Eckert, K.L., B.P. Wallace, J.G. Frazier, S.A. Eckert, and P.C.H. Pritchard. 2012. Synopsis of the biological data on the leatherback sea turtle (*Dermochelys coriacea*). U.S. Department of Interior, Fish and Wildlife Service, Biological Technical Publication BTP-R4015-2012, Washington, D.C.

For additional copies or information, contact:
Sandra L. MacPherson
National Sea Turtle Coordinator
U.S. Fish and Wildlife Service
7915 Baymeadows Way, Ste 200
Jacksonville, Florida 32256
Phone: (904) 731-3336
E-mail: Sandy_MacPherson@fws.gov

Series Senior Technical Editor:
Stephanie L. Jones
Nongame Migratory Bird Coordinator
U.S. Fish and Wildlife Service, Region 6
P.O. Box 25486 DFC
Denver, Colorado 80225
Phone: (303) 236-4409
E-mail: Stephanie_Jones@fws.gov

ISSN 2160-9498 Electronic ISSN 2160-9497
Biological Technical Publications online: http://library.fws.gov/BiologicalTechnicalPublications.html

Table of Contents

List of Figures ix

List of Tables x

Acknowledgments xii

Executive Summary 1

Chapter 1: Identity 2

Nomenclature 2
    Valid Name 2
    Synonymy 2
    Type Locality 3

Taxonomy 3
    Affinities 3
        Diagnosis 4
    Taxonomic Status 4
    Subspecies 5
    Standard Common Names 5
    Definition of Size Categories 5

Morphology 6
    Description 6
    External Morphology and Coloration 12
        Coloration 13
        Eggs 13
    Internal Morphology 13
        Alimentary System 14
        Respiratory System 15
        Circulatory System 15
        Urogenital System 15
        Muscular System 16
    Cranial Morphology 16
        Skull 16
        Post-Cranial Skeleton 17
    Cytomorphology 18
    Biochemistry 19
        Karyotype 19

Chapter 2: Distribution 21

Total Area 21

Differential Distribution 24
    Hatchlings 24
    Juveniles and Subadults 24
    Adults 24

Determinants of Distributional Changes 25

Hybridization 25

Chapter 3: Bionomics and Life History 26

Reproduction 26
    Sexual Dimorphism 26
    Age at Maturity 26
    Courtship and Mating 27
    Nesting Behavior 28
        Emergence from the sea onto the nesting beach 28
        Overland traverse to and selection of a suitable nest site 29
        Excavation of a body pit 30
        Excavation of the nest chamber 30
        Oviposition 30
        Filling the nest 30
        Covering and concealing the nest site 30
        Returning to the sea 30
        Density-dependence 31
    Eggs 32
        Fertility 35
    Reproductive Cycles 35

Embryonic and Hatchling Phases 40
    Embryonic Phase 40
        Embryonic development 40
        Embryo abnormalities 43
        Hatching success and sources of embryonic mortality 43
        Temperature dependent sex determination 46
    Hatchling Phase 47
        Hatching and emergence 47
        Offshore swim 51
        Imprinting and natal homing 52

Juvenile, Subadult and Adult Phases 53
    Longevity 53
    Hardiness 53
    Competitors 54
    Predators 54
    Parasites and Commensals 55
    Abnormalities and Injuries 58

Nutrition and Metabolism 59
    Food 59
    Feeding 63
    Growth 65

Scales	66
Platelets	66
Plastron and extremities	66
Pigmentation	66
Secondary characters	66
Growth rate	66
Metabolism	67
Thermoregulation	70
Osmoregulation	71

Behavior 71
Migrations and Local Movements 71
    Satellite telemetry 73
    Inter-nesting behavior 76
Navigation and Orientation 76
Diving 79
Schooling 81
Communication 81

Sensory Biology 82
Vision 82
Olfaction 82
Hearing 83

Chapter 4: Population 84

Population Structure 84
Sex Ratio 84
Age Composition 84
Size Composition 84
Phylogeography 85

Abundance and Density 85
Average Abundance and Density 85
Changes in Abundance and Density 86

Natality and Recruitment 87
Reproductive Rates 87
Factors Affecting Reproduction 88
Recruitment 88

Mortality 88
Mortality Rates 88
Factors Causing or Affecting Mortality 88
    Direct take 88
    Incidental capture 90
    Longline fisheries 91
    Gillnets and driftnets 92
    Pot fisheries 92
    Trawl fisheries 93
    Regional summaries and general notes 93
    International trade 94
    Marine debris and pollution 94
    Other 95

Population Dynamics 96

Chapter 5: Protection and Management 97
Conservation Status 97
Legal Status 97
Regulatory Measures 98
Management Strategies 99
Gaps and Recommendations 100

Chapter 6: Mariculture 104
Facility Considerations 104
Food and Feeding 105

Literature Cited 107

Appendix A 151
Life stages of the leatherback sea turtle, *Dermochelys coriacea* (photographers in parentheses).

Appendix B 154
Leatherback sea turtle cranial skeleton: skull dorsal, ventral views. Source: Wyneken (2001:23, 24).

Appendix C 156
Leatherback sea turtle post-cranial skeleton. Sources: Fretey (1981:21) adapted from Deraniyagala (1939), and Pritchard & Trebbau (1984:254) with carapace bones (D) adapted from Remane (1936) and the plastral view of the shell with elimination of remnants of mosaic bones (E) adapted from Deraniyagala (1939).

Appendix D 160
Nesting sequence of the leatherback sea turtle. Approach from the sea (Kimberly Maison), site preparation ("body-pitting") and nest chamber excavation (Scott A. Eckert), egg-laying (Alicia Marin), and nesting covering (with measuring) and return to the sea (Carol Guy Stapleton).

List of Figures

Figure 1. Global distribution of the leatherback sea turtle, including northern and southern oceanic range boundaries and sites representative of the species' current nesting range. Extreme northern and southern records (see Table 6 for coordinates) may not represent persistent nesting grounds, but represent known geographic boundaries for successful reproduction. Map created by Brendan Hurley (Conservation International)..22

Figure 2. Generalized leatherback sea turtle life cycle. Source: Chaloupka et al. (2004:150). 23

List of Tables

Table 1. The size (curved carapace length, CCL—*except* Puerto Rico (Culebra) and French Guiana (Ya:lima:po) presented as straight carapace length/width, SCL/SCW) of adult female leatherback sea turtles at their nesting grounds. Table is not comprehensive; locations were selected for geographic representation. 7

Table 2. The mass of juvenile and adult (primarily gravid female) leatherback sea turtles. Gender (F, M) not reported for juveniles (Juv). Table is not comprehensive; locations were selected for geographic representation. 8

Table 3. Reported average yolked egg diameters (mm) and egg masses (g) for leatherback sea turtles. Number of clutches tallied appears in brackets, with number of eggs measured in parentheses. ± 1 SD is noted. 9

Table 4. Straight carapace length and width (mm), and body mass (g) of leatherback sea turtle hatchlings. Data shown are means ± standard deviations (or ranges), with sample sizes (number of hatchlings measured) in parentheses. An asterisk (*) indicates that hatchlings were 3-5 days old at the time of measurement; (**) indicates total length. 10

Table 5. Leatherback sea turtle morphology from two specimens captured at sea. SCL (SCW) = Straight carapace length (width); CCL (CCW) = Curved carapace length (width). 11

Table 6. Published records that define the known northern and southern geographic range for successful egg-laying by leatherback sea turtles. 21

Table 7. Indirect estimates of age at maturity for leatherback sea turtles 27

Table 8. Nesting behavior in leatherback sea turtles. Durations for stages (min) for the Atlantic coast of Costa Rica were recorded during a single nesting at Matina in 1958 (Carr and Ogren 1959). Mean durations in minutes (± 1 SD) for St. Croix, U.S. Virgin Islands represent a composite of 113 nestings at Sandy Point National Wildlife Refuge in 1985 (Eckert and Eckert 1985). Mean durations in minutes (± 1 SE) for Playa Grande, Costa Rica, were collected over 11 nesting seasons (sample size in parentheses). * denotes values given for crawling while both emerging from and returning to the sea. 29

Table 9. Clutch size (yolked eggs only) and average number of yolkless eggs per clutch for leatherback sea turtles. Where available, sample size (number of clutches tallied) appears in parentheses and ± 1 SD is noted. 33

Table 10. Occurrence and duration of nesting seasons for leatherback sea turtles by geographic region......36

Table 11. Internesting periods for leatherback sea turtles, defined as the number of days between consecutive successful egg-laying events within a nesting season. Range of values and number of intervals (n) are also given...37

Table 12. Clutch frequency (number of clutches per season) in leatherback sea turtles. Observed Clutch Frequency is the number of confirmed successful egg-laying events. Estimated Clutch Frequency is calculated by dividing the number of days between the dates of the first and last observed nesting by the internesting period (cf. Frazer and Richardson 1985). Total Clutch Frequency is an estimate that attempts to take into account egg-laying events before and after the first and last observations, respectively (cf. Rivalan). Sample size (=number of clutches, but see Santidrián Tomillo et al. 2009) in parentheses; asterisk (*) indicates a range of mean annual values. 39

Table 13. Remigration intervals for leatherback sea turtles, defined as the number of years between consecutive nesting seasons. In parentheses is the proportion (%) of the nesting cohort exhibiting the remigration interval, or the number (n) of intervals examined. 40

Table 14. Descriptions of the anatomy of embryonic and hatchling leatherback sea turtles. Source: Miller (1985). 41

Table 15. Post-ovipositional embryonic statges in leatherback sea turtles. Source: Deraniyagala (1939). 41

Table 16. Pre-ovipositional embryonic stages, defined as the intra-oviducal period and development prior to the formation of 24 pairs of somites, in the leatherback sea turtles. Source: Miller (1985). 42

Table 17. Incubation duration and hatching success for leatherback sea turtles. Hatching success is generally calculated as the number of hatched eggs (or hatchlings) divided by the number of eggs in a clutch. Emergence success is calculated as the number of hatchlings that emerge from the nest to the beach surface, divided by the number of eggs in a clutch. Nest location refers to whether clutches developed *in situ*, in a hatchery, in Styrofoam® incubators, or were relocated to another location on the beach. Data are shown as mean ± SD. Sample sizes (number of clutches) in parentheses; asterisk (*) indicates a range of annual means. 44

Table 18. Predators of leatherback sea turtles. Taxonomic detail reflects that given in the source reference. Life stage affected: E = egg; H = hatchling; J = juvenile; A = adult. 48

Table 19. Parasites and commensals of leatherback sea turtles. Taxonomic detail reflects that given in the source reference. 56

Table 20. Prey items, targeted and incidental, of wild leatherback sea turtles, as determined by gut content analysis or by direct observation. Taxonomic detail reflects that given in the source reference. Life Stage (Stage): H = hatchling; J = juvenile; A = adult; [blank] = unknown or unreported. Cnidarians are reported in early references as 'coelenterates.' 60

Table 21. Summary of reported metabolic rates (MR) for leatherback sea turtles. Activity levels: Resting = fed (unless noted as fasted), quiescent turtles; Active = continuous non-maximal activity (e.g., swimming, crawling); Max = sustained maximal metabolic rate; Field = at-sea field metabolic rates (FMR, incl. all normal daily activity); Laying = during oviposition; Calculated = MR derived from models based on activity, behavior and environmental factors. Mass values are mean ± SD, unless otherwise noted. Source: adapted from Wallace and Jones (2008). 68

Table 22. Summary of leatherback sea turtle dive and movement parameters during post-nesting migrations and while on putative foraging grounds. Max Duration = Maximum Duration; Max Distance = Maximum Distance traveled during the tracking period. 74

Table 23. Summary of leatherback sea turtle movement parameters recorded during internesting periods. Data shown are means ± SD, sample sizes in parentheses. Max Depth = Maximum Depth; Max Duration = Maximum Duration; Total Distance = Total Distance traveled during the internesting period. 77

Table 24. Diet, maximum longevity, and cause of death of leatherback sea turtles reared in captivity. With the exception of the juvenile stranded in Puerto Rico, all specimens were obtained as eggs or hatchlings. 106

Acknowledgments

The authors are very grateful to the following colleagues, each of whom reviewed at least one chapter of text and made important contributions to the final draft: Larisa Avens, Ana Rebeca Barragán, Rhema Kerr-Bjorkland, Paolo Casale, Claudia Ceballos, Milani Chaloupka, Benoit de Thoisy, Peter H. Dutton, Chan Eng-Heng, Allen M. Foley, Marc Girondot, Matthew H. Godfrey, Brendan J. Godley, Hedelvy J. Guada, Craig A. Harms, Graeme C. Hays, George R. Hughes, Douglas Hykle, T. Todd Jones, Irene Kinan Kelly, Jeff Kinch, Rebecca L. Lewison, Suzanne R. Livingstone, Peter A. Meylan, Jeffrey D. Miller, Richard D. Reina, Pilar Santidrián-Tomillo, Christopher R. Sasso, George L. Shillinger, Amanda L. Southwood, James R. Spotila, Manjula Tiwari, and Anton (Tony) D. Tucker.

The authors are particularly indebted to Sandra L. MacPherson (U.S. Fish and Wildlife Service) and Dr. Kelly R. Stewart (NOAA National Marine Fisheries Service) for their full and careful review of the entire manuscript.

A first draft of this Synopsis was prepared by Peter C.H. Pritchard for presentation at the Western Atlantic Turtle Symposium (WATS II) in Mayagüez, Puerto Rico (October 1987), but never published.

We would like to recognize colleagues who reviewed and made important contributions to several earlier versions of the Synopsis over the course of many years: Sneed B. Collard, Jacques Fretey, Sally R. Hopkins-Murphy, Michael C. James, John A. Keinath, Robert Lockhart, Molly E. Lutcavage, Peter L. Lutz, Nicholas Mrosovsky, John (Jack) A. Musick, Larry Ogren, David W. Owens, Frank V. Paladino, Henri A. Reichart, Anders G.J. Rhodin, Ricardo Sagarminaga, A. Laura Sarti M., Barbara A. Schroeder, Sally E. Solomon, Malcolm Stark, Jeanette Wyneken, and Rainer Zangerl. In all, more than 50 researchers have given of their time, expertise, and sometimes unpublished data to ensure that the Synopsis is as complete as possible. Thank you all!

The Synopsis is current with peer-reviewed literature published to early-2009, at which time the draft went through two rounds of international peer-review and was queued into the Biological Technical Publication series of the United States Fish and Wildlife Service. The Synopsis is a product of U.S. Fish and Wildlife Service Purchase Order No. 20181-0-0169, and U.S. Fish and Wildlife Service Grant Agreement No. 401814G050.

Executive Summary

The leatherback sea turtle (*Dermochelys coriacea;* leatherback) is the largest and most migratory of the world's turtles, with the most extensive geographic range of any living reptile. Reliable at-sea sightings extend from ~ 71° N to 47° S. This highly specialized turtle is the only living member of the family Dermochelyidae. It exhibits reduced external keratinous structures: scales are temporary, disappearing within the first few months and leaving the entire body covered by smooth black skin. Dorsal keels streamline a tapered form. The size of reproductively active females varies geographically (~ 140–160 cm curved carapace length, ~ 250–500 kg); a record male weighed 916 kg. Clutch size also varies geographically (~ 60–100 viable eggs), incubation is typically 60 days (during which time gender is heavily influenced by ambient temperature), *in situ* hatch success generally ranges from 45–65%, and hatchlings (~55–60 mm carapace length) are primarily black with longitudinal white stripes dorsally.

The species has a shallow genealogy and strong population structure worldwide, supporting a natal homing hypothesis. Gravid females arrive seasonally at preferred nesting grounds in tropical and subtropical latitudes, with the largest colonies concentrated in the southern Caribbean region and central West Africa. Non-breeding adults and sub-adults journey into temperate and subarctic zones seeking oceanic jellyfish and other soft-bodied invertebrates. Long-distance movements are not random in timing or location, with turtles potentially possessing an innate awareness of profitable foraging opportunities. The basis for high seas orientation and navigation is poorly understood. Little is known about the biology or distribution of neonates or juveniles, with individuals smaller than 100 cm in carapace length appearing to be confined to waters > 26°C. Distribution of both juveniles and adults most likely reflects the distribution and abundance of macroplanktonic prey. Age at maturity is debated and not conclusively known, but recent estimates (26–32 yr) are similar to that of some other sea turtle genera.

Studies of metabolic rate demonstrate marked differences between leatherbacks and other sea turtles: the "marathon" strategy of leatherbacks is characterized by relatively lower sustained active metabolic rates. Metabolic rates during terrestrial activities are well-studied compared with metabolic rates associated with activity at sea. One diel behavior pattern involves deep diving (> 1200 m).

The species faces two major thermoregulatory challenges: maintaining a high core temperature in cold waters of high latitudes and/or great depths, and avoiding overheating in some waters and latitudes, especially while on land during nesting. Biophysical models demonstrate that leatherbacks are able to thermoregulate in varied environments by combining large body size with low metabolic rates, blood flow adjustments (e.g., counter-current heat exchangers in their flippers), and peripheral insulation (6–7 cm); a suite of adaptations sometimes referred to as 'gigantothermy,' distinct from strict ectothermy and endothermy. The primary means of physiological osmoregulation are the lachrymal glands, which eliminate excess salt from the body.

The leatherback was re-classified in 2000 by the International Union for the Conservation of Nature (IUCN) *Red List of Threatened Species* as Critically Endangered. It remains vulnerable to a wide range of threats, including bycatch, ingestion of and entanglement in marine debris, take of turtles and eggs, and loss of nesting habitat to coastal processes and beachfront development. There is no evidence of significant current declines at the largest of the Western Atlantic nesting grounds, but Eastern Atlantic populations face serious threats and Pacific populations have been decimated. Incidental mortality in fisheries, implicated in the collapse of the Eastern Pacific population, is a largely unaddressed problem worldwide.

Although sea turtles were among the first marine species to benefit from legal protection and concerted conservation effort around the world, management of contemporary threats often falls short of what is necessary to prevent further population declines and ensure the species' survival throughout its range. Successes include regional agreements that emphasize unified management approaches, national legislation that protects large juveniles and breeding-age adults, and community-based conservation efforts that offer viable alternatives to unsustainable patterns of exploitation. Future priorities should include the identification of critical habitat and priority conservation areas, including corridors that span multiple national jurisdictions and the high seas, the creation of marine management regimes at ecologically relevant scales and the forging of new governance patterns, reducing or eliminating causal factors in population declines (e.g., over-exploitation, bycatch), and improving management capacity at all levels.

Chapter 1: Identity

Nomenclature

Valid Name
Dermochelys (Blainville 1816)

Dermochelys coriacea (Vandelli 1761)

Synonymy
This species was first described by Vandelli in 1761 (Fretey and Bour 1980, King and Burke 1997) as *Testudo coriacea*. In 1816, Blainville proposed the genus *Dermochelys* but failed to name *D. coriacea* as the type species (Smith and Smith 1980). This led to some confusion about the correct scientific name for the species but generally since the publication of Boulenger (1889), *Dermochelys coriacea* has been considered the correct name for the leatherback. The leatherback is the only living member of the family Dermochelyidae (Stewart and Johnson 2006).

The history of the familial name is complex (Baur 1889, Pritchard and Trebbau 1984). Sphargidae (Gray 1825) is the oldest name, but when the type genus *Sphargis* (Merrem 1820) was recognized by Baur (1888) to be a junior synonym of *Dermochelys* (Blainville 1816), Lydekker (1889) argued the family should also be subordinated to Dermatochelyidae Fritzinger 1843 (see also Smith and Taylor 1950). Lydekker claimed that due to Aristotle's original Greek spelling, *Dermatochelys* (not *Dermochelys*) was justified, and, hence, the family Dermatochelyidae would be preferred. In fact, *Dermatochelys* Lesueur 1829 (not Wagler 1830, c.f. Pritchard and Trebbau 1984) is a junior synonym to *Dermochelys* Blainville 1816, and the family name based on it has not been used frequently.

The first use of the accepted name Dermochelyidae is commonly credited to Wieland (1902) [who in fact used "Dermochelydidae"], although there are earlier publications (e.g., Baur 1889 [Dermochelydidae], 1890, 1891, 1893; Wieland 1900). It is not uncommon to find variant spellings, often from the (possibly inadvertent) omission of the "y" e.g., Dermochelidae. Another variant, Dermochelydidae, has also been used over the past century (Baur 1889, Wermuth and Mertens 1977). Smith and Smith (1980) give a detailed and lucid discussion of the nomenclatural points involving Dermochelyidae.

The following synonymy is according to Pritchard and Trebbau (1984):

Testudo coriacea sive *Mercurii* Rondeletius, 1554, Libri Pisc. Mar., Lyon: 450. Type locality: Mediterranean Sea.

Mercurii Testudo Gesner, 1558, Medici Tigurini Hist. Animal, Zürich, 4: 1134.

Testudo coriacea Vandelli, 1761, Epistola de Holothurio, et *Testudine coriacea* ad Celiberrimum Carolum Linnaeum, Padua: 2. Type locality: "Maris Tyrrheni oram in agro Laurentiano."

Testudo coriacea Linnaeus, 1766, Syst. Nat., Ed. 12, 1: 350. Type locality: "Mari Mediterraneo, Adriatico varius" erroneously restricted to Palermo, Sicily, by Smith and Taylor (1950).

Testudo coriaceous Pennant, 1769, Brit. Zoology, Ed. 3, 3, Rept.: 7.

Testudo arcuata Catesby, 1771, Nat. Hist. Carolina, Florida, Bahama Isl., 2: 40. Type locality: coasts of Carolina and Florida, as restricted by Mertens and Wermuth, 1955.

Testudini Coriacee Molina, 1782, Sagg. Sulla Stor. Nat. Chili, Bologna, 4: 216 (illegitimate name).

Tortugas Coriaceas Molina, 1788, Comp. Hist. Geog. Chile, Madrid, 1: 237 (illegitimate name).

Testudo Lyra Lacépède, 1788, Hist. Nat. Quad. Ovip., 1: table "Synopsis."

Testudo marina Wilhelm, 1794, Unterhalt. Naturgesch. Amphib.: 133. Type locality: all oceans.

Testudo tuberculata Pennant *in* Schoepf, 1801, Naturgesch. Schildkr.: 144. Type locality: not designated.

Chelone coriacea Brongniart, 1805, Essai Classif. Nat. Rept. 26.

Chelonia coriacea Schweigger, 1812, Königsberg. Arch. Naturwiss. Math., 1: 290.

Chelonias lutaria Rafinesque, 1814, Spec. Sci. Palermo: 666. Type locality: Sicily (*fide* Lindholm 1929).

Dermochelys coriacea Blainville, 1816, Prodrom. Syst. Règn. Anim.: 119.

Sphargis mercurialis Merrem, 1820, Tent. Syst. Amphib.: 19. Type locality: "Mari Mediterraneo et Oceano atlantico" (substitute name for *Testudo coriacea* Vandelli, 1761).

Coriudo coriacea Fleming, 1822, Phil. Zool., 2: 271.

Chelonia Lyra Bory de St-Vincent, 1828, Résumé d'Erpét. Hist. Nat. Rept.: 80 (substitute name for *Testudo coriacea* Vandelli 1761).

Scytina coriacea Wagler, 1828, Isis, 21: coll. 861.

Sphargis tuberculata Gravenhorst, 1829, Delicae Mus. Zool. Vratislav., 1: 9.

Dermochelis atlantica LeSueur *in* Cuvier, 1829, Règn. Anim., Ed. 2, 2: 406 (*nomen nudum*).

Dermatochelys coriacea Wagler, 1830, Natürl. Syst. Amphib.: 133.

Dermatochelys porcata Wagler, 1830, Natürl. Syst. Amphib.: expl. to pl. 1 (substitute name for *Testudo coriacea* Vandelli, 1761).

Sphargis coriacea Gray, 1831, Synops. Rept., pt. 1, Tortoises, etc.: 51.

Chelyra coriacca Rafinesque, 1832, Atlantic Jour. Friend Knowl., 1: 64 (typographical error).

Testudo coriacea marina Ranzani, 1834, Camilli Ranzani de *Testudo coriacea marina*, Bologna: 148.

Dermatochelys atlantica Fitzinger, 1836 (1835), Ann. Wien. Mus., 1: 128.

Testudo (*Sphargis*) *coriacea* Voigt, 1837, Lehrb. Zool., Stuttgart, 4: 21.

Dermochelydis tuberculata Alessandrini, 1838, Cenni Sulla Stor. Sulla Notom. Testuggine coriacea marina, Bologna: 357.

Chelonia (*Dermochelys*) *coriacea* van der Hoeven, 1855, Handboek Dierkunde: 548.

Testudo midas Hartwig, 1861, Sea and its Living Wonders, Ed. 2, London: 152.

Sphargis coriacea Var. *Schlegelii* Garman, 1884, Bull. U.S. Nat. Mus., 25: 303. Type locality: "Tropical Pacific and Indian Oceans" erroneously restricted to Guaymas, Sonora, Mexico by Smith and Taylor (1950).

Sphargis schlegelii Garman, 1884, Bull. U.S. Nat. Mus., 25: 295. Type locality: "Pacific (Ocean)."

Dermatochelys schlegeli Garman, 1884, Bull. Essex Inst., 16, 1–3: 6. Type locality: "Tropical Pacific and Indian Oceans."

Sphargis angusta Philippi, 1889, An. Univ. Santiago, Chile, 104: 728. Type locality: "Tocopilla, Chile."

Dermatochaelis coriacea Oliveira, 1896, Rept. Amph. Penín Ibérica, Coimbra: 28.

Dermochelys schlegelii Stejneger, 1907, Bull. U.S. Nat. Mus., 58: 485.

Dermatochelys angusta Quijada, 1916, Bol. Mus. Nac. Chile, 9: 24.

Dermochelys coriacea coriacea Gruvel, 1926, Pêche Marit. Algérie, 4: 45.

Dendrochelys (*Sphargis*) *coriacea* Pierantoni, 1934, Comp. Zool. Torino: 867.

Dermochelys coriacea schlegeli Mertens and L. Müller, *in* Rust, 1934, Blatt. Aquar.-u-Terr. Kunde, 45: 64.

Type Locality

Vandelli (1761) specified the origin of his specimen as "…*maris Tyrrheni oram in agro Laurentiano*,…" and Linnaeus (1766) indicated "…*habitat in Mari mediterraneo, Adriatico rarius*." Smith and Taylor (1950) restricted the type locality to Palermo, Sicily, without discussion. As Fretey and Bour (1980) observed, the original Vandelli type locality includes a slight element of ambiguity, since "Laurentiano" may refer to the ancient town of Laurentum, 8 km northeast of Lido di Ostia (near Tor Paterno), 13 km southwest of Rome; or it may refer to the present town of Lido di Lavinio, 7.5 km north of Anzio and 22 km southeast of Rome. The type locality should therefore be simply "…coast of Italy (western Mediterranean), on the Tyrrhenian Sea near Rome."

Taxonomy

Affinities

– Suprageneric

Phylum Chordata
  Subphylum Vertebrata
    Superclass Tetrapoda
      Class Reptilia
        Subclass Anapsida
          Order Testudines
            Suborder Cryptodira
              Superfamily Dermochelyoidea
                Family Dermochelyidae

– Generic

Genus *Dermochelys* is monotypic.

– Specific

Diagnosis.—This is a highly specialized sea turtle with reduced external keratinous structures: scales are temporary, disappearing within the first few months after hatching, when the entire body is generally covered by smooth skin (although traces of scales may remain on eyelids, neck and caudal crest); claws are absent (with few exceptions in embryos and newly hatched young); and the rhamphothecae on the upper and lower beaks are thin and feeble. A conspicuous recurved cusp, delimitated both anteriorly and posteriorly by a deep notch, is on the anterior of each upper jaw. The lyre-shaped carapace has seven longitudinal ridges, or keels (sometimes described as five longitudinal ridges, with an additional ridge on each side marking the bridge), two anterior paramedial projections and one posterior medial projection. The plastron has six (three pairs of) weak keels that are also longitudinal. Stout horny papillae line the pharyngeal cavity, but not the choanae.

Unique features in the skull include: unossified epipterygoid; rudimentary descending process on parietal; parasphenoid rudiment in basisphenoid; lack of contact between squamosal-opisthotic, prootic-parietal, pterygoid-parietal, and pterygoid-prootic; no coronoid and a cartilaginous articular. A mosaic of dermal ossicles develops during the first year to cover the carapace. Of the usual dermal elements in the carapace, only the nuchal bone is present, leaving the relatively unexpanded ribs free. Plastron bones are also greatly reduced in size, forming a flimsy ring; and there are normally eight instead of nine elements; the entoplastron is absent. Both the ribs and the plastral bones are embedded in the subdermal cartilaginous layer. Adults, at more than 2 m in total length and often exceeding 500 kg, are the largest Recent Testudines. The black dorsal coloration with white spots is also diagnostic.

Taxonomic Status

In terms of contemporary species, this family is monotypic, and this often results in confusion between familial, generic, and specific characters, especially because the extant form, *Dermochelys coriacea*, is so extraordinary. So unusual are the dermochelyids that Cope (1871) created a special suborder, Athecae, specifically for them. Although variant spellings have been used, e.g., "Athecata" (Lydekker 1889: 223 "amended from Cope") and "Athecoidea" (Deraniyagala 1939), this taxon was in use as late as 1952 by Carr. However, the concept of the Athecae as the sister group to other turtles has been rejected by more recent phylogenetic studies.

A variety of detailed comparative studies, including specimens of *D. coriacea*, have concluded that Dermochelyidae is most closely related to the cheloniid sea turtles. These investigations have involved the skeleton (Baur 1886, 1889; Dollo 1901; Wieland 1902; Versluys 1913, 1914; Völker 1913; Williams 1950; Romer 1956); cranium (Nick 1912; Wegner 1959; Gaffney 1975, 1979); penis (Zug 1966); blood proteins (Frair 1964, 1969, 1979, 1982; Chen and Mao 1981) and sequence data (e.g., Shaffer et al. 1997, Krenz et al. 2005, Near et al. 2005, Naro-Maciel et al. 2008).

Because the family Dermochelyidae includes only a single living species, *D. coriacea*, published diagnoses of the family, genus, and species tend to be very similar. However, several fossil genera of dermochelyids have been described. It is also tempting to define the family in terms of known characteristics, particularly of the soft parts of the living species, even though it is generally impossible to confirm that these characteristics were also shown by the extinct species which, for the most part, are known only from fragmentary fossils.

This caveat should be kept in mind when applying the diagnoses of the family and species presented by Pritchard and Trebbau (1984)—"DERMOCHELYIDAE: A family of turtles characterized by: extreme reduction of the bones of the carapace and plastron (with the neural and peripheral bones of the carapace, and the entoplastron in the plastron, lacking; the pleurals reduced to endochondral ribs, separated by wide fenestrae; and the plastral bones reduced to narrow splints, forming a ring of bones surrounding a great fontanelle); development of a neomorphic epithecal shell layer consisting of a mosaic of thousands of small polygonal bones; claws and shell scutes lacking (scales only present in the first few weeks of life); skull without nasal bones; no true rhamphothecae; parasphenoid overlain by pterygoids; prefrontals in contact dorsally, with descending processes that are moderately separated; unridged tomial surfaces; a generally neotenic and oil-saturated skeleton; extensive areas of vascularized cartilage in the vertebrae, limb girdles, and limb bones; very large body size; and marine habitat."

Until recently the earliest dermochelyids were dated from the Eocene (Europe, Africa, North America: Romer 1956, de Broin and Pironon 1980, Pritchard and Trebbau 1984), but are now confirmed from the Cretaceous (Japan: Hirayama and Chitoku 1996). Subsequent evolution led to several distinct lineages, all but one of which became extinct (Wood et al. 1996).

In the most recent review of fossil dermochelyids (Wood et al. 1996), six genera are recognized: *Cosmochelys* Andrews 1919—Eocene of Nigeria, one species; *Dermochelys* Blainville 1816—Recent cosmopolitan, one species; *Egyptemys* Wood, Johnson-Gove, Gaffney and Maley 1996—Eocene of northern Egypt and North America, two species; *Eosphargis* Lydekker 1889—Eocene of Europe, two species; *Natemys* Wood, Johnson-Gove, Gaffney and Maley 1996—Oligocene of Peru, one species; *Psephophorus* Von Meyer 1847—Eocene through Pliocene of Europe, North Africa and North America, eight species.

Specimens of *Cosmochelys* and *Pseudosphargis* [Koenen 1891—Oligocene of Germany] are mere fragments, and there have been discussions about their true identity (Wood 1973); indeed, *Pseudosphargis* is no longer considered viable (Wood et al. 1996). Likewise, much of the *Psephophorus* material is fragmentary, and it is impossible to be certain about some of the identifications here also. Some fossil dermochelyids are so incomplete that not only have they given rise to discussions about specific and generic identity, but ordinal and class identity have also been questioned, for some specimens have been identified as crocodiles or fish (Deraniyagala 1939, de Brion and Pironon 1980, Pritchard and Trebbau 1984).

Comprehensive studies of dermochelyid fossils have been done on *Eosphargis*; Nielsen (1959) made a detailed study of good material of *E. breineri* from the Eocene of Denmark. It is possible that detailed study of the fossil material will result in conclusions that some of the genera presently recognized are synonymous with *Dermochelys*, the oldest generic name in the family.

According to Dutton et al. (1999), (i) the leatherback sea turtle (*Dermochelys coriacea*; leatherback) is the product of an evolutionary trajectory originating at least 100 million years ago, yet the intraspecific phylogeny recorded in mitochondrial lineages may trace back less than 900,000 years; (ii) the gene genealogy and global distribution of mtDNA haplotypes indicate that leatherbacks may have radiated from a narrow refugium, possibly in the Indo-Pacific, during the early Pleistocene glaciation; and (iii) analysis of haplotype frequencies reveal that nesting populations are strongly subdivided both globally (F_{ST} = 0.415) and within ocean basins (F_{ST} = 0.203–0.253), despite the leatherback's highly migratory nature (see Chapter 4, *Population structure, Phylogeography*, below).

Subspecies

No subspecies are recognized at the present time.

Of the numerous specific names that have been applied to leatherback turtles since 1554 (see *Synonymy*, above), all of those published before 1884 may be considered to represent simply replacement or substitute names rather than a conviction by an author that he had identified a new kind of leatherback turtle. However, Garman (1884a, 1884b) recognized a supposed new variety of the leatherback, that he named *Sphargis coriacea* Var. *Schlegelii*, or *Dermatochelys* (or *Sphargis*) *schlegeli schlegeli*, as a subspecific name, which has been utilized for the leatherbacks of the Indian and Pacific Oceans by many authors subsequently, including Carr (1952), Mertens and Wermuth (1955), Caldwell (1962), Hubbs and Roden (1964), Stebbins (1966), and Pritchard (1967). Moreover, a number of influential authorities preceding Carr (1952) gave *schlegeli* full species ranking. These authorities include Stejneger (1907), Stejneger and Barbour (1917), van Denburgh (1922), Bogert and Oliver (1945), and Ingle and Smith (1949).

None of these authors, from Garman (1884a) to Pritchard (1967), had undertaken analyses of the actual differences between leatherback turtles from different oceans. Museum material was inadequate for this task, and the places where leatherbacks may be found in quantity in the wild had, for the most part, not been discovered. Moreover, Garman's proposal of the new name *schlegeli* was confusing and inconsistent on several counts, and would not be considered acceptable if published today. The only demonstrated aspect of geographic variation relates to the smaller adult size of females from the Eastern Pacific (see Chapter 4, *Population structure, Size composition*, below). While this is of interest, it may derive from some aspect of the environment rather than from genetic differences, and this character alone should not be used to justify subspecific recognition of this population.

If further study should reveal taxonomically valid characteristics in *D. coriacea* in the Eastern Pacific, the name *angusta* should be used rather than *schlegelii*, the former having an Eastern Pacific type locality (Chile), while the type locality of Garman's name *schlegelii*, to the extent that it can be known, is Burma (i.e., the Indian Ocean) based on Tickell's (1862) detailed description of an adult leatherback that had been captured on 1 February 1862 near the mouth of the Ye River in the Province of Tenasserim, Burma.

Standard Common Names

Throughout the world, the leatherback sea turtle is known by many local names. Recently published examples include India, where *doni tambelu* is used (*doni* means "wheel of a bullock cart") (Tripathy et al. 2006), and Papua New Guinea (Kinch 2006), where *hana, hum, kareon,* and *nangobu* are among the tribal language terms for the species. As summarized by Pritchard and Trebbau (1984), the following are common vernacular names for *Dermochelys coriacea* in the Atlantic: leatherback, leathery turtle (English); trunk turtle, trunkback turtle, coffinback, caldong (English-Caribbean); tinglada (Spanish); canal, cardon, siete filos, chalupa, baula, laúd, tortuga sin concha (Spanish-Latin America); machincuepo, garapachi (Spanish-Pacific Mexico); tortuga llaüt (Spanish-Canary Islands); tortue luth (French); cada-arou (Galibi Indians-French Guiana); aitkanti [aitikanti], sixikanti (Suriname); caouana (Marowijne Carib); and tartaruga de couro, tartaruga coriacea (Portuguese-Brazil, Azores, Africa). See also Deraniyagala (1939), Hughes (1974a), Mittermeier et al. (1980), Fretey (2001), and Shanker and Choudhury (2006), among others.

Definition of Size Categories

Hatchling—from hatching to the first few weeks of life, characterized by the presence of the umbilical scar.

Juvenile—umbilical scar absent, with a maximum size of 100 cm curved carapace length (CCL); rarely seen but believed to occur only in waters warmer than 26°C.

Subadult—carapace length > 100 cm CCL to the onset of sexual maturity at 120–140 cm CCL, depending on the population; able to exploit their full biogeographical range.

Adult—sexually mature (> 120–140 cm CCL for gravid females, depending on the population); the size at sexual maturity for males is assumed to be similar to that of females.

Morphology

Description

Informative general descriptions of this species are presented by Deraniyagala (1939), Carr (1952), Loveridge and Williams (1957), Villiers (1958), Pritchard (1971a, 1979a, 1980), Ernst and Barbour (1972), and Pritchard and Trebbau (1984). More recently, Wyneken (2001) described the internal anatomy in detail.

The size (carapace length) of reproductively active females varies geographically, with population averages of ~ 150–160 cm CCL in the Atlantic and Indian Oceans, and ~ 140–150 cm CCL in the Eastern Pacific (Table 1). Comparable data are not available for adult males. From the few measurements recorded in the literature (e.g., Deraniyagala 1939, 1953; Lowe and Norris 1955; Donoso-Barros 1966; Brongersma 1969, 1972; Hartog and van Nierop 1984; Hughes 1974a; Maigret 1980, 1983; James et al. 2007), there would appear to be no obvious difference in average size between the sexes (but see Morgan 1990).

Eckert et al. (1989b) were the first to document the average weight of a nesting cohort at the breeding grounds, and these and later data collected at Western Atlantic sites indicate (nesting) population averages of 327 to 392 kg. There are no comparable data for other geographic regions, or for males (Table 2). The record weight is that of an adult male (916 kg: Morgan 1990), which was ensnared in a fisherman's net off the coast of Wales, U.K. Calculated relationships between body weight and carapace length are variously presented (Hirth 1982, Boulon et al. 1996, Leslie et al. 1996, Georges and Fossette 2006).

The average diameter of a normal-sized viable egg (52–55 mm) varies among populations. Population averages for egg mass also vary geographically, reportedly from 71.8 g to 84.3 g, with the largest eggs associated with Western Atlantic populations and the smallest with Eastern Pacific populations (Table 3). Noticeably undersized yolkless eggs are normally laid together with viable eggs; the former are highly variable in size and shape. Average hatchling size (straight carapace length, SCL) and mass varies geographically, typically from 55 to 65 mm and from 40 to 50 g, respectively (Table 4).

There have been few analyses of the inter-relationships between different morphometric parameters (Table 5). In nesting females there is a strong positive relationship between width and length of the carapace, when measured either along the curve (Hughes 1974a) or straight-line length (Fretey 1978). Benabib (1983) established this for both measuring techniques on the same specimens. Head width and carapace length are also positively related (Hughes 1974a), but these relationships have been described only with linear models and no effort has been made to test for allometry or to test other types of models.

In a recent analysis of 17 morphometric measurements obtained from 49 leatherbacks, Georges and Fossette (2006) used a stepwise backward analysis to show that body mass could be estimated with 93% of accuracy from the standard curvilinear carapace length (SCCL) and body circumference at half of SCCL.

In hatchlings, the interrelationships between different parameters are less clear. Hughes (1974a) concluded that there was no significant relationship between either carapace width and carapace length or head width and carapace length; however, Benabib (1983) found a very significant positive relationship between carapace width and carapace length.

Analyses of morphometric parameters, especially when comparing results that span several decades, may be compromised by the lack of standardized measurement techniques. Divergent values from distinct studies may only reflect discrepancies in equipment, technique or experience (Frazier 1998), rather than biologically significant differences in the sizes of animals. Likewise, important biological differences may be masked by non-standard measuring techniques that make results appear artificially similar. Hughes (1971a) concluded that the differences between measurements made over the curve or in a straight line amount to 6% of lengths and 32% of widths. Hughes (1974a) and Tucker and Frazer (1991) provide equations for converting from straight carapace length (or width) to curved carapace length (or width).

A related point concerns the fact that measurements not only vary from straight to curved, but the end points are not always the same. Measurements may be made along a keel ridge or between keels, at the anteriormost projection of the carapace (paramedial keels) or at the more posterior median keel. To further complicate the situation, the caudal projection is sometimes broken (Godfrey et al. 2001). The challenge led some workers to present two or three different measurements for either curved or straight techniques (e.g., Brongersma 1972, Eckert et al. 1982, Benabib 1983, Eckert and Eckert

Table 1. The size (curved carapace length, CCL—*except* Puerto Rico (Culebra) and French Guiana (Ya:lima:po) presented as straight carapace length/width, SCL/SCW) of adult female leatherback sea turtles at their nesting grounds. Table is not comprehensive; locations were selected for geographic representation.

Location	CCL (cm) Mean ± SD (range)	Sample Size (n)	CCW (cm) Mean ± SD (range)	Sample Size (n)	Reference
Western Atlantic					
Brazil (Espírito Santo)	159.8 ± 10.5 range: 139-182	24	–	–	Thomé et al. (2007)
French Guiana (Ya:lima:po)	154.6 ± 8.98 127-252 SCL	1,328	87.3 ± 6.21 67-109 SCW	1,328	Girondot & Fretey (1996)
Suriname[1]	154.1 ± 6.7 155.6 ± 6.7 range: 128-184	1,840 629	113.2 ± 5.0 114.5 ± 4.9 range: 97-135	801 383	Hilterman & Goverse (2007)
Venezuela (Playa Cipara, Playa Querepare)	151.8 ± 6.2	–	110.0 ± 4.4	–	Rondón et al., unpubl. data
Trinidad (Matura Beach)	157.6 range: 139.7-210.0	104	–	–	Chu Cheong (1990)
Trinidad (Matura Beach)	154.47 ± 5.03 range: 115-196	17,884	112.91 ± 6.97 range: 94-150	17,901	Nature Seekers, unpubl. data 1992-07
Costa Rica (Gandoca)	153.2 ± 7.39 range: 135-198	2,751	112 ± 5.53	2,751	Chacón & Eckert (2007)
Costa Rica (Tortuguero)	156.2 ± 10.6 range: 124.0-180.3	35	–	–	Leslie et al. (1996)
USA (St. Croix, USVI)[2]	152.2 range: 139.4-175.8	19	–	–	Eckert (1987)
USA (Culebra, Puerto Rico)	147.0 ± 5.55 134.2-160.5 SCL	65	–	–	Tucker & Frazer (1991)
USA (Culebra, Puerto Rico)	–	–	83.4 ± 3.4 76-92 SCW	24	Tucker (1988)
USA (Florida: Juno Beach)	151.8 ± 6.63 range: 125.0-173.5	174	109.2 ± 5.03 range: 94-129	174	Stewart et al. (2007)
Eastern Atlantic					
Equatorial Guinea (Bioko Island)	156.06 ± 14.87 range: 120-200	458	–	–	Formia et al. (2000)
Republic of Gabon (Pongara Beach)	150 ± 6 range: 139-169	22	–	–	Deem et al. (2006)
Gabon (Gamba Complex)	150.4 ± 7.6 range: 130-172	819	108.3 ± 6.6 range: 126-144	819	Verhage et al. (2006)
Western Pacific					
Australia	162 ± 6.8	11	–	–	Limpus (2006)
Papua New Guinea (Kamiali, Huon Coast)	166.0 ± 7.8 range: 149.1-173.0	96	119.3 ± 7.15 110-156.5 (sic)	97	Pilcher (2006)
Papua New Guinea (multiple sites)	169.5 ± 8.74 range: 155-186.1	34	–	–	Hamann et al. (2006a)
Eastern Pacific					
Mexico (Michoacán, Guerrero, Oaxaca)	143.8 ± 6.88 range: 120-168	6,466	102.8 ± 17.9 range: 1-121	1,098	Sarti M. et al. (2007)
Mexico (Jalisco)	144.5 range: 135-151	4	–	–	Castellanos-Michel et al. (2006)
Costa Rica (Playa Langosta)	144.9 ± 6.7 range: 125-158	304	104.5 ± 7.8 range: 90-116	304	Piedra et al. (2007)
Costa Rica (Playa Grande)	147 ± 0.48 (SE) range: 133-165	152	105.1 ± 0.39 (SE) range: 93.5-116.8	152	Price et al. (2004)

Table 1, continued

Location	CCL (cm) Mean ± SD (range)	Sample Size (n)	CCW (cm) Mean ± SD (range)	Sample Size (n)	Reference
Indian Ocean					
South Africa (Tongaland)	161.1 ± 7.0 range: 133.5-178.0	122	115.6 ± 6.5 range: 101.5-127.0	120	Hughes (1974a)
Mozambique	157.5 ± 80.4 range: 145.5-175	15	113.3 ± 64.1 range: 100-125	15	Louro (2006)
Sri Lanka	151.9	—	109.7	—	Kapurusinghe (2006)
India (Great Nicobar Island)	155.7	125	113.1	125	Andrews et al. (2006)

[1] mean ± SD was reported by year for Suriname, so that this entry features statistics from the year with the smallest average size and the year with the largest average size; range is reported for the years 2001-2005, combined
[2] USVI = U.S. Virgin Islands

Table 2. The mass of juvenile and adult (primarily gravid female) leatherback sea turtles. Gender (F, M) not reported for juveniles (Juv). Table is not comprehensive; locations were selected for geographic representation.

Location	Mass (kg) Mean ± SD (range)	Sample Size (n)	Gender	Reference
Western Atlantic				
French Guiana (Ya:lima:po)	389.7 ± 61.9 range: 275.6-567.3	182	F (nesting)	Georges & Fossette (2006)
Trinidad (Matura Beach)	327.75 ± 65.134 range: 143-498.5	250	F (nesting)	S.A. Eckert, unpubl. data
Costa Rica (Tortuguero)	346.8 ± 55.4 range: 250-435	22	F (nesting)	Leslie et al. (1996)
USA (St. Croix, USVI)	327.38 ± 45.05 range: 262-446	26	F (nesting)	Eckert et al. (1989b) S.A. Eckert, unpubl. data
USA (St. Croix, USVI)	259-506	102	F (nesting)	Boulon et al. (1996)
Canada	392.6 range: 191.9-640	23	F, M, Juv (bycatch)	James et al. (2007)
Eastern Atlantic				
UK (Wales)	916	1	M (bycatch)	Morgan (1990)
Northern Europe (Norway, Scotland, Ireland)	302.67 ± 85.28 range: 241-400	3	M (capture, stranding)	Brongersma (1972)
Northern Europe (Norway, Scotland, Ireland)	323.33 ± 89.047 range: 224-396	3	F (capture, stranding)	Brongersma (1972)
Eastern Pacific				
USA (California)	349 kg	1	M (capture)	Lowe & Norris (1955)
Indian Ocean				
Sri Lanka	301.6 448.0	1 1	F (nesting) F (nesting)	Deraniyagala (1939)
South Africa (Natal)	340.08 ± 205.28 range: 150-646	5	F (stranding)	Hughes (1974a)
South Africa (Natal)	320 27.3	1 1	M (stranding) Juv (stranding)	Hughes (1974a)

Table 3. Reported average yolked egg diameters (mm) and egg masses (g) for leatherback sea turtles. Number of clutches tallied appears in brackets, with number of eggs measured in parentheses. ± 1 SD is noted.

Nesting Site	Egg Diameter (mm)	Egg Mass (g)	Reference
Western Atlantic			
Suriname (Bigi Santi)	53.0	–	van Buskirk & Crowder (1994)
Trinidad (Matura Beach)	55.0 (30)	–	Bacon (1970)
Trinidad (Matura Beach)	55.0 [12] (120) range: 52.0-59.0	–	Maharaj (2004)
Costa Rica (Matina)	55.4 [1] (66) range: 50.3-59.0	–	Carr & Ogren (1959)
Costa Rica (Playa Gandoca)	53.2 ± 0.93 (3,250)	–	Chacón & Eckert (2007)
Costa Rica (Tortuguero)	54.0 ± 1.4 (613)	84.3 ± 5.2 (613)	Leslie et al. (1996)
USA (St. Croix, USVI)	54.1 (926)	–	Eckert et al. (1984)
USA (Humacao, Puerto Rico)	54.5 ± 1.8 [9] (90)	–	Matos (1986)
USA (Culebra Island, Puerto Rico)	53.1 ± 2.2 (500) range: 45.7-58.8	–	Tucker (1988)
USA (Brevard County)	51.0 [7] (70) range: 47.0-57.0	–	Maharaj (2004)
Eastern Atlantic			
Bioko	55.0 (4) range: 54-56	–	Butynski (1996)
Eastern Pacific			
Costa Rica (Playa Grande)	–	80.9 ± 7.0 (6,638)	Wallace et al. (2006a)
Costa Rica (Playa Grande)	–	76.2 ± 6.6 (30)	Bilinski et al. (2001)
Mexico (Mexiquillo, Michoacan)	53.2 ± 0.31 (3,766) range: 34.8-63.6	79.95 ± 7.85 (3,825) range: 57.2-121.6	L. Sarti M., *in litt.* 22 June 1991
Western Pacific			
Malaysia (Terengganu)	–	71.8 (50)	Simkiss (1962)
Australia (Wreck Rock)	53.2 ± 1.1 (120)	82.0 ± 4.2 (70)	Limpus et al. (1984)
Australia[1]	52.9 (435)	–	Limpus & McLachlan (1979)
Papua New Guinea	52.2 ± 2.3 [17] (340) range: 46-58	–	Hamann et al. (2006a)
Indian Ocean			
South Africa (Tongaland)	53.1 ± 1.49 (165) range: 50-56 [1]	–	Hughes (1974b)
Ceyon [Sri Lanka]	52.5 [3] (18) range: 51-54	61-85	Deraniyagala (1939)
Sri Lanka	53.2 (34)	79.6 (33)	Kapurusinghe (2006)

[1] denotes that value displayed is an average of annual averages

Table 4. Straight carapace length and width (mm), and body mass (g) of leatherback sea turtle hatchlings. Data shown are means ± standard deviations (or ranges), with sample sizes (number of hatchlings measured) in parentheses. An asterisk (*) indicates that hatchlings were 3-5 days old at the time of measurement; (**) indicates total length.

Location	Carapace Length (mm)	Carapace Width (mm)	Body Mass (g)	Reference
Western Atlantic				
French Guiana	65 (12)	50 (12)	–	Bacon (1970)
Suriname	58.3 (25) range: 56-60	41.2 (25) range: 39-44	–	Pritchard (1969, 1971a)
Suriname (Matapica)	59.5 ± 2.0 (360)	–	44.7 ± 3.5 (340)	Hilterman & Goverse (2007)
Suriname (Babunsanti)	59.1 ± 2.0 (100)	–	–	Hilterman & Goverse (2007)
Trinidad	67 (2) range: 66-68	49.5 (2) range: 49-50	–	Bacon (1970)
Costa Rica	62.8 (30)	41.8 (30)	–	Carr & Ogren (1959)
Costa Rica (Tortuguero)	–	–	45.7 ± 0.9 (6)	Thompson (1993)
Costa Rica (Gandoca)	59.6 ± 4.5 (2,621) range: 54-61	–	46.6 ± 6.1 (2,621) range: 39-52	Chacón & Eckert (2007)
USA (Hutchinson Island, Florida)	–	–	42.5 ± 3.0 (26)	Wyneken & Salmon (1992)
*USA (St. Croix, USVI)	–	–	52.6 ± 0.2 (8)	Lutcavage & Lutz (1986)
USA (Culebra, Puerto Rico)	**90.7 ± 4.2 (267) range: 79.1-99.0	38.9 ± 3.5 (267) range: 27.4-49.8	44.7 ± 4.2 (223) 31.5-55.0	Tucker (1988)
Western Pacific				
Malaysia (Terengganu)	57.3 (200) range: 51.0-64.8	–	38.2 (200) range: 28.5-45.6	Chan & Liew (1989)
Australia (Queensland)	56.4-60.5 (20)	–	41.2-53.5 (20)	Limpus & McLachlan (1979)
Australia (New South Wales)	61.0 (39) range: 57.3-65.3	–	–	Limpus (2006)
Eastern Pacific				
Mexico (Mexiquillo, Michoacan)	56.4±0.18 (2,800) range: 50.5-62.8	–	41.2 ± 3.1 (2,937) range: 32.4-50	L. Sarti M., *in litt.* 22 June 1991
Costa Rica (Playa Grande)	56.9 ± 2.1 (218 clutches)	38.8 ± 1.8 (218 clutches)	40.1 ± 2.7 (218 clutches)	Wallace et al. (2006a, 2007)
Costa Rica (Playa Grande)	–	–	40.5 ± 1.0 (8)	Jones et al. (2007)
Indian Ocean				
Sri Lanka	53.5 (55)	32.7 (55)	–	Kapurusinghe (2006)
Ceylon [Sri Lanka]	–	–	range: 32.6-33.6	Deraniyagala (1952)
South Africa (Tongaland)	58.7 (131) range: 54.8-63.4	39.3 (124) range: 36.3-43.5	37.3 (47) range: 27.5-41.0	Hughes (1974a)

Table 5. Leatherback sea turtle morphology from two specimens captured at sea. SCL (SCW) = Straight carapace length (width); CCL (CCW) = Curved carapace length (width).

Location	Specimen Size (Gender)	Part or Organ	Dimension or Mass	Notes	Reference
Western Atlantic					
USA (Louisiana)	Width: 95 cm (♀)	Body	154 cm	Length (max)	Dunlap (1955)
		Front Flipper	205 cm	Tip-to-tip (span)	
		Hind Flipper	117 cm	"Spread"	
		Heart	800 g		
		Alimentary Tract	1,620 cm	Mouth-to-anus	
		Esophagus (alone)	183 cm 4,700 g	Diameter: 15 cm at origin, 7.6 cm "further down"	
		Stomach	203 cm	"Tubular and irregularly dilatated at intervals of 7-12 cm"	
		Liver	8,000 g		
		Kidney	(R) 950 g (L) 870 g		
		Ovary	—	Each ovary had several hundred immature yellow eggs ≤ 6 mm	
Eastern Pacific					
USA (California)	144 cm SCL 97 cm SCW (♂)	Body	63 cm	Depth (max)	Lowe & Norris (1995)
		Head	24.5, 23.7 cm	Length, width	
		Front Flipper	84.3, 29.8 cm; 235 cm	Length, width; Tip-to-tip (span)	
		Hind Flipper	42.8, 26.8 cm	Length, width	
		Tail	17.2, 5.7 cm	Length, width	
		Penis	49.3, 9.6 cm	Length, width	

1983) before handbooks aimed at global (Pritchard et al. 1983, Eckert et al. 1999) and regional (e.g., Demetropoulos and Hadjichristophorou 1995, Chacón et al. 2001, Shanker et al. 2003, Eckert and Beggs 2006) audiences articulated standardized protocols intended to encourage comparable data collection between different populations and different studies.

External Morphology and Coloration

Dermochelys coriacea has a leathery skin instead of the usual outer covering of horny, keratinous scales (Appendix A). It would be an overstatement, however, to contend that there is an absence of all cornified external structures.

In addition to a stratum corneum, a horny beak is present but relatively weak. Claws may occur in embryos or hatchlings, but they are unknown in animals more than a few weeks old; on some occasions, as much as 30% of a clutch may bear claws. In addition, shallow temporary pits develop on the enlarged scales at the distal ends of the first two digits, and when a claw is present it protrudes from such a pit. The "beady" scales of terminal embryos and hatchlings are modified by ecdysis and ontogenetic changes; after the first few months scales are thin and inconspicuous. However, vestiges of scale divisions are often seen on the eyelids, neck and caudal crest of adults. These features have been described in detail in numerous works of Deraniyagala (1930, 1932, 1936b, 1939, 1953). These exceptions to the oft-repeated generalization of "no external keratin" (Carr 1952; Pritchard 1971a, 1979a, 1980; Ernst and Barbour 1972; Pritchard and Trebbau 1984) are not just trivial points, but reflect on ontogenetic and evolutionary considerations. Clearly, the lack of scales and claws on the shell and appendages of juveniles and older animals is not a neotenic (paedomorphic) reduction, but a highly specialized loss of a character virtually ubiquitous in Testudines (Frazier 1987).

Often over 2 m in total length, the great size of this turtle frequently gives the illusion that the body is flattened, but the anterior of the animal is almost barrel-shaped. Deraniyagala (1939) described the plastron as "boat shaped anteriorly" and "apt to be concave posteriorly." A nucho-scapular hump has been consistently described as the highest point of the carapace in both hatchlings and adults; it is supported by the columnar scapulae. Conspicuous on the lyre-shaped carapace are seven longitudinal keels that are irregularly serrate. Comments that there are only five keels on the carapace result from confusion; a narrow line of osteoderms ("platelets") may lie immediately dorsal to each marginal keel, sometimes reducing the conspicuousness of this outermost keel of the carapace (Brongersma 1969).

A pair of paramedial projections, conforming with the paramedial (or costal) keels, extend the anterior of the carapace, and an attenuated caudal projection carries the medial and paramedial keels posteriorly. The caudal projection commonly shows a variety of injuries and abnormalities (Brongersma 1969, Fretey 1982) which, based on studies in Tortuguero, Costa Rica (Reyes and Troëng 2001, Harrison and Troëng 2002), shorten the curved carapace length by an average of 4.75 cm (Stewart et al. 2007).

The marginal keel, below the supramarginal, forms the boundary between the carapace and plastron. The latter has six (three pairs) of feeble longitudinal keels, with the "medial" keel being composed of two close-set ridges separated by a medial groove (Deraniyagala 1930, 1939; Burne 1905; Brongersma 1969, 1970). Versluys (1913) described a "partly paired" median row, as the anterior section is sometimes fused. The anterior ends of the keels, particularly on the plastron, are frequently without sharp protuberances.

The front flippers are long and wide, both in relative and absolute terms. A patagium, or cruro-caudal fold, links the two hind limbs and the tail. The wide, paddle-like hind limbs are posteriorly directed. A "dorsal cutaneous ridge" or "crest" tops the laterally compressed tail, and in both sexes the cloaca is remarkably distant from the posterior of the plastron (Deraniyagala 1939). The tail of the adult male is longer and the cloaca extends further beyond the posterior tip of the carapace (James 2004, James et al. 2007).

No less remarkable is the head with a pair of large posteriorly-pointed cusps, each bordered anteriorly by a deep medial cleft and posteriorly by a deep notch in the anterior of the upper jaw. Brongersma (1970) and Rainey (1981) showed that in hatchlings the cusps terminate in a sharp spine. The anterior of the lower jaw has an equally conspicuous medial cusp, and the sharp recurved point fits neatly into a pit anterior to the choanae. A distinct internal ridge runs parallel to each maxillary margin forming a slot that receives each mandibular edge of the lower beak when the mouth is closed (Deraniyagala 1932, 1939; illustrated by Brongersma 1970). The large head and neck, which grade gradually into the body, are nearly immobile. The eyelid slits are nearly vertical. The nares open almost dorsally. There is no external tympanum.

The outer layer of the body has been described as "…tough, leathery and slightly flexible, composed of rather loose fibrous tissue and containing no cartilage…" (Dunlap 1955). Composed of connective tissue, the "dermal carapace" is as thick as 36 mm and makes up the bulk of the corselet; it is covered by a cuticle with osteoderms which together are only 5 mm thick (Deraniyagala 1932, 1936b, 1939, 1953). External pores pierce the anterior of the carapace between the supramarginal and inframarginal keels, and from 15–33 mm posterior to the edge of the corselet. They occur in hatchlings as well as in adults, and as many as three or four pores may be seen on each side. In the young turtle, each pore is surrounded by four or five scales, but the adult has only four or five lines radiating out from each opening (Deraniyagala 1932, 1936, 1939;

Brongersma 1970). The pores are probably related to Rathke's gland (Rainey 1981).

Coloration.—Adults are matte, or slate, black on the carapace, with interrupted white lines on the keels; white spots, often in three or four longitudinal lines, are between keels. The head has large white blotches, some of which may extend to the jaws; five longitudinal rows of spots may be discernible on the dorsal neck surface. The bases of the flippers have many white spots, and the top of the tail crest is white. White dominates much of the ventral surface, particularly along the keels. A black band may extend from the inguinal area to the cloaca. For details of coloration see Deraniyagala (1930, 1932, 1936, 1939) and Pritchard and Trebbau (1984).

There is tremendous variation in the coloration of individuals within populations, as evidenced by diversity among gravid females on the same nesting beach. White or pale spotting may vary from faint to abundant, so that females may range in coloration from nearly all black to boldly spotted. Some investigators contend that individuals may be recognized by differences in white (Duguy et al. 1980) or pink (McDonald and Dutton 1996) markings on the head. Descriptions of animals that are brown with yellowish markings (Duméril and Bibron 1835, Yañez 1951) are evidently based on mounted specimens where the oil has migrated to the exterior of the body. The appearance of an animal depends on its status; colors will be less intense if it is dry and dusty, more intense if wet.

Adult leatherbacks have a pink spot on the top of the head. In females, this mark has been thought to be a scar or abrasion produced by the male during copulation (Pritchard 1969, Hughes 1974a, Lazell 1976), but Benabib (1983), in the first quantitative study, argued that since the pink crown is constant and there is no evidence of lesions associated with it, this mark is more likely a normal part of the adult coloration. The pink spot is now known to be associated (in both sexes) with the pineal gland. According to Wyneken (2001), "…the ductless pineal gland (epiphysis) is a dorsal extension of the brain; it connects indirectly to the dorsal surface of the braincase, it is located deep to the fronto-parietal scale in cheloniids and the 'pink spot' in *Dermochelys* [and is] responsible for modulating biological rhythms." McDonald et al. (1996) have used the mark to identify adult individuals.

Hatchlings are intense black dorsally, or "blue black" according to Deraniyagala (1939), with white longitudinal keels, except the anterior of the medial keel, which is interrupted with black. The three inner lines extend dorsally onto the neck, where two more lines occur between them. The margins of the flippers, except at the distal ends of the first and second digits, are white. Ventrally, the plastron keels are covered by broad white longitudinal bands with black in between. The throat and bases of the flippers are mainly white (for developmental descriptions, see Chapter 3, *Embryonic and hatchling phase,* below).

Little is known of the coloration of young juveniles. During their first year the carapace is totally dark, but thereafter intense white spots develop; in contrast, the plastron is mostly white with longitudinal black markings paralleling the umbilicus on each side (Deraniyagala 1936b, 1939; Brongersma 1970; Hughes 1974a; Pritchard and Trebbau 1984).

Eggs.—Cross-sections of decalcified and stained egg shell indicate that the shell membranes are about 250 μm thick and that the matrix of the shell is only about half that thickness. There is said to be no change in structure during incubation, and no indication that the membranes detach from the outer shell (Simkiss 1962).

The ultrastructure of *Dermochelys* egg shell was investigated by Solomon and Watt (1985), who presented numerous scanning electron micrographs. Mainly, the exterior of the shell is composed of the spicular aragonite form of calcium carbonate; these crystals are laid down in radial patterns indicating the presence of saucer-shaped nucleation sites of membrane fibers in the mammillary layer (Solomon and Reid 1983). A secondary crystal layer shows a great variety of crystalline forms; interspersed randomly among the aragonite crystals are, in particular, calcite blocks and flattened lozenge-shaped crystals. These may occur singly or stacked with secondary crystal growths. Pores were not observed, but the shell is thin enough that gaseous exchange occurs across it. No outer cuticle was observed.

Infrared spectrophotometry showed a dominant absorption peak at 860 cm (corresponding to aragonite) and another clear peak at 879 cm (calcite), indicating that calcite comprises only about 5% of the crystal. The mechanism for production of even this small proportion of calcite is not understood, but indicates changes in the oviductal environment (e.g., pH, ionic content, temperature, trace elements). It was hypothesized that phosphorus, which is absent from the secondary crystalline layer, is intimately involved in the production of aragonite (Solomon and Watt 1985).

Internal Morphology

The only cryptodires known to lack flaps or ridges around the lateral margins of the choanae are *Dermochelys* and the Cheloniidae. In *Dermochelys,* the choanae are remarkably large and anteriorly placed (Parsons 1968), with no surrounding papillae (Deraniyagala 1939, Parsons 1968, Brongersma 1970). Villiers (1958) referred to unicellular nasal glands. The function of these is unclear, and further anatomical details were not presented. Detailed descriptions of the chondrocranium, nerves and sinuses of the head were given by Nick (1912). The cranial arteries were investigated by Albrecht (1976).

Alimentary System.—The anatomy of the alimentary system has been described by Rathke (1846 *in* Burne 1905), Vaillant (1896), Burne (1905), Dunlap (1955), Rainey (1981), and Hartog and van Nierop (1984). From the pharyngeal cavity to the cardiac sphincter, sharp papillae with horny sheaths line the esophagus, pointing posteriorly, and forming practically all the exposed inner surface (see Dunlap 1955, Villiers 1958). They occur in embryos as well as in adults, decreasing in length and thickness of keratinous armor from the pharynx (8 cm long in adults) to the stomach (where they are soft and only a few mm long). Burne (1905) reported that these papillae are always single at the anterior end of the esophagus, often bifid in the middle, and sometimes trifid at the posterior, or cardiac, end.

There is no possibility of pharyngeal-esophageal gas exchange, for the thick keratinous sheaths provide poor surfaces for efficient gas exchange and the papillae are very poorly vascularized (Brongersma 1970; see also anatomical descriptions in Dunlap 1955 and Hartog and van Nierop 1984). Instead, the papillae are thought to function in retaining food (Bleakney 1965, Brongersma 1970, Hartog and van Nierop 1984). Versluys (1913) argued that a close relationship between *Dermochelys* and the cheloniids is evidenced by the fact that only these turtles have highly developed esophageal papillae.

The anterior part of the alimentary canal seems to be highly variable, or else there has been some confusion in distinguishing different parts. The main constant in descriptions of the esophagus is its horny papillae. Burne (1905) described and illustrated a looped esophagus with the ascending limb rising, nearly parallel to the descending limb, to meet the stomach; all of this was contained within a peritoneal sac. He concluded that the unusually long and bent esophagus and the complicated stomach were somehow related to the well developed mesenteric sac. Dunlap (1955) agreed that the trachea and esophagus are "uncommonly long" (11% of the total length of the alimentary canal), and this was thought to simply accommodate the extension of the neck. The esophagus was said to make a "fish-hook curve" but neither a tight loop nor a mesenteric sac were mentioned.

Villiers (1958) and Bleakney (1965) agreed with the description in Burne (1905), referring to the esophagus as recurved or "J-shaped." Rainey (1981), however, clearly showed a hatchling with an esophagus that completely encircled the anterior stomach, and he stated that the mesenteries supporting the esophagus and stomach are more complex than in the cheloniids. Hartog and van Nierop (1984) added further support to the concept of a relatively long esophagus. They pointed out that its length is not strongly correlated to body size, suggesting that there is great individual variation and/or that the presence or absence of food has a marked effect on gut length and form. Again, there was no mention of either a tight loop or a mesenteric sac in the esophagus. Pritchard and Trebbau (1984) stated that the esophagus is singularly long and looped, and they suggested that it serves as a food storage organ.

Variation in the anatomy of the stomach is apparently even greater. Vaillant (1896) described the stomach to be proportionally longer than in cheloniids and more complex, with a globular sac followed by a tubular section. The latter was U-shaped, twice as long as the former and divided internally by folds, some of which were virtually diaphragms with central perforations. A fibrous fascia enveloped the stomach. Burne (1905) described and illustrated an anterior globular part and a posterior U-shaped tubular part. The tubular stomach was illustrated as tightly looped with two limbs descending and one ascending; it had approximately 13 compartments formed by approximately 13 irregular transverse folds, but no diaphragms perforated in their centers. The globular stomach was enclosed within, and the tubular stomach was included within, a peritoneal sac. Dunlap (1955) reported only that the gastrointestinal lining made an abrupt transition at the cardiac sphincter from the papillae to the glandular mucosa, and that the stomach was irregularly dilated.

Rainey (1981) stated that the stomach was composed of two distant parts, clearly showing loops in the posterior tubular stomach. Hartog and van Nierop (1984) described the stomach as unusually long and made up of a sac-like anterior part and a larger tubular posterior part. They reported that it is the anterior stomach that is U-shaped and muscular, and both legs of the U are tightly connected by mesentery and connective tissue. The tubular stomach is thin and subdivided into compartments by 16 distinct, permanent, transverse folds, each provided with a sphincter muscle. Although there was great variation in the development of these compartments, both within and between stomachs, consistently there were two small but well isolated compartments just anterior to the pylorus. A rich plexus of large vessels was observed between the bends of the tubular stomach (Vaillant 1896). Only a left anterior abdominal vein has been observed (Rathke 1848 *in* Burne 1905, Burne 1905).

According to Vaillant (1896), there is no caecum, but large and small intestines are easily distinguished by external diameter. The wall of the small intestine is very thin and covered with a honeycomb-like mucosa, more complicated than in any other Testudine. A gall bladder duct enters the small intestine in the transverse limb at two places, but the connection is functional only at the site more distant from the gall bladder (as much as 9 cm away) where a slit-like opening is bordered by foliate lips (Burne 1905). What may be "…an extremely vestigeal Meckel's diverticulum…" was observed in the free ventral mesentary some 40 cm posterior of its beginning (Burne 1905).

The liver consists of two broad lobes of equal length, but the right lobe is larger; the two lobes are connected by two narrow bands (Deraniyagala 1930, 1939).

Little is documented about the cloaca. Deraniyagala (1939, 1953) described a young specimen that expelled 20 cc of water, and he considered this as proof that mucosal respiration occurs in the cloaca. However, with a lack of supportive evidence it is difficult to accept that this could contribute significantly to metabolic needs. As Hartog and van Nierop (1984) pointed out, there is no strong relationship between gut length and body size. However, the relative lengths of various parts of the gut do not differ greatly between individuals.

Respiratory System.—Paired lateral folds in the larynx appeared to be "rudimentary vocal cords" (Dunlap 1955). The larynx is notable in that the procricoid cartilage forms a process on the anterior dorsal surface of the crico-thyroid, instead of being completely separate. The first complete tracheal ring is the seventh (Burne 1905); further information is in Rathke (1846 *in* Burne 1905). Around the margins of the trabeculae and extending into the air spaces were bundles of smooth muscle; these would provide the mechanism for active expiration from the depths of the lungs. The alveolae are lined with a rich plexus of thin-walled capillaries, evidently not covered by an alveolar epithelium (Dunlap 1955).

Circulatory System.—The heart was observed to be unusually long and narrow for a Chelonian, due mainly to the ventricle forming a long and stout gubernaculum cordis; this posterior half of the ventricle is virtually solid muscle, without a cavity. The auricular walls are relatively thin (Burne 1905). The anterior of the ventricle has been described as "spongy" having many muscular trabeculae; as the coronary artery is relatively small and the coronary vein is large, it was suggested that a major part of the blood supply comes directly from the ventricle chamber (Dunlap 1955).

The left aorta, notably on the dorsal wall, has a linear row of small outpouchings that pass into the interaortic septum. Also unique to this turtle is the course of the left aorta. It leaves the ventricle on the right side of the muscular "septum" and at the top of the truncus, goes past the opening of the right aorta, and joins the brachiocephalic trunk. The communication between the left aorta and the brachiocephalic trunk is comparable to the Foramen of Panizza in the Crocodylia (Adams 1962), but since these features are based on one specimen, it is not known how constant they are in *Dermochelys*.

The pulmonary artery originates in a special subchamber of the ventricle, and although this shows a tendency toward an advanced four-chambered heart, the separation was thought not to be homologous to the intraventricular septum of crocodiles, birds, and mammals. Shortly after their bifurcation, the pulmonary arteries have distinct muscular thickenings that were thought to be sphincters (Koch 1934, Dunlap 1955). Dunlap postulated that the sphincters close and the heart rate drops as part of an automatic response to diving, which is perhaps stimulated by the extension of the neck.

Evidently unaware of these earlier brief descriptions, Sapsford (1978) described and illustrated the results of dissections of the pulmonary artery. Just distal to the ductus Botalli there is an abrupt thickening of the walls of the pulmonary artery, from 1.5 to 3.9 mm in an adult specimen. At the same time, the external diameter decreases by a factor of 0.5. The thickened wall has a remarkable concentration of smooth muscle, which after an unspecified distance, but evidently several cm, ends abruptly. It was originally thought that this sphincter served to shunt blood away from the lungs during diving/apnea to reduce oxygen consumption in non-vital areas. However, the presence of sphincters in land tortoises raised the possibility that there is another function, the control of heat exchange (loss especially) via the peripherally situated lungs. It was reasoned that the primary function of the pulmonary artery sphincter is thermoregulatory, and that this system was elaborated on as a diving adaptation secondarily as ancestral Testudines adapted to the marine environment.

A countercurrent heat exchanger has been described from the limb bases; it consists of well defined vascular bundles of closely packed vessels with as many as four major veins per artery (Greer et al. 1973). It occurs in hatchlings as well as in adults (Mrosovsky 1980) and has been linked to an ability to "thermoregulate" specifically in heat conservation (see Chapter 3, *Nutrition and metabolism, Thermoregulation,* below). There is also a suggestion that a counter-current heat exchanger exists in the region of the nares "to conserve body heat" (Sapsford and Hughes 1978).

Urogenital System.—The urogenital system has been briefly described by Burne (1905) and Dunlap (1955). Microscopic examination of peripheral portions of the adult kidney revealed what appeared to be nephrogenic tissue in subcapsular islands. Hence, nephrons are thought to be produced throughout life (not only until hatching), which would enable an increase in excretory function during growth. An ability to increase excretory function is of great importance since body mass increases by a factor of 10^4 (Dunlap 1955).

The ureters arise from the medial aspect near the caudal end of each kidney and continue caudally to enter the cloaca by separate lateral openings in close association with the ends of the oviducts. The ureters do not communicate directly wtith the urinary bladder, but open freely into the cloaca (where the urine is refluxed into the urinary bladder). Chemical analysis of urine (from postmortem specimens) showed urea nitrogen = 140 mg dL^{-1}, uric acid = 320 mg dL^{-1}, and chloride = 503 mg dL^{-1} (Dunlap 1955).

The posterior end of a structure thought to be the "interrenal organ" was examined histologically: oval bodies, always associated with hyalinized scars, were thought to be primordial follicles, and it was suggested that this organ may be the true source of ova, while the anatomical "ovary" is only a repository for developing eggs (Dunlap 1955). In immature females the oviducts do not communicate with the cloaca, but they are imperforate, separated by a "hymen" (Burne 1905, Dunlap 1955).

The penis is relatively simple; the glans consists of only a single U-shaped fold, apparently an enlarged continuation of the seminal ridges. Terminating on the inner surface of the fold is the single seminal groove; sinuses are evidently absent. This condition is comparable to that in the other Recent sea turtles and less elaborate than that found in other cryptodires; it led to the conclusion that *Dermochelys* is closely related to the other extant sea turtles (Zug 1966).

Muscular System.—Detailed general descriptions of the muscular anatomy are given by Rathke (1846), Fürbringer (1874) and Burne (1905). Poglayen-Neuwall (1953) did detailed studies of jaw musculature and innervation in a *Dermochelys* young enough to have scales; these findings were then compared with those from other species. Burne (1905) presented several notable observations that distinguish *D. coriacea* from other chelonians. These include: the cervico-capitis takes its origin only from vertebrae IV and V and not from III; the transversalis cervicis inserts onto the basioccipital, as well as onto vertebrae I and II; the sphincter colli inserts onto the scapula; the longus colli has no origin from anterior ribs or the nuchal "plate"; the humero-carpali-metacarpalis I inserts onto the head of metacarpal I, not upon the radius and carpus.

The musculature of the thoracic and lumbar regions is in a degenerate condition, and Burne (1905) was unable to distinguish separate muscle masses. However, muscles extend posteriorly beyond the 9th rib, and he concluded that the degree of degeneration is less than in other chelonians and, thus, that the unique carapace of *D. coriacea* is primitive and not a retrograde specialization. The anterior half of the body cavity is almost all pectoral musculature. Several fibromuscular sheets divide the abdominal cavity into compartments. One sheet originated from the ventral surface of the lung and inserted into the capsule of the right lobe of the liver; it was thought to function as a diaphragm (Dunlap 1955).

Conspicuous fat bodies are present in *Dermochelys*. The green fat of this species occasionally resembles multilocular brown fat, but there is considerable variation in fat color and no knowledge of the primary function of fat bodies. The thickness of "the fat layer" at the juncture of the carapace and plastron, of an adult-sized female caught in Cornwall, England, was 45–55 mm (Brongersma 1972). The hatchling has discrete lenticular, yellow-white fat bodies in both axillary and inguinal regions, which are (relatively) larger than in cheloniids (Rainey 1981).

The high concentration of oil in *Dermochelys* tissues is remarkable; the oil is pervasive even in the skeleton and outer body covering.

Cranial Morphology

Skull.—The most important studies of the skull are those of Nick (1912) and Wegner (1959), as well as Gaffney (1979) who presented eight illustrations and listed another nine publications in which there are valuable illustrations (see also Deraniyagala 1939, 1953). Because it is so unusual, the skull of this species is one of the best studied and illustrated of all the turtles (Gaffney 1979). In comparison with most turtles, many cranial elements are reduced or neotenic, and despite its large size, the bones are of low density and poorly fused; hence, the skull is weak and easily disarticulates post mortem. Its general form is unique. There is no significant temporal emargination, and the supraoccipital process is almost totally occluded dorsally by the skull roof. Deep notches in the midline of the maxillaries as well as the anterior cutting surface of each maxilla produce a conspicuous cusp on either side of the jaw; both the premaxillary and maxillary contribute to the cusp (Appendix B).

Gaffney (1979) discussed the characteristic features of *D. coriacea*, of which many are unusual. The frontal is omitted from the orbital margin, and the postorbital is singularly large, covering a major part of the temporal roof. The medially directed process of the jugal is reduced and does not contact either the palatine or the pterygoid, as is normal in turtles. As the horizontal palatine process of the maxilla is so narrow that it is nearly absent, the palatine extends laterally to the labial ridge of the maxilla, and there is only a primary palate. The crista supraoccipitalis, which is the attachment site for tendons of the adductor mandibulae externus and normally the most prominent external feature of the supraoccipital, is relatively small. The fact that the maxillaries and premaxillaries do not border the internal nares, but slender processes of the palatines and vomer do, was used by Dollo (1903) to argue that an ancestor of *Dermochelys* had a secondary palate similar to that of the cheloniids.

Dermochelys coriacea shares a number of peculiar features with the cheloniids. The foramen palatinum posterius is absent (Gaffney 1979). In the quadrate, the incisura columellae auris, containing the single ear bone, is relatively open. There is no contact between the maxillae and pterygoid. The internal carotid artery gives off the palatine branch from within the cranial cavity, not closely surrounded by bone within the canalis caroticus; this is related to several features in the pterygoid involving reduced, or absent, bony roofs or canals and the absence of foramina (Nick 1912, Albrecht 1976, Gaffney 1979). As in some cheloniids, the basioccipital is exposed dorsally between the exoccipitals for the length of the condylus occipitalis (Gaffney 1979). The processus trochlearis oticum of the prootic is highly reduced. As in the cheloniids, the taenia intertrabecularis develops in the embryo; however, unlike the cheloniids, in *D. coriacea* it does not ossify, whereas the dermal posterior parasphenoid blastema does and persists as a rudiment in the endochondral basisphenoid (Nick 1912, Pehrson 1945, Gaffney 1979). Versluys (1907) was first to show, despite long standing opinions to the contrary, that the parasphenoid does exist in *Dermochelys*, although this was not immediately accepted (Fuchs 1910, Versluys 1910).

In addition, *D. coriacea* has several unique features in its skull. The squamosal does not reach the processus paroccipitalis of the opisthotic (Gaffney 1979). This is the only cryptodire known to lack an ossified epipterygoid, evidently from neoteny (Nick 1912; Gaffney 1975, 1979). Neither the prootic nor the pterygoid contacts the rudimentary processus inferior parietalis; pterygoid contact with the anteroventrolateral portion of the prootic is also absent (Gaffney 1979).

Several other cartilaginous features of the skull are noteworthy. The brain case, with highly reduced bony walls, is secondarily closed by cartilage (Nick 1912). Rostral cartilage, an extension of the nasal septum, develops in embryos (Pehrson 1945). The occipital condyle remains cartilaginous throughout life (Hay 1908).

The sclerotic ossicles commonly number 14, but may be as few as seven, when there may be a gap in the anterodorsal part of the ring. Usually the number of ossicles in each eye is equal, and evidently individual ossicles may expand to fill gaps in the ring. Neighboring ossicles may be subimbricate or fused (Deraniyagala 1932, 1939, 1953). In 31 turtles (6 hatchlings, 2 small juveniles: 17, 27 cm CCL, and 23 subadults and adults [9♀, 8♂, 6 unknown]: 122–173 cm CCL) examined by Avens and Goshe (2008), there were 11–14 ossicles per eye (mean = 12); there was no discernible gap in the ring (L.R. Goshe, pers. comm.).

The mandible also exhibits unique or highly unusual features; the dentary contacts only the surangular and the angular, rather than five different bones. Only the labial ridge is developed on the dentary, for the linguinal ridge is absent (Gaffney 1979). There is no depression in the lateral surface of the dentary for attachment of the adductor mandibulae externus. The coronoid is absent; the articular is unossified; and the prearticular does not contact any other bone, for it is isolated by the cartilaginous articular.

Post-Cranial Skeleton.—A thorough and detailed study of the trunk, limb and dermal skeleton was done by Völker (1913). The vertebrae number: 8 cervical, 10 dorsal, 2 sacral and 18 caudal (Deraniyagala 1939) [n.b. Völker (1913) reported one more sacral and one less caudal]. The neck is relatively short, evidently from secondary shortening; and although some vertebrae are united by thick cartilaginous pads and strong fibrous tissue, they show articulations typical of the Cryptodira (Versluys 1913, Völker 1913). However, Hay (1922) refused to accept that this, or the resemblance of vertebrae with those of other sea turtles pointed out earlier by Vaillant (1877), had phylogenetic significance. As is usual for the Cryptodira, the IVth vertebra is biconvex, those anterior to it are opisthocoelus, those posterior are procoelus. The joint between VI and VII tends toward immobility and sometimes it is almost fused; the joint between VII and VIII is highly variable, sometimes biconvex (Williams 1950).

Cervical ribs are reduced in size, cartilaginous and generally fused to the vertebrae (Romer 1956) (Appendix C). Of the 10 dorsal ribs, the first pair are short and the last pair are vestigial; the others have thin phalanges on both anterior and posterior edges which are widest medially. Compared to the costal bones of other turtles, the ribs of this species are narrow and feeble, but Hay (1898, 1908) thought that their flattened form, with jagged edges, showed that they had once been fused to costal plates. The caudal vertebrae are procoelous and lack chevron bones (Deraniyagala 1939).

Several features distinguish the humerus. Unlike in most other sea turtles, the ectepicondylar foramen persists throughout life, and does not open to form a groove. The deltopectoral crest projects far laterally, and is associated with a strong transverse line of sites for muscle attachment on the ventral surface of the shaft. The lateral tubercle is poorly developed. Hind limb elements, femur, tibia and fibula, are somewhat flattened dorso-ventrally and relatively short (Romer 1956). The phalanges are elongate and lack condyles. The carpus has only one central, although a rudiment of the second radial central may be present in young animals (Versluys 1913, Völker 1913) (Appendix C).

The epiphyses of the long bones remain cartilaginous and unossified throughout life, and they are highly vascularized from the epiphyses to the diaphyses by conspicuous perichondral and transphyseal vessels that traverse relatively thin physeal plates (Rhodin et al. 1981). Conspicuous endochondral and periosteal bone cones are thought to be unchanged throughout life from remodeling. These chondro-osseous characteristics are comparable to those in marine mammals and indicate the potential for rapid growth and an active metabolic rate (Rhodin 1985).

The elements of the pectoral girdle are relatively robust, with a massive coracoid. More remarkable is the pelvic girdle, which lacks the usually large thyroid fenestra in the puboishiadic plate, and instead has a pair of small foramina. The plate remains largely cartilaginous. A well developed epipubis is unique in having a medial fenestra (Versluys 1913, Völker 1913, Deraniyagala 1939, Romer 1956).

The normal testudine dermal skeleton (termed "thecal") is extremely reduced; only a bat-shaped nuchal bone is present in the carapace, and this is separated from the outer shell by a layer of connective tissue (Versluys 1913). Thecal elements of the plastron are also reduced; instead of the usual solid plate, there is a flimsy ring around the periphery, although there is some overlap in the eight splint-like bones. The entoplastron is absent, except as a cartilaginous vestige in some embryos (Deraniyagala 1939). Both the carapace and the plastron have been described and illustrated by Völker (1913), Deraniyagala (1939) and Brongersma (1969).

In contrast, "epithecal" dermal elements are highly developed. About seven months after hatching, osteoderms begin to appear along the keels. Tectiform platelets dominate, but their line is interrupted by flat ossicles. Gradually, smaller, flat ossicles appear between the keels of the carapace, until virtually the entire dorsal surface is covered by a mosaic of interlocking ossicles (Appendix C). Osteoderms on the plastron only develop under the keel ridges, and even then only posterior to the epiplastral region and in interrupted lines. The osteoderms on the neural ridge of an adult female only made up 5 mm of the total 41 mm thickness. Sometimes described as "polygons" the dermal ossicles are irregular in shape; those from between ridges are rarely more than a centimeter wide (Deraniyagala 1939) (see Chapter 3, *Embryonic and hatchling phases, Embryonic phase,* below). A detailed description of the epithecal mosaic is given by Broin and Pironon (1980).

Compared with other, extinct dermochelyids, the plastral armor of *D. coriacea* is highly reduced, and Deraniyagala (1930, 1934, 1939) concluded that the process of reduction in osteoderms appears to be proceeding dorsally in the extant form. The epithecal elements of the plastron are restricted almost completely to six longitudinal rows. Proceeding laterally from the paramedial rows, the osteoderms often become larger but less numerous. In two of the three specimens examined in detail by Brongersma (1969; two adult-sized males and a subadult of unspecified sex), the osteoderms of the plastron showed signs of abrasion and in all cases some platelets had evidently fallen out. There was no explanation for this.

Descriptions of the remarkable anatomical features of the shell and discussions of their phylogenetic relevance have been common and lively during the earlier part of the last century (see Versluys 1913, 1914; Hay 1922). Pritchard and Trebbau (1984) hypothesized that a mosaic of small bones allows the turtle to grow in size more rapidly than would be possible with the normal, heavily ossified turtle shell. In this respect, comparisons with other taxa (e.g., Glyptodonts, Recent Edentates) that also have a mosaic of dermal osteoderms may prove enlightening.

Versluys (1913) summarized information from numerous detailed osteological studies to conclude that the epithecal shell of *Dermochelys* is not a *de novo* structure, but has homologues in both living and fossil turtles. Völker (1913) argued that the peripherals (equal to the "marginal bones") of the typical thecophoran shell are epithecal in origin. This contrasts with Dollo's (1901) view that epithecal elements are unique to the Dermochelyidae, and also with Hay's (1922) view that epithecal elements are found in a variety of testudinates, living and fossil, but nonetheless that *Dermochelys* is in a distinct suborder. Romer (1956) listed a variety of reptiles, including turtles extant and fossil, that have well developed osteoderms, and although there is disagreement about the evolution of dermal ossicles, he concluded, together with earlier authors, that epithecal components are included in the shells of other turtles.

An earlier system of referring to "subdermal" and "true dermal" elements to the shell (Hay 1898, 1908) was rejected in favor of "thecal" and "epithecal" because both classes of elements arise from the dermal layer (Versluys 1913, Völker 1913). Likewise, describing the carapace of *Dermochelys* as "dermal" and that of the other turtles as "skeletal" (Deraniyagala 1932) is imprecise. Also inaccurate is the reference to a "primitive dermal skeleton" (Villiers 1958). Although the carapace of *Dermochelys* is unique among living Testudines, it is not usual to refer to it as a "pseudo-carapace" or "pseudo-dossière" (Fretey 1978, 1982; Fretey and Frenay 1980). Useful illustrations of the postcranial skeleton are in Deraniyagala (1939, 1953).

Cytomorphology

The calculated volume of an erythrocyte (> 900 μm^3) is more than 10 times the volume of a human corpuscle (Frair 1977a). Red cell counts ranged from 447 to 547, averaging $0.503 \times 10^6 \mu l^{-1}$; and packed cell volumes ranged from 32 to 49, with a mean of 42.3 cm^3 per 100 cm^3 [0.423 L per L] (with no significant relation to carapace length). In comparison with other species of sea turtles, the counts were higher and the mean corpuscular volume (MCV) was lower (Frair 1977b).

Montilla et al. (2008) reported hematological values in 13 gravid females nesting at Querepare Beach, Venezuela. Counting of red (RBC) and white (WBC) blood cells were conducted using the Natt and Herricks technique, with the following results: mean RBC value = $0.33 \times 10^3 \mu l^{-1} \pm 0.06$ (0.25–0.43); mean WBC value = $3.15 \times 10^3 \mu l^{-1} \pm 0.7$ (1.9–4.6); PCV = 35.4% as determined through centrifugation; and Mean Corpuscular Volume = 1076.9 fL ± 158.3 (878–1360). WBC differential counts were performed manually using light microscopy and Diff-Quik stains; four types of WBC were identified (heterophils, lymphocytes, eosinophils, monocytes). Deem et al. (2006) reported similar values for PCV, RBC and WBC from 28 nesting leatherbacks in Gabon.

Biochemistry

Chemical analyses of blood (postmortem specimens) showed the following concentrations: non-protein nitrogen = 109 mg dL^{-1}; urea nitrogen = 70 mg dL^{-1}; uric acid = 4 mg dL^{-1}; chloride = 596 mg dL^{-1}; total protein = 4.77 g %; albumin = 2.21 g %; globulin = 2.40 g %; fibrinogen = 0.12 g % (Dunlap 1955). These blood concentrations represent: 50% of the value of urea in urine; 1.25% of the uric acid in urine; and 118.49% of the chloride value in urine.

Deem et al. (2006) reported plasma biochemistry values from 18 adult female leatherbacks nesting in Gabon, including the following ranges: glucose (55–95 mg dL^{-1}), sodium (124–148 mmol L^{-1}), potassium (2.8–5.1 mmol L^{-1}), CO_2 (18–25 mmol L^{-1}), blood urea nitrogen (2–13 mg dL^{-1}), total protein (3.0–6.0 g dL^{-1}), albumin (1.0–2.4 g dL^{-1}), globulins (1.7–3.8 g dL^{-1}), cholesterol (136–497 mg dL^{-1}), triglycerides (232–473 mg dL^{-1}), calcium (4.4–10 mg dL^{-1}), phosphorus (8.9–14 mg dL^{-1}), uric acid (0.2 mg dL^{-1}), aspartate aminotransferase (94–234 U L^{-1}), creatine kinase (20–7086 U L^{-1}) and others. Harms et al. (2007) reported similar values, with the exception of higher calcium (10.1–16.8 mg dL^{-1}) and phosphorus (13.1–20.2 mg dL^{-1}), from 13 nesting leatherbacks in Trinidad, and also included measurements of chloride (104–117 mmol L^{-1}), lactate (0.9–4.2 mmol L^{-1}), and others.

Tests of immunoprecipitation with antiserums show that *D. coriacea* is distinct from the hard-shelled sea turtles, but more like them than other turtles (Frair 1979). Similar results were obtained with electrophoresis and immunoelectrophoresis of serums, and it was reported that *Dermochelys* has the second fastest moving anodal line (albumin) (Frair 1982). These studies resulted in the conclusion that *D. coriacea* is in the same family as the other Recent sea turtles.

Molecular and functional properties of the ferrous and ferric derivatives of the native and PCMB-reacted main myoglobin component (Mb II) have been compared with those of other monomeric hemoproteins, and found to be similar to those of sperm whale myoglobin (Ascenzi et al. 1984).

Studies of six tryptic peptide patterns (hemoglobin fingerprints) in six species of turtles showed that *Dermochelys* often has the simplest pattern, with fewer peptide spots. It was concluded that this turtle arose from the cheloniids because its globins were said to be most similar to those of cheloniids (Chen and Mao 1981). However, the results presented do not show this unequivocally. Cohen and Stickler (1958) reported that this turtle, like several other species, lacks human-like albumen proteins in the serum. Frair (1969) found that compared with fresh serum, serum that has been stored at 4°C for 10 years loses about one third of its reactivity in immunological reactions. This effect was similar to the results with freshwater turtles, but more marked than with other species of sea turtles.

Two unsaturated fatty acids are concentrated in depot fat: the monoene *trans* 16:1tw10 (*trans*-6-hexa-decenoic acid) and the polyene 20:4w6 (Ackman et al. 1971, 1972). In turtles, the monoene is only reported from marine species, in which the polyene is also unusually prominent; as both of these fatty acids are concentrated in jellyfish, they are thought to originate exogenously in the turtles, from coelenterate food items (Ackman et al. 1971, Joseph et al. 1985). The unusually high concentration of another long-chained unsaturated acid, notably 20:1w7, may result from the same food chain effect, as may the occurrence of 22:4w6 (Ackman et al. 1971). An absence of 16:1w9 and a relatively low proportion of 18:1w7 to 18:1w9 was taken as evidence that metabolic chain shortening is not as common as with other turtles, particularly freshwater species. Nearly comparable proportions of the saturated fatty acids 12:0 (lauric) and 14:0 occur in fats of *Dermochelys* (Ackman et al. 1971) and these are thought to have been converted from jellyfish carbohydrates (Joseph et al. 1985).

The diversity of chemical compounds found in the oils is unusual for a marine animal (Ackman and Burgher 1965). Analysis of oil specimens from Sri Lanka and Japan showed saponification values of 199.6 and 181.3, respectively and iodine content of 103.8% and 128.1%, respectively (Deraniyagala 1953). Antibiotic effects have been demonstrated in *Dermochelys* oil (Bleakney 1965), and this potential warrants detailed investigation.

Karyotype.—In an early review of cryptodirian chromosomes, Bickham and Carr (1983) could not report any data for *D. coriacea*. Medrano et al. (1987) examined chromosomal preparations from kidney, spleen, and lung cells of three leatherback hatchlings from artificially incubated eggs. Based on incubation temperature, all were presumed to be males. Using the same nomenclature and categorization as Bickham and Carr (1983), they arranged chromosome types as follows: group A consists of metacentric and submetacentric chromosomes, group B consists of telocentric and subtelocentric chromosomes, and group C consists of microchromosomes. They reported that leatherbacks have a diploid number of 56 chromosomes and identified seven pairs of group A macrochromosomes, 5 pairs of group B macrochromosomes and 16 pairs of group C microchromosomes. No heteromorphic sex chromosomes were found.

Medrano et al. (1987) concluded that this is the same chromosomal configuration shown by other extant sea turtle taxa (2n = 56; c.f. Bickham 1981, 1984); noted that distinct adult morphological characteristics (e.g., shell constitution: Romer 1956; chondro-osseous morphology: Rhodin et al. 1981) represent derived characters; and supported the classifications of Gaffney (1975) and Bickham and Carr (1983) that there are two living families of sea turtle, the Dermochelyidae and the Cheloniidae (see *Taxonomic Status*, above).

Chapter 2: Distribution

Total Area

No other reptile has a geographic range as great as that of the leatherback sea turtle (Table 6, Figure 1). The species is known to nest on every continent except Europe and Antarctica, as well as on many islands in the Caribbean and the Indo-Pacific. Reliable at-sea sightings confirm a range that extends from ~71°N (Carriol and Vader 2002) to 47°S (Eggleston 1971). A record of *Dermochelys* in the Barents Sea is often but erroneously attributed to Bannikov et al. (1977), who reported the species from the Bering Sea; in fact, the Barents Sea sighting was of a loggerhead sea turtle (*Caretta caretta*) (see Brongersma 1972, Kuzmin 2002).

In the Western Atlantic, a regular summer population appears in the Gulf of Maine and as far north as Newfoundland (48°N) (Bleakney 1965, Brongersma 1972, Lazell 1980, Shoop et al. 1981), and there is also a record from Labrador (56°45'N) (Threlfall 1978). There are numerous records from as far south as Rio de la Plata and Mar del Plata, Argentina (38°S) (Freiberg 1945, Frazier 1984).

Eastern Atlantic records include northern Norway (68°46'N), Iceland and the Baltic Sea (Brongersma 1972). An adult female caught at Skreifjorden, Seiland, Finnmark in northern Norway in September 1997 (~71°N, 23°E) is the northernmost record for the species (Carriol and Vader 2002) and the range extends as far south as Angola and Cape Town (34°S) (Hughes 1974a). European and Mediterranean sightings are summarized by Casale et al. (2003) and Frazier et al. (2005).

Indian Ocean records range from the northern limits of the Red Sea (28°N) (Frazier and Salas 1984a) to the waters of the Southern Ocean off South Africa (41°48'S, 22°18'E) (Hughes et al. 1998). There are numerous records from Southeast Asia (Polunin 1975, Hamann et al. 2006a), but fewer from Australia and Tasmania (Limpus and McLachlan 1979, Tarvey 1993). Sightings extend into New Zealand, some as far south as Foveaux Strait (47°S), the southernmost record for the species (Eggleston 1971).

In the Northwest Pacific, there are records from the Japanese coast, some as far north as 44°N (Nishimura 1964a, 1964b), from near Mys Povorotnyg on the Soviet coast (~44°N) (Taranetz

Table 6. Published records that define the known northern and southern geographic range for successful egg-laying by leatherback sea turtles.

Region	Northern Nesting Record	Southern Nesting Record	Reference
Eastern Pacific Ocean	San Felipé, Baja California, Mexico (30° 56' N)	Mulatos, Colombia (2° 39' N)	N: Caldwell (1962) S: Amorocho et al. (1992)
Western Atlantic Ocean	Assateague Island National Seashore, Maryland, USA (38° N)[1]	Torres, Rio Grande do Sul, Brazil (29° S)	N: Rabon et al. (2003) S: Soto et al. (1997)
Eastern Atlantic Ocean	"at the entrance of Bolon de Djinack," Senegal (13° 35' N, 16° 32' W)[2]	between Cabo Ledo (9° 39' S, 13° 15' E) and Cabo de São Bráz (9° 58' S, 13° 19' E), Angola[3]	N: Dupuy (1986) S: Carr & Carr (1991)
Western Indian Ocean	Quirimbas Archipelago National Park, Mozambique (12° 19' S, 40° 40' E)	Storms River mouth, Western Cape, South Africa (34° 01' S, 23° 56' E)[4]	N: Louro (2006) S: George Hughes, *in litt.* 4 October 2009
Eastern Indian Ocean	West Bay, Little Andaman Island, India (10° 38' N, 92° 25' E)[5]	Alas Purwo National Park, Jawa, Indonesia (8° 40' S, 114° 25' E)	N: Choudhury (2006) S: Adnyana (2006)
Western Pacific Ocean	Jamursba-Medi, Papua, Indonesia (0° 20'–0° 22' S, 132° 25'–132° 39' E)	Newcastle, New South Wales, Australia (32° 55' S, 151° 45' E)[6]	N: Adnyana (2006) S: Limpus (2006)

[1] This record is an isolated event not associated with an active leatherback nesting beach, and is not mapped in Figure 1
[2] Márquez (1990) described nesting in Mauritania [north of Senegal] as "minor and solitary," but no locations were given
[3] Huntley (1974, 1978) made similar observations "south of Luanda," but no locations were given
[4] This record is an isolated event not associated with an active leatherback nesting beach, and is not mapped in Figure 1
[5] Jones (1959) reported a daylight nesting near Kozhikode (11° 15' N, 75° 47' E), but nesting on the Indian mainland is extremely rare
[6] This record is an isolated event not associated with an active leatherback nesting beach, and is not mapped in Figure 1

Figure 1. Global distribution of the leatherback sea turtle, including northern and southern oceanic range boundaries and sites representative of the species' current nesting range. Extreme northern and southern records (see Table 6 for coordinates) may not represent persistent nesting grounds, but represent known geographic boundaries for successful reproduction. Map created by Brendan Hurley (Conservation International).

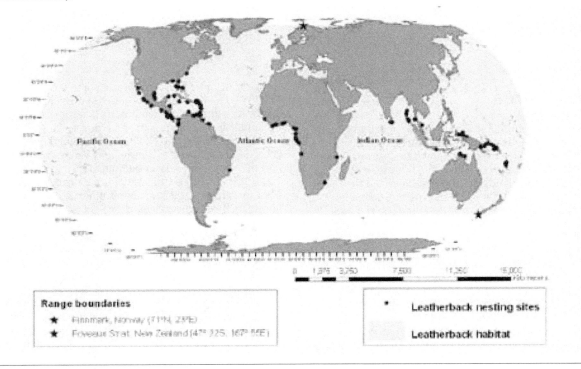

1938), and from near Mys Navarin in the Bering Sea (~62°N) (Terentjev and Chernov 1949, Bannikov et al. 1971, 1977). In the Eastern Pacific, records extend north to British Columbia (MacAskie and Forrester 1962) and the Gulf of Alaska (61°N) (Hodge 1979) and south to Quinteros, Chile (33°S) (Frazier and Salas 1984b).

Despite its extensive range, distribution is far from uniform and large nesting colonies are rare. In the Western Atlantic, nesting occurs as far north as Assateague Island National Seashore, Maryland (38°N) (Rabon et al. 2003) and as far south as Torres, Rio Grande do Sul, Brazil (29°S) (Soto et al. 1997). In the most complete assessment, leatherbacks laid eggs on 470 of 1311 known nesting beaches in the Western Atlantic, but only 2% (10/470) received more than 1000 nesting crawls per year (Dow et al. 2007). The largest colonies are located in French Guiana-Suriname, where a "...stable or slightly increasing..." population laid an estimated 5029 [1980] to 63,294 [1988] nests per year from 1967 to 2002 (Girondot et al. 2007), and Trinidad, where an estimated 52,797 and 48,240 nests were laid at the nation's three largest nesting beaches in 2007 and 2008, respectively, and the population is also believed to be stable or slightly increasing (SAE).

In the Eastern Atlantic, "...widely dispersed but fairly regular..." nesting occurs between Mauritania in the north and Angola in the south, but only Gabon, with about 5865 to 20,499 females nesting annually (Witt et al. 2009), is reported to have a large colony[1]. Field surveys are incomplete, but literature notes on the northern and southern boundaries of egg-laying in this region describe nesting in Mauritania as "...minor and solitary..." (Márquez 1990) and, to the south, as dispersed over "...some 200 km of coast south of Luanda..." in Angola (Hughes et al. 1973, also Weir et al. 2007). All available reports are summarized by Fretey (2001).

In the Western Indian Ocean, the nesting colonies of South Africa have been actively studied since the 1960s. Regular and monitored leatherback nesting is normally restricted to north of the St. Lucia Estuary (28° 22'S, 32°25'E) and some 200 km to the Mozambique border, with "...occasional nesting females encountered on beaches south of St. Lucia..." and a southernmost record at the Storms River mouth (34°01'S, 23°56'E) in the Western Cape (G.R. Hughes, pers. comm.). There was a "...gentle but steady increase..." in the numbers of leatherbacks nesting in the 56-km survey area in Tongaland (KwaZulu-Natal) from five females in 1966–1967 to 124 females in 1994–1995 (Hughes 1996).

---

[1] For conversion between nests laid per year and females nesting annually, the typical clutch frequency is 5 to 7 nests per female per reproductive year.

The IUCN (2001) recognizes Sri Lanka and the Andaman and Nicobar Islands as the last three areas in Southeast Asia with significant nesting; the colony in Nicobar is one of the few that exceeds 1000 individuals in the Indo-Pacific region (Andrews 2000). An estimated 5000 to 9200 nests are laid each year among 28 sites in the Western Pacific, with 75% of these concentrated at only four sites along the northwest coast of Papua, Indonesia (Dutton et al. 2007).

No major nesting is recorded in Australia. As summarized in Department of the Environment, Water, Heritage and the Arts (2008): low density nesting (1–3 nests per year) occurs in southern Queensland (Limpus and MacLachlan 1979, 1994) and the Northern Territory (Limpus and MacLachlan 1994, Hamann et al. 2006a); some nesting has occurred in northern New South Wales (NSW) near Ballina (Tarvey 1993), although no nesting has been reported in Queensland or NSW since 1996 (Hamann et al. 2006a); and nesting in Western Australia is still unknown or unconfirmed (Prince 1994).

In the Eastern Pacific, only remnant populations remain. Mexico, until recently with the largest nesting population in the world (~75,000 reproductively active females: Pritchard 1982), recorded 120 nests (combined) at four index monitoring sites during 2002–2003 (Sarti M. et al. 2007). Contemporary nesting is documented from Colombia (Mulatos, 2°39′N: Amorocho et al. 1992) north to the Baja California peninsula, Mexico (San Felipe, 30°56′N: Caldwell 1962 *in* Seminoff and Nichols 2007).

Both major and minor nesting areas are largely confined to tropical latitudes; exceptions include Florida (United States) and KwaZulu-Natal (South Africa). Recent regional summaries are available for the Western Atlantic (Stewart and Johnson 2006, Dow et al. 2007, Turtle Expert Working Group 2007), Eastern Atlantic (Fretey 2001, Fretey et al. 2007a), Indian Ocean and Southeast Asia (Humphrey and Salm 1996, Zulkifli et al. 2004, Hamann et al. 2006a, Shanker and Choudhury 2006), and Australia (Department of the Environment, Water, Heritage and the Arts 2008), as well as for the Western (Kinan 2002, 2005; Dutton et al. 2007), Northern (Eckert 1993) and Eastern (Spotila et al. 1996, Sarti M. et al. 2007) Pacific Ocean.

Pritchard and Trebbau (1984) summarized global nesting records, including notes on geographic variation. In a review mandated by the United States Endangered Species Act (ESA) of 1973, the United States National Marine Fisheries Service and the United States Fish and Wildlife Service (2007) provided an updated global overview of current species status, including nesting records.

Figure 2. Generalized leatherback sea turtle life cycle. Source: Chaloupka et al. (2004:150).

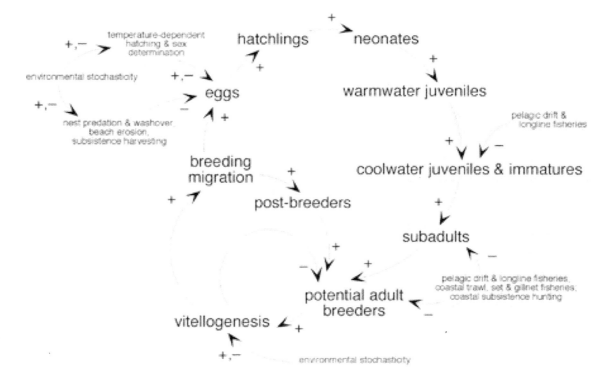

Differential Distribution

In order to successfully complete the life cycle (Figure 2), the leatherback sea turtle relies on developmental habitats that include the nesting beach, as well as coastal and pelagic waters.

Hatchlings

The post-hatchling habitat remains obscure. In a thorough review of the pelagic stage of post-hatchling sea turtle development, Carr (1987) found no evidence that young *Dermochelys,* in contrast to the young of other sea turtle genera, associate with *Sargassum* or epipelagic debris. The striking pattern of light stripes on a black background would appear to make the hatchlings conspicuous in virtually any habitat, although the counter-shading, which develops as the animal grows, might offer some crypsis (Pritchard and Trebbau 1984).

Persistent swimming in captivity prompted Carr and Ogren (1959) to propose that hatchling leatherbacks spend the first hours or days following emergence from the nest in steady travel away from their natal beach. Hall (1987) followed hatchlings offshore from Puerto Rico, noting that they "…swam almost continuously…" in a relatively undeviating course away from land, and Fletemeyer (1980) terminated his attempts to follow hatchlings during their initial journey offshore after becoming exhausted by their unrelenting activity. In the first quantified study, Wyneken and Salmon (1992) observed that having entered the sea, hatchlings swam unhesitatingly away from land—a period referred to as 'frenzy,' during which time the small turtles swim continuously for the first 24 hours before undertaking a diel swimming pattern.

The relatively limited range of swimming styles exhibited by leatherback hatchlings and adults may reflect an oceanic lifestyle, i.e., the need to swim steadily over great distances in order to prey on surface plankton, specifically jellyfish. Shortly after entering the ocean, hatchlings are capable of diving (Deraniyagala 1939, Davenport 1987, Price et al. 2007). Salmon et al. (2004) reported that leatherback hatchlings between 2–8 weeks of age dived deeper and longer with age and foraged throughout the water column on exclusively gelatinous prey.

Juveniles and Subadults

There are few data relevant to the distribution of leatherback juveniles and subadults. Deraniyagala (1936a) suggested that they remain in the open ocean, based on the sighting of a juvenile 20 km from shore. Eckert (2002a) summarized data gleaned from published sources, stranding databases, fishery observer logs and museum records on the location, date, sea temperature and turtle size for 98 small (< 145 cm) specimens from around the world. He concluded that juveniles < 100 cm CCL occur only in waters warmer than 26°C; in contrast, turtles slightly larger than 100 cm were found in waters as cool as 8°C. A juvenile (30.5 cm CCL), feeding on pelagic tunicates (Class Thaliacea), stranded near death in Western Australia in July 2002 after having been "…entrained for some extended time…" in a cold water mass (Prince 2004).

Morphological and physiological characteristics enhance the leatherback's ability to stay warm. These features include a cylindrical body form, large body mass, thick fatty insulation and countercurrent circulation (Greer et al. 1973); adults may also have temperature independent cellular metabolism (Spotila and Standora 1985, Paladino et al. 1990, Spotila et al. 1991, Penick et al. 1998). It is possible that large size (> 100 cm CCL), in reducing the surface area to mass ratio, creates a thermal inertia regime that enables forays into cold water (see Chapter 3, *Juvenile, subadult and adult phases, Hardiness,* below). If leatherbacks are able to efficiently retain metabolically generated heat, as proposed by Penick et al. (1998), then one interpretation of the distributional data is that this capacity is developmentally induced and that heat generation is physiological rather than simply a function of morphology.

The relationship between the distribution of juvenile leatherbacks and temperature is an important clue to understanding life history. It appears certain that leatherbacks spend the first portion of their lives in tropical waters, venturing into cooler latitudes only after reaching 100 cm CCL (Eckert 2002a). As is the case with adults, the distribution of juveniles and subadults is likely closely linked to the distribution and abundance of macroplanktonic prey. For example, the fact that jellyfish "…were abundant throughout the study area…" may explain the presence of subadult and adult leatherbacks off the coast of Angola (Carr and Carr 1991).

Adults

As an adult, *Dermochelys* has the most extensive biogeographical range of any extant reptile, spanning ~71°N (Carriol and Vader 2002) to 47°S (Eggleston 1971). Nesting occurs in primarily tropical latitudes on every continent except Europe and Antarctica, as well as on many islands in the Caribbean and the Indo-Pacific; large nesting colonies are rare (see *Total area,* above).

Foraging, mainly on gelatinous cnidarians and tunicates (see Chapter 3, *Nutrition and metabolism, Food,* below), is reported both on the continental shelf and in pelagic waters. Long distance migration between foraging and nesting grounds is the norm (see Chapter 3, *Behavior, Migrations and local movements,* below).

Determinants of Distributional Changes

There is no information on the geography, sequence, timing, or impetus for distributional changes related to developmental habitats for young *Dermochelys*. Nothing is known of the dispersal or distribution of post-hatchlings in the open sea. Oceanic distribution of juveniles (and adults) most likely reflects the distribution and abundance of macro-planktonic prey, as well as preferred thermal tolerances. According to empirical data collated by Eckert (2002a), juveniles < 100 cm CCL are likely confined to ocean waters warmer than 26°C.

Reproductively active females (and recent data show males, as well) arrive seasonally at preferred nesting grounds in (mainly) tropical latitudes, while non-breeding adults and subadults range further north and south into temperate zones seeking areas of predictable though often ephemeral patches of oceanic jellyfish and other soft-bodied invertebrates.

Long-distance movements are not random but regular in timing and location. While the proximal impetus is unknown, the turtles seem to possess some innate awareness of where and when profitable foraging opportunities will occur (see Chapter 3, *Behavior, Migrations and local movements*, below).

Hybridization

No hybridization involving *Dermochelys* is known.

Chapter 3: Bionomics and Life History

Reproduction

Sexual Dimorphism

There is no apparent sexual size dimorphism in adult leatherbacks (James et al. 2005a); notwithstanding, by far the largest specimen on record is that of a male captured off the coast of Wales, U.K. (916 kg, Morgan 1990). The largest females on record are non-breeding adults weighed after having been captured incidentally in fisheries off South Africa (646 kg, Hughes 1974a) and Nova Scotia (640 kg, James et al. 2007). Sexual size dimorphism occurs in various reptile taxa, including sea turtles (Miller 1997). Leatherbacks may represent a departure from this model, but additional data, especially from females during non-reproductive years and from adult males, are needed.

Apart from sexual size dimorphism, anatomical dimorphisms exist that permit visual distinction between adult males and females. The tail of the adult male is much longer than that of the female, and the cloaca extends further beyond the posterior tip of the carapace (James 2004, James et al. 2007). Furthermore, the adpressed hind limbs extend posteriorly to the cloaca only in male leatherbacks, whereas in females the tail barely reaches half-way down these limbs (Deraniyagala 1939, Reina et al. 2005). Deraniyagala (1939) described the male as having a concave plastron, narrow hips, and a shallow body depth (vertical height of carapace and plastron when the animal is on land) relative to the female, and speculated that the pronounced terminal osteoderm on each ventral ridge on the male might assist in maintaining his position on the female during copulation (as mating is rarely observed, this speculation is difficult to confirm).

No information is available regarding sexual dimorphism in juvenile size classes.

Age at Maturity

Age at maturity has not been conclusively determined, but recent estimates (Avens and Goshe 2008, Avens et al. 2009) extend those posed by earlier studies.

Direct field measurements are problematic; therefore, inferential or correlative analyses have been employed to generate estimates of leatherback age at maturity. For example, estimates have been made based on extrapolations from growth rates of post-hatchlings and young juveniles held in captivity (Deraniyagala 1939, Birkenmeier 1971, Jones 2009), from histological and skeletochronological analyses (Rhodin 1985, Zug and Parham 1996, Avens et al. 2009), population trend analysis of reproductively active females (Dutton et al. 2005), and inference of generation time through DNA fingerprinting (Dutton et al. 2005) (Table 7). These estimates generally indicate that *Dermochelys* may reach sexual maturity at an earlier age than is characteristic of other sea turtle genera (excepting *Lepidochelys*). In the most comprehensive analysis to date (a skeletochronological assessment based on eight known-age, captive reared turtles and 33 wild leatherbacks from the Atlantic, spanning hatchling to adult), Avens et al. (2009) estimate age at maturity to be similar to that of other large sea turtle genera (2–3 decades or longer).

In the absence of field measurements, indirect techniques such as analyses of bone growth patterns, with a known or inferred temporal component, can be used to generate length-age data pairs. Specifically, patterns of bone growth and remodeling that are manifested in lines of arrested growth (LAGs), or growth rings, may represent annual cycles of active growth and cessation of growth. These generated length-age data pairs can then be coupled with growth functions to estimate age at maturity. Based on the presence of what were characterized as two growth rings in the humeral cross-section of an adult female, as well as chondro-osseous development characteristics indicative of rapid growth, Rhodin (1985) hypothesized sexual maturity in leatherbacks at 2–3 years of age. He cautioned against extrapolating captive growth rates to wild turtles, but noted that even if the 2–3 year estimate for sexual maturity was incorrect by the same order of magnitude as the discrepancy between captive and free-living growth studies in other sea turtles, the age at maturity estimate for leatherbacks would be ≤ 6 years (see *Growth*, below).

Zug and Parham (1996) assessed LAGs along the lateral edges of cross-sections of scleral ossicles extracted from Pacific leatherbacks across the body size range from hatchling to adult and, using a growth function, estimated minimum age to maturity at 5–6 years (minimum adult female length) and 13–14 years (average adult female length). Avens et al. (2009) honed this analytical technique by analyzing LAGs at the wide tips of ossicle cross-sections (where LAG lengths are not as vulnerable to lateral compression and resorption as they are

Table 7. Indirect estimates of age at maturity for leatherback sea turtles.

Method	Estimated Age at Maturity	Reference
Extrapolations from young (≤ 2-yr old) juveniles reared in captivity	2-6 years	Deraniyagala (1939, 1953)
	2-3 years	Birkenmeier (1971)[1]
	15 years	Jones (2009)[2]
Histological and skeletochronological analyses	3-6 years	Rhodin (1985)[3]
	5-6 (min) to 13-14 years (mean)	Zug & Parham (1996)[4]
	24.5-29 years (based on 145 cm CCL mean size at first nesting)	Avens et al. (2009)[5]
Population trend analysis and survival rates of nesting females	12-14 years	Dutton et al. (2005)

[1] data refer to a single captive-reared individual and linear growth function: "If this growth rate should continue the Leathery Turtle would be 60 cm at one year, 120 cm at two and 180 cm at three years of age. They would be adult and sexually mature when between two and three years old."
[2] estimate derived from von Bertalanffy growth function applied to captive reared individuals provided with ample food and carefully controlled diet, water quality, and temperature regimes and skeletochronology length-age data from the published literature
[3] estimate derived from analyses of chondro-osseus development and linear growth function
[4] estimates derived from von Bertalanffy growth function and reported as years to minimum reproductive size (min) and years to mean reproductive size (mean)
[5] estimate derived from skeletochronology (scleral ossicles) and von Bertalanffy growth function; sample size of 8 captive, known-age and 33 wild (6 hatchlings, 2 small juveniles (16.6, 27.3 cm CCL), 25 subadults and adults (122-173 cm CCL, mean 147.5 ±13.9; 10 ♀, 9 ♂, 6 unknown)) leatherbacks from North Atlantic waters

laterally) and estimated maturity, using a growth function, at 24.5 to 29 years (based on 145 cm CCL mean size at first nesting). They were the first to validate the core mark and partially confirm LAG deposition frequency, but also recognized that work is still needed to increase the sample size (especially among small and medium-sized individuals), expand regional diversity, and further validate the nature of LAG deposition patterns.

As with any long-lived organism, confirming the recruitment of neophytes into adult populations is difficult via mark-recapture studies because of the extended periods of time required to achieve saturation-tagging of all nesting individuals. Dutton et al. (2005) reported an increase in the nesting population at St. Croix, U.S. Virgin Islands (USVI), which began approximately 12–14 years after a dramatic and sustained increase in hatchling production. Because this increase in nesting adult females included a large proportion of untagged (neophyte) turtles that were genetically related to remigrant nesters, these investigators theorized an age to maturity in this population that agreed well with the estimates of Zug and Parham (1996) (Table 7).

Courtship and Mating

Few direct observations of courtship and/or mating in leatherbacks have been described in the literature. Whether mating occurs at the breeding grounds and/or at some distant locale (with "courtship" in tropical waters representing opportunistic behavior on the part of adult males) remains an unanswered question.

Lazell (1980) suggested that in any given year virtually all the males might migrate to and from the nesting beach, inseminating females prior to their first oviposition and then leaving the breeding grounds before the females completed the laying season. Supporting evidence is available from James et al. (2005b), who tracked adult males from temperate Atlantic foraging grounds to residence areas adjacent to known nesting beaches. James et al. (2005b) also confirmed that males linger at (or travel among) nesting colonies well in advance of the nesting season and remain until the peak of the season.

Carr and Carr (1986) described a leatherback courtship near Culebra Island, Puerto Rico, as a series of lunges at the female by the male as he attempted to position himself atop her carapace. In this account the female repeatedly sounded beneath the male, only to resurface in close proximity in order that he could lunge at her once again. As the movements became more coordinated, he positioned the center of his plastron just posterior to the center of her carapace. Mounted precariously, he curved his thick muscular tail beneath her tail; a semi-erect penis was clearly visible as the pair rolled back and forth, struggling to maintain their balance. There was no obvious embrace. Mating off the coast of Puerto Rico is also reported by Rathbun et al. (1985) and Tucker (1988). Godfrey and Barreto (1998) observed mating off Matapica Beach, Suriname, and reported that local fishermen commonly observed leatherback copulation in the same general area.

In contrast, a study of the age composition of the pantropical barnacle *Conchoderma* attached to leatherbacks nesting on the northern Caribbean island of St. Croix suggested that females arrived asynchronously at the nesting beach (from temperate latitudes outside the biogeographic range of the barnacle) and began nesting within relatively few days of arrival (Eckert and Eckert 1988). Based on this indirect line of evidence, the authors suggested that females do not arrive far enough in advance of their first nesting to accommodate mating on site and concluded that mating occurs prior to or during migration.

In the Eastern Pacific, video images acquired from animal-borne camera systems provided a first glimpse of interactions between males and females off Playa Grande, Costa Rica, at and below the surface of the water (Reina et al. 2005). In these recorded episodes, the interactions began with a collision initiated by a male, typically near the surface, which caused females, apparently in avoidance behavior, to descend to the seafloor where they remained motionless or turned to face the approaching male. Males proceeded to circle, approach, and repeatedly pass over females lying on the ocean bottom, with the male usually making some contact with his body, flippers, and/or head. In addition, male turtles bit females on the head and anterior carapace and struck the females with their front flippers, thus demonstrating physical courtship behavior similar to that of other sea turtle species (see Miller 1997). In one instance, a male's right front flipper appeared clasped to the lateral edge of a female's carapace for 4 min, perhaps indicating successful mounting of the female by the male; whether this encounter resulted in successful mating was not confirmed. In all recorded events, females remained on the bottom until the male was no longer visible in the frame, and typically spent longer periods at the surface following interactions with males, likely replenishing oxygen stores after the physical activity associated with the interaction (Reina et al. 2005). Whether such interactions result in successful mating or represent harassment and avoidance behavior has yet to be determined.

Microsatellites have indicated very infrequent or no multiple paternity within or among successive clutches of a female (Dutton and Davis 1998, Rieder et al. 1998, Dutton et al. 2000). More recent genetic analyses of leatherbacks that nest at Playa Grande, Costa Rica, confirm that while polygyny and polyandry are present, single paternity is the most prevalent mating strategy observed (Crim et al. 2002). These results indicate that the apparent evasion of male leatherback courtship attempts by female leatherbacks reported by Reina et al. (2005) are consistent with the observation that female sea turtles store sperm during a reproductive season, and thus do not need to mate more than once (Owens 1980, Miller 1997, FitzSimmons 1998).

Nesting Behavior

Nesting is seasonal and typically nocturnal, although daylight nesting does occur. Preferred nesting grounds are mainly in the tropics (see Chapter 2, *Total area*, above) and can be described as "… deep, clean, high energy beaches with either a deep water oceanic approach or by a shallow water approach with mud banks but without coral or rock formations…" (Turtle Expert Working Group 2007).

Preferred beaches are generally free of rocks, coral, or other hard abrasive materials that might cause injury to the turtle. Strong waves and tides may assist the females in their emergence from the sea (Reina et al. 2002a), and a steep profile enables the heavy-bodied turtle to attain high ground while minimizing overland effort (Hendrickson and Balasingam 1966, Pritchard 1971a, Hendrickson 1980).

The first detailed examination of nesting beach preferences showed that beaches on which *Dermochelys* specializes are characterized by five interrelated factors: coarse-grained sand, steep sloping littoral zone, obstacle-free approach, proximity to deep water, and oceanic currents impacting the coast (Hendrickson and Balasingam 1966). A South African study revealed that 81.1% of successful nesting emergences were associated with obstruction-free approaches, and because 14.8% of approaches were characterized as "deep" (with respect to water depth) while 66.3% were characterized as "shallow" an obstruction-free approach appeared to be more important than absolute depth (Hughes 1974a).

Whatever factors attract turtles to nesting beaches, the geographic location of the beach must be considered in relation to the immediate offshore areas and dominant currents. Hughes (1974a) summarized the situation at five nesting areas and concluded that offshore currents at major rookeries, during the main period of hatching, would carry hatchlings into waters of 26.5°C to 31.5°C. Research is needed into this aspect of reproductive success—namely, the relationship between the survival rate of hatchlings and the surface temperatures of the oceanic areas into which these animals are carried.

The nesting process is a stereotypic sequence of behaviors for sea turtles in general and is described in detail for leatherbacks by Deraniyagala (1936a, 1939), Carr and Ogren (1959), Pritchard (1971a), Pritchard and Trebbau (1984), and others. Briefly, the sequence of behaviors are as follows: emergence from the sea onto the nesting beach; overland traverse to and selection of a suitable nest site; excavation of a body pit; excavation of the nest chamber; oviposition (egg-laying); filling of the nest chamber; covering and concealing the nest site; and returning to the sea (Appendix D).

The entire sequence, from emergence to return to the sea, requires some 80–140 min (Carr and Ogren 1959, Hughes et al. 1967, Bacon 1970, Pritchard 1971a, Eckert and Eckert 1985, Chua and Furtado 1988, Miller 1997, Reina et al. 2002a) (Table 8).

The following paragraphs describe each phase in more detail.

Emergence from the sea onto the nesting beach.—Tide and lunar cycles, steepness of beach profile, and wave action are thought to influence leatherback nesting behavior (Miller 1997).

Table 8. Nesting behavior in leatherback sea turtles. Durations for stages (min) for the Atlantic coast of Costa Rica were recorded during a single nesting at Matina in 1958 (Carr and Ogren 1959). Mean durations in minutes (± 1 SD) for St. Croix, U.S. Virgin Islands represent a composite of 113 nestings at Sandy Point National Wildlife Refuge in 1985 (Eckert and Eckert 1985). Mean durations in minutes (± 1 SE) for Playa Grande, Costa Rica, were collected over 11 nesting seasons (sample size in parentheses). * denotes values given for crawling while both emerging from and returning to the sea.

Nesting Stage	Matina, Costa Rica (Carr & Ogren 1959)	St. Croix, USVI (Eckert & Eckert 1985)	Playa Grande, Costa Rica (Reina et al. 2002a)
Emergence from the Sea	03	8.5 ± 6.5	22 (range: 7-65) *
Nest Preparation (Body Pit)	17	9.4 ± 6.3	16.5 ± 0.8 (82)
Nest Excavation	05	22.9 ± 8.7	17.4 ± 0.7 (147)
Oviposition (Egg-Laying)	15	10.8 ± 2.9	12.7 ± 0.4 (164)
Filling and Concealing	45	34.0 ± 17.1	47.3 ± 3.6 (173)
Return to the Sea	08	4.2 ± 2.3	22 (range: 7-65) *
Total	93	112.6 ± 28.4	117.8 ± 17.5 (84)

Girondot and Fretey (1996) found that leatherbacks nesting on the estuarian beach of Ya:lima:po[2], French Guiana "...adjusted their internesting return date to be closer to a full or new moon..." producing peaks of nesting for spring tides. No such relationship was identified on the oceanic beach of Pointe-Isère, French Guiana (Fretey and Girondot 1989b). Similarly, Lux et al. (2003) found no such relationship at Playa Grande, Costa Rica. Reina et al. (2002a) reported that the timing of leatherback nesting activities was loosely associated with the timing of the high tide, but that this association did not exist on nights during which both high tides occurred near or during nighttime; nesting occurred throughout the night on such occasions. Pineda et al. (2004) observed no apparent relationship between tidal cycles and leatherback emergence at Mexiquillo, Mexico, but suggested that leatherbacks tended to nest during the darkest periods of the night (i.e., before moonrise and after moonset); a similar phenomenon has been anecdotally supported at Playa Grande, Costa Rica (Lux et al. 2003).

In Trinidad, Bacon (1973) reported "...no significant relationship..." between turtle size (curved carapace length) and crawl length (< 10 m vs. >10 m from tide level to nest site), but shorter crawls were reported to be more common on steeply sloping beaches. In the USVI, Eckert (1987) found no significant difference in distance crawled inland as a result of turtle size (CCL) or prior exertion (previous failed nesting attempts); however, longer crawls were associated with more steeply sloping beach profiles.

Overland traverse to and selection of a suitable nest site.—The locomotor behavior of gravid females during emergence from and return to the sea is described as a simultaneous gait where all four limbs move at once to propel the turtle forward (Wyneken 1997). The resulting tracks are symmetrical, with diagonal grooves formed on the outer portion of the track by the front flippers that frame smaller depressions formed by the rear flippers as well as marks left by the plastron and tail drag in the center of the track (Miller 1997).

Because of the respiratory requirements of embryos, successful *Dermochelys* clutches typically incubate above the natural high tide line. Nest site selection has received some attention, and generally reflects the opposing selection pressures of embryonic mortality resulting from tidal inundation and erosion below the high tide line (Mrosovsky 1983, Whitmore and Dutton 1985, Eckert 1987) and embryonic mortality and hatchling disorientation from nests placed too far inland (Godfrey and Barreto 1995, Kamel and Mrosovsky 2004).

Early studies suggested that leatherbacks use a scatter-nesting approach to minimize nest loss in uncertain environments where erosion and wave wash may claim > 50% of nests per annum (Mrosovsky 1983, Eckert 1987). Whether intra-individual nest site selection patterns exist and are heritable has important implications for nest relocation programs employed by conservation projects worldwide. Specifically, if particular females consistently placed nests in 'doomed' sites, nest relocation programs would be inadvertently selecting for poor nest site selection traits in those individual turtles (Mrosovsky 2006).

Two more recent studies have examined the inter- and intra-individual variation in leatherback nest site selection. Nordmoe et al. (2004) reported that consecutive nest placements along the ocean-to-vegetation axis at Playa Grande, Costa Rica, were statistically independent and that leatherbacks typically nested in the open beach between the high tide line and the vegetation regardless of the site of their previous nest. However, the authors reported a pattern of nest site dependence along the coastal

---

[2] Les Hattes, Les Hattes-Awara, Ya:lima:po-Awa:la and Ya:lima:po are different names for the same nesting beach; throughout the publication, the authors have standardized on the current preference, "Ya:lima:po."

axis, supporting the notion of spatial proximity whereby leatherbacks tend to nest close to the site of their previous nest. Kamel and Mrosovsky (2004) found that individual female leatherbacks demonstrated a preference for nesting at particular distances from the highest spring tide line, but not at particular sections of the beach along the coastal axis.

Excavation of a body pit.—After reaching the dry upper portion of the nesting beach, a nesting leatherback begins to plant, scoop, and sweep from anterior to posterior her enormous front flippers, thus removing and throwing large amounts of sand. As she continues this activity, she effectively removes surface debris from the area, including the driest sand most likely to collapse into the eventual nest chamber. The resulting crater formed by the repeated removal and throwing of sand is referred to as a 'body pit' (Miller 1997).

Between sand-throwing sequences using the front flippers, the hind flippers move in a side-to-side fashion to smooth mounds of sand formed behind the turtle during the sand throwing. The rear half of the turtle's carapace becomes covered in sand, hence the alternative name of "sand bath" given to this phase (Deraniyagala 1936a). The depth of the body pit depends on the thickness of the dry surface sand layer and the size of the turtle; thus, the turtle will continue body pit construction until reaching firmer, wetter, cooler subsurface sand, at which point she will shift to nest (egg) chamber excavation.

Excavation of the nest chamber.—Leatherback turtles use their hind flippers to construct the nest chamber. Initially, the turtle will scoop and flick surface sand away from the area immediately behind her to begin the cavity. As the cavity gains depth, she performs repeated scooping motions with the ventral side of a rear flipper, after which she gently cups, removes, and places the sand next to her. Meanwhile, the second flipper sustains the weight of the rear portion of the turtle over the cavity, until the first flipper is removed, at which point the second flipper flicks forward sand that had fallen on its dorsal side, and is lowered into the cavity to scoop again. These actions are then alternated between flippers until maximum attainable depth is reached.

The shape of the nest cavity is not uniformly cylindrical, but instead the lower portion (egg chamber) generally takes a rounded shape, such that the entire nest is often described as pear- or flask-shaped (see Miller 1997). Double-chambered nests have also been documented (Billes and Fretey 2001, Kamel and Mrosovsky 2004). Billes and Fretey (2001) used thermal curing polyurethane foam to produce castings of the subterranean nest, documenting several variations on the flask shape and reporting a mean depth of 70 cm (SD ±7.84, range = 60–84, n = 23 nests) and a mean volume of the egg chamber (the bottom ~45% of the nest) of 15 litres (SD ± 5.7, range: 6.1–24, n = 11).

Successful excavation relies on the condition of the hind limbs; in cases where they have been injured or partially amputated, the volume of the egg chamber is likely to be inadequate to hold the eggs. This results in the last eggs to be oviposited being insufficiently covered or even exposed at the surface of the nest, and occasionally the female herself will destroy her own (exposed) eggs in the process of covering the nest.

Oviposition.—Generally, after the rear flippers can no longer reach to the bottom of the nest chamber to remove sand, oviposition begins. One rear flipper, usually the one last inserted into the nest to remove sand, sometimes hovers inside the nest chamber during oviposition. Eggs, typically laid in pulses of 1–4, are coated in a clear viscous liquid. During oviposition, leatherbacks appear relatively indifferent to external stimuli, including egg collection, tagging, measuring, attachment of instrumentation, etc.

Filling the nest.—Once oviposition is complete, the female refills the nest chamber by scooping sand into the cavity with her rear flippers. As the cavity is filled, the turtle compacts the sand by shifting the weight of the posterior portion of her body onto her hind flippers with each scoop of sand. This process continues until the cavity is filled back to the level of the body pit or sand surface.

Covering and concealing the nest site.—After filling the nest with sand, leatherbacks perform sand-throwing behaviors essentially identical to those exhibited during body pit excavation. The turtle uses powerful scooping and throwing motions to move large amounts of sand in the general area of the nest chamber. These activities are repeated as the turtle changes direction and moves forward. The end result is that an area much larger than the actual nest site is greatly disturbed in no discernible pattern, which likely makes detection and locating of the clutch more difficult for potential egg predators.

Deraniyagala (1936a) characterized the apparent effectiveness of this nest covering behavior in concealing (sometimes referred to as the 'camouflage' stage) the nest site as follows: "Throughout this phase the turtle did not appear to move from the nest and it was only by comparing the animal's position with a haversack I had laid down when first she commenced to dig, that it became apparent that she had moved quite two metres during ten minutes…after she had gone, three of us dug for an hour with our hands but were unable to locate the eggs."

Returning to the sea.—After a relatively unpredictable duration of nest covering, the leatherback begins her return to the sea, utilizing the same simultaneous gait demonstrated during her initial emergence from the sea. The return may or may not follow a straight route, and disorientation by coastal lighting may be a significant distraction. Small, quickly executed circles are sometimes noted.

These circles were observed in 30% of descent crawls at Matura Bay, Trinidad, during 1971 and 1972 (Bacon 1973); circling is also reported from mainland Atlantic (Pritchard 1971a, Schulz 1975) and Pacific (Cornelius 1976) coasts. While the function of circling is unclear, it is speculatively attributed to orientation or sea-finding, perhaps evoked by changes in ambient illumination. The duration of the return to sea depends on the distance between the tide line and the nest site, and may range between < 1 min to > 60 min (Reina et al. 2002a). Circling is also sometimes noted in hatchlings (see *Behavior, Navigation and orientation*, below).

The ratio of successful to unsuccessful nestings, the latter defined as a landing that does not result in oviposition ("false crawl"), varies both temporally and geographically. Aborted nesting attempts may be caused by the presence of predators, erosion bluffs and other obstacles on the beach, unsuccessful nest excavation (e.g., nest collapse due to dry sand), or human disturbances.

At some sites in the Western Atlantic (i.e., Sandy Point National Wildlife Refuge, St. Croix), the successful to unsuccessful nest attempt ratio varies annually, largely as a consequence of beach conditions: 53.6% to 74.6% of total nesting attempts resulted in the deposition of eggs between 1982 and 1988 (USVI Division of Fish and Wildlife, unpubl. data). Less variability was reported in the Gulf of Uraba region of Colombia, where 90.6% and 86.2% of crawls resulted in egg-laying in 2006 and 2007, respectively (Patino-Martinez et al. 2008). In the Eastern Atlantic (Gamba Complex, Gabon), Verhage and Moundjim (2005) found similarly high successful to unsuccessful nest ratios: 2002–2003 (607:25), 2003–2004 (203:10), 2004–2005 (128:0) and, in the east Pacific (Michoacán, Mexico), 88%, 95.5% and 91.1% of emergences resulted in the deposition of eggs in three seasons (Sarti M. et al. 1986, 1987, 1989a). In the Indian Ocean, Sivasundar and Devi Prasad (1996) reported from the Andaman Islands that most nests (85/105) were laid in three or fewer attempts.

Tucker (1988) showed how the mean ratio of nests to false crawls varied as the laying season progressed (10:1 in March, 19.5:1 in April, 5.3:1 in May, 4.1:1 in June, 6.2:1 in July) and implicated a variety of causal factors including erosion berms and rocks, nest collapse (dry sand), water in the bottom of the nest, and "...flashlight spooked."

Leatherbacks have long been described as more tolerant of disturbances during nesting than are other sea turtle species (e.g., Deraniyagala 1936a, Carr and Ogren 1959, Hughes et al. 1967). During the core phases of the nesting process, but particularly during oviposition, leatherbacks generally are unresponsive to potential disturbances, including human or predator activity. Notwithstanding, gravid females have been known to return to the sea before laying a full complement of eggs and without covering the nest after having been disturbed by flashlight (Pritchard 1969, Bacon 1973) and Pritchard (1971a) attributed longer internesting intervals in Suriname (vs. French Guiana) to disturbance "...by over-enthusiastic taggers..." obliging females "...to postpone their nesting to the following night." On Culebra Island (Puerto Rico), disturbance during approach accounted for 28% of the unsuccessful nesting attempts observed (Tucker and Hall 1984). In the Eastern Pacific, fewer than 8% of nesting attempts were aborted at Playa Grande and Playa Langosta, Costa Rica (Chaves et al. 1996, Reina et al. 2002a).

Density-dependence.—Whether nesting beach carrying capacity (the number of nests a beach may support) exists has received empirical and theoretical attention. In 2007, at Grande Riviere, Trinidad, 23,869 body pits were counted on 800 m of beach; at Matura Beach the tally was 16,911 body pits on 3 km of beach (SAE). In Michoacán, Mexico, the site of what was previously considered the largest nesting aggregation of leatherbacks in the world (Pritchard 1982), 5021 crawls, including 4796 nests, were recorded along 4.5 km of beach in Mexiquillo, Michoacán, Mexico, in a single season (1986–1987) (Sarti M. et al. 1989b).

In many areas the annual number of nests laid has declined significantly in recent decades and historical nesting densities may never be known. For example, at least 13,000 leatherback nests were reported in 1984 on 17.8 km of beach at Papua, Indonesia (formerly Irian Jaya) (Bhaskar 1985) while today, Yusuf et al. (2006) estimate that "...some 3000 leatherback sea turtle nests..." are laid every year at this site (18 km of beach at Jamursba-Medi). Referencing turtles (vs. nests), Hitipuew et al. (2007) estimated 300–900 females nesting annually during peak nesting season at Jamursba-Medi, compared with about 1000–3000 females before 1985. More dramatic declines are reported from Malaysia, where Hendrickson and Balasingam (1966) reported maximum densities of 4000 nests/km (2500 nests/mi) at Terengganu, but by 1972 (the peak year between 1967 and 1987), nest density had been reduced to an estimated 866 nests/km (Chua 1988b). By 1995, nesting levels were < 1% of levels recorded in the 1950s, with zero nests laid in 19 of 27 monitored beaches (Chan and Liew 1996).

In French Guiana, nightly nest density reached a maximum concentration of 256 females per km at Ya:lima:po Beach in 1986 (Fretey and Girondot 1987). In 1987, an April to October survey of 10 beaches in French Guiana recorded 49,000-plus nests and a nightly maximum of 255 females per km^2 (Fretey and Girondot 1988). The maximum number of nests recorded at the major nesting beach in French Guiana (Ya:lima:po) was 60,000 in 1992 (Girondot and Fretey 1996). Girondot et al. (2002) employed a computer simulation model to examine potential density-dependent nest destruction effects on population fluctuations of leatherbacks nesting at Ya:lima:po Beach, French Guiana, which revealed that density-dependent nest destruction does occur. The authors determined that the maximum number of nests deposited on the beach for which total hatchling production continues to increase was 95,000 nests, well beyond the maximum number of 60,000 nests observed.

Using experimentally-derived parameters, Caut et al. (2006b) improved upon the Girondot et al. (2002) theoretical model to determine that the effective carrying capacity of the major nesting beach in French Guiana (Ya:lima:po) was approximately the same as the maximum nest density observed for this beach (~60,000 nests). Thus, while density-dependent nest destruction may affect leatherback nest success, this phenomenon is not common worldwide because very few leatherback nesting colonies are sufficiently large (Troëng et al. 2004, Dow et al. 2007) to have significant density-dependent effects.

Eggs

Leatherback eggs are the largest of any sea turtle species, and among the largest eggs of any oviparous amniote. The number of yolked eggs in a single clutch ranges from 20 to > 100 (average 60–100 eggs; Table 9). Clutch sizes of Eastern Pacific leatherbacks are smaller than those of leatherbacks from other regions of the world. Leatherback egg mass varies less than clutch size (Wallace et al. 2007), and ranges from 66–82 g across nesting rookeries; likewise, there is relatively little variation with respect to egg diameter (Table 3). Leatherbacks typically lay spherical eggs with pliable egg shells and because they are not turgid at oviposition, they drop from the cloaca into the nest without breakage (Miller 1985).

Leatherback eggs are comprised of three main components: yolk (fertilized ovum, energy and nutrients), albumen (water and proteins), and shell and associated membranes (Wallace et al. 2006a). Leatherback egg composition has been limited to two studies (Simkiss 1962, Wallace et al. 2006a). Water composition of leatherback eggs in both studies was similar, but Simkiss (1962) reported similar proportions of yolk and albumen in eggs (46.8% yolk, 48.9% albumen) from leatherbacks nesting in Terengganu, Malaysia, whereas Wallace et al. (2006a) reported that yolk and albumen mass comprised 33% and 66%, respectively, of egg mass from leatherbacks nesting in Costa Rica. Underlying causes for such differences are unclear.

As in other oviparous amniotes, including other sea turtles, leatherback egg shells are the interface between the internal environment within which the embryo develops and the external environment consisting of influential biological (e.g., other eggs, bacteria, fungi) and physical (e.g., oxygen, carbon dioxide, water, temperature) factors. Wallace et al. (2006a) reported that the water vapor conductance of leatherback egg shells was intermediate between values for parchment-shelled eggs of most squamates and rigid-shelled eggs of crocodilians and birds, but similar to conductance values for other pliable-egg shells of other sea turtle species. The egg shell facilitates the diffusion of respiratory gases and water vapor into and out of the egg that permits embryonic development, and it is composed of an inner organic membrane and an outer inorganic or mineral layer of calcium carbonate deposited as aragonite. The soft egg shells of sea turtles are structurally modified at the level of the mammilary layer to encourage the growth of long needle-shaped aragonite crystals; gaseous diffusion occurs between the crystal masses without the need for specific pores (Solomon and Reid 1983).

Using scanning electron microscopy, phosphorus analysis (microanalytical techniques and atomic absorption spectrophotometry), and infrared analysis, Solomon and Watt (1985) observed that in addition to the aragonite crystals, calcium carbonate may also be deposited as calcite in the egg shells of leatherback turtles. Leatherback egg shells (collected in Suriname) exhibited a variety of crystal forms consistent with the presence of both aragonite and calcite within the organic matrix; phosphorus was not detected (Solomon and Watt 1985). In contrast, eggs collected from Terengganu, Malaysia, showed traces of phosphorus in the range of 100–2000 ug g^{-1} of egg shell material; i.e., 0.01–0.2 wt % (Chan 1989). Based on research showing that stress results in delayed oviposition in birds, and that delayed eggs show an "…extra cuticular deposit of calcium…" (often in the form of calcium phosphate), stress associated with harassment at the Terengganu rookery was implicated (Chan and Solomon 1989).

Yolk mass increases significantly with whole egg mass, but comprises a smaller fraction (33%) of whole egg mass than yolk mass of other sea turtle eggs (~49%) and other reptile eggs (~90%) (Wallace et al. 2006a). Variation in yolk mass was small (7.5 g over a 30 g range of egg mass), in accordance with the findings of Rostal et al. (1996), who found little variation in ova size detected using ultrasonography. No analyses of leatherback egg yolk composition with respect to organic compounds (e.g., lipids, proteins, carbohydrates) have been conducted. However, Simkiss (1962) found that yolk was the main store of calcium for the developing leatherback embryo, but that a sizeable portion of calcium was also contributed by the egg shell. In addition, Bilinski et al. (2001) reported that yolk and albumen calcium were replenished by egg shell calcium stores during embryonic development.

Albumen provides a large proportion of water as well as proteins with immune functions to the developing embryo. Not only does albumen comprise a relatively high proportion of leatherback egg mass, it also contains a high proportion of solids relative to albumen of other reptile eggs, and a similar proportion to that of avian eggs. Further, leatherback hatchling mass increases with yolk mass and was approximately twice the yolk mass at any given egg mass, thus indicating that albumen contributed significantly to hatchling wet mass (Wallace et al. 2006a).

Anomalies and 'yolkless eggs.'—Leatherbacks exhibit egg anomalies that include oval, pear-shaped, and elliptical eggs, as well as dumb-bell and elongate shapes that may enclose multiple yolks (Gosse 1851, Miller 1985). The most unusual anomalies are the 'yolkless eggs' (yolk-deficient eggs in Whitmore and Dutton 1985; shelled albumen gobs, or SAGs in Wallace et al. 2004), which are distinguished from eggs both by the absence of yolk and in their smaller and irregular sizes. They typically appear in a clutch during the latter half of oviposition. In one study they represented, on average, 31.03% of the total clutch (248 nests) and ranged from 0.3 to 45 mm in diameter (Chacón et al. 1996).

The majority of the yolkless eggs are spherical or slightly ovoid, but fused eggs and twisted shapes are also observed. They contain albumen and occasionally a minute quantity of yolk; there is no vitelline membrane present (Miller 1985). Follicular rupture during oogenesis may account for the yolk fragments. Area-specific water vapor conductance rates of egg shells and 'yolkless egg' shells were not statistically different; indicating that shell material is similar for both (Wallace et al. 2006a).

Due to the high variability in the size and number of yolkless eggs in leatherback clutches, Wallace et al. (2007) suggested that recording their cumulative mass in a given clutch was a more appropriate representation of maternal investment than counting all individual yolkless eggs. Nonetheless, the majority of studies have reported yolkless egg counts rather than masses (Table 9). In St. Croix, USVI, the total weight of yolkless eggs averaged 1100 g per clutch (Eckert et al. 1989b); in Playa Grande, Costa Rica, the average was 947 g (SD ± 393.8 g) per clutch (n = 334 clutches, 146 females) and varied widely within and among females (Wallace et al. 2007). In general, the number of yolkless eggs in a clutch comprises roughly 30–50% of clutch size (number of eggs in a clutch), and the total mass of yolkless eggs in a clutch is approximately 20% of the mass of the egg clutch (Wallace et al. 2007).

Whether yolkless eggs have any function is unknown. Early speculations were that they might facilitate gas exchange and/or buffer temperature fluctuations within the nest environment, but Wallace et al. (2004) found no differences between oxygen levels and temperatures in the upper chamber (where yolkless eggs are located) and in other regions of the nest. Caut et al. (2006a)

Table 9. Clutch size (yolked eggs only) and average number of yolkless eggs per clutch for leatherback sea turtles. Where available, sample size (number of clutches tallied) appears in parentheses and ± 1 SD is noted.

Nesting Site	Clutch Size	Yolkless Eggs	Reference
Western Atlantic			
Brazil (Espírito Santo)	87.7 ± 18.9 (260)	22.1 ± 13.4 (260)	Thomé et al. (2007)
French Guiana (Silébâche Beach)	88.1 (19)	29.1 (19)	Pritchard (1971a)
French Guiana (Awala Ya:lima:po)	87.8	24.7	Caut et al. (2006b)
Suriname	86.0 (30)	25.1 (8)	Pritchard (1969)
Suriname (Bigi Santi)	84.1 (385)	24.4 (385)	Schulz (1975)
Suriname (Babunsanti)	86.6 ± 18.4 (188)	31.6 ± 20.9 (188)	Hilterman & Goverse (2007)
Venezuela (Playa Parguito)	80.6 ± 16.4 (73)	–	Hernández et al. (2007)
Trinidad (Matura Beach)	85.7 ± 15.39 (48)	31 (range: 12-52)	Maharaj (2004)
Trinidad (Grande Riviere Beach)	83.1 ± 8.85 (55)	35 (range: 8-64)	Maharaj (2004)
Costa Rica (Matina)	67.3 (6)	30.0 (4)	Carr & Ogren (1959)
Costa Rica (Playa Gandoca)	81.2 ± 17.9 (5,260)	32.1 ± 14.2 (5,260)	Chacón & Eckert (2007)
Costa Rica (Tortuguero)	83.0 (206)	38.0 (206)	Leslie et al. (1996)
Costa Rica (Tortuguero)	80.2 ± 17.6 (20)	28.4 ± 10.3 (20)	Campbell et al. (1996)
USA (St. Croix, USVI)	82.0 ± 17.5 (227)	36.9 (227) 1,100 g (46) [1]	Eckert et al. (1989b)
USA (Humacao, Puerto Rico)	78.4 ± 12.6 (9)	30.8 ± 18.3 (9)	Matos (1986)
USA (Culebra Island, Puerto Rico)	77.1 ± 16.0 (124)	35.2 ± 13.6 (124)	Tucker (1988)
USA (Brevard County, Florida)	83.14 ± 11.22 (39)	33.2 (range: 15-82)	Maharaj (2004)
USA (Florida)	73 ± 18.26 (208)	24.9 ± 12.6 (208)	Stewart & Johnson (2006)

Table 9, continued

Nesting Site	Clutch Size	Yolkless Eggs	Reference
Eastern Atlantic			
Gabon (Gamba Complex)	74.7 ± 15.6 (15)	25.9 ± 11.17 (26)	Verhage et al. (2006)
Eastern Pacific			
Costa Rica (Playa Naranjo)	65.6 (6)	–	Cornelius (1976)
Costa Rica (Playa Langosta)	65.3 ± 15.9 (48)	39.4 ± 22.1 (48)	Chaves et al. (1996)
Costa Rica (Playa Langosta)	64.5 ± 15.7 (131)	–	Piedra et al. (2007)
Costa Rica (Playa Grande)	64.7 (1,389)	38.5 (1,389)	Reina et al. (2002a)
Costa Rica (Playa Grande)	61.8 ± 16.3 (334)	947 g ± 393.8 (334)[1]	Wallace et al. (2007)
Mexico (Jalisco)	66 (8)	–	Castellanos-Michel et al. (2006)
Mexico (Michoacán, Guerrero, Oaxaca)	62.0 ± 17.9 (1,098)	–	Sarti M. et al. (2007)
Western Pacific			
Malaysia (Terengganu)	82.3 (627)	–	van Buskirk & Crowder (1994)
Australia (East coast)	87.0 (5)	42.4 (5)	Limpus & McLachlan (1979)
Australia (New South Wales)	97.7 (3) range: 94-104	–	Limpus (2006)
Australia (Queensland)	86.1 ± 15.7 (16) range: 64-121	–	Limpus (2006)
Australia (Wreck Rock)	82.8 ± 13.1 (14)	46.5 ± 14.5 (13)	Limpus et al. (1984)
Indonesia (Papua)	72 (25)	67 (25)	Bhaskar (1987)
Indonesia (Papua: Jamursba-Medi)	79.6 ± 16.3 (48)	–	Tapilatu & Tiwari (2007)
Indonesia (Papua: Warmon)	76.2 ± 16.1 (51)	–	Tapilatu & Tiwari (2007)
Papua New Guinea (Kamiali, Huon Coast)	94.6 ± 27.28 (44) range: 16-150	–	Kisokau (2005)
Papua New Guinea (Kamiali, Huon Coast)	94.7 ± 21.9 (94) range: 43-156	–	Pilcher (2006)
Papua New Guinea (multiple sites)	88.2 ± 20.2 (37) range: 42-118	–	Hamann et al. (2006a)
Indian Ocean			
South Africa (Tongaland)	104 ± 25.6 (59) range: 60-160	–	Hughes (1974b)
Sri Lanka	100.5 (30) range: 29-140	–	Ekanayake & Ranawana (2001)

[1] denotes average total mass of yolkless eggs (per clutch)

reported that the proportion and hydration status of yolkless eggs in a clutch were related to hatching success and depredation rate of eggs by a burrowing insect.

Wallace et al. (2007) found that yolkless egg mass varied negatively with clutch size and positively with egg mass in leatherback clutches, and concluded that this pattern supported the hypothesis that yolkless eggs are 'production over-runs' of oviducts producing copious albumen for egg clutches. The authors suggested that when production of albumen and shell material exceeds the number of yolks (ova) available for a given clutch, the excess albumen is deposited to a greater degree into the eggs and into yolkless eggs, whereas in larger clutches, the albumen is allocated to a larger number of eggs than in smaller clutches. These results, and the findings that shells from yolkless and yolked eggs appear to have the same functional structure and that leatherback albumen appears to be relatively important to embryonic development (Wallace et al. 2006a), provide support for the 'yolkless eggs as production over-runs' hypothesis.

Chua and Furtado (1988) observed that the number of yolkless eggs decreased as the number of eggs and the number of clutches increased in Malaysia, but Hughes et al. (1967) reported no correlation between the numbers of yolked and yolkless eggs per clutch ($n = 24$ clutches) in South Africa.

The precise role of the yolkless eggs in the reproductive biology of *Dermochelys* has yet to be defined. Whether hypotheses presented here—or other possibilities, such as the space left unoccupied by the progressively dessicating yolkless eggs providing much-needed 'wiggle room' for the large hatchlings—are ultimately accepted, will require additional research.

Fertility.—Attempts to quantify infertility are hindered because of difficulties inherent in recognizing early embryonic death (Limpus et al. 1984). A white spot develops on a fertile leatherback egg at 4–5 days of incubation, regardless of temperature (26°–31°C) (Chan 1989). Whitmore and Dutton (1985) classified eggs as infertile if there was no visible embryo and no white circle on the egg shell. Using this index, they reported 6.1% (SE = 2.3, $n = 30$ clutches) infertility in *in situ* leatherback clutches in Suriname, and 5.4% (SE = 0.2, $n = 54$ clutches) if data from nests reburied on the beach or transferred to Styrofoam® boxes were included. Mean infertility was higher in leatherback clutches than in green turtle (*Chelonia mydas*) clutches; in 1982, the majority (61%) of leatherback clutches had 1–10% infertility while the majority (74%) of green turtle clutches had 1% or less (Whitmore and Dutton 1985). Using the less rigorous criterion of no visible embryo, infertility was estimated at 11.3% ($n = 9$ clutches) in Suriname (Whitmore and Dutton 1985) and 13.4% ($n = 6$ clutches) in South Africa (Hughes and Mentis 1967).

When 35 of 627 clutches failed to develop, Balasingam (1967) concluded that infertility among leatherbacks nesting at Terengganu, Malaysia, was 5.5%. Nearly two decades later, after the population had experienced a severe decline, Chan et al. (1985) estimated infertility at 22%. In their study, four of 18 clutches produced no hatchlings and, upon excavation and examination, the eggs showed no evidence of embryonic development after 70 days of incubation and were in "…good condition [with] thick albumin as in fresh eggs."

In an Australian study, the contents of at least two eggs from each of five clutches were examined at oviposition in order to establish fertility. Blastodiscs (embryonic stage 6; Miller 1985) were present in all cases, yet three of these clutches showed no sign of embryonic development after two months of incubation, prompting Limpus et al. (1984) to conclude that the failure of these eggs was not a fertility problem but simply a failure of fertile eggs to develop beyond oviposition, perhaps a consequence of poor gas exchange.

True detection of the presence of an embryo during the initial stages of development is only possible using microscopy techniques. Using this approach, Bell et al. (2003) discovered that 93.3% (± 2.5%, $n = 819$) of females at Playa Grande, Costa Rica, were fertile, but that within-female fertility declined during the nesting season and that mean fertility differed significantly among females. Previous studies of infertility rates might have over-estimated infertility because detection of microscopic embryos was not achieved.

Reproductive Cycles

Nesting season typically lasts 3–6 months and varies geographically (Table 10). Individual leatherbacks demonstrate nesting region philopatry, but nesting beach fidelity varies according to nesting populations and may be less developed than in other sea turtle species (see *Behavior, Navigation and orientation*, below), perhaps because of the dynamic nature of preferred nesting beaches (see *Reproduction, Nesting behavior*, above).

The phenology of leatherback nesting seasons roughly approximates a bell curve distribution of nests laid over time that may be detected and described empirically from comprehensive beach coverage (Western Pacific: Benson et al. 2007c, Hitipeuw et al. 2007; Eastern Pacific: Reina et al. 2002a, Sarti et al. 2006; Indian Ocean: Andrews et al. 2006; Western Atlantic: Chacón and Eckert 2007, Girondot et al. 2007, Ordoñez et al. 2007). Long-term datasets confirm that nesting season contracts as populations decline. In the 1980s, nesting at Mexiquillo Beach, Mexico, extended from mid-October to late March; two decades later (2001–2002), nesting began in late November and ended in late January "…with no evident peak in nesting activity…" (Sarti M. et al. 2006).

Acquiring robust estimates of nest numbers is important for deriving indices of abundance, and population sizes and trends. But because comprehensive survey effort may be challenging for logistical reasons, a variety of statistical methods have been employed to describe nesting phenology. Hilterman and Goverse (2007) combined different nest count datasets to develop a straightforward correction scheme to account for the proportion of nests missed given different survey methods, thereby generating estimates of total annual leatherback nesting in Suriname. Gratiot et al. (2006) used a least squares adjustment of a symmetrical, sinusodial model that was designed to extrapolate complete distributions of leatherback nesting in French Guiana from incomplete data. Girondot et al. (2006, 2007) developed models using interpolation and extrapolation of asymmetrical logistic functions and Gaussian link to describe the nesting phenology for *Dermochelys* nesting in French Guiana. Godgenger et al. (2009) used a similar model with Poisson link for a low density nesting beach in Congo. A synthesis model was recently applied to low and high density leatherback nesting beaches in Central Africa (Godgenger et al. 2008).

Contrary to early speculation that leatherbacks nest once per season (Dunlap 1955), females deposit, on average, about six clutches of eggs per season (with significant interannual variation, Rivalan 2003), the intervening interval being most often 9–10 days (range: 7–15 days) (Table 11). Due to physiological constraints associated with egg production, the

Table 10. Occurrence and duration of nesting seasons for leatherback sea turtles by geographic region.

Nesting Site	Nesting Season (Peak)	Reference
Western Atlantic		
Brazil (Espírito Santo)	September–February (November)	Thomé et al. (2007)
French Guiana	March–August (June)	Girondot & Fretey (1996)
Suriname	April–August (June)	Hilterman & Goverse (2007)
Venezuela (Playa Parguito)	March–September (June)	Hernández et al. (2007)
Trinidad	March–August (April–May)	Bacon (1970)
Colombia (Gulf of Uraba region)	February–July (May)	Patino-Martinez et al. (2008)
Panama (Playa Chiriqui)	March–July (May)	Ordoñez et al. (2007)
Costa Rica (Gandoca)	March–July (May)	Chacón & Eckert (2007)
USA (St. Croix, USVI)	March–August (May)	Boulon et al. (1996)
USA (Florida)	March–June (May)	Stewart & Johnson (2006)
Eastern Atlantic		
Angola	September–March (November–December)	Weir et al. (2007)
Congo	November–April (December–January)	Parnell et al. (2007)
Gabon (Mayumba)	October–March (December)	Billes et al. (2003)
Gabon (Pongara)	October–March (December)	Deem et al. (2007)
Côte d'Ivoire	October–February (January)	Peñate et al. (2007)
Eastern Pacific		
Costa Rica (Playa Grande)	October–March (December)	Reina et al. (2002a)
Costa Rica (Playa Langosta)	October–March (December)	Piedra et al. (2007)
Mexico (Jalisco)	"mainly" November–December	Castellanos-Michel et al. (2006)
Mexico (Michoacán, Guerrero, Oaxaca)	October–March (December)	Sarti M. et al. (2006, 2007)
Western Pacific		
Australia (Wreck Beach)	October–March (December)	Limpus et al. (1984)
Malaysia (Terengganu)	May–September (July)	Chua & Furtado (1988)
Viet Nam	June–September	Dung (2006)
Indonesia (Papua: Jamursba-Medi)[1]	May–September (July)	Hitipeuw et al. (2007)
Indonesia (Papua: Warmon)[1]	October–March (December)	Hitipeuw et al. (2007)
Papua New Guinea	October–March (December)	Benson et al. (2007c)
Vanuatu	October–March (December)	Petro et al. (2007)
Indian Ocean		
South Africa (Tongaland)	October–February (December)	Hughes (1996), Nel (2006)
Mozambique	October–February (November–January)	Magane and João (2003)
Sri Lanka	April–August (May)	Kapurusinghe (2006)
India (Andaman & Nicobar Islands)	September–April (December–January)	Andrews et al. (2006)

[1] nesting is described as "year-around" (Hitipeuw et al. 2007)

Table 11. Internesting periods for leatherback sea turtles, defined as the number of days between consecutive successful egg-laying events within a nesting season. Range of values and number of intervals (n) are also given.

Location	Mean (days)	Range (n)	Reference
Western Atlantic			
Suriname	10.3	7-13 (36)	Pritchard (1971a)
Suriname	10.4	7-13 (141)	Schulz (1975)
Suriname	–	9.4-9.6[1]	Hilterman & Goverese (2007)
French Guiana (Ya:lima:po)	9-10[2]	6-15	Fretey & Girondot (1989a)
USA (St. Croix, USVI)	9.6	7-15 (411)	Eckert (1987)
USA (St. Croix, USVI)	9.6	9.4-9.8[1]	Boulon et al. (1996)
USA (Humacao, Puerto Rico)	9.5	8-11 (12)	Matos (1986, 1987)
USA (Culebra, Puerto Rico)	9.2	7-12[3] (140)	Tucker (1988)
USA (Florida)	10.1 ± 1.2	8-14[3] (131)	Stewart (2007)
Eastern Atlantic			
Gabon (Gamba Complex)	ca. 10[4]	(151)	Verhage et al. (2006)
Eastern Pacific			
Costa Rica (Playa Grande)	9[2]	6-14 (1,613)	Steyermark et al. (1996)
Costa Rica (Playa Grande)	9.5	(3,683)	Reina et al. (2002a)
Costa Rica (Playa Langosta)	9[2]	(229)	Chaves et al. (1996)
Costa Rica (Playa Langosta)	9.6	(904)	Piedra et al. (2007)
Mexico (Michoacán, Guerrero, Oaxaca)	9.7	8-14	Sarti M. et al. (2007)
Western Pacific			
Malaysia (Terengganu)	9-10	0-49[5] (> 2,000)	Chua & Furtado (1988)
Papua New Guinea (Kamiali)	11	–	Benson et al. (2007c)
Papua New Guinea	14.7 ± 10.01	2-45[5] (31)	Kisokau (2005)
Indonesia (Papua)	9.5	(467)	Bhaskar (1987)
Australia	9.1 ± 0.75	9-11 (6)	Limpus (2006)
Indian Ocean			
South Africa (Tongaland)	9.7	8-12 (22)	Hughes (1974a)
India (Great Nicobar Island)	10.1	8-14	Bhaskar (1993)
India (Great Nicobar Island)	12.5	7-47[5] (82)	Andrews et al. (2006)

[1] denotes range of mean annual values
[2] denotes mode
[3] excludes intervals greater than or equal to: 16 days (Tucker 1988), 15 days (Stewart 2007)
[4] "The distribution of inter-nesting intervals for the 151 leatherbacks recorded show peaks around 10, 20 and 30 days...suggesting an nesting interval of around 10 days." (Verhage et al. 2006)
[5] denotes observed periods between sightings of individual turtles but, for intervals longer than ca. 14 days, nesting events during the intervening period are assumed to have occurred unobserved

minimum period between consecutive nesting events (the internesting period) is six days (Miller 1997). Considering this minimum internesting period, nesting beach monitoring efforts may assume that any internesting period of greater than 14 days probably included another nesting event that went undetected (Frazer and Richardson 1985, Reina et al. 2002a, Rivalan et al. 2006).

Reported values of clutch frequency for leatherbacks vary according to the thoroughness of detection capabilities of a given monitoring program. Observed clutch frequency (OCF), defined as the number of observed, confirmed nesting events for an individual turtle, may be an underestimate of the true value if the probability of a nesting leatherback escaping detection is high. To address this bias, techniques are available to determine estimated clutch frequency (ECF). Frazer and Richardson (1985) calculated ECF by dividing the number of days between the dates of the first and last observed oviposition by the mean internesting period for the population or the individual, preferably the latter. Steyermark et al. (1996) performed the same calculation, but added one to the resulting number to account for the first nest. Reina et al. (2002a) used this ECF methodology at Las Baulas, Costa Rica, given the nearly complete survey coverage at that location. ECF is often biased because it is unable to account for nests that occurred before the first day or after the last day of observed nesting (Briane et al. 2007; but see subsampling method of Reina et al. 2002a).

The ECF method is not useful in situations where direct observations are difficult or impossible due *inter alia* to small size of monitored area, high density of nesting turtles, and/or observer error. To calculate ECF in a situation where direct counts are impossible, Rivalan et al. (2006) computed what they termed 'Total Clutch Frequency (TCF)' by adapting the 'stopover duration' method used in studies of population density of migratory birds (Schaub et al. 2001). This method relies on parameter estimates of capture probabilities, survival probabilities, and duration of residence of individuals prior to first detection that are derived from capture-recapture models. Briane et al. (2007) developed a further method for computing the distribution of TCF by combining information on OCF and monitoring effort with estimates of capture probability to estimate TCF and nesting female population sizes. They also evaluated the effect of including one-time nesters on population estimates of TCF. Table 12 summarizes reported OCF, ECF and TCF for the species worldwide.

Endocrine, ovarian, and behavioral cycles of leatherback reproduction show patterns similar to those of other sea turtle species (e.g., Miller 1997). Ultrasonography of gravid leatherbacks revealed that the proportion of females that had mature preovulatory follicles decreased and that ovum size did not vary significantly as the nesting season progressed (Rostal et al. 1996). In addition, plasma testosterone and estradiol declined throughout the nesting season, but plasma progesterone and calcium showed no such decrease (Rostal et al. 1996). These authors concluded that vitellogenesis is complete prior to the arrival of the female at the nesting beach. For these reasons, and because female leatherbacks are able to store sperm during a nesting season (Crim et al. 2002), they are likely to mate only early in the season and become less receptive as the season progresses. Satellite tracking reveals that male leatherbacks migrate from high latitude foraging grounds in Canada to putative breeding grounds near documented nesting beaches in the Caribbean during the early portion of the nesting season (James et al. 2005b).

Santidrián Tomillo et al. (2009) estimated annual reproductive output to be 252 ± 141 hatchlings per female ($n = 61$ females). The combination of the clutch size, clutch frequency, and the non-breeding duration between consecutive nesting seasons (remigration interval) determines the long-term reproductive output (in terms of total eggs produced) for individual females. Remigration intervals exhibited by most populations of leatherbacks are 2–3 yr (range 1–6 yr), but in some populations 3–4 yr (range 1–11 yr) intervals are more common (Table 13). There is some evidence that remigration intervals are affected by changing climatic conditions (Saba et al. 2008a, Reina et al. 2009).

Conceptually, the remigration interval represents the minimum amount of time necessary for a female to acquire and assimilate sufficient resources to remigrate to breeding areas and reproduce again, and thus has important consequences for population dynamics. Because empirical measurements of leatherback prey abundance and distribution are rare (but see Witt et al. 2007a), remigration interval has been used as a proxy for resource availability (Rivalan et al. 2005a, Wallace et al. 2006b, Saba et al. 2007). Inter-individual and inter-population differences in remigration intervals are proposed to reveal differences in foraging habitat quality and/or variability in resource acquisition and assimilation abilities of leatherbacks (Hays 2000; Rivalan et al. 2005a; Wallace et al. 2006b; Saba et al. 2008a, 2008b).

Wallace et al. (2006b) speculated that differences in resource availability between putative foraging grounds of leatherback populations in the Eastern Pacific and the North Atlantic resulted in observed differences in adult size, reproductive output, and population trajectory. Saba et al. (2008a, 2008b) supported this hypothesis with an analysis of leatherback reproductive output and body size modeled against primary productivity on foraging grounds for selected populations. For a review, see Wallace and Saba (2009).

Price et al. (2004) reported that delayed remigration by leatherbacks to Costa Rican nesting beaches resulted in no apparent increase in reproductive output or in growth rates, leading the authors

Table 12. Clutch frequency (number of clutches per season) in leatherback sea turtles. Observed Clutch Frequency is the number of confirmed successful egg-laying events. Estimated Clutch Frequency is calculated by dividing the number of days between the dates of the first and last observed nesting by the internesting period (cf. Frazer and Richardson 1985). Total Clutch Frequency is an estimate that attempts to take into account egg-laying events before and after the first and last observations, respectively (cf. Rivalan). Sample size (=number of clutches, but see Santidrián Tomillo et al. 2009) in parentheses; asterisk (*) indicates a range of mean annual values.

Location	Observed Clutch Frequency	Estimated Clutch Frequency	Total Clutch Frequency	Reference
Western Atlantic				
French Guiana (Ya:lima:po)	1.1-2.5* (9,579) max = 11	max = 14	8.3 ± 0.9 SE	Rivalan (2003)—TCF Rivalan et al. (2006)—OCF
Suriname	1.6-3.1* (9,158)	4.1-4.9* (2,575)	–	Hilterman & Goverse (2007)
Venezuela (Playa Cipara)	1.99 (369)	2.4 (369)	4.4 (155)	Rondón, Buitrago & Guada (unpubl. data)
Venezuela (Playa Querepare)	1.78 (216)	2.2 (216)	4.4 (93)	Rondón, Buitrago & Guada (unpubl. data)
USA (St. Croix, USVI)	5.26 3.9-6.0*, max = 11	–	–	Boulon et al. (1996)
USA (St. Croix, USVI)	4.9 (83) range: 0-9	–	–	Eckert (1987)
USA (Culebra, Puerto Rico)	5.2-7.0* (80) range: 1-10	5.8-7.5* (80) range: 1-11	–	Tucker (1988), Tucker & Frazer (1991)
USA (Florida)	1.8 ± 1.2	4.2 ± 1.7	–	Stewart (2007)
Western Pacific				
Terengganu, Malaysia	5.5 range: 1-10	–	–	Hamann et al. (2006a)
Papua New Guinea	2.2 (25) range: 1-6	–	–	Kisokau (2005)
Eastern Pacific				
Costa Rica (Playa Grande)	3.5-3.6* (621) range: 1-10	4.9-5.1* (621) range: 1-13	–	Steyermark et al. (1996)
Costa Rica (Playa Grande)	3.2-5.6* (1,383) max = 13	6.4-7.9* (399) max = 14	–	Reina et al. (2002a)
Costa Rica (Playa Grande)	–	9.45 ± 1.63 (61 females)	–	Santidrián Tomillo et al. (2009)
Costa Rica (Playa Langosta)	3.3 (229) range: 1-9	–	–	Chaves et al. (1996)
Costa Rica (Playa Langosta)	2.9-4.6* range: 1-11	–	–	Piedra et al. (2007)
Mexico (Michoacán, Guerrero, Oaxaca)	–	5.5 range: 3-12	–	Sarti M. et al. (2007)
Indian Ocean				
South Africa (Tongaland)	–	6.23 (218) 8.31 (216)[1]	–	Hughes (1974b)
Mozambique (Bazaruto Archipelago)	2 (11) range: 0-5	–	–	Louro (2006)
Mozambique (Ponta Malongane)	2.25 (11) range: 0-10	–	–	Louro (2006)
India (Andaman & Nicobar Islands)	4.9 (27) range: 1-7	–	–	Bhaskar (1993)
India (Andaman & Nicobar Islands)	3.96 (82)	–	–	Andrews et al. (2002)
India (Great Nicobar Island)	2.4 (177) range: 1-10	–	–	Andrews et al. (2006)

[1] total number of nests divided by an estimated total number of females for the lowest and highest years reported

Table 13. Remigration intervals for leatherback sea turtles, defined as the number of years between consecutive nesting seasons. In parentheses is the proportion (%) of the nesting cohort exhibiting the remigration interval, or the number (n) of intervals examined.

Location	Mean Remigration Interval (years)	Range	Reference
Western Atlantic			
French Guiana	2 (88%)	–	Pritchard (1972)
French Guiana	1 (3%), 2 (57%), 3 (22%), 4 (11%), 5 (6%)	–	Chevalier & Girondot (1998)
Suriname	2	–	Schulz (1975)
Suriname	1 (1.0%), 2 (67.5%) 3 (15.4%), 4-5 (16.0%)	–	Hilterman & Goverse (2007)
Venezuela (Playa Cipara, Playa Querepare)	2.5 (n = 50)	–	Rondón et al., unpubl. data
USA (St. Croix, USVI)	2 (61.4%) 3 (30.3%)	1-11	Boulon et al. (1996) Dutton et al. (2005)
Western Pacific			
Malaysia (Terengganu)	2	–	Chua & Furtado (1988)
Eastern Pacific			
Costa Rica (Playa Grande)	3.7 (n = 92)	–	Reina et al. (2002a)
Costa Rica (Playa Grande)	3.7 (n = 448)	1-9	Santidrián Tomillo et al. (2007)
Mexico (Mexiquillo)	3	–	Garcia-Muñoz (2000) *in* Sarti M. et al. (2007)
Indian Ocean			
South Africa (Tongaland)	2 (44.8%) 3 (29.2%)	1-12	Hughes (1996)

to conclude that remigration for reproduction occurs after a leatherback reaches a threshold level of energy acquisition. In contrast, Rivalan et al. (2005a) reported that leatherbacks at French Guiana with 3-year remigration intervals laid more clutches, on average, than did leatherbacks with 2-year remigration intervals, and proposed that this represented a trade-off between current and future reproductive effort.

Embryonic and Hatchling Phases

Embryonic Phase

Embryonic development.—Early investigations into the embryology of the leatherback sea turtle dealt largely with skeletal aspects (Rathke 1848 *in* Burne 1905, Parker 1868) and later efforts provided insight into other systems (Table 14), but not until Deraniyagala (1932, 1939) was a relatively complete serial description of development published. After examining embryos from eggs obtained in Sri Lanka between 1928 and 1936, Deraniyagala (1939) defined 12 post-ovipositional stages beginning with 24 pairs of somites (Table 15).

Miller (1982, 1985) studied in precise detail the development of five sea turtle species in Australia, including *D. coriacea*, and described 16 pre-ovipositional stages (the intra-oviducal period and development prior to the formation of 24 pairs of somites) (Table 16). Using a progressive series of stages based on changes in key morphological structures, he concluded that from oviposition to the formation of the carapace, morphological differences between the embryos of different sea turtle species are slight. However, as the carapace begins to develop, the differences between the Cheloniidae and Dermochelyidae become increasingly obvious.

Pehrson (1945) did a detailed study of the embryonic skull, from 17 to 29 days old, concentrating on the parasphenoid and intertrabecular. At 17 days the trabecles are partly chondrofied, and they are the only elements in the orbital portion of the skull that are identifiable. By 19 days the trabecles are about the only part of the skull where cartilage is well formed, although the basal plate is partly cartilagenous. Blastemic tissue forms primordea of the nasal and inter-orbital septa, planum septale, and the isolated otic capsules. Preblastemic concentrations of nuclei are in primordeal sites of the posterior of the pterygoids, and apparently also the anterior parasphenoid (which is anterior to the hypophysis).

Table 14. Descriptions of the anatomy of embryonic and hatchling leatherback sea turtles. Source: Miller (1985).

Organ/System	Aspect	Group	Reference
Nose	Structure of nasal region	Embryo	Parsons (1970)
Eye	Structure of orbit, eyeball and retina	Hatchling to adult	Underwood (1970)
Stomach	Development	Embryo	Sjögren (1945)
Branchial arches	Temporary epithelial structures	Embryo	Raynaud et al. (1980, 1983)
Skeleton	Carapace	Embryo (20 mm)	Simkiss (1962)
Skeleton	Carapace	Hatchling	Parker (1868), Deraniyagala (1939)
Skeleton	Plastron	Embryo	Rathke (1848) in Burne (1905), Parker (1868)
Skeleton	Plastron	Embryo (25 mm)	Deraniyagala (1939)
Skeleton	Girdles	Embryo	Simkiss (1962)
Skeleton	Skull	Embryo	Pehrson (1945)

Table 15. Post-ovipositional embryonic statges in leatherback sea turtles. Source: Deraniyagala (1939).

Stage	Description
A	10-day embryo. 5.5 mm long; 12 anterior somites to behind fore limbs, 12 more to base of tail; open ventrally; choroid fissure and ectodermal branchial grooves present; tail bent upwards.
B	13-day embryo. 7.5 mm long; somites as before, better definition; visceral arches with branchial nodes; tail curved downwards; allantois trilobed.
C	15-day embryo. 9.5 mm long; somites as before, anterior ones reduced; posterior two branchial grooves partially covered by anterior visceral arches.
D	18-day embryo. 9.6 mm long; head enlarged; visceral arches widened, some displayed a conspicuous branchial node; limbs bud-like; tail thick and stumpy.
E	19-day embryo. [size not given]; completely closed ventrally; olfactory capsules with rims unclosed; visceral grooves vestigial; limbs with terminal discs; tail elongate, motile, and with a terminal hook.
F	21-day embryo. 12.5 mm long; somites as before; body closed ventrally; eyes pigmented; choroid fissure closed; visceral grooves absent; limbs with end plates; carapace begins as lateral ridge and ends as prominence above hind limb; characters of the order Testudinata commence.
G	24-day embryo. 13 mm long; oro-nasal groove closed; premaxillo-maxillary cusps appear; tissues differentiate out from mesoderm; Family characters commence.
H	25-day embryo. 19 mm long; eyes protuberant; sclerotic plates commence; corselet margin defined; carapace ridges tuberculate; tail with dorsal crest; limbs paddle-shaped.
I	26-day embryo. 24 mm long; black pigment on carapace which is confluent with neck and tail; supracaudal crest begins; eyelid well defined; rostral point present.
J	27-day embryo. 31 mm long; pholidosis begins; ear, subdermal, nuchal, and plastral bones ossify; Family characters complete.
K	48-day embryo. 65 mm long; nucho-scapular hump appears; oral papillae present; complete ring of sclerotic bones on eyeball; pholidosis and color complete; ribs ossified from vertebrae to under costal ridges; external generic characters nearly complete.
L	58-65 days. Embryos 82-85 mm long, ready to hatch; fore flippers as long as carapace and fore flipper tips rounded in outline; rudiments of claws at times present on first and second digits; ossification almost complete as in adult; ring of sclerotic bones usually open antero-dorsally; nucho-scapular hump at a lower level than middle of carapace; anterior margins of carapace and plastron level, corselet feebly compressed; nearly all external specific characters present.

Table 16. Pre-ovipositional embryonic stages, defined as the intra-oviducal period and development prior to the formation of 24 pairs of somites, in the leatherback sea turtles. Source: Miller (1985).

Stage	Description
1	Approximately intra-oviducal day 3. A single furrow forms the initial cleavage of the embryonic area.
2	Approximately intra-oviducal day 4. The embryonic area contains approximately 100 large blastomeres.
3	Approximately intra-oviducal day 5. The embryonic area contains at least 300 large blastomeres.
4	Approximately intra-oviducal day 7. The embryonic area includes small blastomeres surrounded by large blastomeres.
5	Approximately intra-oviducal day 8-9. The embryonic area consists of small blastomeres of nearly uniform size; peripheral cleavage furrows reduced or absent.
6	Stage at oviposition. Dorsally, embryonic disk situated eccentrically and posterior to ovoid pellucid area; shape of blastopore appears as strong-to-weak crescent, opening anteriorly; some extra-embryonic mesoderm visible in pellucid area posterior to embryonic disk; notochordal plate may have irregular radii extending from its margin.
7	$1.2 \pm 0.5\%$ of incubation period. Dorsally, the blastopore forms a posteriorly opening crescent; margins of blastopore almost completely apposed; head fold is shallow transverse groove across anterior embryonic disk; neural groove not evident; area of notochord forms elongated triangle; embryonic disk round-to-oval; extra-embryonic mesoderm extends along lateral borders.
8	$2.8 \pm 0.5\%$ of incubation period. Embryonic shield oval; dorsally, blastopore is an inverted U-shape; area of notochord is a thick triangle, pointed anteriorly; head fold is a semicircular furrow at the apex of the neural groove, which appears as a shallow channel; entire embryonic plate appears thicker, with thickest region oriented along the anteroposterior axis; lateral borders of embryonic shield convergent with extra-embryonic mesoderm; posteriorly, boundary between extra-embryonic mesoderm and embryonic shield is indistinguishable.
9	$3.8 \pm 0.5\%$ of incubation period. Blastodisk is an elongated oval with the chordamesodermal canal located at posterior end; neural groove and neural folds are distinct; head fold forms a crescent anterior of the neural groove; extra-embryonic mesoderm surrounds the embryonic disk.
10	$4.8 \pm 0.5\%$ of incubation period. Two or three pairs of somites present; dorsally, head fold forms deep inverted U-shape anterior to neural groove; anteriorly, raised neural folds meet behind head fold; posteriorly, neural folds are separate to the neurenteric canal; head process slightly raised; ventrally, border of anterior intestinal portal is forming.
11	$5.7 \pm 0.5\%$ of incubation period. Five or six pairs of somites present; neural folds fused behind head but remain open along the body length; optic vesicles lie lateral to prosencephalon; amnion extends dorsally to first somite.
12	$6.7 \pm 0.5\%$ of incubation period. Eight to 10 pairs of somites; anterior neuropore remains open; neural folds of brain not fused along midline; otic vesicles just visible; neural folds not fused in posterior one-fifth of body; heart is present as a pair of endocardial tubes; posterior embryo wide and flattened; dorsally, amnion covers one-half total length.
13	$7.6 \pm 0.5\%$ of incubation period. Twelve or 13 pairs of somites; anterior neuropore closed; neural folds are parallel ridges along body length, fused in head region; otic vesicle developed as a depression circumscribed by a low ridge; optic vesicles prominent; heart S-shaped; mandibular and hyoid arches recognizable; neurenteric canal conspicuous; lateral body folds present; amnion extends posteriorly over all somites to neurenteric canal.
14	$8.6 \pm 0.5\%$ of incubation period. Fifteen to 17 pairs of somites; anterior neuropore closed; neural folds fused anteriorly and along entire body length; lenses forming; otic vesicle distinct; first pharyngeal cleft evident; mandibular arch a small bulge; heart beating; lateral body folds conspicuous; small tail bud; dorsally, amnion covers the neurenteric canal.
15	$11.5 \pm 1\%$ of incubation period. Nineteen to 21 pairs of somites; first pharyngeal cleft open, second and third clefts indicated as grooves; mouth open; lens recognizable; lateral body walls are ridges extending laterally; amnion covers entire body; caudal amniotic tube present.
16	$13.4 \pm 1\%$ of incubation period. Twenty-three to 27 pairs of somites; first two pharyngeal clefts distinct and open, third marked by depression; small limb buds; lens present; wide choroid fissure; otic vesicle present; mandibular process directed caudally; tail process extends beyond base of hindlimbs; tail mesoderm unsegmented; blood vessels visible; cranial and cervical flexure.

At 21 days cartilage has developed on the anterior of the planum septale and surrounding elements forming an anterior orbital portion to the skull. The otic capsules have fused with the parachordal plate, but this complex is still separated from the anterior orbital portion—except by the notochord. A blastemal primordium of the vomer has developed immediately ventral to that of the anterior parasphenoid. A blastema of the rostral cartilage is immediately anterior of the anteroventral tip of the nasal septum.

Pehrson's (1945) 29-day old specimen had a carapace length of 13.5 mm, and in size it is most comparable to Deraniyagala's (1932) "corrected" 25-day specimen. At this stage all "dermal" [viz. thecal] bones are developed in the skull, having assumed their definitive structures and shapes. While the anterior parasphenoid has undergone regression, the posterior parasphenoid is distinguishable for the first time at this stage. The first indication of the taenia intertrabecularis is visible at this point. Seen at 21 days, the rostral cartilage is not evident at 29 days. No evidence was found for the intertrabecule, in contrast to the cheloniids.

Leatherback embryos have large glomerulae external to the pronephros (Fraser 1950). In hatchlings, the kidneys are oblong, broad, dorsoventrally flattened and lobate, with surface convolutions similar to those of adults (Burne 1905, Miller 1985). With the exception of these studies, descriptive and experimental work on the urinogenital system of the Dermochelyidae has been generally neglected (Fox 1977), as has study of the development of the alimentary canal (Miller 1985), with the exception of the stomach (Sjögren 1945). Comparatively speaking, the development of the skeleton, in particular the plastron and carapace, is rather well known (Rathke 1848 *in* Burne 1905, Parker 1868, Deraniyagala 1939, Pehrson 1945, Simkiss 1962).

Simkiss (1962) reported that the calcium content in a newly hatched *Dermochelys* is more than four times that in a fresh egg yolk. Accumulation of embryonic calcium occurs near the end of incubation; by the time the embryo is 80 mm long, it contains more than three times the calcium in fresh yolk, and the incubated yolk, albumen and membranes have 50% more calcium than does fresh yolk. During incubation the allantochorion becomes well vascularized and must be instrumental in the transport of calcium from the outside of the egg contents to the embryo. The Ca:Mg ratio in the newly hatched *Dermochelys* has more than twice as much Mg as expected.

These findings led Simkiss (1962) to speculate that the accumulated calcium not only comes from outside the yolk, but from sea water outside of the egg, thus also accounting for the unexpectedly high concentration of Mg. Unfortunately, he concluded that the egg shell does not change structurally during incubation, and hence could not supply the amounts of Ca or Mg that have accumulated in the newly hatched turtle. Subsequent studies, however, leave little reason to doubt that the egg shell is the sole source of the extramembranal Ca and Mg (Bustard et al. 1969, Solomon and Baird 1979).

Miller (1985) provides a useful review of biochemical changes in sea turtle eggs and embryos in general. Studies relating specifically to *Dermochelys* are scarce.

Most recently, Renous et al. (1989) identify 22 embryologic stages between formation of the first somites and hatching. They find "…evidence of a great homogeneity in the embryonic development stages of Chelonians…[but] some peculiarities in the leatherback…" including, among other things, four pharyngeal clefts which seem to close somewhat later than in other [marine and freshwater turtle] species and transient epithelial structures that appear on the posterior edge of the pharyngeal arches.

Embryo abnormalities.—Twelve (0.14%) hatchlings excavated from *in situ* nests on Culebra Island, Puerto Rico, had visible abnormalities (Tucker 1988). These defects included incompletely closed cranium, limb deformity, no lower mandible, pronounced kertosis, hydrocephalic, and amelanistic conditions. Albino and amelanistic hatchlings are occasionally reported (e.g., Trinidad: Downie and Reilly 1992). In Suriname, malformed jaws, eyes and plastron were more common in clutches reburied on the beach or transferred to Styrofoam® boxes than in natural nests (Whitmore and Dutton 1985). In Sri Lanka, drowning resulted when a hare-lip admitted water into the mouth of one hatchling (Deraniyagala 1939).

Twin embryos are reported from Sri Lanka (Deraniyagala 1932), South Africa (Hughes et al. 1967), Malaysia (Chan 1985), Suriname (Whitmore and Dutton 1985), and the West Indies (Tucker 1988, Eckert 1990). The common yolk sac of twins in Sri Lanka was 39 mm and that of a normal embryo 43 mm (Deraniyagala 1939). Twins may be comparable in size, or one may be considerably larger than the other. Data from a long-term population study in St. Croix (USVI) suggest that the occurrence of twin embryos among the leatherback turtles is rare (0.038–0.200 pairs of twins per female per year) and that the production of multiple pairs of twins may be precipitated by factors intrinsic to individual females (Eckert 1990).

Hatching success and sources of embryonic mortality.—Emergence success (often mistakenly reported as hatching success) hovers near 50% worldwide (Table 17), and is lower than that of any other sea turtle species (Miller 1997). Some investigators (Whitmore and Dutton 1985; Chan 1989, 1993) have implicated infertility, based on the staging of unhatched leatherback eggs after hatchling emergence and defining eggs with no embryo present as 'infertile.' However, Bell et al. (2003) report a fertility rate of 93.3% after staging

Table 17. Incubation duration and hatching success for leatherback sea turtles. Hatching success is generally calculated as the number of hatched eggs (or hatchlings) divided by the number of eggs in a clutch. Emergence success is calculated as the number of hatchlings that emerge from the nest to the beach surface, divided by the number of eggs in a clutch. Nest location refers to whether clutches developed *in situ*, in a hatchery, in Styrofoam® incubators, or were relocated to another location on the beach. Data are shown as mean ± SD. Sample sizes (number of clutches) in parentheses; asterisk (*) indicates a range of annual means.

Location	Incubation Duration (days)	Hatching Success (%)	Emergence Success (%)	Nest Location	Reference
Western Atlantic					
Brazil	–	65.1 ± 26.9 (185)	–	*In situ*	Thomé et al. (2007)
French Guiana (Ya:lima:po)	–	–	38.2 (86)	*In situ*	Caut et al. (2006a)
Suriname (Krofajapasai)	–	52.4 ± 27.1 (46)	–	*In situ*	Whitmore & Dutton (1985)
Suriname (Krofajapasai)	–	68.7 ± 17.7 (13)	–	Relocated	Whitmore & Dutton (1985)
Suriname (Krofajapasai)	–	59.9 ± 23.2 (11)	–	Styrofoam® boxes	Whitmore & Dutton (1985)
Suriname (Babunsanti)	60.9-64.8* (338)	21.6-34.9* (380)	–¹	*In situ*	Hilterman & Goverse (2007)
Suriname (Matapica)	62.7-67.3* (97)	58.3-63.47* (151)	–¹	*In situ*	Hilterman & Goverse (2007)
Venezuela (Playa Parguito)	58.5 ± 1.8 (18)	47.2 ± 23.8 (18)	–	*In situ*	Hernández et al. (2007)
Venezuela (Playa Parguito)	58.3 ± 1.5 (3)	27.8 ± 25.5 (4)	–	Relocated	Hernández et al. (2007)
Venezuela (Playa Parguito)	58.1 ± 2.1 (21)	33.1 ± 15.6 (21)	–	Hatchery	Hernández et al. (2007)
Venezuela (Playa Cipara, Playa Querepare)	–	80.19 ± 16.9 (32)	–	*In situ*	Rondón et al., unpubl. data
Venezuela (Playa Cipara, Playa Querepare)	–	52.7 ± 29.0 (46)	–	Relocated	Rondón et al., unpubl. data
Venezuela (Playa Cipara, Playa Querepare)	–	59.9 ± 27.9 (903)	–	Hatchery	Rondón et al., unpubl. data
Trinidad (Matura Beach)	66 (8)	65.26 (28)	–	*In situ*	Maharaj (2004)
Colombia (Gulf of Uraba)	–	75.7 ± 1.9 (86)	–	*In situ*	Patino-Martinez et al. (2008)
Colombia (Gulf of Uraba)	–	69.4 ± 3.3 (29)	–	*In situ*	Patino-Martinez et al. (2008)
Costa Rica (Tortuguero)	–	53.2 (72)	–	*In situ*	Leslie et al. (1996)
Costa Rica (Tortuguero)	–	13.8-46.5* (256)	11.6-39.4 (462)	*In situ*	Tröeng et al. (2007)
Costa Rica (Gandoca)	–	–	41.0 ± 25.8 (818)	*In situ*	Chacón & Eckert (2007)
Costa Rica (Gandoca)	59.7 ± 9.7 (2,254)	–	42.6 ± 35.14 (2,254)	Hatchery	Chacón & Eckert (2007)
USA (St. Croix, USVI)	64.0 ± 3.2 (160)	–	64.1 ± 21.1 (178)	*In situ*	Eckert & Eckert (1990a)
USA (St. Croix, USVI)	62.6 ± 2.6 (272)	–	53.7 ± 20.1 (290)	Relocated	Eckert & Eckert (1990a)
USA (St. Croix, USVI)	–	67.0 (56.9-76.4*)	–	*In situ*	Boulon et al. (1996)
USA (St. Croix, USVI)	63.2	60.4 (50.5-69.0*)	–	Relocated	Boulon et al. (1996)
USA (Culebra, Puerto Rico)	–	75.1 (72.2-76.8*)	71.1 (68.7-72.9*)	*In situ*	Tucker (1988)

Table 17, continued

Location	Incubation Duration (days)	Hatching Success (%)	Emergence Success (%)	Nest Location	Reference
USA (Florida)	66.9 ± 7.8 (177)	67 ± 24.7 (208)	–	In situ	Stewart & Johnson (2006)
Eastern Atlantic					
Benin (Grand-Popo)	–	46.6	–	Hatchery	Fretey et al. (2002)
Gabon (Gamba Complex)	–	68.70 (95)	–	In situ	Verhage et al. (2006)
Gabon (Gamba Complex)	–	–	49.17 (15)	Hatchery	Verhage et al. (2006)
Western Pacific					
Malaysia (Rantau Abang)	–	65.1 (100) range: 0-95	–	In situ	Siow (1982)
Malaysia (Rantau Abang)	–	46.2 ± 11.5	–	Hatchery	Chan & Liew (1996)
Indonesia (Papua)	–	43 (25)	34.7 (25)	In situ	Bhaskar (1987)
Indonesia (Papua: Warmon)	61.5 ± 4.7 (13)	47.1 ± 23.6 (52)	–	In situ	Tapilatu & Tiwari (2007)
Indonesia (Papua:Jamursba)	61.0 ± 5.1 (38)	25.5 ± 32.0 (48)	–	In situ	Tapilatu & Tiwari (2007)
Papua New Guinea	–	–	58 (10) range: 5.4-88	In situ	Kisokau & Ambio (2005)
Papua New Guinea (Kamiali, Huon Coast)	66.8 ± 10.2 (9)	60.6 ± 20.23 (32)	–	In situ	Pilcher (2006)
Australia (Queensland)	–	15.3 ± 17.6 (7)	–	–	Limpus (2006)
Australia (New South Wales)	–	40.3 (3) range: 0-78	–	–	Limpus (2006)
Eastern Pacific					
Costa Rica (Playa Grande)	–	–	54.2 ± 23.2 (164)	Hatchery	Reynolds (2000)
Costa Rica (Playa Grande)	–	–	50.4 ± 9.2 (53)	In situ	Reynolds (2000)
Costa Rica (Playa Grande)	–	19.8 (22)	–	In situ	Bilinski et al. (2001)
Costa Rica (Playa Grande)	–	7.4 (251 eggs)	–	Styrofoam® boxes	Bilinski et al. (2001)
Costa Rica (Playa Grande)	–	71.6 (847 eggs)	–	Styrofoam® boxes	Bell et al. (2003)
Costa Rica (Playa Grande)	–	–	41.0 ± 25.2 (334)	Hatchery	Wallace et al. (2007)
Costa Rica (Playa Grande)	59.3 ± 2.5 (416)	0.44 ± 0.27 (416)	0.38 ± 0.27 (414)	In situ	Santidrián Tomillo et al. (2009)
Costa Rica (Playa Langosta)	–	47.9 (26)	31.6 (26)	In situ	Piedra et al. (2007)
Costa Rica (Playa Langosta)	–	51.4 (33)	26.5 (33)	Relocated	Piedra et al. (2007)
Mexico (Mexiquillo)	58.0 ± 5 (28)	67.0 ± 25 (151)	66.4 (151)	In situ	L. Sarti M., in litt. 5 June 2008 (data from 1988-89)
Indian Ocean					
South Africa (Tongaland)	62.5—72	76.2 ± 15.7 (39)	68.9 ± 18.6 (39)	In situ	Hughes (1974b)
Sri Lanka	59.6 (55)	–	–	–	Kapurusinghe (2006)

[1] emergence success was generally 1-1.5% lower than hatching success at both Babunsanti and Matapica

leatherback embryos at Playa Grande, Costa Rica, at various points during development using light microscopy; these authors conclude that eggs previously described as 'infertile' had embryos present that were invisible to the naked eye.

Embryonic mortality in leatherbacks shows two peaks: one peak occurs early and the second late in incubation, depending on the nesting population (Whitmore and Dutton 1985, Bell et al. 2003). Intrinsic factors (e.g., developmental genetics, gamete quality) responsible for early stage embryonic mortality are undefined, but trauma during the critical period of extra-embryonic membrane organization (48 hr–2.5 wk) is known to result in death to early stage, pre-carapace embryos (Limpus et al. 1979, Blanck and Sawyer 1981). Chan et al. (1985) reported that leatherback eggs are able to "…tolerate rough handling…" only up to five hours after oviposition, after which time care must be taken to prevent bumping, rotation, and disorientation of the vertical axis. Other extrinsic factors (hydric environment, gaseous context, temperature, and depredation) may also contribute to mortality.

During 1981–1982 on Krofajapasi beach, Suriname, mortality in size classes < 10 mm accounted for about half of all embryo deaths in both natural and reburied nests (Whitmore and Dutton 1985). Likewise, the majority of leatherback embryos at Playa Grande, Costa Rica, tend to die in early stages of development (before Stage 6 of Miller 1985) (Bell et al. 2003, Wallace et al. 2004). In contrast, data from two long-term nesting studies in the West Indies indicate that mortality at full term constitutes the largest proportion of embryonic deaths in both *in situ* and reburied clutches (Tucker 1988, Eckert and Eckert 1990a). Between 1982 and 1985, only 0.2% of the yolked eggs per clutch contained dead embryos less than 10 mm in size ($n = 468$ clutches) (Eckert and Eckert 1990a).

In Suriname, the proportion of late stage embryo (> 30 mm) deaths rose in nests that had been washed over or incubated in Styrofoam® boxes (Whitmore and Dutton 1985). On St. Croix, mortality of embryos > 30 mm was more common in clutches that had been reburied at oviposition as a precaution against erosion, as opposed to those left to incubate *in situ* (Eckert and Eckert 1990a). While the cause of late stage embryo death in these cases, particularly at pipping, remains unknown, it does not appear to reflect early trauma.

Wallace et al. (2004) hypothesized that detrimental conditions of the nest environment during peak embryonic metabolism (e.g., low oxygen/high carbon dioxide concentrations, high temperatures) might contribute to late stage embryonic mortality. Oxygen levels tend to decrease and carbon dioxide levels and nest temperatures increase at about the midpoint of incubation (Reynolds 2000, Wallace et al. 2004, Ralph et al. 2005), due to associated onset of metabolically active somatic growth of embryos. Oxygen levels in leatherback nests at Playa Grande, Costa Rica, appeared to be artificially ventilated by twice daily vertical excursions of the subterranean water table due to effects of tidal pumping (Wallace et al. 2004, Sotherland et al. 2007)—whether decreased oxygen levels or increased carbon dioxide levels reach lethal levels in leatherback nests on beaches where tidal pumping is not a factor, such as at most Caribbean beaches, thus influencing hatching success, requires further study.

Biotic (e.g., clutch size, egg mass, embryonic oxygen consumption) and abiotic (e.g., sand grain size, moisture content, gas exchange) characteristics of the nest environment influence embryonic development (Miller 1985, Ackerman 1997). Incubation duration is inversely correlated with nest temperature (Standora and Spotila 1985, Mrosovsky 1994, Wallace et al. 2004) due to the temperature dependence of embryonic development (Miller 1985). High rainfall can result in prolonged incubation periods and cooler, male-producing temperatures in leatherback nests (Grenada: Godfrey et al. 1996; Suriname: Houghton et al. 2007).

Temperature dependent sex determination.— Sexual differentiation in *Dermochelys* is stongly influenced by ambient incubation temperature, a phenomenon known as Temperature-dependent Sex Determination, or TSD (reviewed by Standora and Spotila 1985, Mrosovsky 1994). Specifically, the sustained temperature to which the embryo is exposed during the middle trimester of incubation (thermo-sensitive period) determines the eventual gonadal differentiation and sex of the hatchling (Wibbels 2003).

The transitional range of temperatures (TRT) refers to the range within which a given clutch will be a mixture of males and females; thus, the lower and upper bounds of this range represent the temperatures at which a clutch is 100% male or 100% female, respectively. For leatherbacks in Suriname, the TRT is 28.75°–29.75°C (Rimblot-Baly et al. 1986–1987); similarly, at Playa Grande, Costa Rica, the TRT is 29°–30°C (Binckley et al. 1998).

The "pivotal temperature" (1:1 sex ratio) defined by Mrosovsky and Yntema (1980) may differ with species and locale. Pivotal temperatures for leatherbacks have been estimated from the relationship between constant incubation temperature and embryo gender obtained from gonadal histological methods (Mrosovsky et al. 1984, Rimblot-Baly et al. 1986–1987, Godfrey et al. 1996, Binckley et al. 1998). The relationship between hatchling sex ratio and incubation duration at constant temperature has been used to estimate sex ratio from incubation length *in situ* (e.g., Mrosovsky et al. 1984, Godfrey et al. 1996, Binckley et al. 1998, Goverse et al. 2006).

The pivotal temperature for leatherback embryos is estimated at 29.25°–30.50°C in Suriname and French Guiana (Mrosovsky et al. 1984, Dutton et al. 1985, Lescure et al. 1985, Godfrey et al. 1996, Chevalier et al. 1999) and in Malaysia (Chan and Liew 1995). The most precise estimates are 29.51°C (SE = 0.02) (Suriname and French Guiana) and 29.43°C (SE = 0.10) (Playa Grande, Costa Rica) (Hulin et al. 2009).

Hatchling sex ratios are influenced by seasonal conditions, resulting, for example, in a preponderance of males during cool wet months and a preponderance of females during warm dry months (French Guiana: Lescure et al. 1985). In Suriname, clutches laid in May averaged 30% female, while those laid in June averaged 100% female (Dutton et al. 1985). The average ratio over 11 years was estimated at 49.0% female, but variation among years is expected (e.g., gravid females arrived late in 1982 and the ensuing ratio was 60.5% female, Godfrey et al. 1996).

Throughout the species' range, most studies report a female bias among hatchlings. In the Western Atlantic, the percentage of females ranged from 53.4 to 69.7% (Suriname: Mrosovsky et al. 1984, Godfrey et al. 1996). In the Eastern Pacific, nests produced 100%, 93.5% and 74.3% female hatchlings during 1993–1996 (Costa Rica: Binckley et al. 1998). In Malaysia, 100% of all hatchlings produced between July and October 1986 were female (Chan and Liew 1995). However, recent research in Suriname (Goverse et al. 2006) suggests a more complex scenario, with sex ratios shifting over time and predominantly males produced at three of four study beaches.

Metabolic heating due to embryonic development can create an increasing spatial temperature gradient from the center to the periphery of leatherback clutches (Godfrey et al. 1997, Wallace et al. 2004, Ralph et al. 2005). Godfrey et al. (1997) demonstrated that temperature in the clutch center becomes elevated relative to the periphery early in development, but that eggs on the periphery did not experience temperatures > 0.5° C than the surrounding sand until day 45 of incubation. However, there were no significant differences in the amount of metabolic heating between the centers and peripheries of clutches during the thermosensitive period. For metabolic heating to affect sex ratios of leatherback hatchlings, sand temperature surrounding egg clutches would have to be at or just below the pivotal temperature (Godfrey et al. 1997).

Studies in freshwater turtles have focused on the physiological, biochemical, and molecular cascades initiated by the temperature signal, and the findings have been confirmed in sea turtles. Increased aromatase (the enzyme that converts androgen to estrogen) activity at higher incubation temperatures induced higher estrogen production and feminization of embryos (Desvages and Pieau 1992). Embryonic stages sensitive to temperature with regard to sex determination are the same as those where aromatase is itself sensitive to temperature (Desvages et al. 1993). In addition, Standora and Spotila (1985) proposed a genetic component to sex determination in turtles, including *Dermochelys*, and suggested that temperature may act as a modifying agent affecting gene action.

Several authors have cautioned against artificial incubation techniques that potentially bias sex ratios (Mrosovsky and Yntema 1980, Morreale et al. 1982, Mrosovsky 1983, Dutton et al. 1985, Rimblot et al. 1985). Chan and Liew (1995) speculated that hatchery practices at Rantau Abang, Malaysia, may have inadvertently led to production of 100% female hatchlings, thus exacerbating the downward spiral of that population.

Hatchling Phase

Hatchlings emerge from the nest following approximately 60 days of incubation (Table 17). Mean carapace length, carapace width, and body mass of leatherback hatchlings around the world are similar (Table 4). Leatherback hatchlings are the largest of all sea turtle hatchlings, weighing around 40 g or approximately 50% of egg mass. Leatherback hatchling mass increases with whole egg mass, and in a similar pattern to yolk mass, but also might derive body mass from water and solids in the albumen of a typical leatherback egg (Wallace et al. 2006a). These patterns are more similar to those found in altricial bird eggs than other reptile eggs. Leatherback hatchlings increase body mass roughly 20% due mainly to ingestion of seawater after entering the ocean (Reina et al. 2002b, Jones et al. 2007). Post-natal ontogenetic changes have been documented by Deraniyagala (1936b).

Leatherback eggs and hatchlings face many predators, both on the natal beach and at sea (Table 18). Mortality is believed to be high once hatchlings enter the sea, but survival has not been quantified. In some areas, sharks reportedly frequent the waters off the nesting beach during hatching season (Carr and Ogren 1959, Fretey 1977). Hatchlings have been found in the stomachs of carnivorous fishes in the Western Atlantic (French Guiana: Fretey 1981; USVI: Nellis and Henke 2000; Florida: Vose and Shank 2003). Spotila et al. (1996) assumed survivorship from Day 1 to one year to be 0.25, based on findings for well-studied populations of freshwater turtles (Congdon et al. 1993, 1994).

Hatching and emergence.—Hatching is accomplished by the turtle piercing the egg shell using a pointed rostral caruncle or egg tooth (Deraniyagala 1939), a process also referred to as pipping. The work required during ascent and emergence from the nest cavity is done in concert, i.e., any resumption of activity by one member usually stimulates a period of energetic group effort (Carr and Ogren 1959). Because it is unlikely that a single hatchling would, on its own, make the long vertical trip from the bottom of the nest to the surface of the beach, the adaptive value

Table 18. Predators of leatherback sea turtles. Taxonomic detail reflects that given in the source reference. Life stage affected: E = egg; H = hatchling; J = juvenile; A = adult.

Predator	Location	Life Stage	Reference
Invertebrates			
Ants			
Dorylus spininodis (army ant)	Gabon	E	Ikaran et al. (2008)
Unspecified	Suriname	E	Whitmore & Dutton (1985)
	Equatorial Guinea	E	Rader et al. (2006)
	Sri Lanka	E, H	Kapurusinghe & Ekanayake (2002)
Flies (larvae)			
Dipteran larvae	French Guiana	E	Fretey & Frenay (1980)
	Mexico (Pacific)	E, H	Alvarado et al. (1985), Cruz et al. (1986)
Megaselia scalaris	Suriname	E	Whitmore & Dutton (1985)
Locusts (larvae)			
Acrididae	Suriname	E	Whitmore & Dutton (1985)
Crickets			
Scapteriscus didactylus (mole cricket)	French Guiana	H	Maros et al. (2003, 2006), Caut et al. (2006a)
	Suriname	E	Hilterman & Goverse (2007)
Crabs			
Ocypode quadratus [=*quadrata*] (ghost crab)	French Guiana	E, H	Pritchard (1971a), Fretey & Frenay (1980), Maros et al. (2003), Caut et al. (2006a)
	Suriname	H	Whitmore & Dutton (1985)
	Trinidad	E	Maharaj (2004)
	USA (St. Croix, USVI)	H	Eckert et al. (1984)
	USA (Puerto Rico)	H	Tucker (1988)
	Costa Rica	H	Hirth & Ogren (1987)
	Equatorial Guinea	E	Rader et al. (2006)
	Gabon	E, H	Verhage et al. (2006), Livingstone (2007)
	Sri Lanka	E, H	Kapurusinghe & Ekanayake (2002)
	Indonesia (Papua)	H	Adnyana (2006)
Ocypode occidentalis	Mexico (Pacific)	E, H	López & Sarti (1988)
Vertebrates			
Fishes			
Caranx latus (horse-eye jack)	USA (St. Croix, USVI)	H	Nellis (2000), Nellis & Henke (2000)
'Carnivorous' fishes	French Guiana	E, H	Fretey (1981)
Gray reef shark	Palau	J/A (?)	Engbring et al. (1992)
	Ceylon [Sri Lanka]	A	Deraniyagala (1939)
L. griseus (gray snapper)	USA (Atlantic: Florida)	H	Vose & Shank (2003)
Megalops atlanticus (tarpon)	USA (St. Croix, USVI)	H	Nellis (2000), Nellis & Henke (2000)
Shark	Barbados	J, A	Horrocks (1987, 1989, 1992)
	Indonesia (Papua)	H	Adnyana (2006)
Sphyraena sp. (barracuda)	Sri Lanka	J	Deraniyagala (1939)

Table 18, continued

Predator	Location	Life Stage	Reference
Reptiles			
Crocodilus porosus	Solomon Islands	A	Pritchard (1981)
	Papua New Guinea	A	Quinn et al. (1983), Lockhart (1989), Hirth et al. (1993), Kinch (2006)
Varanus cepedianus	Ceylon [Sri Lanka]	E	Deraniyagala (1953)
Varanus indicus	Papua New Guinea	E	Kinch (2006)
Varanus kabaragoya [= salvator]	Ceylon [Sri Lanka]	E, H	Deraniyagala (1953)
	India (Andaman Isl.)	E, H	Kar & Bhaskar (1982), Sivasundar & Devi Prasad (1996)
Varanus niloticus	Equatorial Guinea	E	Rader et al. (2006)
	Gabon	E, H	Livingstone & Verhage (2006)
Varanus sp.	Tongaland	E	Pritchard (1971a)
	Indonesia (Papua)	H	Adnyana (2006)
"water and land monitors"	Sri Lanka	E, H	Kapurusinghe & Ekanayake (2002)
Birds			
Buzzards	Costa Rica	H	Carr & Ogren (1959)
Casmerodius albus (white heron)	Mexico (Pacific)	H	Villaseñor (1988)
Coragyps atratus (vulture)	French Guiana	H	Mrosovsky (1971), Fretey (1981), Fretey & Lescure (1981)
	Costa Rica	E, H	Hirth & Ogren (1987), Leslie et al. (1996)
	Trinidad	E	Maharaj (2004)
Corvus albus (crow)	Equatorial Guinea	E	Rader et al. (2006)
Crows, Gulls, Hawks	Ceylon [Sri Lanka]	H	Deraniyagala (1939, 1952), Kapurusinghe & Ekanayake (2002)
Fregata magnificens (frigatebird)	Mexico (Pacific)	H	Villaseñor (1988)
Gull	Scotland	A	Stephen (1961) *in* Brongersma (1972)
	Indonesia (Papua)	H	Adnyana (2006)
Gypohierax angloensis	Equatorial Guinea	E	Rader et al. (2006)
Haliastus indus (Brahmini kite)	Indonesia (Papua)	H	Adnyana (2006)
Hawk	Ceylon [Sri Lanka]	H	Deraniyagala (1952)
	French Guiana	H	Fretey (1981), Fretey & Lescure (1981)
	Costa Rica	H	Carr & Ogren (1959)
Haliaetus leucogaster (sea eagle)	Indonesia (Papua)	H	Adnyana (2006)
Larus atricilla (gull)	USA (Puerto Rico)	H	Tucker (1988)
Larus argentatus (gull)	Mexico (Pacific)	H	Villaseñor (1988)
Nyctanassa [= *Nycticorax*] *violacea* (night heron)	USA (St. Croix, USVI)	H	Eckert & Eckert (1983), Tucker (1988), McDonald-Dutton et al. (2000)
Pandion haliaethus (eagle)	Mexico (Pacific)	H	Villaseñor (1988)
Sterna maximus (tern)	Mexico (Pacific)	H	Villaseñor (1988)
Mammals			
Atilax paludinosus (mongoose)	Gabon	E, H	Verhage et al. (2006)
Atherurus africanus (porcupine)	Equatorial Guinea	E	Rader et al. (2006)
Canis vulgaris (common dog)	Mexico (Pacific)	E, H	López & Sarti (1988)
Canis adjustus (striped jackal)	South Africa	E	Hughes (1996)

Table 18, continued

Predator	Location	Life Stage	Reference
Canis familiaris (domestic dog)	French Guiana	E, H	Fretey & Frenay (1980), Fretey (1981)
	Suriname	A *	Crossland (2003) * attack, harassment
	Trinidad	E, H	Maharaj (2004)
	Panama (Caribbean)	E, H	Ordoñez et al. (2007)
	Colombia (Caribbean)	E	Patino-Martinez et al. (2008)
	Costa Rica	H	Carr & Ogren (1959)
	USA (St. Croix, USVI)	H	Eckert et al. (1984), McDonald-Dutton et al. (2000)
	Mexico (Pacific)	E	Cruz & Ruiz (1984)
	Ceylon [Sri Lanka]	E, H	Deraniyagala (1939), Kapurusinghe & Ekanayake (2002)
	India (Andaman & Nicobar Islands)	E, H	Andrews et al. (2006)
	Papua New Guinea	E, H	Kinch (2006), Pilcher (2006)
	Indonesia (Papua)	E	Hitipeuw et al. (2006, 2007)
	Equatorial Guinea	E	Rader et al. (2006)
	South Africa	E	Hughes et al. (1967)
Cattle	USA (Puerto Rico)	E *	Tucker (1988) * trampled
	Colombia (Caribbean)	E *	Patino-Martinez et al. (2008) * trampled
Civettictis civetta (African civet cat)	Gabon	E (H?)	Livingstone & Verhage (2006)
Dasypus novemcinctus (armadillo)	USA (Florida)	E	Engeman et al. (2003)
Didelphis marsupialis (opossum)	Trinidad	E	Maharaj (2004)
Felis bengalensis (tiger)	Malaysia (Terengganu)	A	Fitter (1961)
Genetta sp. (genet cat)	Unspecified	H	Pritchard (1971a)
Herpestes auropunctatus (mongoose)	USA (St. Croix, US Virgin Islands)	H	Eckert & Eckert (1983), McDonald-Dutton et al. (2000)
Mellivora capensis (honey badger)	South Africa	E, H	Hamann et al. (2006a)
Ictonyx sp. (polecat)	unspecified	H	Pritchard (1971a)
Pantera onca (jaguar)	Suriname	A	Pritchard (1979a), Autar (1994)
	French Guiana	A	Fretey (1977, 1982)
	Costa Rica	A	Troëng (2000), Troëng et al. (2007)
Leopard (?)	Ceylon [Sri Lanka]	H	Deraniyagala (1939)
Mandrillus leucophaeus (drill)	Equatorial Guinea	E	Rader et al. (2006)
Nasua nasua (S. American coati)	French Guiana	E, H	Fretey (1981)
Nasua narica (white-nosed coati)	Costa Rica	E, H	Hirth & Ogren (1987), Leslie et al. (1996)
Orcinus orca (killer whale)	St. Vincent	A	Caldwell & Caldwell (1969)
	USA (Pacific: California)	A	Pitman & Dutton (2004)
	Mexico (Pacific)	A	Sarti et al. (1991)
Procyon cancrivorus (raccoon)	French Guiana	E, H	Fretey (1981), Pritchard (1973)
Procyon lotor (raccoon)	Costa Rica	E	Hirth & Ogren (1987)
	USA (Florida)	E	Engeman et al. (2003)
Rats	India (Great Nicobar Is)	H	Kar & Bhaskar (1982)
Sus scrofa sulawensis (wild pig)	Irian Jaya [Papua, Indonesia]	E, H	Bhaskar (1985), Starbird & Suarez (1994), Yusuf et al. (2006), Hitipeuw et al. (2006, 2007), Tapilatu & Tiwari (2007)
	Ceylon [Sri Lanka]	E	Deraniyagala (1939, 1952)
Viverra civetta (African civet cat)	Gabon	E, H	Verhage et al. (2006)

of group effort (proto-cooperative hatching and emergence responses) appears significant. Carr and Ogren (1959) characterized the emergence of a group of hatchlings as "…a survival unit in which undercrowding can result in entombment, and which by its explosive group emergence avoids the dangers attending a protracted, one-by-one leaving of the nest site."

In general, sea turtle hatchlings emerge from the nest 1–7 days after pipping (Lohmann et al. 1997). Blood lactate levels in leatherback hatchlings were highest for actively digging hatchlings relative to those resting on the bottom of the nest or at the sand surface; furthermore, leatherback blood lactate concentrations related to nest emergence were the lowest among three species of sea turtle hatchlings (Milton and Lutz 2003).

If the beach surface is approached during the heat of the day or during rain, thermal inhibition of activity promotes quiescence and encourages nocturnal nest emergence (Mrosovsky 1968). Leatherback hatchlings lose limb coordination and experience the onset of spasms at extremely high ambient temperatures (33.4° and 40.2° C, respectively) (Drake and Spotila 2002).

At Sandy Point National Wildlife Refuge (USVI), 79.4% of emergences occurred between 1800 and 2100 hr in 1985 (Eckert and Eckert 1985) and similar patterns were noted in subsequent years (Brandner et al. 1990). On Culebra Island, Puerto Rico, 64–85.7% of all emergences occurred "between nightfall and midnight" (Tucker 1988). Based on generally early evening (1830–2000 hr) or post-rainfall emergences on the Pacific coast of Costa Rica, Drake and Spotila (2002) concluded that hatchlings tended to emerge once sand temperatures decreased below a certain threshold. They reported that the threshold temperature above which *Dermochelys* hatchlings would not be expected to emerge is 36°C, and that hatchling emergence occurred during slow rates of temperature declines when temperatures had already dropped below this threshold.

Delayed emergence that results in overwintering in the nest is common in many freshwater turtle species (Gibbons and Nelson 1978), but is not known to occur in leatherbacks or in other sea turtle species. Risk features of the environment do not change appreciably during the potential hatching period, thus an immediate emergence is favored because of the potential benefits of early feeding and growth (Gibbons and Nelson 1978).

Once hatchlings emerge from the nest, they spend a variable amount of time resting before quickly traversing the beach to the sea. Terrestrial locomotion is labored, and features an unstable gait that involves the simultaneous movement of all four limbs and forward over-balancing during each limb cycle (Carr and Ogren 1959; Davenport 1987; reviewed by Wyneken 1997). As the limbs move backward, the body is pushed forward until the turtle's center of gravity moves ahead of the ground contact areas of the tips of the foreflippers. At this point the hatchling over-balances, rocks forward onto the anterior portion of the plastron and the leading edges of the foreflippers, and the hind limbs leave the ground. Forward movement of the limbs is initiated immediately and continues until both sets are at right angles to the body, at which time they are pressed downward and backward against the sand and the cycle is repeated. On sloped beach profiles, considerable distance is gained when, as is often the case, over-balancing is accompanied by 'tobogganing,' i.e., hatchlings slide downhill on the anterior part of the plastron (Davenport 1987). A typical, alternating, reptilian gait is also sometimes used (Hughes et al. 1967).

Offshore swim.—Having entered the sea, hatchlings swim unhesitatingly away from land, a period referred to as 'frenzy' (Wyneken and Salmon 1992; also see *Behavior, Navigation and orientation*, below). As during emergence from the nest, blood lactate in leatherbacks increases during crawling and frenzy swimming; however, in contrast to other sea turtle species, there were no significant differences in lactate levels among different activities (e.g., resting, crawling, frenzy or post-frenzy swimming) for *Dermochelys* (Milton and Lutz 2003).

In vitro studies suggest that leatherback hatchlings swim continuously for the first 24 hours, and then undertake a diel swimming pattern in which they decrease swimming to 15–45% of nighttime. In contrast, loggerhead and green sea turtle hatchlings eventually cease all swimming activities during noctural periods (Wyneken and Salmon 1992). Furthermore, the cost of locomotion is up to 20% lower for leatherback hatchlings than for other sea turtle hatchlings, due to the lowest swim speeds, stroke rates, and metabolic rates (Wyneken and Salmon 1992). For a review of aquatic locomotion of sea turtle hatchlings, see Wyneken (1997).

Hatchlings appear capable of forward swimming only and use a synchronized beating of the foreflippers whether moving slowly or quickly; the hind limbs make no contribution to propulsion (Davenport 1987). Two swimming speeds are observed: subsurface and fast (30 cm s^{-1}) or near-surface and slow (8 cm s^{-1}). Intermediate velocities are transitory and there are no periods of rest without movement. Neither alternate foreflipper action ('dog-paddling') nor gliding appear to be used. During fast swimming, power is developed on both the upstroke and downstroke of the limb cycle. During slow swimming, power is only developed during the upstroke, a consequence of the orientation of the axis of the limb beat, which is opposite in direction to that of cheloniid sea turtles. Peak velocity did not exceed six body lengths s^{-1}, which is slightly lower than that exhibited by green sea turtles; however, leatherbacks appear to sustain their vigorous swimming for long periods of time, whereas green turtles slow down considerably within a few limb cycles (Davenport 1987).

Shortly after entering the ocean, leatherback hatchlings are capable of diving. Price et al. (2007) reported that leatherback hatchlings achieve a respiratory pattern of a single breath followed by a long respiratory pause as well as low respiratory frequency (similar to the pattern exhibited by nesting adults) upon emergence from the nest. Deraniyagala (1939) observed: "Unlike the Chelonioidae, the young animal can dive with ease and makes for deep water traveling at about 30 cm beneath the surface thereby avoiding both gulls and wave crests. Once every 10 or 15 metres it rises for air..." In a videotape of hatchlings swimming offshore in the South China Sea, it appeared that all subsurface swimming was of the vigorous type, with no equivalent of the "routine swimming" observed in green turtles (Davenport 1987).

Hall (1987) followed hatchlings offshore Puerto Rico, noting that they "...swam almost continuously..." in a relatively undeviating seaward course at speeds of 18.3–48.8 cm sec^{-1} (mean = 33.1, n = 5), the 48.8 cm sec^{-1} individual being a hatchling that emerged naturally from the nest as opposed to being excavated following the successful emergence of siblings. Fletemeyer (1980) confessed to terminating his attempts to follow wild leatherback hatchlings during their initial journey offshore after becoming exhausted by their unrelenting activity (as compared to the relatively easy task of tracking loggerhead hatchlings, Fletemeyer 1978). Persistent swimming in captivity prompted Carr and Ogren (1959) to propose that hatchling leatherbacks spend the first hours or days following emergence from the nest in steady travel away from their natal beach.

Ontogeny of activity and energetics of leatherback hatchlings differ from those of other sea turtle species. Bels et al. (1988) video-documented the activity periods of captive leatherback hatchlings and observed that between Week 1 and Week 5 significantly more time was spent swimming than resting. By Week 7, rest periods became increasingly longer and swimming periods correspondingly shorter; by Week 8 there were no significant differences between the times allotted to these two activities. Salmon et al. (2004) reported that leatherback hatchlings between 2–8 weeks of age dived deeper and longer with age, performed V-shaped dives (down to 18 m), and foraged throughout the water column on exclusively gelatinous prey, in contrast to green turtle hatchlings, which swam and foraged mainly near the surface.

Leatherback resting tidal volumes increased during the first six days post hatching, while those of olive ridley sea turtle (*Lepidochelys olivacea*) hatchlings did not (Price et al. 2007). Leatherback oxygen consumption rates during active swimming decreased 53% over the first month of development, while factorial aerobic scope (ratio between active metabolic rate and resting metabolic rate) of leatherback hatchlings did not increase significantly, while olive ridley oxygen consumption declined only 35% but factorial aerobic scope increased significantly (Jones et al. 2007). Therefore, differences between hatchlings of leatherbacks and other sea turtle species in ontogeny of energetics and activity might reflect differences in life history and ecology, where leatherbacks exhibit a 'marathon'-style activity (oceanic, vertical, water column foraging behavior strategy) while others exhibit a 'sprinting'-style activity (float-and-wait, superficial foraging sit-and-wait strategy) (Wyneken 1997, Jones et al. 2007).

The activity during the frenzy period is fueled by residual yolk not consumed during embryonic development (Wyneken 1997). Bels et al. (1988) concluded that the activity frenzy requisite to transport hatchlings offshore continues for about seven weeks, at which time swimming becomes relatively less intense and feeding and growth may assume increased importance. The yolk sac, internalized soon after hatching, fuels this prolonged swimming or frenzy stage.

Birkenmeier (1971) reported that leatherback hatchlings contain "...an astonishingly large amount of yolk..." and measured one yolk sac weighing 5 g and measuring 30 mm across. Lutcavage and Lutz (1986) measured hatchling weight at 47.6–54.2 g (n = 8) and reported that yolk sacs weighed about 2% of total body weight. Jones et al. (2007) applied measurements of energy expenditure at different activity levels to model diel energy expenditure based on time-activity budgets during frenzy and post-frenzy swimming (Wyneken and Salmon 1992), and determined that leatherback hatchlings could be sustained for up to 3 weeks post-emergence on residual yolk reserves alone.

The post-hatchling habitat remains obscure (see Chapter 2, *Differential distribution*, above). Hatchling leatherbacks forage on gelatinous prey (Salmon et al. 2004), and use both visual and chemosensory cues to locate prey in the water column, with visual cues likely being most important (Constantino and Salmon 2003).

Imprinting and natal homing.—Natal beach homing, or the phenomenon whereby adults return to nest in the same general region from which they themselves emerged as hatchlings, has been confirmed for various species of sea turtles, including leatherbacks (Dutton et al. 1999, 2005), via genetic analyses (Lohmann et al. 1997). However, the mechanisms by which hatchling sea turtles imprint on natal beaches in order to return as reproductive adults are not completely understood (also see *Behavior, Navigation and orientation*, below). Imprinting, adult learning, and genetics may play varying roles within populations, species, and genera.

Owens et al. (1982) and Lohmann et al. (1997) summarized hypotheses concerning imprinting, or the ability of sea turtles to learn an identifying cue or set of cues characteristic of the natal beach. The social facilitation model proposed by Hendrickson (1958) hypothesized that no specialized information is acquired by hatchlings, but rather juveniles approaching sexual maturity would exhibit an increase in stochastic movement, thus increasing the likelihood of encounters with experienced conspecifics. The net effect would be that virgin males and females would join remigrants to the nesting beach, realize a successful mating and nesting experience, and then "learn" this particular nesting beach by acquiring such characteristics as site fixation (Owens et al. 1982).

Another model involves the imprinting of hatchlings during development and/or as the young turtles traverse the beach, enter the sea, and swim away. The components of this scenario typically include olfactory or chemical cues that must be retained by the turtles for the decade(s) preceding sexual maturity. While salmon are known to use olfactory cues to recognize natal spawning grounds, it appears unlikely that sea turtles use chemical cues to navigate to natal beaches, and only limited evidence suggests a role of chemical cues in natal beach recognition (Lohmann et al. 1997). Recent findings have revealed the ability of some juvenile sea turtles to navigate to specific foraging grounds using geomagnetic cues (Lohmann et al. 2004). Whether adult leatherbacks use geomagnetic cues to navigate to natal beaches is unknown.

Sea turtle hatchlings have been tagged, or otherwise marked for subsequent identification, in a variety of ways (see Eckert and Eckert 1990b for review), but few attempts have been made to tag or mark leatherback hatchlings. In 1970, Hughes (1971a) implanted a fine piece of stainless steel wire under the skin of the right foreflipper in 22 leatherback hatchlings from Tongaland, Natal. The hatchlings were released immediately. Although many stranded hatchlings were recovered, none bore an implant (Hughes 1971b, 1974b). In 1984, 24 hatchlings from the USVI were tagged with subcutaneously inserted binary-coded wires and held in captivity to assess tag longevity: there was no outward evidence of physical disability among tagged individuals, but tagged turtles died significantly sooner than did untagged controls (Eckert and Eckert 1990b).

Juvenile, Subadult and Adult Phases

Longevity
There are no reliable data on maximum longevity for *Dermochelys*, or any other sea turtle species. Leatherbacks typically fare poorly in captivity (see Chapter 6, *Mariculture, Facility considerations* below) and little can be deduced regarding longevity in the wild from existing studies. The maximum age estimate obtained through skeletochronology is 43 years in an average-sized nesting female (155 cm CCL) (Avens et al. 2009).

Despite potentially high levels of tag loss associated with traditional flipper tagging methods (Rivalan et al. 2005b), tagged adult females have returned to monitored nesting grounds for 18 years (South Africa: Hughes 1996) and 19 years (USVI: P.H. Dutton, pers. comm.). An adult female washed ashore "freshly dead" in New Jersey after having been tagged on the nesting beach in French Guiana in 1970, 19 years earlier (Pritchard 1996). Hughes (1996) also reported 28 females with recorded breeding histories spanning 10 to 16 years. Also see *Nutrition and metabolism, Growth,* below.

Hardiness
The leatherback is well adapted to pelagic life with a streamlined body form (keeled, posteriorly tapered carapace) and long, powerful foreflippers. The species also exhibits a broad thermal tolerance and the most extensive range of any modern reptile ($\sim 71°$ N to $47°$ S; Chapter 2, *Total area*, above). Adults have been sighted north of the Arctic Circle in Europe and juveniles have stranded in Scotland, Wales, and England, U.K. (Brongersma 1972). Early speculation (Babcock 1939) was that leatherbacks straying northward in the Gulf Stream became benumbed after entering cold New England waters have proved erroneous.

Eckert (2002a) summarized data on the locations, water temperatures, dates, and body sizes of juvenile leatherbacks worldwide from published reports, strandings, fisheries observer records, museums, and personal communications. Latitudinal distribution was from $56.75°$ N to $33.58°$ S; most records were from the Northern Hemisphere. He reported a positive correlation between body size and latitude, noting that turtles < 100 cm CCL were found only in water warmer than 26°C, and concluded that high latitude foraging grounds were not available to smaller juveniles. Witt et al. (2007a) also reported a positive relationship between body size (including juvenile body sizes) and latitude for leatherbacks in the Northeast Atlantic.

Bleakney (1965) summarized sightings from New England and eastern Canada and noted that both juveniles and adults were in vigorous health, capable of navigating the North Atlantic and quite able to leave the Gulf Stream, penetrate the Labrador Current, and navigate away again by late September. Individuals do not easily succumb to cold or starvation; specimens dead in far northern waters commonly have jellyfish in their esophagus and are almost invariably found to have been suffocated in fishing nets, damaged by ships' propellers, or with plastic blocking their gut (Davenport et al. 1990). Also see Chapter 4, *Mortality, Factors causing or affecting mortality,* below).

Leatherbacks are vulnerable to abrasion and injury on rocks, coral reefs, and other obstacles.

Nesting colonies are most often associated with beaches providing unobstructed marine access (see *Reproduction, Nesting behavior;* above).

Flipper and carapace damage is widely observed, especially with respect to nesting females. Notched and frayed foreflippers are the most common; in addition, rear flippers are sometimes frayed or amputated, rope or net entanglement may leave shoulders deeply scarred, and gaping semi-circular wounds, typically to a shoulder, often testify to shark attack. Carapace damage may include loss of or damage to the caudal peduncle, scratching and abrasion, and, more rarely, mutilation in the form of impact wounds or propeller slashes. Gravid females missing parts of or entire (front or rear) flippers are still observed to nest successfully. Injuries to the head and jaw are also noted (see *Juvenile, subadult and adult phases, Abnormalites and injuries,* below).

Once on shore, females may succumb to the hypersaline waters of coastal swamps or encounter log or root jams that prevent them from returning to the sea; instead, they perish from exhaustion (Pritchard 1973). Between April and June 1977, a study of four nesting beaches in French Guiana revealed that 0.5% to 6.5% of gravid females died on the nesting beach from heat exhaustion, entrapment in mangrove roots, and related incidents (Fretey 1977).

The extent to which disease affects the survival prospects of wild leatherback turtles is unknown. Wolke (1981) reported a case of enteritis. Ogden et al. (1981) diagnosed hematogenous septic arthritis and osteomyelitis involving the elbow, distal humerus, and proximal radius and ulna in a 135 cm adult stranded on the New England coast after it had been struck in the head by a boat propeller. Rothschild (1987) documented avascular necrosis of bone in Oligocene and Eocene members of the Dermochelyidae and suggested decompression syndrome as the etiology of this bone pathology; the extent to which the phenomenon debilitates modern deep-diving dermochelids is unknown. Bacterial infections have been documented for leatherbacks, including *Vibrio damsela* (Aguirre 2006). Huerta et al. (2002) reported the first confirmed case of fibropapillomatosis in a leatherback.

A blockage of the intestine was found in specimens of *Dermochelys* that washed up dead in New Jersey. Of 10 specimens examined in 1982, four (all of them adult females) had enteroliths obstructing the ileocaecal valve. Between 3 and 5 cm along the largest diameter, the enteroliths were yellow to brown in color and had a consistency of hard clay; concentric "growth rings" were revealed by cross sectioning. This enterolith consisted of amorphous basophilic material, intermingled with degenerating cells that had hyperchromatic nuclei and extensive eosinophilic cytoplasm (W. Madway, pers. comm.). Morphologically the cells resembled those from the intestinal epithelium. No focus was found within any enterolith (Schoelkopf *in litt.* to J.G. Frazier, 6 April 1986). Davenport et al. (1993) describe a faecolith from a stranded turtle.

In captivity, diagnosed diseases are confined largely to fungal and bacterial infections. For example, leatherbacks are prone to infection via dermal abrasions and lesions caused by contact with tank walls (Jones et al. 2000). Jones (2009) reported that mortality in captive juvenile leatherbacks was usually due to subacute or chronic bronchopneumonia with secondary infections of the liver and kidneys, and interstitial nephritis.

Competitors

Leatherback sea turtles travel widely and forage over an extensive oceanic area. There are no documented competitors for food resources; interspecific competition may be minimized by the fact that the trophic system of which leatherbacks are a part is largely independent of the more commonly recognized trophic systems supporting whales, tunas, etc. (Hendrickson 1980). *Dermochelys* occupies a unique trophic niche based on a specialized diet of medusae and other gelatinous plankton (e.g., siphonophores, salps).

The ocean sunfish (*Mola mola*) is another known medusivore and competitive interaction between leatherbacks and sunfish has been suggested (Shoop and Kenney 1992), but poorly characterized (Desjardin 2005). Based on remote sensing data, Hays et al. (2009) hypothesized vertical niche portioning with the sunfish having "...a far more extensive capacity for foraging on target prey throughout the water column to depths greater than 500 m."

Leatherbacks often nest coincidentally with other sea turtle species, but competition for nest sites is not known to occur.

Predators

The large body size of adult leatherbacks reduces the threat of predation by most animals. On land, gravid females are periodically ambushed and killed by crocodiles (*Crocodilus* spp.) and large cats (*Felis bengalensis, Panthera onca*); at sea, depredation on adults by killer whales (*Orcinus orca*) and crocodiles (*Crocodilus* spp.) is documented (Table 18).

A variety of injuries to adult leatherbacks have been reported, some attributed to pelagic or coastal sharks (e.g., Fretey 1982). In a typical account, a 305.5 kg female leatherback washed ashore alive in 1989 on the Atlantic coast of Barbados after her right front flipper had been severed at the shoulder by a shark (Horrocks 1989). Engbring et al. (1992) reported an aggressive defensive display by an adult *Dermochelys* apparently under attack by a gray reef shark in Palau. Exceptionally deep diving (> 1000 m) by gravid leatherbacks (Eckert et al. 1989b, Hays et al. 2004a) may represent a flight response to predators.

The harassment of an adult turtle in Scottish waters included "…being attacked by gulls…evidently trying to pick out its eyes…" (Stephen 1961).

Juveniles are also vulnerable to attack at sea. Deraniyagala (1939) described a young animal (8.5 cm CCL) caught about 3 km from the edge of the continental shelf on the west coast of Sri Lanka with punctures and slashes on its limbs and shell. On the basis of the wounds, he suggested that two kinds of fishes had attacked it, the last being a barracuda, *Sphyraena* spp. Two small juveniles (20–30 cm CCL) were stranded in Barbados (the most oceanic of the major West Indian islands), each with a front flipper bitten off (Horrocks 1987, 1992). Because observations on immature *Dermochelys* are rare, it is unknown how representative these accounts are.

Naturally-occurring predators on eggs and hatchlings vary greatly in different areas (Table 18), and attacks are most severe at oviposition and at hatching and emergence. The nesting crawl is erased within several days by wind and/or tidal erosion, rainfall, and animal (including human) activity and few predators are able to locate the eggs outside the first several days of incubation and the last few days before hatchling emergence (Carr and Ogren 1959). Invasive and feral species, such as the wild pig (*Sus scrofa sulawensis*) in Indonesia and the mongoose (*Herpestes auropunctatus*) in the Caribbean, also consume eggs and hatchlings (Table 18).

Quantitative studies of nest depredation are uncommon. Hilterman and Goverse (2007) reported the mean annual proportion of yolked eggs per nest depredated by mole crickets (*Scapteriscus didactylus*) to be 37.4–41.4% at Babunsanti Beach and 11.2–13.7% at Matapica Beach in Suriname. In Trinidad, 41.7% and 56.4% of nests were disturbed by "…erosion or predators…" at Matura and Grande Riviere beaches, respectively, with the primary predators listed as opossums (*Didelphis marsupialis*), ghost crabs (*Ocypode quadrata*), and Black Vultures (*Coragyps atratus*) and depredation statistics were provided for each (Maharaj 2004).

Tunnels of crabs (Ocypodidae) are thought to give access to dipteran flies, whose larvae (maggots) feed on eggs (Fretey and Frenay 1980). Infestation rates of dipteran larvae in *Dermochelys* eggs may be high, although it is not known whether they precede or follow the death of the embryo (Benabib 1983). At San Juan de Chacagua, Oaxaca, Mexico, 0.3% of the normal-sized eggs transplanted to hatcheries became infested with maggots; however, there was no evidence of crab tunnels in infested nests (Adame and Salim 1985). A previous study on this beach found that 70.9% of all natural nests were infested with maggots, involving an average of 6.7% of each clutch; in contrast, only 44% of the transplanted nests, involving an average of 2.7% of the clutch, were infested (Cruz and Ruiz 1984). In Mexiquillo, Michoacán, Mexico, 59% of the nests, or 5.5% of the eggs and hatchlings, were infested with maggots (Alvarado et al. 1985). A second study on the same beach reported an average of 1.2% of the clutch was unhatched and infested with maggots; the numbers of maggot-infested hatchlings left in the nest was 0.8% of the clutch (Cruz et al. 1986), or a total of 2% of the average clutch was infested by maggots.

Of 35 leatherback nests marked and monitored throughout the incubation period at a 6-km section of beach in the Gamba Complex of Protected Areas, Gabon, Livingstone (2007) documented 56% (n = 9) of unhatched nests destroyed by crabs (*Ocypode* spp.). Also in Gabon, underground predation by army ants (*Dorylus spininodis*) was found to be "…one of the main hazards to leatherback nests in Pongara [National Park], with 67% of the marked nests affected in some extent…" (Ikaran et al. 2008).

At Jamursba-Medi and Warmon beaches in Papua, Indonesia (formerly Irian Jaya), field research suggests that low hatchling production results from nest destruction due mainly to seasonal beach erosion and widespread wild pig (*Sus scrofa sulawensis*) predation (Starbird and Suarez 1994, Hitipeuw et al. 2006). Similarly, Yusuf et al. (2006) estimate that wild pigs "…destroy more than 80% of nests every year…" at Jamursba-Medi Beach. Dogs (*Canis lupus [C. l. familiaris]*) in Morobe Province, (which hosts 50% of leatherback nesting activity in Papua New Guinea) are credited with up to 80% of depredated nests (Kinch 2006, Pilcher 2006).

Sivasundar and Devi Prasad (1996) reported that 68.7% of all nests laid on Little Andaman Island (India) were destroyed by water monitor lizards (*Varanus salvator*). A decade later, Andrews et al. (2006) estimated that feral dogs in the Andaman and Nicobar Islands, the most important nesting site for *D. coriacea* in the Northern Indian Ocean, depredated over 70% of eggs and hatchlings at some locations: e.g., "…feral dogs in North Andaman Island predated over 90% of the nests between December 2000 and March 2001."

In the Western Atlantic, Fretey (1981) reported the loss of nearly 1000 hatchlings in a single night's emergence at Ya:lima:po, French Guiana, to dogs. Patino-Martinez et al. (2008) estimated 5–6.6% of clutches lost to domestic and feral dogs at study sites in the Gulf of Uraba, Colombia; and Ordoñez et al. (2007) reported 54.3% of leatherback nests lost to dogs in 2003 at Chiriqui Beach, Panama.

Parasites and Commensals

Internal parasites include mainly Platyhelminthes (flatworms, tapeworms, flukes) and more rarely Annelida (segmented worms) and Nematoda (roundworms) (Table 19). Amoebae resembling *Entamoeba histolytica* were found in the intestine of a specimen off southeastern Louisiana, in the Gulf of Mexico (Dunlap 1955).

Extensive reviews of Cestoda (tapeworms) and Trematoda (flukes) in reptiles and endoparasitic helminths in turtles have listed only one endoparasite from *Dermochelys*: *Astrorchis*

Table 19. Parasites and commensals of leatherback sea turtles. Taxonomic detail reflects that given in the source reference.

Species	Location	Reference
Protozoa		
cf. *Entamoeba histolytica*	captive	Dunlap (1955)
Annelida (segmented worms)		
Ozobranchus branchiatus	Mexico (Pacific)	Sarti M. et al. (1987)
Platyhelminthes (flatworms)		
"Helminth specimens"	Pakistan	Firdous (1989)
Turbellaria (flatworms)		
Turbellaria (unspecified)	Netherlands	Hartog & van Nierop (1984)
Trematoda (flukes)		
Calycodes anthos	Newfoundland (Canada)	Threlfall (1979)
Cymatocarpus sp.	Newfoundland (Canada)	Threlfall (1979)
Enodiotrema carettae	Italy	Manfredi et al. (1996)
Enodiotrema instar		
Pyelosomum [= *Astrorchis*] *renicapite*	Newfoundland (Canada)	Threlfall (1979)
	Indian Ocean	Mohan (1971)
	France	Heldt (1933)
	England	Penhallurick (1990)
	USA (Puerto Rico)	Dyer et al. (1995)
Unspecified	USA (Atlantic: Florida)	Yerger (1965)
	Norway, Scotland, Ireland	Brongersma (1972)
	England	Hartog & van Nierop (1984)
	France (Mediterranean)	Petit (1951)
	USA (Gulf Mex.: Louisiana)	Dunlap (1955)
Nematoda (roundworms)		
Unspecified	Norway	Brongersma (1972)
Arthropoda		
Crustacea		
Malacostraca (isopods)		
Excorallana acuticauda (isopod)	USA (St. Croix, USVI)	Williams et al. (1996)
Maxillopoda (barnacles)		
Balanus trigonus	USA (St. Croix, USVI)	Eckert & Eckert (1988)
Chelonibia testudinaria	Mexico (Pacific)	Benabib (1983), Sarti et al. (1987)
	Sri Lanka, presumably	Deraniyagala (1939)
Conchoderma auritum	USA (St. Croix, USVI)	Eckert & Eckert (1988)
	Mexico (Pacific)	Benabib (1983)
Conchoderma virgatum	France	Brongersma (1972)
	USA (St. Croix, USVI)	Eckert & Eckert (1988)
	USA (Culebra, Puerto Rico)	Tucker (1988)
	South Africa	Hughes (1974b)
	Mexico (Pacific)	Benabib (1983)
Conchoderma sp.	Norway	Brongersma (1972)

Table 19, continued

Species	Location	Reference
Lepas anatifera	USA (St. Croix, USVI)	Eckert & Eckert (1988)
	Mexico (Pacific)	Benabib (1983)
Lepas sp.	USA (Culebra, Puerto Rico)	Tucker (1988)
Platylepas coriacea	Australia	Monroe & Limpus (1979)
Platylepas hexastylos	USA (St. Croix, USVI)	Eckert & Eckert (1988)
	USA (Culebra, Puerto Rico)	Tucker (1988)
Platylepas hexastylos	USA (Atlantic: Georgia)	S.A. Eckert, unpubl. data
	Mexico (Pacific)	Benabib (1983)
Platylepas sp.	Trinidad	Bacon (1970, 1971)
	South Africa	Hughes (1974b)
Platylepas sp.	Mexico (Pacific)	Benabib (1983)
Stomatolepas dermochelys [= *S. elegans*]	Canada (Pacific)	Zullo & Bleakney (1966)
	England	Brongersma (1972), Penhallurick (1990)
	USA (St. Croix, USVI)	Eckert & Eckert (1988)
	USA (Culebra, Puerto Rico)	Tucker (1988)
	Norway	Carriol & Vader (2002)
	Australia	Monroe & Limpus (1979)
	New Zealand	McCann (1969)
	Mexico (Pacific)	Benabib (1983)
Unspecified	Scotland	Brongersma (1972)
Chordata		
Pisces		
Echeneis naucrates	South Africa	Hughes (1974b)
	USA (St. Croix, USVI)	Eckert & Eckert (1988)
	USA (Florida)	Yerger (1965)
	Mexico (Pacific)	L. Sarti M., pers. comm.
Naucrates doctor	France (Corsica)	Delaugerre (1987)
	Norway	Willgohs (1957), Carriol & Vader (2002)
	France	Brongersma (1972)
	England	Penhallurick (1990)
	USA (Atlantic: Maine)	Moulton (1963)
	South Africa	Hughes (1974b)
Remora [= *Echeneis*] *remora*	France	Duguy (1968), Brongersma (1972)
	England	Penhallurick (1991)
	USA (St. Croix, USVI)	Eckert & Eckert (1988)
	Australia	Limpus & McLachlan (1979)
	Mexico (Pacific)	L. Sarti M., pers. comm.
	Costa Rica (Pacific)	B. Wallace, unpubl. data

renicapite (Leidy 1856) recorded from no other host (Hughes et al. 1941a, 1941b, 1942; Ernst and Ernst 1977). Twenty-five specimens of the digenean *Astrorchis renicapite* were found in the intestine of a stranded leatherback in Puerto Rico (Dyer et al. 1995). Threlfall (1979) reported two new records of diagenean trematodes in *Dermochelys*, both from Newfoundland, Canada. A male turtle had three specimens of *Calycodes anthos* (Braun) in its intestine, and a female had a single specimen of *Cymatocarpus* sp. (possibly *C. undulatus* Loos) in its gall bladder. These flukes are previously known only from cheloniids (Hughes et al. 1941b, 1942; Ernst and Ernst 1977).

Firdous (1989) reported helminth specimens in the alimentary canal of a stranded leatherback in Pakistan. Three species of trematodes (Digenea) were collected from the liver and intestines of a leatherback stranded on the coast of Lampedusa, Italy (Manfredi et al. 1996), and unidentified trematodes have been reported from several North Atlantic adult *Dermochelys*.

Williams et al. (1996) document the occurrence of at least one species of isopod (*Excorallana acuticauda*) associated with leatherbacks nesting in the USVI (Table 19). Blood was found in the gut, suggesting that the isopod was feeding on its host. The authors speculated that the true extent of such associations is unknown, given that most isopods would fall off when a female comes ashore to nest.

A variety of sessile coronuloid barnacles of the subfamilies Chelonibiinae and Platylepadinae, as well as stalked Lepadid barnacles (*Conchoderma* spp., *Lepas* spp.), have been documented on *Dermochelys* (Table 19). Eckert and Eckert (1988) documented the increase of settlement of multiple barnacle species on individual leatherbacks as the nesting season progressed in St. Croix. They reported two cosmopolitan lepadomorph species (*Conchoderma auritum* and *Lepas anatifera*), as well as the pantropical *Conchoderma virgatum*, increased as the season progressed, while balanomorph species (*Balanus trigonus*, *Platylepas hexastylos*, *Stomatolepas dermochelys*) presumably settled on leatherbacks in more temperate latitudes prior to the turtles entering Caribbean waters.

The northernmost record for *Stomatolepas elegans* is Finnmark, Norway (~ 71° N) (Carriol and Vader 2002), and this barnacle species on a leatherback has also been reported as far south as New Zealand (41° 01' S, 176° 06' W) (McCann 1969).

The only quantitative report of barnacle infestations is that of Benabib (1983) for 81 nesting females in Mexiquillo, Mexico. Rates of infestation for six body parts were presented for sessile (*Chelonibia* spp. and *Platylepas* spp.), stalked (*Conchoderma virgatum*), and combined barnacle fauna. The carapace was most often colonized: 94% of the females had sessile, 46% had stalked, and 45% had both types of barnacles. In decreasing order, the sessile barnacles colonized the shoulders (62% of the females), front limbs (57%), hind limbs (56%), head (51%), and neck (25%). Stalked barnacles colonized the head (18% of the females), hind limbs (12%), neck (11%), front limbs (8%), and shoulders (7%). No female was unaffected.

Anecdotal observations of pilot fishes (*Naucrates*; Carangidae) and disk fishes or shark suckers (*Echeneis* and *Remora*; Echeneidae) attached to or associated with free-swimming leatherbacks are commonplace in the literature (Table 19). In New South Wales, Australia, a "whaler shark" maintained a position above an adult-sized turtle that was about 3 m deep; in addition to several remoras, about 10 black kingfish (estimated 27 kg each, species not given) swam with it (Sands *in* Limpus and McLachlan 1979). Fretey (1978) provides an interesting review, addressing especially the echeneids.

Abnormalities and Injuries

Injuries to leatherbacks, thought to have been made in the marine environment, have been reported from many localities. There are a few observations of wounds on animals in temperate latitudes (Brongersma 1969, 1972), but most accounts are of wounds on nesting females: Australia (Limpus and McLachlan 1979), Colombia (Kaufmann 1973), French Guiana and Suriname (Pritchard 1971a, Fretey 1982), Mexiquillo, Mexico (Benabib 1983), South Africa (Hughes et al. 1967), Sri Lanka (Deraniyagala 1939, 1953), and Trinidad (Bacon 1970, Bacon and Maliphant 1971), among others. The preponderance of injury reported from nesting females is more likely a matter of access (by researchers), not special suseptability.

Injuries to the limbs have been depicted in the earliest illustrations of *Dermochelys* (Borlase 1758, Ranzani 1832), but quantitative data are scarce. Detailed information is available from two studies: 6791 females in French Guiana (Fretey 1982) and about 80 females in Mexico (Benabib 1983). In French Guiana, damage to limbs accounted for 75% of the total number of injuries, and although front and hind limbs had almost equal rates of injury, the left limbs were damaged nearly twice as often as the right. Amputations of phalanges, or even more proximal limb bones, were common, and although the injuries presumably occurred at sea, the causes were unknown.

Damage to the head was recorded in less than 0.4% of the French Guiana females and included gaping holes in the jaws and numerous parallel lacerations on the crown that ran almost in line with the long axis of the body. The variety of injuries seen on nesting females in French Guiana is remarkable. Other rates of injury to these animals include damaged: eyes, 0.2% of the females; shoulder 0.6%; carapace, 0.6%; tail, > 0.1 %; caudal projection, 0.2%; and neck, 0.06%. More than 8% of all nesting females had some kind of conspicuous external damage to either limbs or head or other parts of the body. Although eye damage is thought to occur on land, as a result of collisions with mangrove and other trunks, and supracaudal wounds are assumed to be from sharks (Fretey 1982), the true causes of these injuries are unknown.

In Mexico, 76% of the nesting females had injured limbs, although major damage was rare. As in French Guiana, the left flipper was more often damaged than the right, but the difference was not statistically significant. The caudal projection was truncated or injured in 28% of these females (Benabib 1983). It was pointed out that large wounds need not be the work of large predators but may have occurred when the turtle was small. The straight cuts of the caudal projection were thought to be not from predation but from a boat propeller, and some injuries were thought to have been made from the turtle banging against rocks or the bottom while coming onto the beach (Benabib 1983, see also Bacon 1970).

The occurrence of billfish (Istiophoridae), such as marlin (*Makaira*) and sailfish (*Istiophorus*), bills broken off in various sea turtles, including *Dermochelys*, is summarized by Frazier et al. (1994). Two records not included are those of Fretey (1982), who documented a rostrum of either *Makaira* sp. or *Tetrapturus* sp. in the shoulder of a female nesting in French Guiana, and Eckert et al. (1994), who described the distal portion of the bill of a blue marlin (*Makaira nigricans*) protruding vertically from the carapace of a female nesting on St. Croix, USVI. When the animal returned to St. Croix to lay her fifth nest of the season, the wound, originally 2 x 3 cm at the skin surface with a depth of 6 cm and located directly over the left lung, was smaller and appeared to be filling in. These events are not likely to have been caused by the fish attempting to attack the sea turtle.

Nutrition and Metabolism

Food
According to every review of leatherback prey items, individuals at all life stages consume gelatinous organisms related to the Cnidaria (jellyfish), Ctenophora, and Urochordata (Tunicata). Other putative prey items appear to be opportunistically (i.e., commensals or other organisms associated with gelatinous zooplankton) or accidentally ingested.

Brongersma (1969) provided the first detailed review of all literature references to the diet of *Dermochelys* and observed that early reports were replete with speculation and uncritical repetition of statements of questionable accuracy. He summarized stomach content analyses of 26 leatherbacks examined by other investigators, added two observations of actual feeding, and concluded that the most credible reports of the normal food of the leatherback referred almost exclusively to Cnidaria (Table 20).

The conclusion that the diet "…consists chiefly of jellyfish and their parasites and symbionts…" (Bleakney 1965) was further corroborated by gut content analysis published by Hartog and van Nierop (1984). In a review of the foraging ecology and nutrition of leatherbacks, all available data subsequent to Bleakney's (1965) and Brongersma's (1969) conclusions have confirmed that leatherbacks feed primarily on scyphomedusae, pelagic tunicates, and associated organisms (Bjorndal 1997).

Based on the leatherback's oceanic habitat, its speed and strength, and its "…powerful jaws armed with maxillary cusps…" (Ray and Coates 1958), some early authors (e.g., Ray and Coates 1958, Villiers 1958, Worrell 1963) believed *Dermochelys* to be primarily a fish eater. There is scant evidence to support this notion: Burne (1905) found a small teleost in the mouth of a Japanese leatherback; Heldt (1933) found the urohyal bone of a fairly large fish between the oesophageal papillae of a Tunisian leatherback; Navaz and de Llarena (1951) found a partially digested juvenile horse mackerel (*Trachurus*) among the oesophageal papillae of a leatherback caught off France; and Bleakney (1965) found a partially digested young fish (*Urophycis*) in the stomach of a leatherback caught off Nova Scotia. Atkins (1960) reported that a Norwegian fishing vessel caught a leatherback on a shark line baited with herring (Clupeidae). Brongersma (1969), however, considered that records of fish in leatherback digestive systems were based on accidental or casual ingestion of dead fish, or of fish habitually associated with preferred food taxa. For example, juvenile *Trachurus* and *Urophycis* are known to associate closely with cnidarians (Mansueti 1963). There have been no direct observations of leatherbacks catching healthy, active fish, or showing any inclination to do so.

Several authors (e.g., Deraniyagala 1939, 1953; Ingle and Smith 1949; Smith 1951; Neill 1958) include crustaceans, often specified as "prawns" in the diet of the leatherback. Brongersma (1967) considered the frequent entanglement of leatherbacks in lobster lines as possible evidence that the turtle might prey on lobsters or crabs when in shallow water, but later discarded this hypothesis (Brongersma 1969). The only first-hand reports of crustaceans in leatherback stomachs refer to species habitually associated with jellyfish or tunicates, such as amphipods (*Hyperia* spp.) (Sears 1887, Vaillant 1896, Bouxin and Legendre 1947, Willgohs 1956, Bleakney 1965). In the guts of two adult male leatherbacks, one taken from the waters of England and the other from The Netherlands, Hartog and van Nierop (1984) found 306 and 376 specimens of *Hyperia galba*, respectively. Capra (1949) reported the amphipod *Phronima sedentaria* (a commensal of tunicates) in an Italian leatherback.

Gudynas (1980) reported the crab *Libinia* from the stomach of a leatherback from Uruguay. *Libinia spinosa* commonly resides inside the bell of Discomedusae off the coast of Uruguay (Vaz

Table 20. Prey items, targeted and incidental, of wild leatherback sea turtles, as determined by gut content analysis or by direct observation. Taxonomic detail reflects that given in the source reference. Life Stage (Stage): H = hatchling; J = juvenile; A = adult; [blank] = unknown or unreported. Cnidarians are reported in early references as 'coelenterates.'

Species	Location	Stage	Reference
Ctenophora			
Ocryopsis, Mneniopsis sp.	USA (Florida)	J	Salmon et al. (2004)
Cnidaria			
Hydrozoa			
Aequorea sp.	England	A	Hartog & van Nierop (1984)
Aequorea (*pensilis?*)[1]	Scotland	A	Hartog & van Nierop (1984)
Obelia dichotoma	Netherlands	A	Hartog & van Nierop (1984)
Scyphozoa			
Aurelia aurita?	Netherlands, England, Scotland	A	Hartog & van Nierop (1984)
Aurelia sp.	USA (Pacific: Washington)		Eisenberg & Frazier (1983)
Chrysaora hysoscella	Netherlands, Scotland (?)	A	Hartog & van Nierop (1984)
Cyanea capillata	Netherlands, Scotland	A	Hartog & van Nierop (1984)
	Scotland		Clarke *in* Brongersma (1969)
	Norway		Grandison *in* Brongersma (1969)
	Canada (Atlantic)		Bleakney (1965)
Cyanea lamarckii	Netherlands, England	A	Hartog & van Nierop (1984)
Cyanea sp.	England	A	Brongersma (1972)
Pelagia noctiluca	England	A	Hartog & van Nierop (1984)
Rhizostoma cuvieri	Tunisia		Heldt (1933)
Rhizostoma octopus	Netherlands, England	A	Hartog & van Nierop (1984)
	France (Mediterranean)	A	Duron-Dufrenne (1987)
Rhizostoma pulmo	France	A	Duron and Duron (1980)
Stomolophus sp.	USA (Atlantic: Georgia)		J. Webster, pers. comm.
Stomolophus fritillarius	Trinidad	A	Bacon (1970, 1971)
Unspecified	Mexico (Pacific)	A (♀,♂)	L. Sarti M., pers. comm.
	USA (Atlantic)		Sears (1887)
	France		Vaillant (1896), Duguy (1968)
	Sri Lanka		Deraniyagala (1930)
	Ireland	A	Brongersma (1972)
	Malta	A	Hartog (1980)
Siphonophora			
Physalia physalis	Trinidad	A	Bacon (1971)
Apolemia uvaria	England, Malta	A	Hartog (1980), Hartog & van Nierop (1984)
Mollusca			
Cephalopoda			
Squid	USA (Atlantic)		Sears (1887)
Gastropoda			
Pteropod	Ireland	A	Brongersma (1972)

Table 20, continued

Species	Location	Stage	Reference
Crustacea			
Amphipoda			
Hyperia galba[1]	England, Netherlands	A	Hartog & van Nierop (1984)
	France		Vaillant (1896), Bouxin & Legendre (1947)
	Scotland		Clarke *in* Brongersma (1969)
Hyperia medusarum[1]	Canada (Atlantic)		Bleakney (1965)
	Norway		Grandison *in* Brongersma (1969)
Hyperia sp.[1]	USA (Atlantic)		Sears (1887)
	Norway		Willgohs (1956)
Phronima sedentaria[2]	Italy		Capra (1949)
Decapada			
Carcinus maenas[3]	Netherlands	A	Hartog & van Nierop (1984)
Libinia sp.[1]	Uruguay	A (?)	Gudynas (1980)
	USA (Atlantic: Georgia)	A	S.A. Eckert, unpubl. data
Chordata			
Urochordata (Tunicata)			
Ascidiacea			
Unspecified	Japan		Burne (1905)
	France		Harant (1949)
Thaliacea			
Pyrosoma sp.	Italy insular North Pacific		Capra (1949), Iverson & Yoshida (1956), Jones & Shomura (1970), Balazs & Gilmartin, unpubl. data *in* Davenport & Balazs (1991)
	New Zealand		Davenport & Balazs (1991)
Salps	Madeira		Brongersma (1968)
Vertebrata			
Pisces			
Argenina siaiis (Pacific argentine), otolith	USA (Pacific)	A	Anon. (1988)
Engrulis mordax (anchovy), 2 otoliths	USA (Pacific)	A	Anon. (1988)
"Teleosts"	Japan		Burne (1905)
	Tunisia		Heldt (1933)
Trachurus trachurus[1]	Spain		Navaz & de Llarena (1951)
Urophycis sp.[1]	Canada (Pacific)		Bleakney (1965)
Unspecified	England	A	Brongersma (1972)
	Mexico (Pacific)		Montoya *in* Pritchard (1971a)
Plantae[4]			
Chlorophyta (green algae)			
Cystosira fibrosa	France		Vaillant (1896)
Enteromorpha prolifera	Netherlands	A	Hartog & van Nierop (1984)
Ectocarpus sp.	France		Vaillant (1896)
Fucus sp.	USA (Atlantic: Maine)		Ray & Coates (1958)
Unspecified	England, Ireland	A	Brongersma (1972)
Chromophycota (brown seaweed)			
Halidrys siliquosa	France		Vaillant (1896)

Table 20, continued

Species	Location	Stage	Reference
Anthophyta (flowering plants)			
Zoster sp. (seagrass)	France		Vaillant (1896)
Unspecified	Tunisia		Heldt (1933)
"Seaweed"	Japan		Burne (1905)
Monera			
Cyanophyta (bluegreen algae)	Sri Lanka		Deraniyagala (1930)

[1] generally assumed to have been ingested incidentally with Scyphozoa
[2] assume ingested incidentally with the tunicate, Pyrosoma (Brongersma 1969)
[3] assume ingested with the green alga, *Enteromorpha prolifera* (Hartog and van Nierop 1984)
[4] Brongersma (1969) suggests: "algae and pieces of sea-grass are swallowed more or less accidentally together with other food"

Ferreira Guadalupe 1972); thus, the presence of this neritic crab in leatherback digesta strengthens the evidence that *Dermochelys* specializes on soft-bodied pelagic invertebrates (Frazier et al. 1985). In February 1989, an adult female leatherback tagged in French Guiana stranded on the Georgia coast; *Libinia* and several unidentified medusae were found in the animal's stomach (SAE). *Libinia* is commensal on the jellyfish *Stomolophus* and it is likely that the crab, which was found intact and undigested in the hindgut, was incidentally ingested. Murphy et al. (2006) reported fragments of *L. dubia* and *L. emerginata* in stomach contents of stranded leatherbacks along the coast of South Carolina (United States).

The claims that leatherbacks eat echinoderms (Audubon 1834) and sponges (Nöel-Hume and Nöel-Hume 1954), subsist on molluscs and cuttlefish (Pritchard 1964), or are able to tear mussels and oysters from rocks (Kappler 1887) cannot be substantiated. As Bleakney (1965) observed, the jaws of the leatherback are quite different from those of turtle species known to feed on hard-shelled prey. There is no evidence to support the claim that leatherbacks eat molluscs in the wild except for the single observation of Sears (1887) that a leatherback from Essex County, Massachusetts, had what appeared to be partially digested squid in its intestine, and the fact that adult leatherbacks are occasionally taken on longline hooks baited with squid in the West Indies (Eckert et al. 1992) and octopus in Australia (Limpus 1984). The presence of gastropods, bivalve shells, and fragments of crabs and holothurians in the stomach of a leatherback taken off the British Isles (Glüsing 1973) may reflect confusion with the stomach contents from, possibly a loggerhead sea turtle (Hartog and van Nierop 1984).

Similarly, claims that the leatherback is even partially an herbivore are unlikely to be valid. Indigenous communities of the Suriname coast once believed the leatherback to be herbivorous (Schulz 1964), while others have described the species as omnivorous, consuming both plant and animal material (Audubon 1834, de Sola 1931, Carr 1952, Ray and Coates 1958). Fragments of ingested plant matter (e.g., *Cystosira fibrosa*, *Ectocarpus* sp., *Fucus* sp., *Halydrys siliquosa*, *Zostera* sp.) are sometimes reported (Table 20), but quantities are invariably small and it seems likely that vegetable matter is ingested incidentally to feeding on other foods.

In summary, leatherbacks appear to feed predominately on pelagic medusae. This specialized diet is unique among sea turtles and among most marine vertebrates, with the possible exception of the ocean sunfish *Mola mola* (see *Juvenile, subadult and adult phases, Competitors*, above). Most leatherback diet items are from subtropical, temperate and boreal latitudes where the preferred prey, at least in the Western Atlantic, appears to be *Cyanea* spp., *Aurelia* spp., and *Stomolophus* spp. (Bleakney 1965, Lazell 1980, James and Herman 2001, Murphy et al. 2006). Elsewhere, jellyfish representing several species have been found in the stomachs of leatherbacks from France, England, Scotland, Ireland, Norway, The Netherlands, Malta, Tunisia, and Sri Lanka (Table 20). The necropsy of an adult female shot off the coast of California in July 1988 revealed "...2 lbs of jellyfish in the esophagus [suggesting] that the animal was feeding at time of death..." (Anonymous 1988).

Hartog and van Nierop (1984) subjected the digesta of six leatherbacks from Scotland, England, and The Netherlands to microscopic examination; only six species of Scyphozoa occur in shallow waters of the British Isles and the North Sea, and all six were represented among the leatherbacks examined. Davenport and Balazs (1991) compiled a list of direct observations (of feeding) or stomach contents containing *Pyrosoma* spp., a widely distributed pelagic colonial tunicate. Duron-Dufrenne (1978) reported that leatherbacks off the French coast consumed approximately 200 kg per day of *Rhizostoma* spp. Brongersma (1969) speculated that floating gooseneck barnacles, swarms of pteropods, "Portuguese Man-O-War" jellyfish (*Physalia physalis*) and *Velella* may be opportunistically consumed; Bacon (1970) also reported consumption of *P. physalis*. *Chrysaora fuscenscens*, *C. colorata* (sea nettles), and *Aurelia* spp. are known prey items for leatherbacks foraging off the United States' Pacific coast (Benson et al. 2007b). In addition to the documentation of prey provided by internal examination, corroborating evidence is available from reports of leatherbacks feeding in the wild (see *Feeding*, below).

Compared with other types of prey, gelatinous organisms like jellyfish have relatively low energy content per unit wet mass, due to high ash content and high water content (Doyle et al. 2007). Lutcavage and Lutz (1986) estimated that leatherbacks would have to consume the equivalent of their entire body mass daily in jellyfish just to meet basic metabolic demands. Doyle et al. (2007) measured energy densities of three jellyfish species (*Cyanea capillata, Chrysaora hysoscella, Rhizostoma octopus*) that are known or putative leatherback prey in the northeastern Atlantic Ocean, and reported that the values for jellyfish were much lower than those for other foodstuffs, such as fish and algae. The authors speculated that leatherbacks might preferentially consume the highest energy parts of jellyfish, i.e., the gonads, in order to maximize energy intake for biomass consumed (see *Metabolism*, below).

Analytical methods have been employed to elucidate trophic status of leatherbacks. Using stable isotope analyses, Godley et al. (1998) demonstrated that leatherbacks occupied a trophic position that was intermediate to more carnivorous loggerhead and herbivorous green sea turtles, and that leatherbacks appeared to forage in more offshore locations than do loggerhead or green sea turtles; the latter conclusions were also reported by Wallace et al. (2006c). Caut et al. (2008) used stable isotope analyses to discern differences in remigration intervals among leatherbacks nesting in French Guiana, and proposed that the differences were related to time spent in different foraging areas.

An unusual fatty acid, *trans*-6-hexadecenoic acid, has been isolated from the depot fat of the leatherback (Hooper and Ackman 1970) in the same proportions as it occurs in at least two pelagic medusae: *Cyanea capillata* (Sipos and Ackman 1968) and *Aurelia aurita* (Hooper and Ackman 1972). The acid does not appear to have any specific metabolic or functional value in higher animals (Ackman et al. 1972). Hooper and Ackman (1972) interpret the presence of this and other unusual unsaturated fatty acids in leatherback turtles as confirmation of their dietary association with jellyfish. In examining an adult male leatherback, significant levels of the arachidonic acid 20:4w6 in jellyfish total lipid and in the leatherback neutral lipid and phospholipid fractions of all tissues sampled suggested that arachidonic acid assumes more importance in food chain relationships involving leatherback turtles than in other marine food webs, such as those involving fish (Holland et al. 1990).

There are very few data on the diet of hatchlings or young juveniles in the wild. Salmon et al. (2004) observed diving and feeding behavior of leatherback and green turtle post-hatchlings in the open ocean. The authors reported that nine of 20 leatherbacks were observed feeding at depths between 0.5 and 14 m, with two feeding on ctenophores (*Ocyropsis* or *Mnemiopsis*), one on gelatinous (probably molluscan) eggs, and six on "moon" jellyfish (*Aurelia* spp.).

Hartog and van Nierop (1984) did not consider the leatherback to be a deliberately selective feeder. They postulated that the turtles feed rather indiscriminately on all slow-moving or floating objects of some size, a propensity that also predisposes them to swallow anthropogenic debris, especially floating plastic (Mrosovsky 1981).

Feeding

Foraging areas generally occur at remote distances from nesting beaches, and mostly but not exclusively at temperate latitudes. While leatherbacks are generally considered to be oceanic foragers (Bjorndal 1997, Godley et al. 1998, James et al. 2005a, Eckert 2006, Wallace et al. 2006c), as leatherback behavior and movements have been better studied, it has become apparent that coastal, continental shelf habitats are also important for leatherbacks, especially in the North Atlantic (James et al. 2005a, 2007; Eckert et al. 2006a; Murphy et al. 2006). Little is known of the relative importance of these foraging grounds, the fidelity of individual turtles to specific foraging areas, or the existence or distribution of foraging populations of any age/size class. Most of what is known consists of observations derived from satellite telemetry; we review these studies in *Behavior, Migrations and local movements*, below, and only present brief references here.

Bleakney (1965) summarized 88 sightings of leatherbacks in New England (United States) and Nova Scotian (Canada) waters between 1824 and 1964. He concluded that these individuals were not strays due to their apparent vigorous activity in cold water and because they were present in predictable seasonal abundances, perhaps to prey on *Cyanea capillata artica*. Summarizing more recent data, including the tag returns of Pritchard (1976), Lazell (1980) hypothesized that Atlantic leatherbacks routinely moved into temperate and boreal waters to feed on *Cyanea*, and wintered in the Gulf of Mexico and Florida (United States) for the same reason. These early conclusions have since been amply corroborated by satellite telemetry and tag returns confirming that Caribbean-nesting leatherbacks journey to foraging grounds in the North Atlantic after their breeding season has ended (see *Behavior, Migrations and local movements*, below).

Early knowledge of foraging behavior and geography was based largely on prey items identified from the digestive tracts of stranded and dead individuals (Table 20), and from opportunistic observations of foraging animals. For example, leatherbacks appear to congregate off the west coast of France during seasonal concentrations of *Rhizostoma pulmo*; in 1978 an adult was photographed capturing and swallowing *Rhizostoma* in the region of Pertuis d'Antioche (Duron and Duron 1980; see also Duguy 1968). In England, a leatherback was sighted in waters "...thick with jellyfish and mackerel..." (Brongersma 1969) and leatherbacks are reported off southern Ireland and in Cardigan Bay "...especially when jellyfish (usually *Rhizostoma* or *Cyanea*) are abundant..." (Davenport et al. 1990). Similarly, an unusual abundance of leatherbacks off the Cornish coast, England, in 1988 was linked to high local densities of *Rhizostoma* and *Chrysaora* (Penhallurick 1990, 1991).

Houghton et al. (2006) found correlations between leatherback aggregations and jellyfish (*Rhizostoma* spp.) distribution at the ocean surface in the Irish Sea over a period of several decades. Witt et al. (2007b) defined putative leatherback foraging grounds in the Northeast Atlantic by identifying spatio-temporal distributions of gelatinous organisms and characterizing distributions of leatherback sightings, strandings, and captures. The areas identified by this model agreed relatively well with foraging grounds suggested by satellite telemetry (Ferraroli et al. 2004). Few data are available from the Mediterranean. Based on museum collections and published literature, Lazar et al. (2008) characterized the southern Adriatic Sea as a "...summer foraging habitat for leatherbacks within the Mediterranean."

In the western Atlantic, Collard (1990), Grant and Ferrell (1993), and Grant et al. (1996) reported leatherback presence coinciding with high abundance of jellyfish (including *Aurelia* spp. and *Stomolophus* spp.). In Nova Scotia, Canada, James and Herman (2001) reported leatherbacks repeatedly lifting their heads out of the water while attempting to bite/swallow large jellyfish bells and tentacles (*Aurelia* spp. and *Cyanea* spp.).

In the Gulf of Mexico, aerial surveys have shown leatherbacks associated with the jellyfish *Stomolophus* (e.g., Lohoefener et al. 1989). Leary (1957) observed a concentration of an estimated 100 adult and juvenile leatherbacks associated with a dense school of *Stomolophus meleagris* off the coast of Texas. Sneed Collard (University of West Florida, pers. comm.) also reported a "coincidence" of leatherbacks and maximum jellyfish abundance, especially *Aurelia*, in the Gulf.

In the Caribbean, adult leatherbacks consume locally occurring jellyfish (*Physalia physalis, Stomolophus fritillarius*) in the coastal waters of Trinidad where Bacon (1970, 1971), noting the dramatic increase in their numbers during February and March, speculated that the leatherback nesting season, which commences in March, may be determined by a local increase in prey abundance.

Similar observations are reported from the Pacific Ocean. In 1981, a leatherback was seen consuming *Aurelia* in waters off Washington state, in the United States; when the turtle lifted its head to assist in swallowing, tentacles were clearly exposed in its open mouth (Eisenberg and Frazier 1983). Benson et al. (2007b) reported spatio-temporal associations of leatherback and jellyfish (*Chrysaora* spp. and *Aurelia* spp.) distributions that occur seasonally due to fluctuating oceanographic conditions (i.e., upwellings and subsequent relaxation events) in the region. In 1973, in southern Queensland, an adult leatherback was reported swimming along a rocky shoreline "...among numerous jellyfish *Catostylus mosaics*..." and off Kempsey, New South Wales, Australia, where leatherback sightings "...coincided with [the] arrival of abundant *Rhizostoma* jellyfish..." (Limpus and McLachlan 1979).

Sometimes feeding is not actually observed, but is inferred from ambient circumstances. The few available data "...indicate a direct correlation..." between the abundance of arctic jellyfish (*Cyanea*) and the presence of leatherbacks in Massachusetts (Lazell 1980). Keinath et al. (1987) noted that leatherbacks may congregate off the mouth of the Chesapeake Bay to feed on an abundance of *Aurelia aurita* and *Chrysaora quinquecirrha* that flush from the Bay. Aerial surveys document leatherbacks in Virginia waters, especially May to July during peak jellyfish (*Aurelia, Chrysaora*) abundance (Musick 1988). Hoffman and Fritts (1982) recorded a coincidence of leatherback and *Physalia* sightings during aerial surveys of east central Florida.

While foraging has most often been observed (or inferred) at the surface, Hartog (1980) speculated that foraging might occur at depth after finding nematocysts from deep water siphonophores in leatherback stomach samples. Davenport (1988) also speculated that leatherbacks might forage at depth on bioluminescent prey (e.g., *Pyrosoma* spp.), based on examples of such prey species being found in leatherback gut contents and in direct observations of feeding events. Limpus (1984) concluded that the turtles may be feeding "at considerable depth" after a subadult (1.2 m carapace length) was caught on a handline baited with octopus hanging at a depth of 50 m in Western Australia.

Leatherbacks have a propensity for deep, prolonged diving (see *Behavior, Diving*, below), which likely reflects adaptive significance of foraging at depth. Notwithstanding, while on temperate foraging grounds, leatherbacks tend to spend most of their time near the surface (Western Atlantic: Eckert 2006, James et al. 2006a; Eastern Pacific: Benson et al. 2007b) and jellyfish are often observed near the surface in these areas. Leatherbacks may also bring prey from depth to the surface to facilitate ingestion (James and Mrosovsky 2004, James et al. 2005c).

Diel dive behavior patterns may be indicative of foraging strategies. Based on studies of diving by adult females nesting in the USVI, Eckert et al. (1986, 1989b) proposed that the observed internesting dive behavior reflected nocturnal feeding in the deep scattering layer (DSL). Night dives were shorter, shallower, more frequent, and less variable in depth and duration than day dives; night diving was continuous, with dive depth and duration averaging 54 m and 10 minutes, respectively. Similar dive patterns have been reported for leatherbacks during internesting periods (Myers and Hays 2006) and post-nesting migrations for leatherbacks from Grenada, West Indies (Hays et al. 2004a), and for leatherbacks during southward migrations from foraging grounds in Nova Scotia, Canada (James et al. 2006a).

In the Caribbean, the strata comprising the DSL consist primarily of vertically migrating zooplankters, chiefly siphonophore and salp colonies (Michel and Foyo 1976). Davenport (1988) added that nets trawled at 800–1500 m in tropical and subtropical eastern Atlantic waters caught primarily gelatinous and often bioluminescent animals (medusae, ctenophores, salps, siphonnophores), in particular the large pelagic tunicate *Pyrosoma* spp. He suggested that this abundance may also be available to deep diving leatherbacks, particularly in the tropics where surface supplies of jellies are poor.

The diel diving behavior trend with leatherbacks tracking vertically migrating gelatinous prey does not appear to be universal for all sites where leatherback diving has been observed. Southwood et al. (1999) reported no significant patterns in diel dive parameters for internesting leatherbacks off Playa Grande, Costa Rica, and James et al. (2006a) reported very small diel dive behavior differences in leatherbacks at a high latitude foraging ground in Nova Scotia, Canada. James and Herman (2001) and James et al. (2005a) document daytime feeding through direct observation of leatherbacks swallowing large *Cyanea capillata* at the surface.

Fossette et al. (2007) reported that leatherbacks off French Guiana tended to travel at night and showed diurnal activity that the authors speculated resembled foraging behavior; this diel pattern in diving versus travel behavior was the opposite to that observed in the USVI (see Eckert 2002b). Corroborating earlier studies of diving in shallow internesting habitats (Eckert et al. 1996), Fossette et al. (2007) hypothesized that the shallower depths available to turtles off French Guiana constrained not only their diving behavior, but also the depths at which their jellyfish prey could be found.

Myers and Hays (2006) used a beak sensor and datalogger combination to record simultaneously mouth-opening events and dive profiles for about six hours for a gravid female during an internesting period off Grenada, West Indies. Despite no obvious evidence of prey manipulation, the authors reported suggestive evidence of attempted feeding on vertically migrating organisms, noting that the turtle opened its mouth more frequently during dive descent (86.6%) vs. ascent (5.6%) and hypothesizing that the animal was using gustatory cues to sense its immediate environment, perhaps including prey detection. Likewise, Fossette (2008) used beak sensors to record mouth-opening events for four leatherbacks during internesting periods off French Guiana and observed that 'beak-movement' dives by leatherbacks occurred during deeper, longer dives, and during a high proportion of W-shaped dives (dives with rapid vertical fluctuations during an extended bottom time); the authors speculated that the pattern was indicative of opportunistic attempts at foraging on patchily distributed prey.

Southwood et al. (2005) recorded ingestion events using stomach temperature pills and data loggers during the internesting period for leatherbacks off Playa Grande, Costa Rica, and suggested that these "ingestion events" may have represented drinking and/or prey ingestion, as well as mechanisms for cooling core body temperatures in warm tropical waters following highly energetic nesting activities. Wallace et al. (2005) concurred with the latter hypothesis and speculated that the animals were not foraging because rates of energy expenditure and patterns of diving activity suggested energy conservation, but admitted that energy conservation and foraging are not mutually exclusive. Animal-borne video footage of leatherbacks during the internesting period at Playa Grande showed ingestion events when no prey were visible [in the video], and no attempted feeding on occasions when potential prey were visible, as well as periods of inactivity while resting motionless on the ocean floor (Reina et al. 2005).

The actual feeding mechanism of *Dermochelys* has been described by Duron-Dufrenne (1978). The seizure of the prey is associated with a powerful inrush of ambient water into the turtle's mouth and throat, driven by a strong depression of the extensive and muscular hyoid structure. The excess water taken in needs to be expelled quickly, because its retention in the digestive tract would interfere by excessively diluting the digestive secretions, and by moving the intestinal content through the digestive tract at an excessive rate (Hartog and van Nierop 1984). While excess water is expelled up the throat and through the mouth, regurgitation of the prey is avoided by a dense concentration of stiff spines that line the first 1–2 m of the digestive tract, all of which are oriented toward the stomach. The water content of the prey itself is chemically bound (Doyle et al. 2007), and cannot be expelled by simple compression in the gastric cavity until the initial phase of digestion has taken place, in which this water is liberated and the mesogleal collagen and elastic (oxytalan) fibers and the interfibrillary substance (mucopolysaccharides) are broken down (Bouillon and Coppois 1977).

Growth

Deraniyagala (1936b) retained several leatherback hatchlings, taken as they emerged from their nest in Ceylon (now Sri Lanka) in August 1933, to document growth and post-natal changes. The last of the brood expired in captivity 662 days later after its water supply became contaminated with sewage. Ontogenetic changes, including the loss of the infantile scales, the development of a mosaic layer of bony platelets, and changes in pigmentation, morphology, and proportion are summarized in the sections below. Sections *"Scales"* through *"Secondary characters"* are adapted from Deraniyagala (1936b).

Scales.—The infantile scales reached their limit of expansion when the turtlet was about 18 days old. Each scale then commenced to constrict the skin beneath into a polygonal boss. Ecdysis of these strong, infantile scales began about the twenty-second day and ended about the forty-sixth, leaving the animal covered with a network of scale marks which altered in outline especially upon the corselet ridges. The scales themselves were but feebly renewed as a comparatively fine cuticle which was shed in patches, at intervals. The shed skin showed scale boundaries which became more and more indistinct with age as the majority of scales thinned out and disappeared, leaving the adult comparatively smooth skinned.

Platelets.—The first indications of osseous platelets occurred when a uniserial row of tubercles appeared upon each corselet ridge; later, the rudiments were visible through the cuticle, in the 157 day old animal. At this stage there were no platelets in the interspaces. The marginal platelets were both larger and closer to one another than those of the supramarginal ridges. In the 308 day turtle, transverse folds of skin interrupted the carapace ridges into lengths each containing several platelets; in the 562 day animal, the corselet mosaic had extended some distance down each bridge. It is probable that by now the platelets of the interspaces had begun to develop in either side of all carapace ridges, for in the 624 day specimen the base of each ridge appeared swollen.

In the 662 day specimen, with the exception of a patch on each side of the nucho-scapular hump and on the posterior parts of the two interspaces above the supramarginal and costal ridges, the platelet mosaic of both carapace and plastron was numerically complete. It is of interest to note that this process was achieved at a considerably earlier date in the plastron than the carapace. The plastral platelets were probably numerically complete in the 169 day old animal, whereas the carapace mosiac was incomplete in the 662 day old animal. As soon as ossification was complete upon the carapace ridges their scale traces disappeared and it is evident that the animal becomes smooth skinned soon after the osseous mosaic is completed.

Plastron and extremities.—The plastron commenced to project beyond the vertical through the front of the carapace, about the time the animal commenced ecdysis, viz., when 18 days old. When the animal was about one year old, the anterior edges of both carapace and plastron were again at the same vertical level; thereafter the carapace overlapped the plastron to a small degree. The limbs also altered in outline and proportions and their tips gradually became more acute. The 308 day old animal showed a moderate cruro-caudal fold of skin, with a relative increase in the distance between the plastron and cloaca. These features are all conspicuous in the adult, the last reaching its maximum development in the male when the tail undergoes secondary sexual elongation.

Pigmentation.—Towards the forty-sixth day the white dorsal spots and bands appeared comparatively enlarged and more or less retained their proportions until the animal was 600 days old. Thereafter they commenced to decrease. It is probable that, in the present instance, the slow disappearance of white dorsal pigment is due to the comparative lack of sunlight, for the animal was kept in a shed. It is suggested that under natural conditions this pigment will probably diminish at a faster rate, as the animal floats at the surface exposed to sunlight. Since no adult has yet been noted with white bands upon the carapace ridges, the loss of these marks is probably correlated to the assumption of secondary sexual characters.

In the adult, the white spots of the carapace decrease considerably in size, but generally persist upon a slaty background surrounded by diffuse black polygons which denote the former boundaries of the polygonal infantile scales. Ventrally the broad black bands, so conspicuous in the newly hatched, soon diminish, and eventually might only persist as a feeble reticulation upon the bridges and parts of the plastral margin. The white spots upon the ventral surface of the neck, limbs and tail enlarge and fuse to form large areas more or less reticulate with black, which generally fades with increasing age and eventually disappears.

Secondary characters.—Adults are comparatively smooth skinned although scale traces may persist upon the eyelids, neck and caudal crest. The scale traces do not disappear until after the completion of the corselet mosaic of platelets. The foreflippers develop acute tips and the posterior pair are subtriangular. Connecting the hind limbs and tail is a strong cruro-caudal fold of skin. The white dorsal bands of pigment persist upon the head, neck and caudal crest, but disappear completely from the carapace ridges. The plastron is either entirely white, or possesses a dark reticulation along the margins. The general outlines of the adult female are more or less akin to those of the adolescent, but the male displays stronger differentiation in possessing a concave nasal profile, domed skull, comparatively depressed body and elongate tail.

Growth rate.—The distribution of juveniles is poorly known (Eckert 2002a) and specimens have not been accessible for capture-recapture methodologies designed to measure growth directly. In an attempt to mark wild hatchling leatherbacks with a view to determine their age at first maturity, Balasingam (pers. comm. to P. Pritchard) clipped about 2 mm off the posterior tip of 100 Malaysian hatchlings in 1957 and two adults with posteriorly truncated carapaces were observed to nest at the same site in 1974, suggesting maturity in 17 years. However, this mutilation is not particularly rare in any large leatherback population. Fretey (1982) reported 10 specimens from French Guiana with similar mutilations, even though no hatchlings had been marked in this way at any Atlantic site.

Several lines of evidence suggest that leatherbacks may have the fastest juvenile growth rates of any sea turtle species (see *Reproduction, Age at maturity*, above). Based on similarities between the chondro-osseous morphology of leatherback humerii and that of marine mammals, some investigators emphasize the potential for rapid growth and suggest that age to maturity might be as young as 2 or 3 years (Rhodin 1985, Rhodin et al. 1996). Based on an observed weekly growth increment (in captive post-hatchlings) of about 1.2 cm, and assuming that this rate would continue to maturity, Birkenmeier (1971) also estimated maturity at between 2 and 3 years of age (Table 7). In both studies the authors regressed growth over time as a linear function (vs. curvilinear regression), which might have contributed to overestimates of growth rate.

Jones and colleagues successfully raised leatherback hatchlings to > 24 months in captivity, which facilitated collection of many important physiological and energetics data, including growth rates (Jones et al. 2000, Jones 2009). These investigators used the von Bertalanffy Growth Function to extrapolate age to mean size (curved carapace length) at maturity at 15 years based on growth rates (> 0.11 cm day^{-1} for hatchlings, 0.8 cm day^{-1} for juveniles) of post-hatchling juveniles reared under carefully controlled conditions (Jones et al. 2000, Jones 2009).

The most recent study uses skeletochronological analysis of scleral ossicles from wild individuals spanning hatchlings to adults, including both males and females, stranded along the Atlantic and Gulf coasts of the United States. By validating the core mark and making informed assumptions about LAG frequency (based on a comparative analysis of Kemp's ridley, *Lepidochelys kempii*, scleral ossicles and humeri to validate the annual deposition of marks in the ossicles and examination of ossicles from the eight turtles in Jones et al. 2000), Avens et al. (2009) estimated age at maturity in *Dermochelys* to be 24.5 to 29 years (at 145 cm CCL, mean size at first nesting).

Direct measurements of growth in wild leatherbacks are few, consisting solely of information available from long term nesting beach studies that include measurements of sexually mature females. For example, Price et al. (2004) reported growth rates for nesting leatherbacks at Playa Grande, Costa Rica, over an 8-year period to be 0.2 cm CCL yr^{-1} (range: –1.5–2.0 cm yr^{-1}) and 0.2 cm CCW yr^{-1} (range: –1.6–1.7 cm yr^{-1}). Growth rates in this study did not vary with remigration interval duration, nor was there an apparent trade-off between growth rates and reproductive output. However, the authors did report a negative relationship between leatherback body size and growth rates, with "… smaller turtles growing significantly faster than larger ones…" (Price et al. 2004).

Metabolism

Metabolic rates (MR) influence all aspects of leatherback ecology and life history, including *inter alia* energy budgets, diving physiology, and thermoregulation. In this section we review metabolic rates for *Dermochelys* in relation to those of other taxa, including other sea turtle species. Published data relevant to MR are summarized in Table 21; for a review see Wallace and Jones (2008).

Studies of MR demonstrate marked differences between leatherbacks and other sea turtles. Wyneken (1997) reported that leatherbacks were intermediate between loggerhead and green sea turtles both in factorial aerobic scope as well as resting metabolic rates (RMR), and concluded that these differences reflected divergent modes of locomotion and behavior that related to species-specific life history demands: the 'sprinting' strategy of the loggerheads and greens that use burst swimming characterized by high MR followed by periods of relative inactivity, in contrast to the 'marathon' strategy of the leatherbacks, characterized by relatively lower sustained active metabolic rates (AMR).

In a study of the ontogeny of MR and activity in leatherback and olive ridley hatchlings, Jones et al. (2007) found that while factorial aerobic scope increased with age for both species, factorial aerobic scope in olive ridley hatchlings was greater than in leatherback hatchlings. Furthermore, olive ridley maximum metabolic rates (MMR) and AMR during routine swimming were similar, whereas leatherback AMR during routine swimming was only 10% greater than RMR. Based on these results, Jones et al. (2007) concluded that these inter-specific differences in relationships between MMR, AMR, and RMR reflected divergent early life history strategems; the float-and-wait, superficial foraging of the olive ridley versus the active, oceanic, vertical, water column foraging of the leatherback.

All published MR for adult sea turtles are from *Chelonia* (e.g., Prange and Jackson 1976) and *Dermochelys* (there are no published MR values for juvenile *Dermochelys*). In general, MR associated with vigorous activities on a nesting beach (e.g., crawling, bodypitting) are 2–4 times higher than MR associated with 'resting' activities on a nesting beach (e.g., quiescent nest construction and oviposition) (Lutcavage et al. 1990, 1992; Paladino et al. 1990, 1996).

In an early attempt to calculate MR, Mrosovsky and Pritchard (1971) concluded that metabolism did not

Table 21. Summary of reported metabolic rates (MR) for leatherback sea turtles. Activity levels: Resting = fed (unless noted as fasted), quiescent turtles; Active = continuous non-maximal activity (e.g., swimming, crawling); Max = sustained maximal metabolic rate; Field = at-sea field metabolic rates (FMR, incl. all normal daily activity); Laying = during oviposition; Calculated = MR derived from models based on activity, behavior and environmental factors. Mass values are mean ± SD, unless otherwise noted. Source: adapted from Wallace and Jones (2008).

Activity	N	Mass (kg)	$\dot{V}_{O_2}$ (ml min^{-1})	Mass-Specific MR (W kg^{-1})	Temp (°C)	Method	Reference
Active	8	0.053 ± 0.002	0.25	1.58	24	Respirometry	Lutcavage & Lutz (1986)
Laying[1]	3	305 ± 24	76.3	0.08	21-24 (air)	Respirometry	Lutcavage et al. (1990)
Resting[2]	6	340	443	0.39	no data	Respirometry	Paladino et al. (1990)
Active[2]	6	380 ± 70	1,398	1.23	no data	Respirometry	Paladino et al. (1990)
Max[2]	5	380 ± 70	1,715	1.51	no data	Respirometry	Paladino et al. (1990)
Resting[3]	3	358 ± 10	390	0.36	22-27 (air)	Respirometry	Lutcavage et al. (1992)
Laying[4]	3	300 ± 5	261	0.33	23 (air)	Respirometry	Paladino et al. (1996)
Resting[4]	10	354 ± 5	425	0.40	23 (air)	Respirometry	Paladino et al. (1996)
Active[4]	10	366 ± 5	1,050	1.12	23 (air)	Respirometry	Paladino et al. (1996)
Resting	10	0.045 ± 0.003	0.18	1.34	24	Respirometry	Wyneken (1997)
Active	10	0.047 ± 0.005	0.37	2.63	24	Respirometry	Wyneken (1997)
Max	10	0.044 ± 0.003	0.44	3.34	24	Respirometry	Wyneken (1997)
Field[5]	4	278.5 ± 19.7	329	0.40	14-28	Doubly Labeled Water	Wallace et al. (2005)
Resting	8	0.040 ± 0.001	0.23	1.92	29 (air)	Respirometry	Jones et al. (2007)
Max	8	0.040 ± 0.001	0.30	2.50	26	Respirometry	Jones et al. (2007)
Resting	8	0.048 ± 0.001	0.12	0.86	29 (air)	Respirometry	Jones et al. (2007)
Max	8	0.048 ± 0.001	0.26	1.81	26	Respirometry	Jones et al. (2007)
Resting	8	0.078 ± 0.001	0.21	0.90	29 (air)	Respirometry	Jones et al. (2007)
Max	8	0.078 ± 0.001	0.33	1.43	26	Respirometry	Jones et al. (2007)
Calculated[6]	NA	300	576	0.65	NA	Biophysical Model	Bostrom & Jones (2007)
Calculated[7]	9	312 ± 18	230	0.24	no data	Behavioral Inference	Bradshaw et al. (2007)

[1] Lutcavage et al. (1990)—Mass was not measured directly but inferred from curved carapace length to mass relationships.

[2] Paladino et al. (1990)—Mass was reported as a range (250-430 kg, n = 6). We used the midpoint of this range. Resting oxygen consumption rate is from turtles restrained in a cargo net, active oxygen consumption rate is from turtles covering nests and crawling on the beach, and maximum oxygen consumption rate is from the highest oxygen consumption peaks during crawling and nest covering.

[3] Lutcavage et al. (1992)—Mass presented is the mean of turtles for which metabolic rate data were acquired in the study. The resting oxygen consumption data refer to turtles restrained in a cargo net.

[4] Paladino et al. (1996)—Resting oxygen consumption rate data were from turtles restrained in a cargo net and the active measurements were during vigorous exercise while turtles were pulling 100 kg sleds or actively covering their nest.

[5] Wallace et al. (2005)—We recalculated mass based on turtles for which FMR were obtained. The temperature range presented is the range of water temperatures presented in the study. The oxygen consumption rate value (ml min.$^{-1}$) was calculated from W kg^{-1} using 20.3 kJ per L O_2 metabolized.

[6] Bostrom and Jones (2007)—Metabolic rate estimates were based on a 300 kg turtle maintaining 0.7 m s^{-1} swim speed. The oxygen consumption rate value (ml min^{-1}) was calculated from W kg^{-1} using 20.3 kJ per L O_2 metabolized.

[7] Bradshaw et al. (2007)—Mass data were not measured directly but inferred from curved carapace length to mass relationships. No temperature data were provided.

vary appreciably between leatherback, green, and olive ridley sea turtles, and suggested that "...a lack of relationship between oxygen consumption and body size may be characteristic of turtles." From the equation $dT\, dt^{-1} = k(T_{ambient} - T_{body})$, they predicted an oxygen consumption rate of 0.066 ml g^{-1} h^{-1} for adult female leatherbacks on the nesting beach, based on a weight of 374 kg, a rate of heat loss of 0.0055°C min^{-1}, and a constant $k = 0.002$.

In contrast, a later study of nesting females at Tortuguero, Costa Rica, reported on-beach RMR that were intermediate between the RMR of green turtles and other reptiles scaled to leatherback size and RMR of mammals, whereas leatherback AMR is more similar to mammal RMR (Paladino et al. 1990). Lutcavage et al. (1990, 1992) reported leatherback RMR roughly similar to, but somewhat lower than, those reported by Paladino et al. (1990). Subsequent studies of adult female leatherback MR also reported similar RMR and AMR values (Paladino et al. 1996).

Metabolic rates during terrestrial activities in leatherbacks are well-studied compared with metabolic rates associated with daily activity at sea. In the only study of free-ranging adult sea turtle metabolic rates, Wallace et al. (2005) measured at-sea MR for gravid leatherbacks during their approximately 10-day internesting periods off Pacific Costa Rica: the results were similar to leatherback MR measured during quiescent phases of the nesting process (i.e., oviposition, nest chamber construction, or restraint on the beach) and lower than MR during vigorous activity (i.e., nest-covering, crawling on land) for both leatherback and green sea turtles.

Kooyman (1989) used the RMR for green sea turtles, as determined by Prange and Jackson (1976) but scaled to the size of *Dermochelys*, for a calculation of aerobic dive limits (ADL) in leatherbacks. More recent studies have reported MR obtained by using behavioral inferences from diving data (Bradshaw et al. 2007) and biophysical models (Bostrom and Jones 2007). Using dive data from adult female leatherbacks (Hays et al. 2004a), Bradshaw et al. (2007) developed an analytical technique that enabled statistical estimation of ADL, and thus diving MR (DMR), from an asymptotic relationship between dive duration and maximum dive depth. DMR were lower than FMR measured for free-swimming adult female leatherbacks and higher than predictions from allometric relationships of reptile FMR (Bradshaw et al. 2007).

Bostrom and Jones (2007) created a biophysical model that highlighted the crucial role of behavioral adjustments in swimming activity that affect metabolic heat production to achieve high T_{body}–$T_{ambient}$ differentials for leatherbacks. Comparisons with empirical studies appeared to confirm several of the model's predictions of necessary adjustments in swimming behavior to achieve certain MR and T_{body} (Bostrom and Jones 2007).

While leatherback MR are clearly not endothermic in a mammalian sense, questions remain about the relationship between leatherback MR and the MR of other sea turtles and of reptiles in general. This ambiguity arises from the unique physiological and anatomical traits of leatherbacks as well as from incongruences such as (i) adult leatherback RMR are higher than those of reptiles (including green sea turtles) scaled to leatherback sizes (Paladino et al. 1990, 1996), (ii) in other studies, adult leatherback RMR conformed more closely to those of other reptiles and sea turtles (Lutcavage et al. 1990, 1992), and (iii) FMR of leatherbacks during consistent, at-sea diving behavior were similar to adult leatherback RMR measured during nesting (Wallace et al. 2005).

To address this issue, Wallace and Jones (2008) compared allometric relationships between body size (mass) and RMR (ranging from hatchlings to adults, Table 21) for leatherbacks and green turtles to each other and then to similar equations for other reptiles and for mammals. The results revealed that the relationship between body mass and RMR in leatherbacks is similar to that of green turtles, and presumably other sea turtles, and that the relationship between body mass and RMR in sea turtles appears to be similar to that of other reptiles but fundamentally different from that of mammals (Wallace and Jones 2008).

Finally, some research has related metabolism to diet and caloric intake. Based on lengthy observations of leatherbacks feeding off the west coast of France, Duron-Dufrenne (1978) concluded that a fully grown adult consumed close to 50 large specimens of *Rhizostoma pulmo* per day, representing a total content of some 200 liters, or about 8–10 kg protein per day (Duron and Duron 1980). The contention that 200 liters of jellyfish represents about 8–10 kg protein is disputed by Hartog and van Nierop (1984), who argue that *R. pulmo* is only 0.53–2.5% organic matter (the increase reported during breeding season) and therefore the intake of 200 liters of jellyfish provides roughly 1–5 kg of organic matter per day. Based on an average of 2.5 kg, consisting of about equal parts fat and protein, the authors calculate an energy intake of 11,000–16,250 kcal per day, or 2.5 to 4 times the daily energy consumption of a man performing heavy labor.

Lutcavage and Lutz (1986) reported a standard metabolic rate (SMR) for hatchling leatherbacks (0.286 $1O_2$ kg^{-1} h^{-1} at 24°C) about three times greater than that published for hatchling green sea turtles (0.099 ml O_2 g^{-1} h^{-1} at 25°C, Prange and Ackerman 1974). Hatchling leatherbacks swam continuously in the respirometer, raising the possibility that higher metabolic rates are the result of activity per se, and not an intrinsic difference between species (Lutcavage and Lutz 1986). The same study predicted that the average hatchling leatherback (53 g) would need to consume 55.3 g of jellyfish per day for maintenance and growth. Assuming an intraspecific scaling relationship between metabolic rate and biomass, the authors applied a range of scaling factors, from a general value of 0.75 (Schmidt-Nielsen 1985) to the value reported for green sea turtles (b = 1.0, Prange and Jackson 1976), to predict that a 250 kg adult leatherback would require the energetic equivalent of 64.8–260 kg jellyfish per day to satisfy its energy needs, based on the energy content of *Cassiopeia* jellyfish. However, this jellyfish species is a benthic jellyfish inhabiting shallow tropical water, and thus is an unlikely food source for the leatherback, which typically feeds in the water column and offshore (see *Nutrition and metabolism, Food*, above). Pelagic hydromedusae may function as macroplankton traps (Frazier et al. 1985), providing more energy by weight and decreasing the number of items required by the turtle per day (Lutcavage and Lutz 1986).

Thermoregulation

Cold temperatures restrict the geographic ranges of reptiles, including those of most sea turtle species. Pritchard (1969) first suggested that the physical peculiarities of the leatherback—its great size, barrel-like shape, and thick layer of oily connective tissue under the shell—would all assist in the retention of metabolic heat, and it was thus conceivable that the ability of the leatherback to sustain high levels of activity even in cold waters (for example, MacAskie and Forrester (1962) reported vigorous activity in 11.7°C water in the Queen Charlotte Islands) might derive from the species having evolved a degree of endothermy. Brongersma (1972) summarized northern records and concluded that leatherbacks could tolerate surface temperatures as low as 11°C. In 1984, in Trinity Bay, Newfoundland, Canada, a leatherback was observed by fishers throughout an entire day swimming in open water among ice where water temperatures were ~ 0°C (Goff and Lien 1988).

Because of the vast geographic range and depth leatherbacks inhabit, this species faces two major thermoregulatory challenges: maintaining a high core temperature in cold waters of high latitudes and great depths, and avoiding overheating while in tropical waters, especially while on land during nesting. To meet these thermoregulatory demands, leatherbacks possess several unique anatomical and physiological adaptations, including counter-current heat exchangers in their flippers that conserve heat while in cold T_{water} and possibly dissipate heat in tropical T_{water} (Greer et al. 1973), and thick subdermal insulation (6–7 cm: Goff and Lien 1988, Davenport et al. 1990). Goff and Stenson (1988) speculated that brown adipose tissue acts as a "thermogenic organ."

Coagulation of blood increases dramatically below 23°C, suggesting a relaxed selection for hemostatic function below this temperature, perhaps because *Dermochelys* rarely experiences such low body temperatures under natural conditions (Soslau et al. 2004). Circulating serotonin has been identified in the blood of several endothermic species, and its presence in leatherback blood lends anecdotal support for serotonin's function in regulating skin blood flow (Maurer-Spurej 2007).

Pritchard (1969) speculated that endothermy might be a major factor in accounting for the extended range of this species, and the term 'endothermy' has been used many times since as the proposed physiological explanation for leatherback thermoregulation (e.g., Mrosovsky and Pritchard 1971, Frair et al. 1972, Greer et al. 1973). Although it has been pointed out that the differences between body and environmental temperatures reported in various studies do not necessarily indicate an ability to thermoregulate (Neill and Stevens 1974), adult *Dermochelys* at least, are capable of metabolic heat production such that they need not rely solely on thermal inertia from their large size and well insulated body (Standora et al. 1984, Spotila and Standora 1985, Paladino et al. 1990, Bostrom and Jones 2007, Wallace and Jones 2008). There are suggestions that behavioral thermoregulation, such as basking, is also important (Sapsford and Hughes 1978, Sapsford and Van der Riet 1979, Eckert et al. 1986), but this is unlikely given the thermal lag associated with their large body size as well as the negligible vascularization of the carapace (Penick 1996).

Large body size has been recognized as essential to thermoregulation of leatherbacks for many decades (Mrosovsky and Pritchard 1971, Frair et al. 1972, Paladino et al. 1990). Leatherbacks less than 100 cm in carapace length appear to be restricted to $T_w \geq 26°C$ (Eckert 2002a), suggesting that the thermal advantage of large body size conferred upon adult leatherbacks is a prerequisite for exploiting colder water habitats.

Paladino et al. (1990) created a biophysical model, which demonstrated that leatherbacks are able to thermoregulate in varied environments by combining large body size with low MR, blood flow adjustments, and subdermal insulation. This suite of thermoregulatory adaptations, which the authors termed 'gigantothermy,' is distinct from both strict ectothermy and endothermy. Moreover, the gigantothermy model supported previous predictions from purely mathematical models of low (i.e., ectothermic) MR of extremely massive dinosaurs (Spotila et al. 1973).

While acknowledging the importance of body size and metabolism, recent work has focused more attention on behavioral thermoregulation by leatherbacks, which is a well established thermoregulatory strategy for other reptiles. Southwood et al. (2005) measured body temperatures (T_{body}) of free-ranging leatherbacks in tropical waters and observed that T_{body} responded to swimming activity patterns (i.e., AMR) and to different water temperatures (T_{water}), in accordance with predictions of the gigantothermy model for leatherbacks in tropical seas. Biophysical modeling of leatherback MR demonstrates the pivotal role of adjustments in swimming activity (a proxy for metabolic heat production) in achieving substantial T_{body}-T_{water} differentials (Bostrom and Jones 2007).

Wallace and Jones (2008) reported that leatherback RMR are similar to allometric expectations of reptilian RMR scaled to leatherback size, and fundamentally different from mammalian RMR; they concluded that leatherbacks are not endotherms *per se* but a unique brand of poikilotherm. They suggest that leatherbacks do not have unique mechanisms for heat generation, rather they conclude that thermoregulation depends on an integrated balance between adaptations for heat production (e.g., metabolic and behavioral modifications) and retention (e.g., large thermal inertia, blood flow adjustments, insulation, and behavioral modifications) to achieve and maintain preferred differentials between T_{body} and T_{water} in varied thermal environments.

There appears to be no period of hibernation or dormancy in leatherbacks. Cold-stunning, a common response by loggerhead and green sea turtles to frigid water temperatures, is unknown in *Dermochelys* (Witherington and Ehrhart 1989, Shaver 1990).

Osmoregulation

As marine reptiles, leatherbacks face significant challenges with respect to salt and water balance. Reptilian kidneys (including those of leatherbacks) are incapable of producing urine that is hyperosmotic to the blood (Bentley 1976, Lutz 1997). Jellyfish prey is essentially isoosmotic with seawater (Potts 1968)—some of the water resulting from ingestion and digestion of jellyfish may be expelled physically, the rest may be absorbed by the lining of the intestinal tract. The primary means of physiological osmoregulation is the lachrymal glands, which eliminate excess salt from the body.

Carr (1952) hypothesized that the lachrymal glands serve a dual purpose: to perform essential osmoregulatory functions, and to lubricate the eyeball during terrestrial nesting activities when sand is omnipresent. In *Dermochelys* these glands are highly vascular and extremely large compared to other sea turtles, constituting a significant proportion of the volume of the posterior part of the head of an adult leatherback (Schumacher 1973). The glands comprise 0.398% of total body mass in post-hatchlings, and are capable of producing a highly concentrated secretion (six times the osmolarity of the blood and twice that of seawater: Reina et al. 2002b) in response to a jellyfish diet (Hudson and Lutz 1986). This efficient osmoregulatory ability allows leatherback hatchlings to drink seawater to replenish body mass lost immediately after emerging from the nest and to continue to gain body mass after spending time in the ocean (Reina et al. 2002b).

Leatherbacks exhibit high water turnover rates as hatchlings (Reina et al. 2002b) and as adults (Wallace et al. 2005), especially when compared to mammals and terrestrial reptiles.

Behavior

Migrations and Local Movements

In an early reference to the species' vast range, Garman (1884b) observed, "Though [the leatherback turtles'] proper home may be said to extend not more than 35° on each side of the Equator, they are found straggling as many as 15° farther to the north or south." A century later, Pritchard (1980) indicated in a distribution map the occurrence of non-breeding records well outside the limits of the tropics in North and South America, northern Europe, southern Africa, Japan, Australia, and New Zealand, and Lazell (1980) hypothesized, based on the seasons of occurrence of animals in nesting and feeding areas and on tag recoveries reported by Pritchard (1976), that the primary nesting areas were in the Wider Caribbean Region and that post-nesting females dispersed northwards, perhaps following concentrations of jellyfish, especially *Cyanea*. He proposed that this would lead the turtles to the waters of the northeastern United States and eastern Canada, or occasionally to Britain, Scandinavia, or the (former) Soviet Union.

By relating leatherback sightings data and proxy prey distribution data off Western Europe, Witt et al. (2007a) concluded that sea surface temperatures of 10°–12°C appeared to mark the northern boundary of leatherback distribution. McMahon and Hays (2006) observed that leatherbacks typically did not move farther northward than the northern limit of the 15°C isotherm in the North Atlantic. Eckert (2006) concluded that southward movements preceded cooling water temperatures and proposed that the timing of movement away from high latitude foraging areas anticipated the formation of prey-concentrating oceanic features at lower latitudes. James et al. (2005a, 2005b) illustrated regional fidelity to foraging areas, in that some turtles returned to these same locations each year.

Individuals show behavioral differences during distinct phases of their foraging migration cycle. Hays et al. (2004a) noted that adults dived deeper and for longer durations during oceanic migrations, and surmised that these differences might reflect geographic differences in foraging opportunities. James et al. (2005b, 2006b) documented differences between diving and movement behavior while on northern foraging grounds and during southward migrations (e.g., differences in diel diving patterns were more pronounced during southward migrations than on northern foraging grounds), again suggesting place-based differences in resource availability. Eckert (2006) reported that while deep diving predominates in warm oceanic waters, lack of deep diving in the low latitude Mauritania

Upwelling is likely indicative of food availability in surface waters. Recent studies have highlighted new approaches, specifically hierarchical state-space models (SSM) (Jonsen et al. 2006) and switching state-space models (SSSM) (Jonsen et al. 2007, Bailey et al. 2008), to quantitatively analyze movement data and distinguish behavior patterns.

The movements and migrations of hatchlings and juveniles and, to a large extent, adult males, are poorly understood. In recent years, James et al. (2005a, 2005b, 2005c) have documented round-trip migrations of adult male leatherbacks from Nova Scotia to areas off known nesting beaches in the Caribbean Sea. Therefore, not only do adult males occupy similar foraging sites as adult (and subadult) females, but males undertake similar migrations to Caribbean breeding areas.

While telemetry-based studies of juveniles have not been conducted, a growing body of evidence suggests that thermal and geographic range is largely determined by body size. Eckert (2002a) collated available information on juvenile and subadult leatherback biogeography globally and surmised that body size appeared to constrain geographic distribution of these animals to tropical and subtropical latitudes. The smallest subadult leatherback found off Nova Scotia (~44°–47°N) measured 111.8 cm CCL; this was the only turtle < 125 cm ever officially documented in that area (James et al. 2007).

The following sections summarize what is known about migrations and local movements (almost exclusively of adult animals) by geographic region, as well as by methodological approach (flipper tagging, strandings data, aerial surveys), followed by special attention to the results of satellite telemetry studies.

In reference to the Western Atlantic, Lazell (1980) wrote, "By far the quickest route to major *Cyanea* grounds for the bulk of the known breeding population of Atlantic leatherbacks is northward with the season in the western Atlantic to the Gulf of Maine, and Georges and Browns Banks, then south in autumn through the bays and sounds of New England." Subsequent telemetry data in a wide variety of studies support this idea in that many Caribbean nesting leatherbacks do return directly to higher latitudes to feed. Lazell went on to propose that "…wintering in the Gulf of Mexico and Florida waters would maximize *Cyanea* eating opportunities in that season…" a contention unsupported by modern telemetry-based studies (see *Satellite telemetry*, below).

Peak leatherback occurrence in United States, Canadian, and European waters is typically between July and September, with highest occurrence during August (Shoop and Kenney 1992, Epperly et al. 1995, Murphy et al. 2006), observations that would later be confirmed by telemetry-based studies (e.g., Eckert 2006; Houghton et al. 2006; McMahon et al. 2005; James et al. 2006a, 2007; Witt et al. 2007a, 2007b). Fishermen interviewed in all major ports in Nova Scotia spoke of the "turtle season" as extending from June to October, with leatherbacks reported between July and October (Bleakney 1965); similarly, all reported sightings and incidental captures of leatherbacks in Newfoundland, Canada (1976–1985) occurred between July and October (Goff and Lien 1988).

Bleakney (1965) reported that sea turtles were commonly seen off Georges Bank along the edge of the Gulf Stream, and hypothesized that they moved inshore throughout the summer months to feed. More recently, long-term monitoring of leatherback presence in Nova Scotia via sightings, strandings, entanglements, and satellite telemetry work has confirmed this strong seasonality, with leatherbacks typically arriving in July and departing for southern latitudes in October-November (James et al. 2005a, 2005b, 2006a, 2007). Similarly, Stewart and Johnson (2006) summarized results of aerial surveys in the northwest Atlantic showing peak occurrences from June to November, with most sightings shoreward of the 200 m isobath.

Tag returns (from subsequent live encounters or strandings) provided the first direct evidence of movements by adults between boreal, temperate and tropical latitudes of the Western Atlantic. Several individuals tagged while nesting in French Guiana and the Caribbean Sea have subsequently stranded in more northern latitudes, often the northeastern United States (Pritchard 1976, 1985; Eckert et al. 1982; Lambie 1983; Boulon et al. 1988). Conversely, an adult tagged in Chesapeake Bay in May 1985 was killed in Cuba in July 1986 (Barnard et al. 1989). More than 25 turtles captured on foraging grounds in Nova Scotia, Canada, over the course of eight years had been tagged originally on Caribbean nesting beaches, including Costa Rica, Panama, Colombia, Venezuela, Grenada, Trinidad, Suriname, and French Guiana (James et al. 2007).

Some tag returns illustrated movements more accurately described as east-west, including gravid females tagged while nesting in French Guiana and later recovered in Ghana (Pritchard 1976) and Morocco (Girondot and Fretey 1996), West Africa. Similarly, a gravid female tagged in Costa Rica was later recovered in Morocco (Troëng et al. 2004). Carr and Meylan (1984) reported that a leatherback tagged while nesting at Tortuguero, Costa Rica, in July 1979 was recaptured in August 1983 off the south coast of Cuba. A nester tagged at Jupiter Beach, Florida, was recaptured near Cayo Arcas, Gulf of Campeche (Hildebrand 1987) and a nester tagged at Sandy Point, St. Croix, was recaptured near Cayos Triangulos, also in the Gulf of Campeche, two years later and more than 3000 km west of the tagging site (Boulon 1989).

While tag return records provide valuable information on the subject of ocean range, the probability that a tagged animal will subsequently be captured and the tag returned is low relative to the number of tags deployed. Pritchard (1976) reported the recovery of six tagged adult female leatherbacks from French Guiana out of more than 2000 animals tagged. Jacques Fretey tagged an additional 10,221 adult females between 1977 and 1979 on nesting beaches in French Guiana, with a single recovery reported from Venezuela (Meylan 1982). Similarly, thousands of leatherbacks have been tagged at Terengganu, Malaysia, since 1967, but only 35 long distance recoveries are documented (Meylan 1982). The majority of these have been from the Philippines, but there are also records from Japan, Taiwan, Hainan Island (China), and Kalimantan (Indonesia).

Based on stranding data and live sightings (1977–1987) for Cape Cod Bay, Prescott (1988) predicted that leatherbacks moved north offshore, possibly in the Gulf Stream, in early spring, and that the return migration in the summer and into the fall brought them inshore. The prediction is not entirely supported by telemetry-based studies, but high abundance of leatherbacks and leatherback strandings do occur in South Carolina in April and May (Murphy et al. 2006). Leatherbacks are frequently sighted during aerial surveys of the Chesapeake Bay, especially during the summer months and at the mouth of the Bay where they appear to be foraging (Keinath and Musick 1993). Lazell (1980) argued that the medusae-rich waters off New England were critically important habitat for *Dermochelys*.

In the Eastern Pacific, aerial surveys off California, Oregon, and Washington (United States) show that most leatherbacks occur in slope waters, while fewer occur over the continental shelf. Recorded sea surface temperatures at the Oregon and Washington sightings ranged between 13°–18.5°C, with the majority in the 15°–16°C range (Brueggeman 1992). The data suggest that leatherbacks occur north of central California during the summer and fall when sea surface temperatures are highest (Dohl et al. 1983, Brueggeman 1992). Starbird et al. (1993) summarized sightings ($n = 96$; 1986–1991) within 50 km of Monterey Bay, California, collected primarily from recreational boat skippers using the area, and concluded that leatherbacks enter the bay when sea surface temperatures warm to 15°–16°C (peak: August), "…probably to eat seasonally abundant scyphomedusae."

Benson et al. (2007b) synthesized aerial and shipboard survey data off California from 1990–2003 to describe spatio-temporal leatherback distribution and abundance patterns, confirming that neritic waters off the Pacific coast of the United States are important foraging areas for leatherbacks and that late summer and early fall encompass the period for peak leatherback occurrence in California waters. Given the connection between these foraging areas and Western Pacific nesting sites—confirmed by satellite telemetry (Benson et al. 2007a), genetic analysis (Dutton et al. 2007), and egg shell isotope signatures (Paddock et al. 2007)—this timing mirrors the reproductive-migratory cycle of spring-summer nesting in the Northern Atlantic, followed by summer-fall migration and foraging (see above).

In the Western Pacific, Bustard (1972) reported "…an important migration route…down the east coast of Australia judging by personal sightings and reports of capture in shark nets." Similar behavior was suggested for the east coast of Africa after an adult female tagged in KwaZulu-Natal was captured at Beira, Mozambique, about 1000 km to the north (Hughes, pers.comm. *in* Meylan 1982).

Satellite telemetry.—Advances in satellite telemetry have been the key to unlocking the mysteries of leatherback long distance migrations. In the first documented satellite telemetry study of a leatherback, an adult female tagged with a satellite transmitter while nesting at Ya:lima:po, French Guiana, on 17 July 1986, traveled 820 km in 23 days, or an average of 35.65 km day^{-1} (Duron-Dufrenne 1987). The consecutive fixes obtained implied directed movement northward, and the frequency of fixes during the first day, coupled with their subsequent infrequency, suggested that the turtle spent less time at the surface once it swam away from shallow coastal waters. Keinath and Musick (1993) tracked a nesting female tagged with a satellite transmitter from Sandy Point, St. Croix, that traveled 515 km and ventured some 200 km south of St. Croix before the transmitter was removed 18 days later when the turtle emerged to nest on Culebra Island, Puerto Rico, about 90 km northwest of St. Croix.

Since these pioneering efforts, satellite telemetry studies of leatherback movements at sea are reported from every ocean basin (Table 22). In general these migrations are several thousand km in length and interact with several major oceanographic features. For example, post-nesting females departing Caribbean and South American breeding grounds for North Atlantic foraging grounds compensate for the effects of crossing the powerful Gulf Stream in order to maintain their course (Ferraroli et al. 2004; Hays et al. 2004a, 2004b; Gaspar et al. 2006). Eckert and Sarti M. (1997) made a similar observation for leatherbacks leaving Pacific Mexico and Costa Rica. Shillinger et al. (2008) report rapid, directed movements by leatherbacks while they crossed the equatorial current region followed by slower dispersal travel in the low energy South Pacific Gyre.

In contrast, leatherbacks that nest in South Africa appear to interact with strong offshore currents more passively, spending time entrained in these currents and oriented to mesoscale eddy systems (Luschi et al. 2003, 2006a, 2006b; Sale et al. 2006; Lambardi et al. 2008). For apparent purposes of foraging, leatherbacks regularly orient to and remain in mesoscale eddy features, which are presumed to aggregate prey, for extended periods

Table 22. Summary of leatherback sea turtle dive and movement parameters during post-nesting migrations and while on putative foraging grounds.

Tagging Site	Mean Depth (m)	Maximum Depth (m)	Mean Duration (min)	Maximum Duration (min)	Travel Rates (km/h)	Maximum Distance (km)	Reference
Western Atlantic							
French Guiana (Ya:lima:po)	87.0 ± 3.1 3 turtles [1] 80.7 ± 2.9 2 turtles [2]	1,185	23.2 ± 0.8 [1] 26.3 ± 0.8 [2]	83.8	2.1 ± 0.2 [1] 1.8 ± 0.3 [2]	3,948-5,038 5 turtles	Fossette et al. (2008a)
French Guiana	–	–	–	–	1.5	820	Duron-Dufrenne (1987)
Grenada (Levera)	76.7 ± 65.3 (1,190 dives) 4 turtles	441.5 ± 163.1	25.9 ± 8.3	–	–	–	Hays et al. (2004a)
Grenada (Levera)	–	1,230	–	–	–	–	Hays et al. (2004b)
Grenada (Levera)	–	–	–	–	mode: 1.4 9 turtles	–	Hays et al. (2006)
Trinidad	–	>747	–	–	mean: 1.2-1.9 9 turtles	561-13,909	Eckert (2006)
USA (Culebra Isl. Puerto Rico)	–	402-501 2 turtles	–	–	mean: 3.4	19-400	Lutcavage et al. (1999)
Canada (Nova Scotia)	mode: 20-25 (1,312 dives) 1 turtle	96	6.0 ± 1.7	–	–	–	James et al. (2006c)
Canada (Nova Scotia)	~30 [3] 18-40 [4] 15 turtles	>400	~5 [3] 13-28 [4]	34	–	–	James et al. (2006a)
USA (Florida)	–	–	–	–	mean: 1.0 10 turtles	1,691-13,793	Eckert et al. (2006a)
Uruguay	–	1,186	–	86.5	–	–	López-Mendilaharsu et al. (2008)
Eastern Atlantic							
Ireland	–	1,280	–	–	–	>1,400	Doyle et al. (2008)
Western Pacific							
Indonesia (Papua)	–	–	–	–	–	4,784-20,558 19 turtles	Benson et al. (2007a)
Papua New Guinea	–	–	–	–	–	123-9,438 9 turtles	Benson et al. (2007b)
Mexico	–	>750 m (5 of 10 turtles)	–	–	–	–	Eckert (1999)
Eastern Pacific							
Costa Rica (Playa Grande)	–	744	–	–	–	2,780 8 turtles	Morreale et al. (1996)
Costa Rica (Playa Grande)	–	–	–	–	2.3-2.9 46 turtles	2,161-17,133	Shillinger et al. (2008)
Indian Ocean							
South Africa (Maputaland)	–	–	3.2-4.0 1 turtle	–	mean: 3.2	–	Hughes et al. (1998)
South Africa (Maputaland)	–	–	–	–	max: 6.0 3 turtles	6,195-18,994	Luschi et al. (2003)

Table 22, continued

Tagging Site	Mean Depth (m)	Maximum Depth (m)	Mean Duration (min)	Maximum Duration (min)	Travel Rates (km/h)	Maximum Distance (km)	Reference
South Africa (Maputaland)	–	849.8	5.5-16.9 4 turtles [5]	82.3	mean: 3.3	6,195-18,994	Sale et al. (2006), Lambardi et al. (2008)
South Africa (Maputaland)	–	940	10.4 ± 3.2 (SE) 9 turtles	–	–	–	Luschi et al. (2006a,b)

[1] without harness attachment vs. [2] with harness attachment
[3] on foraging grounds vs. [4] during migration
[5] same turtles as in Luschi et al. (2003)

(Luschi et al. 2003, Ferraroli et al. 2004, Eckert 2006, Gaspar et al. 2006, Hays et al. 2006, Doyle et al. 2008).

Leatherback nesting populations generally show diverse post-nesting migratory routes, thus apparently taking advantage of several foraging grounds. In the Western Atlantic, satellite tracking data have revealed an array of putative foraging grounds across the North Atlantic, including Canada and the northeastern United States, Western Europe, and West Africa (e.g., Ferraroli et al. 2004; Hays et al. 2004a, 2004b, 2006; James et al. 2005a, 2005b; Eckert 2006; Eckert et al. 2006a; Doyle et al. 2008). Moreover, adults perform migrations from Nova Scotian foraging grounds to Caribbean breeding grounds and back to Nova Scotia within a calendar year, thus demonstrating foraging site fidelity (James et al. 2005a, 2005b, 2005c). Migration cues from northern foraging grounds toward tropical breeding grounds appear to be related to individual turtles' geographic position (latitude, longitude) and oceanographic conditions (Sherrill-Mix et al. 2007).

In the South Atlantic, leatherbacks are found in the convergence zone off Argentina and Uruguay (Chebez and Balboa 1987; López-Mendilaharsu et al. 2007, 2008). While some of these turtles might come from nesting grounds to the north, possibly Brazil (Thomé et al. 2007) or further north (Fretey and Girondot 1989a, Girondot and Fretey 1996), recent reports of tag returns demonstrate that at least a portion of these turtles cross the Atlantic from nesting grounds in western or southwestern Africa (Billes et al. 2006) where nesting occurs at least as far south as Angola (Hughes et al. 1973, Fretey et al. 2007a). Satellite telemetry confirms post-nesting migrants leaving Gabon, heading west toward South America (Billes et al. 2006, Witt et al. unpubl. data); in contrast, a leatherback originally tagged while nesting in Gabon later stranded in South Africa, suggesting multiple migratory pathways (Fretey et al. 2007b).

In the Western Pacific, Benson et al. (2007a) reported migrations from Papua (Indonesia) to the United States, which requires crossing the North Pacific Subtropical Gyre and entering the California Current. One post-nesting female traveled from Jamursba-Medi (Indonesia) to Oregon (United States), a total of 20,558 km, among the longest movements ever recorded for an ocean-going vertebrate. Not only do leatherbacks from Papua cross the Pacific to forage off the west coast of the United States, but they also move into tropical foraging grounds in the Sulu and Sulawesi Seas, as well as northward toward the South China Sea (Benson et al. 2007a). In addition, leatherbacks from Papua New Guinea migrate south-southeast toward New Caledonia and New Zealand (Benson et al. 2007c). Benson et al. (2007b) reported apparent foraging site fidelity in Monterey Bay, California, among individuals across consecutive years.

In the Eastern Pacific, early speculation that migratory corridors existed along the northwestern seaboard of the Americas (e.g., with post-nesting females traveling north from Mexican rookeries, Stinson 1984) has evolved into the realization that leatherbacks leaving nesting beaches in the Eastern Pacific generally share a south-southwest heading toward the equator, where they then disperse throughout the southeastern Pacific (Morreale et al. 1996, Eckert and Sarti M. 1997). Saba et al. (2008a, 2008b) and Shillinger et al. (2008) speculate that a coastal migratory strategy has been largely selected against by persistently high levels of bycatch mortality in nearshore gillnet fisheries off the coasts of the Pacific Americas (Frazier and Brito Montero 1990, Eckert and Sarti M. 1997, Kaplan 2005). For a review, see Wallace and Saba (2009).

Shillinger et al. (2008) tracked 46 post-nesting female leatherbacks from Playa Grande, Costa Rica, over a period of four years; only one diverged from the oceanic migration behavior displayed by all the others, including those tracked earlier from these same beaches (Morreale et al. 1996). While most tracks outward from Pacific Mexico are also oceanic, Eckert and Sarti M. (1997) did track turtles to coastal areas off South America, perhaps indicative of a relic migratory behavioral polymorphism in these populations (Saba et al. 2008a, 2008b). Future tagging studies on previously tracked individuals are necessary to demonstrate foraging site fidelity, as has been documented in the North Atlantic (James et al. 2005a, 2005b, 2005c) and North Pacific (Benson et al. 2007b), which would be required to support the idea of intra-population behavioral polymorphisms and the selection against coastal migration in East Pacific populations.

In an interesting contrast, adult females departing beaches in Maputaland, South Africa, do not appear to migrate to specific foraging grounds (Hughes et al. 1998; Luschi et al. 2003, 2006a, 2006b; Sale et al. 2006). Instead, they enter the Agulhas Current system off the South African coast, which includes a major coastal upwelling, a longshore current, and reflection eddies on the Atlantic Ocean side (Lambardi et al. 2008). The strategy may represent a relatively lower level of energy expenditure than that exhibited by other leatherback populations in the Atlantic and Pacific oceans, and may partially account for the relatively larger body (Table 1) and clutch (Table 9) sizes of the South African population (Saba et al. 2008a). The South African pattern is somewhat akin to Florida, where Eckert et al. (2006a) tracked 10 post-nesting females from Melbourne and Juno beaches and found that most remained on the continental shelf for much of the year, venturing into oceanic waters only in the winter.

Given that Smith (1849) described five species of sea turtles from Cape Town waters, it is not surprising that modern research techniques have demonstrated regular trans-oceanic basin movements of leatherbacks around the Cape from the Indian Ocean to the Atlantic. Recent satellite studies have shown that many leatherback females, after having completed a nesting season in Tongaland (KwaZulu-Natal), sweep down the east coast of South Africa, passing in some cases over 500 km south of Cape Agulhas, and then move deep into the Atlantic, journeying past Namibia and reaching at least as far as 800 nautical miles (nm) offshore Angola (Luschi et al. 2006b).

Inter-nesting behavior.—During an active breeding season, leatherbacks tend to stay within roughly 100 km of their nesting beaches, remain relatively close to the coast (typically on the continental shelf), and sometimes show patterns of seasonal residency (Chan et al. 1991, Morreale 1999, Eckert 2006, Eckert et al. 2006a, Benson et al. 2007c, Hitipeuw et al. 2007, Witt et al. 2008). Transiting during internesting appears to be conducted at shallow depths to maximize swim efficiency (Eckert 2002b). Dive depths depend on local bathymetric features: leatherbacks routinely dive to 50–100 m, but exhibit extreme dive profiles (> 1000 m) where bathymetry permits (e.g., some areas of the insular Caribbean: Eckert et al. 1986, 1989b; Eckert 2002b; Hays et al. 2004a; Myers and Hays 2006; Myers et al. 2006).

Dives are much shallower during internesting periods in areas where the continental shelf extends substantially from the coast, thus limiting depths available to leatherbacks (Rantau Abang, Malaysia: Eckert et al. 1996; Playa Grande, Costa Rica: Southwood et al. 1999, 2005; Wallace et al. 2005; French Guiana: Fossette et al. 2007, 2008a, 2008b; Georges et al. 2007; Gabon: Georges et al. 2007) (Table 23). Whether leatherbacks actively forage during the internesting period has been a research question for decades (see *Nutrition and metabolism, Feeding*, above).

Differences have been observed in activity levels during internesting periods between North Atlantic and Eastern Pacific leatherbacks. According to Fossette et al. (2007, 2008b), internesting leatherbacks off the Guiana Shield, South America, maintained consistently high levels of diving activity, showing little to no sign of cessation of activity or resting, while leatherbacks off Pacific Costa Rica exhibited prolonged resting periods on the ocean floor (Reina et al. 2005, Southwood et al. 2005) and energy conservation through relatively low metabolic rates during internesting periods (Wallace et al. 2005). Fossette et al. (2007, 2008b) hypothesized that these differences might reflect energetic constraints relative to resource availability on foraging grounds of the Eastern Pacific vs. the North Atlantic (Wallace et al. 2006b, 2006c; Saba et al. 2008a).

Intra-seasonal movement (> 100 km) among nesting beaches is also documented, specifically between sites in French Guiana and Suriname (Schulz 1971, Pritchard 1973, Fossette et al. 2007, Georges et al. 2007), Panama and Costa Rica (Chacon and Eckert 2007), among Caribbean islands (Eckert et al. 1989b, Bräutigam and Eckert 2006, Georges et al. 2007), and Pacific coast beaches in Costa Rica and Mexico (Santidrián Tomillo et al. 2007, Sarti M. et al. 2007). Similarly, Witt et al. (2008) and Georges et al. (2007) documented the trans-boundary movements of leatherbacks that nested in Gabon that also occupied waters of the Republic of the Congo to the south.

Navigation and Orientation

Leatherbacks are among the most widely traveled of the extant sea turtles, yet the underlying orientation and navigation mechanisms are unknown. The primary cue leading hatchlings to the sea is light, specifically the brightness differential between the open ocean horizon and the darker landward view (Mrosovsky 1972a, 1977; Lohmann et al. 1997). Seaward orientation is understood to rely on a complex phototropotactic system with stimulation in different parts of a single retina being associated with turning in opposite directions (Mrosovsky et al. 1979). In contrast to guidance systems that demand fine resolution of stimuli, sea-finding depends on the integration of information over space (wide field of view) and over time (averaging illumination over about one second) (Mrosovsky 1978).

Hatchlings may be disoriented landward by artificial beachfront lighting, such as from residential and commercial development (Raymond 1984, Witherington and Martin 1996; see *Sensory Biology*, below). Villanueva-Mayor et al. (2003) found that leatherback hatchling dispersion on the beach was wider in the absence of moonlight and, when artificial light was present, hatchlings deviated significantly (in the direction of the artificial light)

Table 23. Summary of leatherback sea turtle movement parameters recorded during internesting periods. Data shown are means ± SD, sample sizes in parentheses.

Tagging Site	Mean Depth (m)	Maximum Depth (m)	Mean Duration (min)	Maximum Duration (min)	Travel Rates (km/h)	Total Distance (km)	Reference
Western Atlantic							
USA (St. Croix, USVI)	50.2-122.1 2 turtles	475	10.4-14.5	21.3-37.4	–	–	Eckert et al. (1986)
USA (St. Croix, USVI)	61.6 ± 59.1 (5,096 dives) 6 turtles	1,300 [1]	9.9 ± 5.3	37	–	–	Eckert et al. (1989b)
USA (St. Croix, USVI)	–	–	2.3 1 turtle		mean: 1.2 max: 9.4	515	Keinath & Musick (1993)
USA (St. Croix, USVI)	64.0-93.0 2 turtles	490	10.2-10.3	23.3-29.3	mode: 1.9 [2] max: 7.8 [2]	490±142 [3] 5 turtles	Eckert (2002b)
USA (Florida)	–	–	–	–	1.08±0.55— 2.93±1.8 10 turtles	–	Eckert et al. (2006a)
French Guiana (Ya:lima:po)	–	–	–	–	–	560 ± 134 10 turtles	Georges et al. (2007)
French Guiana (Ya:lima:po)	9.4 ± 9.2 (20,607 dives) 11 turtles	83.8	4.4 ± 3.4	28.2	–	546 ± 154	Fossette et al. (2007)
French Guiana (Ya:lima:po)	11.8 ± 6.3 (1,009 dives) 4 turtles	–	6.6 ± 2.6	–	–	–	Fossette et al. (2008b)
Grenada (Levera)	51.7 ± 39.9 (2,548 dives) 4 turtles	–	11.0 ± 6.1	–	–	–	Hays et al. (2004a)
Grenada (Levera)	54.7 ± 37.9 (8,711 dives) 11 turtles	–	11.1 ± 4.6	–	–	–	Myers & Hays (2006)
Grenada (Levera)	114.9 ± 49.6 1 turtle	–	10.8 ± 2.8	–	–	–	Myers et al. (2006)
Grenada (Levera)	–	–	–	–	–	656 ± 144 9 turtles	Georges et al. (2007)
Eastern Atlantic							
Gabon (Mayumba)	–	–	–	–	–	384 ± 116 13 turtles	Georges et al. (2007)
Gabon (Mayumba)	–	–	–	–	–	96-453 9 turtles	Witt et al. (2008)
Western Pacific							
Malaysia (Rantau Abang)	26.7-45.1 3 turtles	48.0-62.0	7.9-12.1	18.0-27.7	–	–	Eckert et al. (1996)
Indonesia (Papua)	–	–	–	–	–	180-250 7 turtles	Hitipeuw et al. (2007)
Papua New Guinea	–	–	–	–	–	123-9,348 9 turtles [4]	Benson et al. (2007b)
Eastern Pacific							
Costa Rica (Playa Grande)	19 ± 1 4 turtles	124	7.4 ± 0.6	67.3	–	–	Southwood et al. (1999)
Costa Rica (Playa Grande)	16.0 ± 13.3 (465 dives) 11 turtles	–	7.1 ± 6.6	–	–	–	Reina et al. (2005)

Table 23, continued

Tagging Site	Mean Depth (m)	Maximum Depth (m)	Mean Duration (min)	Maximum Duration (min)	Travel Rates (km/h)	Total Distance (km)	Reference
Costa Rica (Playa Grande)	33 ± 13 6 turtles	146	10.1 ± 2.4	67.3 [5]	mean: 1.9 [2] max: 6.4 [2]	–	Southwood et al. (2005)
Costa Rica (Playa Grande)	14.6 ± 4.6 (23,402 dives) 23 turtles	200	7.8 ± 2.4	44.9	–	–	Wallace et al. (2005)

[1] leatherbacks dived beyond the depth recording capacity of the data loggers, but the authors were able to determine a maximum depth of 1300 m using dive duration and rates of ascent and descent
[2] data reported are actual swim speeds, rather than travel rates as estimated by satellite locations
[3] similarly (see 2), data reported are actual swim distances traveled, including submerged (dive) distances, in contrast to surface to surface data provided by satellite-telemetry
[4] some distances include post-nesting travel distances
[5] same turtle as in Southwood et al. (1999)

from their natural course to the sea. Disorientation can be fatal by lengthening exposure time to predators, bringing hatchlings into contact with vehicle traffic and domestic animals, and leaving them vulnerable to the morning sun.

Secondary sea-finding cues may include geotropism (detecting the downward incline of the beach into the surf line), surf sound, and/or geomagnetism. Standora et al. (2000) reported that leatherback hatchlings oriented to surf sounds, but oriented to beach incline when surf sound and slope were in conflict. Schnars and Standora (2004) reported that additive effects of geotropism and surf sound more strongly influenced sea-finding ability in leatherback hatchlings than did geomagnetism, unless the geomagnetic manipulation was very strong (~1 gauss).

Upon entering the sea, leatherback hatchlings maintain seaward orientation using incoming waves as a cue (Lohmann et al. 1990). Beyond the wave refraction zone, leatherback hatchlings rely on an internal and light-independent "magnetic compass" to maintain orientation in the open ocean (Lohmann and Lohmann 1993). Laboratory experiments have revealed that loggerhead sea turtle hatchlings establish a magnetic directional preference by swimming or crawling toward a light source, or by swimming into waves (Lohmann et al. 1997). Because hatchlings crawl across the beach toward the lower, brighter horizon and then swim offshore into oncoming waves, the initial orientation to light and the trek to the sea probably establish the magnetic directional preference, but experimentation on *Dermochelys* has not been undertaken.

En route to the sea, hatchling leatherbacks sometimes interrupt their course by making small, quickly executed circles that seem important in reestablishing bearings (Carr and Ogren 1959). These circles are neither universal (Pritchard and Trebbau 1984) nor unique to *Dermochelys*, but will occur under certain conditions in cheloniid sea turtles (Mrosovsky and Kingsmill 1985). Detailed studies have found that fewer than 8% of hatchlings in natural circumstances make these circles, rejecting the hypothesis that the behavior is a required component of a successive sampling system (Mrosovsky and Shettleworth 1975).

As is characteristic of sea turtles, gravid leatherbacks return repeatedly, within and between years, to specific nesting grounds (see Chapter 4, *Natality and recruitment*, below). Based on early colonization of new beaches in Suriname, Pritchard (1979b) suggested that the "homing mechanism" in leatherbacks may allow them to select a beach of a certain type, rather than a particular spot that may represent the location at which they hatched. He later concluded, after documenting the deposition of consecutive nests 100–120 km apart, that reproductive philopatry in the leatherback may be weaker than that of other sea turtles (Pritchard 1982). Clearly, natural forces of erosion and accretion in some parts of the world, such as the Guianas (northeast coast of South America), force leatherbacks to contend with unpredictable alterations in the configuration of suitable nesting beaches. These environments may, in turn, foster a more flexible approach to homing and beach fidelity.

Recent results from genetic analyses show a matrilinear pedigree structure within a nesting population of leatherbacks (St. Croix, USVI), confirming natal homing in *Dermochelys* (Dutton et al. 2005) and, in general, leatherbacks do show philopatry to a general beach area and some degree of nest site fidelity within a particular nesting beach (Kamel and Mrosovsky 2004, Nordmoe et al. 2004). In a quantified study in the northern Caribbean, Eckert et al. (1989b) concluded that there was insufficient evidence to suggest that leatherbacks show weaker reproductive philopatry than do other sea turtles. Notwithstanding, there is no shortage of anecdotal data on long distance, intra-seasonal movements that result in egg deposition in more than one Caribbean country (Bräutigam and Eckert 2006), and gravid females are known to nest freely among the continental beaches of the Western

Atlantic (Guianas: Pritchard 1973, Chevalier and Girondot 1998, Caut et al. 2006a, Gratiot et al. 2006, Girondot et al. 2007, Hilterman and Goverse 2007; Central America: Troëng et al. 2004; United States: Stewart 2007) and the Eastern Pacific, where the apportion of nesting among index beaches changes from year to year in Mexico (Sarti M. et al. 2006). Using Global Positioning System (GPS) tags deployed on nesting females along Florida beaches, Stewart (2007) found that individual turtles deposited their nests up to 139.8 km apart within a single nesting season.

The long-distance migrations of leatherbacks between nesting and foraging grounds require significant navigational abilities. As described above, leatherbacks demonstrate directed movements, often against strong ocean currents, to reach putative foraging destinations or oceanographic features likely to aggregate prey.

Morreale et al. (1996) tracked leatherbacks from Costa Rica toward the Galapagos Islands, and hypothesized that they were using environmental (possibly geomagnetic) cues from the Cocos-Galapagos Ridge feature. Shillinger et al. (2008) demonstrated that the apparent relationship between leatherback migratory routes and this bathymetric feature was actually due to the influence of ocean currents on leatherback movements, and those current-corrected tracks showed that leatherbacks maintained a relatively constant south-southwest heading away from Costa Rican nesting beaches toward the Southeastern Pacific. Gaspar et al. (2006) reported similar influences of currents on leatherback movements and also showed directional movements by leatherbacks even when confronting contrary current directions. Thus, migrating leatherbacks appear to possess a compass sense, possibly related to geomagnetic cues from the magnetic field of the Earth, enabling them to maintain an overall directional heading while traveling, despite other potential influences on their direction of travel.

Biogenic magnetite, a possible transducer of the earth's magnetic field, has been discovered in a variety of marine genera, including green sea turtles. From green turtle dura tissue, Perry (1982) reported numerous opaque magnetic particles composed of very pure magnetic crystals; scanning electron microscopy revealed unique spherical crystals not previously reported in biological samples. Kirschvink (1980) reported preliminary data documenting "something magnetic" in the heads of three loggerhead sea turtle hatchlings. The systematic examination of tissue obtained from hatchlings expired in the nest, or adults stranded dead on accessible beaches, may provide important information on the subject of leatherback navigational abilities. The fact that blind females have found and climbed the nesting beach in French Guiana (Fretey 1982) indicates that senses other than vision are used in migration, navigation, homing, and nesting beach selection.

Diving

Over their remarkably broad geographic ranges, leatherbacks demonstrate shifts in behavior from relatively shallow diving during internesting periods, to deep, prolonged diving and relatively rapid movements during migrations, to shorter, shallower dives with longer surface intervals on foraging grounds (see *Migrations and local movements*, above). To perform active, deep, and prolonged dives, leatherbacks employ a specialized suite of physiological, anatomical, and behavioral adaptations that is convergent in many respects with the adaptations of other air-breathing taxa (e.g., diving birds and mammals).

In the first study to successfully employ the use of remote sensing equipment to study leatherback diving behavior at sea, Standora et al. (1984) reported that the time spent at or near the surface peaked between 0900–1200 hrs and that day dives were similar in duration to day surface intervals, while night dives were twice as long as night surfacings. Their study was based on the behavior of a subadult animal over a period of 18 hrs off the coast of Rhode Island (United States). Another brief (< 24 hrs) study used radiotelemetry techniques to monitor the behavior of three subadult leatherbacks (122–128 cm CCL) and one adult (141 cm CCL) captured in Rhode Island waters. Again, surfacing behavior generally peaked during mid-day, but no consistent pattern emerged with respect to submergence behavior (Keinath 1986). Neither study reported dive depth information. More recently, studies of the at-sea behavior of adult leatherbacks that include dive depth and durations have demonstrated that leatherbacks are consummate breath-hold divers.

Eckert et al. (1986, 1989b) measured dive parameters in leatherbacks during natural behaviors. In these studies, the researchers secured time-depth recorders (TDR) to eight turtles nesting on Sandy Point National Wildlife Refuge, St. Croix, to monitor dive behavior during the internesting interval. As each turtle returned some 10 days later to deposit another clutch of eggs, the TDR was removed. The turtles dived continuously, day and night, averaging 100 dives per 24-hr period. Leatherbacks dived beyond the depth recording capacity of the data loggers, but the authors were able to determine a maximum depth of nearly 1300 m using dive duration and rates of ascent and descent.

The capacity to achieve depths > 1200 m has since been confirmed using data logging technology with greater recording ranges (Hays et al. 2004a, Doyle et al. 2008). In addition, Fossette et al. (2007) and López-Mendilaharsu et al. (2008) report dive durations greater than one hour. The ecological significance of these extremely deep and long dives is still unclear, but water column searching, thermoregulation, predator evasion, and foraging have been postulated as reasons for such dives

(Eckert et al. 1989b, Hays et al. 2004a, James et al. 2005c, Myers and Hays 2006, Houghton et al. 2008). Regardless, most dives are within the top 300 m of the water column and under 30–40 min in duration (Morreale et al. 1996; Hays et al. 2004a, 2004b; James et al. 2005c, 2006b, 2006c). Tables 22 and 23 summarize leatherback dive depths and dive durations from all published studies.

A useful physiological parameter that may provide estimates of physiological constraints on activity is the aerobic dive limit (ADL), which refers to the dive duration beyond which blood lactate levels increase above resting levels (Kooyman et al. 1980). The ADLs of leatherbacks have been calculated in several studies using various types of physiological and behavioral information. The first estimate of leatherback ADL was 44 min (Kooyman 1989), and was derived from green turtle MR (Prange and Jackson 1976, Jackson and Prange 1979) and total oxygen stores of loggerheads (Lutz and Bentley 1985).

Based on measurements of total oxygen stores and MR of nesting turtles, Eckert (1989) estimated that leatherback ADL was about 17 min (a value similar to the ADL derived empirically (20 min) from examining frequency distributions of dive duration), while Lutcavage et al. (1990, 1992) estimated that leatherback ADL was between 5–70 min. Subsequently, Southwood et al. (1999) recorded one of the longest dive durations for a leatherback (67.3 min) and refined the ADL estimate to between 33–67 min based on heart rates and dive patterns of free-swimming adult female leatherbacks during the internesting period.

Recently, using a novel approach intended to estimate diving MR, Bradshaw et al. (2007) statistically inferred (from dive duration and depth data, as opposed to direct measurements of blood lactate levels) calculated ADL (cADL) values (mean: 38 min, range: 19–48 min) for leatherbacks that were similar to previous results. However, ultimately, actual measurements of MR of free-swimming leatherbacks are necessary to accurately calculate ADLs. Using at-sea MR measurements, Wallace et al. (2005) reported cADLs for internesting female leatherbacks to be between 11.7 and 44.3 min. Leatherbacks sometimes exceed their cADLs during exceptionally prolonged dives, which demonstrates their remarkable physiological capacity for breath-hold diving (Fossette et al. 2008a, López-Mendilaharsu et al. 2008). Further measurements of at-sea MR with concomitant data on diving behavior are warranted to elucidate leatherback diving physiology and behavior.

Investigations of oxygen transport and aerobic metabolism suggest that leatherback turtles rely on enhanced blood and tissue O_2 stores rather than lung O_2 stores during deep dives. Eckert (1989) calculated oxygen stores for adult leatherbacks from lung inflation volumes (49 ml kg^{-1} body wt at 30 cm H_2O inflation pressure), blood hemoglobin (9.2 g dL^{-1}), and muscle myoglobin (6.0 mg g^{-1} wet muscle mass). Lung volumes were smaller, blood hemoglobin roughly equivalent, and myoglobin concentrations about double the values reported for other sea turtle species. Lutcavage et al. (1990) also reported high concentrations of hemoglobin (15.6 ± 1.8 g dL^{-1}) and hematocrit (39% ± 1.2%), pectoral muscle myoglobin (4.9 g dL^{-1}) twice that of other sea turtles, and a relatively low tidal volume, the latter suggesting that leatherbacks have small lungs.

In contrast, Paladino et al. (1996) reported that measurements of leatherback tidal volume and other respiratory parameters indicated that leatherback lung volume was larger than expected based on allometric predictions of sea turtle lung volumes scaled to leatherback size. Regardless, all authors concur that leatherbacks rely both on lung and body O_2 stores, but, similar to deep-diving marine mammals, leatherbacks rely on body O_2 stores to a greater extent than do other sea turtle species (Lutz 1988; Eckert 1989; Lutcavage et al. 1990, 1992; Paladino et al. 1990, 1996). In contrast, loggerhead and green sea turtles show no special adaptations for increased oxygen capacity in blood or tissue; the lung functions as the major oxygen storage tissue (Berkson 1967, Lutz and Bentley 1985).

In addition to oxygen stores, leatherbacks possess other important adaptations for apneic diving. For example, a muscular sphincter has been identified in the leatherback pulmonary artery, which is presumably an adaptation for shunting blood away from the lungs after they collapse under pressure at depth (Wyneken et al. 2003). The respiratory physiology of the species, specifically large tidal volumes and adjustments in breath frequency depending on activity (Lutcavage et al. 1992, Paladino et al. 1996) indicates rapid and thorough exchange of respiratory gases, which would enable a leatherback to efficiently exhale carbon dioxide generated during an extended breath-hold dive and replenish oxygen stores on inhalation.

Southwood et al. (1999) reported patterns in leatherback heart rates during dives that were consistent with a typical dive response (i.e., decreased heart rate during descent and at bottom for oxygen conservation, increased heart rate during ascent and at the surface to optimize gas exchange). In fact, their efficient cardio-respiratory adaptations ensure that leatherbacks can avoid anaerobiosis and that their activity is predominantly fueled by aerobic respiration (Paladino et al. 1996, Wallace and Jones 2008). Additionally, the semi-flexible carapace and plastron of leatherbacks likely enhances the compressibility of the body under high hydrostatic pressure at depth.

Dive durations and ADL detailed above, and heart rates reported by Southwood et al. (1999), have been used to assess acceptable heart rates and periods of apnea in nesting leatherbacks undergoing anesthesia with ketamine and medetomidine (Harms et al. 2007). The median period of apnea immediately following induction of anesthesia was 22 min, with a maximum of 28 min, exceeding routine dive durations but well under the maximum recorded dive duration of 67 min (Southwood et al. 1999). Heart rates under anesthesia ranged from a mean minimum of 16 beats per minute (bpm) to a mean maximum of 21 bpm (Harms et al. 2007), comparable to a surface swimming mean of 24.9 bpm and diving mean of 17.4 bpm (Southwood et al. 1999), with one transient episode of anesthesia bradycardia at 8 bpm comparing with a minimum dive bradycardia of 3.6 bpm. Electrocardiograms recorded during anestesia revealed that the QRS complex is nearly isoelectric in the frontal plane, but the maximum R and S amplitudes occurred in lead aVf (Harms et al. 2007).

Schooling

There is no indication that leatherback turtles consciously organize to form schools or flotillas. They may, however, aggregate in a food patch (see *Nutrition and metabolism, Feeding,* above) or in the vicinity of a nesting beach.

During an aerial survey in December 1956, Leary (1957) observed a school of about 100 adults and juveniles approximately 70 m from the beach in the northwestern Gulf of Mexico. The turtles were not closely aggregated, but the group extended parallel to the coast for about 48 km; their distribution correlated with dense schools of the jellyfish *Stomolophus.*

Over the course of a three-year survey, Schroeder and Thompson (1987) documented 128 sightings of leatherbacks in the Cape Canaveral area of Florida (United States). Sightings during the summer of 1983 were not only numerous (45.3% of total leatherback sightings), but were noticeably concentrated just north of the Cape between 29°N and 29°45′N. Shoop and Kenney (1992) reported that leatherbacks were found farther north and in colder water on average than loggerhead turtles, with areas of highest density around Long Island Sound and the Gulf of Maine (United States).

Based on the contention that seasonal movements are strongly influenced by the abundance and distribution of coelenterates (Pritchard 1971a, 1976; Lazell 1980; Shoop et al. 1981), Schroeder and Thompson (1987) suggested that the seasonal abundance of leatherbacks off the Atlantic coast of Florida may have been indicative of prey abundance. Epperly et al. (1995) reported that peak density of leatherbacks in waters off North Carolina (United States) occurred in spring and early summer, and Grant et al. (1996) concluded that leatherback density in these areas coincided with jellyfish abundance. Likewise, Murphy et al. (2006) reported a peak density in the spring of 175 leatherbacks over 605 km of transect, or 0.29 leatherbacks per km in waters off South Carolina (United States) and described the distribution of leatherbacks as being clumped, rather than dispersed uniformly or randomly, probably in response to the presence of *Stomolophus* aggregations in the area.

In Australia, where most sightings reported are of single leatherback turtles, data from the shark netting off the Gold Coast suggest that they occasionally school (Limpus and McLachlan 1979). On 27 December 1971, six leatherbacks were recorded in these nets, yet none had been recorded in the previous two months. Four more captures (possibly of the same turtles) were recorded three days later, but none for a further 18 days. Twenty adults were observed on one occasion 500 m from the beach at Bribie Island in southern Queensland (Limpus and McLachlan 1979). In the Eastern Pacific, groups of gravid female leatherbacks, not uncommonly interspersed with adult males, are routinely observed during the breeding season off the nesting beaches in Michoacán, Mexico (L. Sarti M., pers. comm.).

Houghton et al. (2006) and Witt et al. (2007a) described leatherback distributions with respect to prey abundances in the Irish Sea and off Western Europe, respectively. Despite the lack of directed sampling of jellyfish distribution and abundance, Houghton et al. (2006) used aerial surveys of jellyfish near the surface to generate 'prey landscapes' which described > 20% of leatherback distribution data based on historic sighting records between Ireland and Wales, U.K. Witt et al. (2007a) synthesized leatherback sightings data from nine European countries and constructed gelatinous zooplankton distributions in this area using Continuous Plankton Recorder Survey data. These authors observed overlap in concentrations of leatherback presence with concentrations of prey presence, and these areas coincided with areas suggested as potential foraging sites due to characteristics of leatherback behavior within unique oceanographic features based on satellite telemetry (Ferraroli et al. 2004).

Communication

Virtually nothing is recorded about auditory sensitivity, much less auditory communication (see *Sensory Biology,* below). How males and females locate mates and whether reproductive readiness is signaled audibly in some way is unknown; courtship and/or mating has been documented only rarely (see *Reproduction.* above).

It has been said that leatherback turtles roar or bellow, or even cry in pain (Carr 1952, Villiers 1958). Deraniyagala (1941, 1953) argued that leatherbacks do not bellow or produce vocal sounds, but rather make a breathing sound common to other sea turtles (see also Pritchard 1969, Pritchard and Trebbau 1984). Fishers who closely observed a passing leatherback off the coast of Skye (Scotland) in September 1959, described the noise made during the leatherback's breathing as a "wheezing sound" reminiscent of "…a cow with pleurisy…" and also spoke of "…a series of loud roaring whistling noises..." (Brongersma 1968). Spectrographic analysis of the airborne sounds shows most energy concentrated between 300 and 500 Hz, and although there is variation in the sounds, there is little evidence that they have any special function (Mrosovsky 1972b).

Sensory Biology

How sea turtles perceive and respond to their environment is governed by the senses they use to gather ambient information—these senses include vision, olfaction, hearing and touch. Despite the fundamental importance of these sensory systems, they are poorly studied in sea turtles. Data relevant to leatherbacks are particularly scarce.

Vision.—As is typical of sea turtles, leatherback hatchlings are strongly photo-attracted and will readily move toward light when attempting to find the sea after emergence from the nest (e.g., Mrosovsky and Shettleworth 1975, Mrosovsky 1978, Villanueva-Mayor et al. 2003). There has been less research on leatherbacks than on other sea turtles relative to the frequency (e.g., color) or quality (e.g., intensity) of the light used in sea-finding (see Lohmann et al. 1997 for a summary). Post-hatchling leatherbacks seem less photo-attracted once they are in the water (Gless et al. 2008), and this tendency is also apparent in other species (Lohmann et al. 1997).

Adults are also photo-attracted. While on the nesting beach, both hatchlings and adults can be oriented and led by flashlight, and Witzell (1999) noted that chemiluminescent light sticks associated with swordfish longlines increased the probability of leatherback bycatch when fished at night (but see Gless et al. 2008). Such attraction would seem advantageous to a species that may feed nocturnally on luminescent prey (Eckert et al. 1989b, Crognale et al. 2008).

Studies of visual spectral sensitivity in leatherbacks show a strongly reduced sensitivity to long wavelengths (Eckert et al. 2006b, Crognale et al. 2008), particularly when compared to green and loggerhead sea turtles (Levenson et al. 2004). For the oceanic, deep-diving leatherback, the favoring of short (blue) wavelengths is logical given the rate of attenuation associated with longer wavelengths. In contrast, green and loggerhead sea turtle vision is adapted for shallow or clear water where the capacity to see long wavelengths (red) is more advantageous.

Crognale et al. (2008) speculate that the increase in short wavelength detection capability may be reflective of a capacity in leatherbacks to see well in low amplitude light, either through an increase in rod receptors, or possibly through the use of cones with enhanced short wavelength visual pigments.

These features would enhance a leatherback's capacity to see under low light conditions, such as at night or during deep dives in the open sea. These authors showed that leatherback visual responses are relatively slow reacting. Whereas green and loggerhead turtles detect flickering light at rates up to 36 Hz, leatherbacks were unable to detect flickering lights above 12 Hz. Such capacity is symptomatic of eyes that rely heavily on rods for light detection, again reinforcing the concept that the leatherback eye is capable of functioning well under low light conditions and where long wavelength light (orange-red) detection is less necessary.

It is interesting that, in contrast to the results of Crognale et al. (2008), the physical properties of the leatherback eye are not particularly well adapted for low light vision. The lens is relatively small when compared to other oceanic vertebrates (Levenson et al. 2004, Brudenall et al. 2008), which would limit light-gathering capability. According to Brudenall et al. (2008), the leatherback's pupil size allows about the same level of light gathering capacity as that of the green turtle, but, at the same time, because the outer segment of its photoreceptor cones are wider, the optical sensitivity of the leatherback is proposed to be four times higher than that of the green turtle—suggesting that each photoreceptor has the capacity for greater light absorption. In another study, Oliver et al. (2000) showed that the retina of the leatherback exhibits an area temporalis, or an area of highly concentrated ganglia designed to enhance visual acuity forward and below the turtle.

Leatherback ocular anatomy, like that of other sea turtles, reflects the requirements of aquatic vision (Bartol and Musick 2003, Brudenall et al. 2008). Visual acuity on land is thought to be poor (Birkenmeier 1971, Hartog and van Nierop 1984). An intriguing observation of Brudenall et al. (2008) is that the leatherback has an iris dilator muscle and a prominent iris sphincter muscle, features not reported before for leatherbacks. She notes that these features may be used to produce an anterior lenticonus to enable accommodation (focus) or that they may enhance the capability of the eye to focus light underwater.

Leatherbacks are clearly specialized for low light conditions when compared to other sea turtles; however, their level of enhancement for low light detection falls short of what is reported for oceanic mammals and fish. This makes sense in terms of niche because leatherbacks specialize on slow moving luminescent prey, whereas oceanic mammals and fish specialize on fast moving cryptic prey.

Olfaction.—There are no quantitative assessments of the olfactory capabilities of leatherbacks. Constantino and Salmon (2003) described a positive response to pureed jellyfish extract, based on increased biting motions.

Hearing.—Hearing capacity in leatherbacks has never been evaluated. A few studies of in-air sensitivity in green and loggerhead sea turtles show a general range in hearing from 100–1000 Hz (Ridgeway et al. 1969, Bartol et al. 1999). No studies, either in-air or in-water, have been conducted on leatherbacks.

Chapter 4: Population

Population Structure

Sex Ratio
The extent to which the sex ratios of hatchlings leaving the natal beach reflect the sex ratios of wild juveniles and adults at sea is unknown. After an exhaustive survey of Northeast Atlantic sea turtle sightings dating from the 13th century, Brongersma (1972) concluded, "It is impossible to draw any conclusions from these scanty data [some 163 records] with regard to the sex ratio of Leathery Turtles that reach European Atlantic waters."

A more recent effort to determine population-level sex ratios was undertaken by the Turtle Expert Working Group (TEWG) of the United States National Marine Fisheries Service (NMFS). Using data from the United States Sea Turtle Stranding and Salvage Network (STSSN) and information from other studies, the Turtle Expert Working Group (2007) published an assessment of the leatherback turtle population in the Atlantic Ocean. From a total of 2181 STSSN records, 344 reported gender and 60% of those were female. These records were primarily of subadults and adults (> 100 cm CCL); only three were of juveniles < 50 cm. The sex ratios within the STSSN data were also analyzed based on geography and month to determine if a preponderance of gravid females near the coast during a nesting season influenced the sex ratio; no such influence was evident. Finally, the Turtle Expert Working Group (2007) reviewed global data on sex ratios gathered from published and unpublished studies and found that most studies reported a slight female bias (range: 51.9–66.7%).

In a study of adult leatherbacks captured either intentionally for satellite telemetry or incidental to fishing operations in Atlantic Canada, James et al. (2007) reported a female bias of 1.86:1 (65% female, $n = 80$). They contrasted this with annual reports noting a male bias of 0.78:1 (43.8% female, $n = 28$) (Duguy et al. 1999 to 2007 *in* James et al. 2007) among adult leatherbacks encountered off the coast of France. Similarly, Murphy et al. (2006) reported a female bias of 2.3:1 among 23 leatherbacks (all size classes) necropsied after stranding on the coast of South Carolina (United States) between 1980 and 2003.

Estimates and comparisons of sex ratios at population (or ocean basin) levels should be viewed with appropriate caution, especially when based on limited data sets, as natural sex ratios often vary widely both temporally (within and among years) and spatially (by nesting location).

Age Composition
There are no data available to estimate the overall age composition of leatherback sea turtle populations, nor to evaluate survivability among age classes. Wild growth rates are unknown and age at maturity has not been determined conclusively (see Chapter 3, *Reproduction, Age at maturity*, above).

Size Composition
The size composition of leatherback populations is poorly understood, and information relevant to turtles < 100 cm CCL is almost non-existent. Eckert (2002) summarized juvenile and small subadult (< 145 cm CCL) sightings, but found relatively few sightings of turtles < 100 cm CCL.

A few studies note size ranges and frequency distributions from at-sea observations of subadult and adult animals (> 100 cm CCL) using stranding or capture information. Murphy et al. (2006) reported size information on 105 of 141 leatherback carcasses stranded in South Carolina (United States) since 1980—with a mean size of 151.7 cm CCL (range 116–185), 27 were juveniles and 78 were adults (1:2.9) based on the size of nesting females at St. Croix, USVI, most of which are > 144 cm (Boulon et al. 1996).

A study from Nova Scotia reports that eight male leatherbacks captured for satellite telemetry ranged in size from 140.0–168.5 cm CCL (mean: 151.5, SD = 8.94) (James et al. 2005b). James et al. (2007) reported the size distribution of 99 live-captured (inclusive of the eight males reported earlier) and 21 dead turtles from the waters of Nova Scotia, Canada, to be 111.8–171.8 cm CCL (mean: 148.1, 95% CI: 143.7–152.5) and summarized a similar range of sizes from 82 turtles reported from the coast of France (mean: 139.8 cm CCL, 95% CI: 127.6–152.0).

Brongersma (1972) summarized over 100 early sightings, strandings, and captures from European waters and, while measurement method (curved vs. straight line) was not reported, mean size (assuming carapace length, not total length) was 148.25 cm ± 10.8 (range: 128–170 cm, $n = 21$). Casale et al. (2003) summarized reports of sightings, captures, and strandings of leatherbacks in the Mediterranean

Sea: curved and unspecified carapace lengths ranged from 112–190 cm (mean: 145.5 ± 17.2, $n = 83$ turtles), curved carapace lengths (only) ranged from 115–190 cm (mean: 145.5 ± 16.4, $n = 44$).

The most complete datasets are those relating to the size distribution of gravid females on the nesting grounds (Tables 1 and 2). Mean carapace length differs slightly between nesting colonies, with the most dramatic difference between Eastern Pacific populations and those nesting elsewhere in the world. There is a growing consensus that the smaller size (as well as slower growth and reduced reproductive output) of these populations may be due to relatively poorer quality foraging habitats in the southeastern Pacific Ocean (Saba et al. 2007; see Chapter 3, *Reproduction, Reproductive cycles,* above).

Phylogeography

D. coriacea is the sole surviving species of an evolutionary lineage (Dermochelyidae) that diverged from other turtles during the Cretaceous or Jurassic Period, 100–150 million years ago (Zangerl 1980). The species is characterized by low genetic diversity and shallow mtDNA phylogeny compared to the cheloniid sea turtles (Bowen and Karl 1996), a finding that Dutton et al. (1999) attribute to a genetic bottleneck during the most recent Ice Age, hypothesizing that *D. coriacea* survived (while other species were lost) by virtue of a refugium in the Indo-Pacific. Global sequence divergence (mtDNA) is relatively low, even at large geospatial scales. Dutton et al. (1996) reported a sequence divergence between Atlantic and Pacific populations of 0.0081, significantly lower than that reported for green sea turtle populations (0.071–0.074).

Leatherbacks have extensive home ranges, move great distances between foraging and nesting areas, and appear to exhibit weaker nesting beach fidelity than other sea turtle species (see Chapter 3, *Behavior,* above). These life history traits may also contribute to reduced differentiation between leatherback nesting populations than has been found in other sea turtle species.

Currently available data are consistent with the natal homing paradigm for sea turtles and reveal varying degrees of population structuring. Dutton et al. (1999) found a shallow gene genealogy and strong population structure worldwide ($F_{ST} = 0.42$, $P < 0.001$), as well as within the Atlantic Ocean ($F_{ST} = 0.25$, $P < 0.001$) and Indian-Pacific Ocean ($F_{ST} = 0.20$, $P < 0.001$). Some geographically distant populations, however, were indistinguishable, including Florida, Atlantic Costa Rica, French Guiana-Suriname, and South Africa (Dutton et al. 1999).

In the Pacific basin, Eastern Pacific nesting populations (Mexico, Costa Rica) comprise one genetic population (Dutton et al. 1999). Nesting populations from Indonesia to Vanuatu, spread across 4000 km of the West Pacific, comprised a single genetic population distinct from those in the Eastern Pacific or mainland Malaysia (Dutton et al. 2007). These findings indicate that, like the oceanic olive ridley sea turtle, leatherback females may be less nest-site specific or more prone to nest-site relocation (Bowen and Karl 2007), or perhaps these are recently founded populations that have not had sufficient time to differentiate.

Research is ongoing using additional nuclear markers (microsatellites) and longer mtDNA sequences and including additional nesting populations that promises to allow more accurate resolution of population boundaries for leatherbacks (Dutton 1996, Dutton et al. 2003, Bowen and Karl 2007, National Marine Fisheries Service and United States Fish and Wildlife Service 2007, LaCasella and Dutton 2008).

Abundance and Density

Average Abundance and Density

Carr (1952) wrote that "…the leatherback appears to nest nowhere in numbers…" and noted that P.E.P. Deraniyagala was one of the very few herpetologists who had ever seen one nesting. However, a few years later, Carr himself discovered an important nesting colony in Costa Rica (Carr and Ogren 1959) and around the same time an important rookery in peninsular Malaysia was announced (Wells 1960). Even so, Fitter (1961) estimated that the world population of *D. coriacea* may be "…as few as 1000 pairs…" of which perhaps 85–95% nested in Terengganu, Malaysia.

Pritchard (1971a) estimated 29,000 to 40,000 breeding females as follows: 15,000 for French Guiana; 8000 for Pacific Mexico; 4000 for Terengganu; 1000 for Matina, Costa Rica; and 200–400 each for Trinidad, Suriname, Tongaland (South Africa), and Sri Lanka (and adjacent parts of southern India). The high estimate of 40,000 assumed colonies not yet discovered at the time of Pritchard's writing. Sternberg (1981) identified a total of 64 beaches on which leatherback nesting had been recorded; the great majority of these characterized as "minor" or "abundance unknown."

Based on an aerial survey of the Pacific coast of Mexico, Pritchard (1982) concluded, "It is difficult to make even an approximate estimate of the Mexican Pacific leatherback population; the density of tracks found on the survey was such that it was not practical to make an actual count, and in any case 'ground truth' data, especially as regards the interval since the last heavy rain (which would have washed out or blurred all tracks and nests on the beach at the time) were not available." Nevertheless, he revised the earlier global estimate to 115,000 reproducing females, including an estimated 75,000 in Pacific Mexico, 12,000 in Central America and unsurveyed parts of Mexico, 4000 in the Vogelkop Peninsula of Papua, Indonesia (formerly Irian Jaya), and 3000 for other parts of Melanesia (Papua New Guinea, Vanuatu, Solomon Islands, Fiji).

In a summary of leatherback nesting worldwide submitted to the Second Western Atlantic Turtle Symposium (WATS II), Pritchard (1987) argued that the global estimate should be raised once again. He did not specify a new estimate, but he noted that the population nesting in Terengganu, Malaysia, was reported at 15,525 females (based on a decade of intensive tagging: T.H. Chua, unpubl. data), that Fretey and Lescure (1979) had confirmed earlier estimates of ~15,000 breeding females in French Guiana, that new information was available suggesting the importance of other Western Atlantic rookeries (Guyana: Pritchard 1987; Colombia and Central America: Carr et al. 1982, Ross 1982, Meylan et al. 1985; Dominican Republic: Ross 1982), as well as South Africa (Hughes 1982), and that additional data had become available from the Eastern Pacific, including Laura Sarti-Martínez's estimate (in Alvarado and Figueroa 1987) that ~2000 leatherbacks had nested at Playa Mexiquillo (Mexico) the previous year. The estimate of 15,525 females in Terengganu (given by Chua, unpubl. data) is likely to be erroneous. Chua (1988a) estimated the number of nesting females per annum (1967–1976) as ranging from 1067 to 3103; Chan and Liew (1996) published similar estimates for the 1950s.

A decade later it became clear that the world's largest nesting colonies had collapsed—the Eastern Pacific due largely to acute extraterritorial bycatch issues (Sarti M. et al. 1996, Eckert and Sarti M. 1997) and Malaysia due to fisheries interactions and chronic over-exploitation of eggs (Chan and Liew 1996). In response, Spotila et al. (1996) revised the global estimate to 34,500 (range 26,200–42,900) breeding females based on data from 28 rookeries around the world and cautioned that leatherbacks, at least in the Pacific, teetered on the edge of extinction (Spotila et al. 2000).

With data available to 2005 and taking into account apparently rising populations at some Atlantic sites, the Turtle Expert Working Group (2007) estimated 34,000–94,000 adult leatherbacks (males and females) in the North Atlantic system. The largest nesting colonies are located in French Guiana and Trinidad. However, estimates in French Guiana vary depending on statistical treatment and census technique, and are complicated by spillover in adjoining Suriname (Hilterman and Goverse 2007, Kelle et al. 2007). In French Guiana-Suriname, an estimated 5029 [1980] to 63,294 [1988] nests were laid annually from 1967 to 2002; the population is described as "…stable or slightly increasing…" (Girondot et al. 2007). In Trinidad, an estimated 52,797 and 48,240 nests were laid at the nation's three largest nesting beaches (combined) in 2007 and 2008, respectively (SAE).

Dow et al. (2007) mapped all known nesting beaches in the Wider Caribbean Region, including Brazil: 470 sites in all. They reported only 10 colonies with more than 1000 crawls (successful and unsuccessful nesting emergences combined) per year, mostly clustered in the southern latitudes (French Guiana, Panama, Suriname, Trinidad) and four additional sites (Costa Rica, Guyana, Suriname, USVI) with 500–1000 crawls per year. Large colonies were rare and more than half (58%) of all known nesting beaches supported very small colonies (< 25 crawls per year).

In the Eastern Atlantic, only Gabon is reported as a large colony. Estimates there have steadily risen, based on increasingly comprehensive surveys, from ~ 6300–7800 females nesting annually (Billes et al. 2003, Fretey et al. 2007a) to ~ 5865–20,499 females nesting annually (Witt et al. 2009).

Hamann et al. (2006a) summarized data available in all countries of the Indian Ocean and Southeast Asia region, concluding that only Sri Lanka and the Andaman and Nicobar Islands of India host more than 100 nesting females per year. Hamann et al. (2006a) listed several countries in this region, including the Philippines, Japan, India (mainland), Thailand, Vietnam, Myanmar, Bangladesh, Seychelles, Somalia and Kenya, as no longer supporting leatherback nesting or reporting such nesting as very rare. There is a small population (50–60 females nesting annually) in South Africa (Nel 2008). Nesting in Australia is largely confined to the Northern Territory and no nesting has been recorded on the east coast of Australia since 1996 (Hamann et al. 2006a); nesting in Western Australia is unknown or unconfirmed (Prince 1994).

In the Western Pacific, 28 nesting sites in Papua New Guinea, Solomon Islands, Vanuatu, and Indonesia (Papua) collectively host ~ 5000–9200 nests per year, with ~75% of nesting activity concentrated at four sites along the northwest coast of Papua (Dutton et al. 2007).

Changes in Abundance and Density

Major Western Atlantic nesting populations appear to be stable or increasing, including the region's largest colony in French Guiana-Suriname, described as "…stable or slightly increasing…" over the past three decades (Girondot et al. 2007). In an assessment of population trends for 11 of the primary nesting colonies of the region (where sufficient data for a trend analysis were available), the Turtle Expert Working Group (2007) reported that nine colonies (including Brazil, Thomé et al. 2007) were increasing. In contrast, Eckert and Bjorkland (2005) concluded that the nesting populations of the insular Eastern Caribbean had, on balance, experienced dramatic declines since World War II; half of the 30 nations and territories in their review were characterized as having "…virtually no capacity to contribute to the survival of the species due to the near extirpation of local nesting colonies or a lack of adequate nesting habitat."

In the Eastern Atlantic, most data are insufficient to speculate on population trends. According to the Turtle Expert Working Group (2007), research and conservation initiatives in the 29 geopolitical units of the Atlantic coast of Africa are relatively young, and available data on leatherbacks tend to be largely descriptive or very recent, making it difficult to identify status and trend. A 4-year study in the Republic of Congo indicates that leatherback nesting is low, but the trend may be increasing (Godgenger et al. 2009). An eight-year time series analysis of 62 beach segments in Cameroon, São Tomé & Príncipe, Gabon, and Congo concluded an overall stable trend (Godgenger et al. 2008). No nesting is reported from the shores of the Mediterranean Sea.

In the Western Pacific, the important nesting colony on the northwest coast of Papua, Indonesia (formerly Irian Jaya) has gradually declined since 1981 to an estimated 3000–4000 nests annually (Hitipeuw et al. 2007). In the Eastern Pacific, Mexico was once credited with more than half the world population (Pritchard 1982); however, Mexico has witnessed an acute decline of more than 90% of its breeding females (Sarti M. et al. 1996, Sarti M. et al. 2007). Similar data collected in 1988 in Pacific Costa Rica show nesting numbers have plummeted 95% (Santidrián Tomillo et al. 2007, 2008).

In the Indian Ocean, Nel (2008) characterized the South African population as "…stable, with a possible marginal increase…" but cautioned that it is "…very small, and vulnerable, [and] recovering very slowly." Significant declines in the number of reproductively active females are reported in India (Cameron 1923, Kar and Bhaskar 1982, Shanker and Choudhury 2006) and Thailand (Polunin 1977). In some cases there are only anecdotal accounts; in Kerala (India), fishermen report that at the turn of the century, "…about 40…" leatherbacks were caught annually when attempting to come ashore or while at sea, while by 1915, only "…about two…" were caught annually (Cameron 1923). In other cases, detailed information has been published. For example, in Terengganu, Malaysia, a decline in both the number of turtles visiting the beach and their clutch frequency was recorded between 1967–1976 and 1984–1988. Based on mean values, the number of females visiting this site dropped 86%. The decline was attributed largely to fisheries interactions and excessive egg collection (Chua 1988a, 1988b; Chan and Liew 1996). The most recent data for the number of leatherback nests laid in Terengganu is: 6 (2004), 1 (2005), 5 (2006), 0 (2007), and 9 (2008) (E.H. Chan, pers. comm.).

There is little information on densities at sea. Murphy et al. (2006) reported that from 1994 to 2003, 1131 leatherbacks were seen during 50 nearshore aerial surveys of South Carolina (United States) waters that covered 30,250 km or 0.04 per km. The highest concentration during a single flight was in May 2002, with 175 leatherbacks seen over 605 km or 0.29 per km. Total annual leatherback observations ranged from 17 to 414, with the mean per flight ranging from 5.3 to 69.0.

There are no data on changes in population abundance or density at foraging grounds, or among size (age) classes other than breeding-age females at their nesting beaches.

Natality and Recruitment

Reproductive Rates

Clutch frequency (the number of clutches produced by a female during a reproductive year) on average ranges between 5 and 7, with a maximum Observed Clutch Frequency (OCF) of 13 (Table 12; Reina et al. 2002a). Average clutch size varies among populations: typically 75–85 eggs in the Atlantic and Western Pacific, 60–65 eggs in the Eastern Pacific, and 100+ in the Indian Ocean (Table 9; Chapter 3, *Reproduction, Reproductive cycles*, above).

Like most sea turtle genera, *Dermochelys* rarely nests every year. The average internesting interval is 2–3 years, but can be much longer (Table 13), and the interval is likely influenced by environmental conditions. At St. Croix (USVI), females nesting at Sandy Point National Wildlife Refuge most commonly (61.4%) return to renest every two years and less commonly (30.3%) every three years. A small percentage renest after four (6.9%) and five (0.7%) years (Boulon et al. 1996), for a population average of 2.5 years. In contrast, Eastern Pacific colonies nesting in Costa Rica and Mexico exhibit longer intervals, reportedly due to comparatively poorer quality foraging conditions in the southeastern Pacific Ocean (Saba et al. 2007, 2008a, 2008b). At Playa Grande, Costa Rica, the renesting interval is 3.7 ± 0.2 years (Reina et al. 2002a); in Mexico it is reported to be 3 years (Reina et al. 2002, Sarti M. et al. 2007). Reproductive longevity is not well known (see Chapter 3, *Juvenile, subadult and adult phases, Longevity*, above).

Emergence success and hatching success rates vary widely (Table 17) but rarely exceed 65%, and are typically below 50% at well studied rookeries. Causal factors vary, but nest environment, handling (*in situ* vs. relocated), and beach dynamics (cycles of erosion and accretion) are implicated. In large colonies, density-related nest destruction by later nesting females is certainly involved (Girondot et al. 2002, Caut et al. 2006b).

A rough calculation of annual hatchling production may be made using these typical production values. For turtles that nest every other year with an average clutch size of 85 eggs, emergence success of 50%, and an average of 6 nests per season, she might be expected to produce 255 hatchlings every other year, representing an annual reproductive potential of 127.5 hatchlings. For Eastern Pacific leatherbacks, a similar calculation using a renesting interval of 3.7 years and a clutch size of 65 eggs, the annual reproductive potential is 52 hatchlings per year. Mortality may be high on nesting beaches due to a wide variety of terrestrial and avian predators, as well as offshore (Nellis and Henke 2000) (see Chapter 3, *Juvenile, subadult and adult phases, Predators*, above).

Some mention should be made of male reproductive rates as they influence gene flow through sea turtle populations. There is little information on male reproductive patterns, but one intriguing study suggests that some males may breed (or seek to breed) annually. James et al. (2005b) observed that one of nine males tracked by satellite telemetry from foraging (Nova Scotia, Canada) to breeding (Galera Point, Trinidad) grounds returned to Galera Point the following year. Trinidad supports nesting by one of the largest colonies of leatherbacks in the world (Turtle Expert Working Group 2007) and primary nesting habitat is bisected on the northeast coast by Galera Point, suggesting that this male was seeking opportunities to mate as he arrived a few weeks before the nesting season and remained in the area until peak egg-laying season.

Factors Affecting Reproduction

There are few quantitative studies on factors affecting reproduction in leatherbacks. Research by Saba et al. (2007, 2008a, 2008b) in the Pacific and Rivalan (2003) in the Atlantic has the potential to significantly expand our understanding of the linkages between oceanic productivity and reproductive cycling and output, but these studies rely primarily on large-scale population comparisons rather than any potential effect of environment on the individual female.

Factors affecting reproductive success on the nesting beach are discussed for eggs and hatchlings, and adults, in Chapter 3 section *Embryonic and hatchling phases* and *Juvenile, subadult and adult phases, Predators*, respectively, above).

Recruitment

Recruitment, defined here as survivorship and recruitment into the adult population, requires at least a basic understanding of annual or stage-based survival rates from hatchling to adult. Given the uncertainty of age at first reproduction, and the challenges inherent in defining hatchling production and monitoring juveniles in high seas developmental habitats, determining recruitment values for leatherbacks is an unresolved challenge.

Mortality

Mortality Rates

Sea turtle life histories, not unlike those of other long-lived marine organisms, are characterized by high juvenile (and low adult) mortality, delayed sexual maturity, and comparatively high fecundity (Musick 1999). Unfortunately, few long-term field studies of sea turtle populations have amassed sufficient data to quantify survival in nature (for early summaries see Hirth and Schaffer 1974; Bjorndal 1980; Richardson 1982; Frazer 1983a, 1983b). Most information on mortality rates is limited to nesting beach studies of adult females and hatchlings (see *Factors causing or affecting mortality*, below). Spotila et al. (1996) estimated survival in the first year to be 0.0625. No data are available on juvenile or subadult mortality rates in leatherbacks, which is understandable given the very low probability of encountering these life stages (Eckert 2002a).

Age and size at maturity, as well as juvenile and adult survivorship rates, may vary among populations, indicating that appraisals of longevity may be population-specific. Chua (1988a) estimated a yearly mortality (1 – survival rate = 0.11) for leatherbacks nesting at Terengganu, Malaysia; however, the study was flawed by the use of a capture-mark-recapture stochastic method (Jolly 1965) which assumed that no marks (flipper tags) were lost over the course of the study and that all individuals within the population were equally catchable during any given sampling year. Both of these underlying assumptions were violated during the 10 years (1967–1976) (Chua 1988a).

More recently, Dutton et al. (2005) used an open robust design mark-recapture model (Kendell and Bjorkland 2001) to evaluate adult female survival for the nesting colony at Sandy Point National Wildlife Refuge, USVI. This population is growing at approximately 13% per year and female adult annual survival was calculated to be 89.3% (95% CI: 0.87–0.92). In Florida, using six years of mark-recapture data and the same open robust design model (Kendall and Bjorkland 2001), annual survival for nesting females was estimated at 95.6% in a population growing at 11.3 ± 1.9% per year (Stewart 2007).

At Playa Grande, Costa Rica, Santidrián Tomillo et al. (2007) used a Cormack-Jolly Seber model to estimate annual survival rate. While many of the same assumptions that invalidated Chua's (1988a) study are also applicable to this analysis, the authors addressed them by using an archival tagging methodology (Passive Integrated Transponder [PIT] tags with presumed 100% retention) and included an estimate of missed coverage probability. In this declining population, adult female survival was calculated at 78% (95% CI: 0.75–0.80).

Factors Causing or Affecting Mortality

Both biotic and abiotic factors are responsible for the death of leatherback turtles and their eggs. In addition to direct take by human and non-human predators, other potentially lethal threats reviewed in this section include incidental capture at sea by fishing vessels, entanglement in or ingestion of persistent marine debris, international trade, and the degradation of nesting habitat from industrialization and urbanization along the coast.

Direct take.—Since there are many references to the killing of leatherbacks by humans, we have attempted in this section to provide an overview of common take scenarios. Most take occurs at the nesting beach where gravid females are killed (for meat, oil, and/or eggs), legally or illegally, in virtually every country where nesting occurs. Especially comprehensive regional reviews are available in Behler et al. (1996), Fleming (2001), Fretey (2001), Kinan (2002, 2005), Bräutigam and Eckert (2006), Hamann et al. (2006a), Shanker and Choudhury (2006), National Marine Fisheries Service and United States Fish and Wildlife Service (2007), Seminoff et al. (2007b), and Turtle Expert Working Group (2007).

In the Western Atlantic, the oily meat is not widely favored and is often prepared by sun-drying or stewing (Eckert and Eckert 1990c). The meat has variously been described as expensive and as representing a sizable income for vendors (Ross and Ottenwalder 1983), and as a "...low status food..." and rarely eaten, having been fed in large quantitites to prisoners in the 1940s (Pritchard 1971b).

The flesh is occasionally described as highly poisonous, provoking nausea, vomiting, diarrhea, weakness, boils, fever, sore lips and throat, hallucinations, coma, and death within 12 hours to two weeks (Chevalier and Duchesne 1851, Halstead 1956, Wills 1966). In Taiwan, the meat is consumed despite its reputation for having a foul taste (Mao 1971). A fisher in Trinidad explained to Bacon and Maliphant (1971) that the leatherback "...is really the doctor for all the other sea turtles. When a turtle gets sick the leatherback takes all its disease out of him. So that is why [the leatherback] is covered with spots and his meat is not good to eat." Similar taboos exist in the Western Pacific, where leatherbacks are avoided as "bad spirits" (Petro et al. 2007). On Bioko Island, off the west coast of Africa, leatherback eggs are collected but killing an adult is rare as it may bring "a big storm to Bioko" (Butynski 1996).

In contrast, Ray and Coates (1958) described the meat as "extraordinarily tender" after dining on a leatherback killed off the coast of New England (United States). Similarly, a leatherback entangled in a fishing net and later consumed at hotel restaurants in Santa Barbara, California, was described as "very fine eating" (van Denburgh 1905). In some regions the consumption of leatherback meat is commonplace. For example, Anvene (2003) reported that 90% of the citizens of Bata (Equatorial Guinea) eat turtle meat; he estimated "...that > 25 turtles are eaten monthly, approximately five leatherbacks and the rest green turtles." In Paiawa (Papua New Guinea), leatherbacks were once "regularly killed and smoked" and the flesh and eggs traded with mountain peoples residing in the interior for pig meat (Kinch 2006).

Less common today are reports of leatherbacks killed for sport (Bacon and Maliphant 1971), for ceremony (Nabhan 2003), or for shark bait (Bacon 1970). Pritchard (1969) commented on a 1967 encounter with a fisherman from Silébâche Beach (French Guiana) who claimed that "...during offshore shark fishing, he usually caught during the 2- to 3-month season about one leatherback per day, which he killed and cut up for shark bait and for any shelled eggs it might contain."

Eggs have been collected, systematically or opportunistically, throughout the species' range for generations (e.g., Western Atlantic: Carr and Ogren 1959, Rebel 1974, Ross 1982, Meylan 1983, Bacon et al. 1984, Ogren 1989, Fleming 2001, Godley et al. 2004, Bräutigam and Eckert 2006, Hilterman and Goverse 2007; Eastern Pacific: Márquez et al. 1981; Indo-Pacific: Nuitja and Lazell 1982, Quinn and Kojis 1985, Lockhart 1989, Eckert 1993, Hirth et al. 1993, Starbird and Suarez 1994, Kinan 2002, 2005, Kinch 2006, Hitipeuw et al. 2007; Africa: Hughes et al. 1973, Sounguet et al. 2004), irrespective of the legality of the practice. Sarti M. et al. (2007) implicate egg collection 25 years ago "...on most of the important nesting beaches of the Mexican Pacific..." in the population's slow response to contemporary conservation efforts.

In West Africa, egg poaching is widespread and often described as approaching 100% of eggs laid (Bal et al. 2007, Peñate et al. 2007). Fretey (2001) confirms leatherback nesting in 26 West African countries; in all but one country for which data were available, eggs are consumed as part of traditional practice but are rarely sold.

Along the north coast of Papua New Guinea, the largest remaining nesting colonies in the Pacific are "...subjected to intense egg harvest..." (Philip 2002), with 40% of surveyed households along the Huon Coast, Morobe Province, consuming leatherback eggs "in the last year" (Kinch 2006). Betz and Welch (1992) reported large-scale egg harvest during the 1980s in Papua, Indonesia (formerly Irian Jaya); e.g., at Warmon Beach (north Vogelkop coast), Starbird and Suarez (1994) reported harvest of 60% of nests laid. Similarly, commercial exploitation of eggs at Jamursba-Medi Beach has been intense for many years. Between 1984 and 1985, four to five boats were observed visiting this beach weekly, and returning with 10,000–15,000 eggs per boat; during peak nesting season, the beach would become crowded with temporary dwellings that housed egg collectors and traders (Hitipeuw et al. 2007).

Perhaps the most infamous example of over-exploitation is Terengganu, Malaysia, where turtle flesh is shunned by Islamic custom but eggs have been harvested in great numbers for decades, an enterprise which has precipitated the dramatic decline of one of the world's most important nesting colonies (Brahim et al. 1987). Between 1967–1976 and 1984–1988, based on mean values, there was an 86% drop in the number of turtles visiting this well studied rookery (Chua 1988b); today the colony is nearly extirpated (Chan and Liew 1996).

The oil has historically been used for varnish and as a sealant on the hulls of small boats and dhows (Deraniyagala 1930) in Taiwan (Mao 1971), India

(Bhaskar 1981), Mozambique (Louro et al. 2006), and Larak Island, Persian Gulf (Kinunen and Walczak 1971), among other places. It has also fueled oil lamps (Pritchard 1979b).

The oil has also been used for medicinal purposes and purported aphrodisiac qualities. In the northern villages of Grenada, West Indies, "kawang oil" is legally (in season) bottled and sold as a vitamin supplement; reputed to keep the consumer "young and strong," it can be drunk undiluted or cut with water, lime juice, and spices (Eckert and Eckert 1990c). In other parts of the Caribbean, the viscous, yellow fluid was sought as a remedy for respiratory infections and other ailments (Rainey and Pritchard 1972, Eckert et al. 1992, Montiel-Villalobos et al. 2006), being associated with "remarkable curative powers" (Hastings 2003). The species was nearly extirpated in the British Virgin Islands as a result of persistent exploitation for oil and meat (Cambers and Lima 1990), but the species is now "...showing signs of recovery coincident with the implementation of an effective moratorium on adult take..." (McGowan et al. 2008).

In central western Africa, leatherback oil is used, either pure or mixed with honey, to treat convulsions, malaria, indigestion, fever, fainting spells, liver problems, traumas caused by shock, tetanus, sprains, fractures, and bruises, as well as to induce vomiting (summarized by Fretey et al. 2007c). The authors contend that "...up to forty litres of oil can be extracted from a dead adult turtle exposed to full sunlight."

It is rare that leatherbacks are regularly and deliberately caught at sea, as once occurred in Peru (Pritchard and Trebbau 1984), but sources of mortality away from the nesting beach include harpooning, gunshot, and boat strikes. Isolated incidences of harpooning have been documented in Norway, Scotland and France (Brongersma 1972), the Canadian Atlantic (Bleakney 1965, Zullo and Bleakney 1966, Threlfall 1978), and off the east (Moulton 1963) and west (Stinson 1984) coasts of the United States. The French account is based on a museum specimen said to have been harpooned, but the incident apparently lacks documentation; the Maine animal was not killed by the blow and was recaptured a week later. In 1979, fishermen diving for sea urchins off Baja California, Mexico, killed a curious leatherback with a machete and harpoon and hauled it ashore (Stinson 1984).

In the Kai Islands, Indonesia, members of eight villages hunt leatherbacks in the open sea using traditional dugout sailboats and harpoons during the oceanic calm period (October–February) (Suarez and Starbird 1996). A more recent survey (November 2003–October 2004) of the Kei Islands found that at least 29 leatherbacks (18 females, 11 males) were hunted from seven villages during the survey period (Lawalata et al. 2005).

A subadult was shot in the Indian River Lagoon of Florida in 1954 (Caldwell 1959), an adult male and adult female were shot in the waters of Labrador in 1973 (Threlfall 1978), and a "free-swimming" animal was later shot off Newfoundland (Goff and Lien 1988). In Ireland, a specimen 183 cm in total length washed ashore after "...some nautical oaf had put a couple of 303 bullets through its head..." and gunshot wounds are also reported from leatherbacks stranded in the Netherlands (adult male total length 244 cm) and France (total length 200 cm) (Brongersma 1972). In 1981, a 185.5 kg leatherback washed ashore at Encinitas, California, with its throat slit and a fractured skull; 0.22 caliber bullets were removed from the turtle and five additional bullet wounds (one in the skull, another in a rear flipper, and three in the abdominal wall) were old and healed (Stinson 1984). On 28 July 1988, a leatherback shooting was reported from Laguna Beach, California; the autopsy revealed seven impacts from an automatic gun and a postmortem propeller strike (Anonymous 1988).

Propeller wounds have been observed on leatherbacks stranded dead or injured in Germany and France (Brongersma 1972), Ameland Island, Netherlands (Hartog and van Nierop 1984), South Africa (Nel 2008), and along the eastern (Ogden et al. 1981, Rhodin and Schoelkopf 1982, Dwyer et al. 2003) and western (Stinson 1984) seaboards of the United States. In Florida, ~20% ($n = 574$) of leatherback strandings between 1980 and 2007 had propeller wounds (A. Foley, pers. comm.). It is difficult to discern whether these wounds were inflicted pre- or post-mortem. In an incident off Scotland, a male (carapace 138.5 cm CCL) was taken aboard the ring-net boat "Hercules" with a fractured skull, perhaps "...caused by a blow from a ship's propeller..." it was brought to Glasgow, Scotland where it later died (Brongersma 1972).

In the Eastern Pacific, van Denburgh (1924) reports that an adult (157.5 cm CCL) was gaffed and brought ashore south of Santa Cruz, California (United States), in 1923 after having been stunned by a ship's propeller. In 1929, an adult (159 cm CCL) was brought to Monterey, California, with head injuries received from a fishing boat's propeller and another was struck off San Francisco (Myers 1933). In May 1967, a 360-kg adult collided with a 25-ft cabin-cruiser in the Catalina Channel (Channel Islands, California, United States), shearing the boat's rudder from the hull and breaking the turtle's back (*San Diego Union*, 25 May 1967).

Fretey (1977) commented on increased cargo ship traffic in the waters of French Guiana, and noted that only ship propellers could inflict the deep wounds observed on some nesting females.

Incidental capture.—Leatherbacks are vulnerable to injury and death as bycatch in artisanal and commercial fisheries. They are ensnared by a wide variety of active and abandoned fishing gear, and may bruise or bleed from the face and mouth after being dropped on the deck of a fishing vessel from a trawl net or purse seine. Nesting turtles are sometimes observed entangled in discarded fishing line and embedded hooks, presumably from accidental interactions with fishers. For example, between 2002 and 2005, 9.0–16.9% of females nesting in Suriname "…had injuries that showed evidence of being fisheries related…" (Hilterman and Goverse 2007), including holes in their carapace "…where wooden sticks had been used to force [the turtles] from fishing nets…" (Crossland 2003). A review of strandings on nesting beaches in southern Gabon and northern Congo estimated that 50% of leatherbacks evaluated "…may have died due to fisheries or boat related activity…" (Parnell et al. 2007).

The fisheries most often implicated in leatherback bycatch are longlines and tangle nets (setnets, gillnets, driftnets). Gear technology research by NMFS has resulted in the replacement of J-hooks and squid bait by circle hooks and fish-type bait in shallow-set longline fisheries in the United States, with positive results (Watson et al. 2005; Swimmer and Brill 2006; Gilman et al. 2006, 2007; but see Read 2007), and Regional Fishery Management Organizations (RFMOs) have adopted several resolutions to reduce sea turtle bycatch and mortality in commercial fisheries. Useful summaries relevant to United States' waters are found in Witzell (1984), National Research Council (1990), Lee et al. (1995), Gerrior (1996), National Marine Fisheries Service and United States Fish and Wildlife Service (1992, 1998, 2007), National Marine Fisheries Service (2001a, 2001b), and Turtle Expert Working Group (2007).

Stinson (1984) reviewed 304 sea turtle sightings (some of multiple animals) in the northeastern Pacific between 1872 and 1983. Of 127 records positively identified as leatherbacks, 17 (13.4%) of these specified entanglement in a pilchard seine, purse seine, gillnet, driftnet (set for thresher sharks and swordfish), crab pot line, or simply a "fishermen's net"; one specimen was caught with hook and line. The data are viewed as an underestimate, and in most cases the turtle was injured, debilitated, or killed as a consequence of the encounter. Ramírez and Gonzáles (2000) reported that 18 (85.7%) turtles accidentally caught by longliners in the Gulf of Mexico due to "…entangling with monofilament fishing line…" were leatherbacks (also see *Marine debris and pollution*, below).

Longline fisheries.—Leatherback bycatch in longline fisheries is documented in the northeastern Caribbean Sea (e.g., Cambers and Lima 1990, Tobias 1991, Fuller et al. 1992) and Gulf of Mexico, where the leatherbacks may be attracted to lights associated with longlining for tuna, causing them to become entangled in the gangion or caught on a hook (Hildebrand 1987). Observer data collected between 1979 and 1981 showed that 74% of turtles hooked by Japanese tuna longliners in the Gulf of Mexico were leatherbacks; 22 were released alive (Roithmayr and Henwood 1982). Similarly, Ramírez and Gonzáles (2000) reported 79.6% of turtles captured in the Mexican tuna longline fishery in the Gulf of Mexico (1994–1995) to be leatherbacks. Leatherbacks are also captured in southern Brazil by tuna longliners (Barata et al. 1998, Kotas et al. 2004).

In the Eastern Pacific, Alfaro-Shigueto et al. (2007) document leatherback bycatch in the coastal gillnet and artisanal longline fisheries targeting mahi mahi (*Coryphaena hippurus*), sharks and rays in Peru.

In the central North Pacific, the Hawaii-based shallow-set longline fishery was closed in 2001 due to its interactions with leatherbacks; the fishery was then modified and re-opened in 2004 with measures to minimize bycatch and post-hooking mortality (National Marine Fisheries Service 2004). Since 2004, the fishery has reduced interaction rates by 82% (Gilman et al. 2007, National Marine Fisheries Service 2008).

Based on logbook records (1997–2001), an estimated 400 sea turtles may be incidentally captured in Australian longline fisheries (tuna, billfish) each year; more than 60% of these are leatherbacks (Robins et al. 2002). Mortality rates are unknown but presumed relatively low, perhaps 10–40 individuals per year based on published estimates of mortality elsewhere (summarized by Department of the Environment, Water, Heritage and the Arts 2008).

A global analysis integrating catch data from over 40 nations and bycatch data from 13 international observer programs, estimated that > 50,000 leatherbacks "…were likely taken as pelagic longline bycatch in 2000…" (Lewison et al. 2004). Based on estimates of immediate and delayed mortality as a result of interaction with longline gear (8–27% for leatherbacks, Lewison et al. 2004), many thousands of leatherbacks may die from their encounters with longline gear every year. In a follow-up study, Beverly and Chapman (2007) used effort data from Lewison et al. (2004) and bycatch data from Molony (2005) to estimate a bycatch rate approximately 20% of that estimated by Lewison et al. (2004).

In the Western and Central Pacific, Kaplan (2005) estimated that coastal sources led to a 13% annual mortality rate, compared with a point estimate of 12% from longlining; in the Eastern Pacific, coastal sources accounted for a 28% annual mortality rate, compared with 5% from longlining. Given the gaps in information for Pacific populations of leatherback turtles, including adequate bycatch data, Kaplan (2005) concluded that a large level of uncertainty exists in the face of competing risk factors. Dutton and Squires (2008) emphasized the integration of a broad suite of approaches into a holistic strategy that extends beyond reducing fishery bycatch mortality to reconcile conservation efforts with comercial use of marine resources.

Gillnets and driftnets.—In the southern latitudes of the Wider Caribbean Region, the world's largest leatherback nesting colonies are threatened by incidental capture in gillnets. In a national survey, gillnet fishing was conducted year-round by 71% of the fishermen interviewed; > 3000 adult leatherbacks were estimated to have been caught in the gillnet fishery in 2000 with ~ 27–34% mortality (Lee Lum 2006). Drift gillnets are also considered a serious threat in the Guianas (Bellail and Dintheer 1992, Hilterman and Goverse 2007) and Brazil (Thomé et al. 2007). Marcovaldi et al. (2006) report that leatherbacks comprise ~70% of all sea turtles captured in Brazilian driftnet shark fisheries. Fallabrino et al. (2006) and Laporta et al. (2006) report leatherbacks drowned in bottom gillnets set for shark and molluscs, respectively, off Uruguay.

Relevant data are scarce from Eastern Atlantic range States, but incidental capture and mortality associated with artisanal gillnets is reported from the Republic of Congo (including juveniles, range: 89–180.3 cm CCL, n = 50, Bal et al. 2007, Godgenger et al. 2009) and Benin (Dossa et al. 2007). Fretey (2001:89) references leatherbacks "…caught in fishing nets [in Morocco], including females which previously nested in French Guiana." Carr and Carr (1991) note that "most" subadult and adult leatherbacks caught in Angola during non-nesting months "…were caught incidentally in gillnets set for fish in inshore waters…" and Weir et al. (2007) made specific reference to a leatherback caught in "submerged monofilament netting" during more recent surveys of Angola.

In a rare Mediterranean report, a leatherback became "…entangled in the ropes of a trammel net…" off the coast of Syria in August 2004; it was released alive (Rees et al. 2004). Lazar et al. (2008) describes gillnets as the dominant threat to leatherbacks in the Adriatic Sea.

In the Eastern Pacific, Frazier and Brito Montero (1990) estimated that "…at least several hundreds…" of leatherbacks died per annum in tangle nets set for swordfish in Chilean waters. From 2000 to 2003, a dockside observer program in Peru documented 133 leatherbacks incidentially captured in artisanal fishing gear, including 101 (76%) in gillnets; 58.6% of the leatherback bycatch was retained for human consumption (Alfaro-Shigueto et al. 2007). Observer data from an experimental shark gillnet fishery off Oregon and Washington (United States) indicated that during the 1988 season, 13 leatherbacks were caught in 68 net sets, a catch rate of 0.19 turtles per set (Stick and Hreha 1989). After encountering and reporting a dead leatherback (~137 cm carapace) with "…gillnet chafe marks on its back, flippers and head…" off Newport Beach, California, in September 1982, commercial fishermen Bob and Mary Hitt commented to Stinson (1984), "We used to see about 10–12 turtles a year, but since the drift gillnetters we have not seen a live turtle in at least three years."

Balazs (1982) documented the death of leatherbacks in driftnets set in the central Pacific (35°–45°N), catch rates in a Yap trial fishery were high, and observer data indicated that at least 250 leatherbacks are killed per annum in the North Pacific squid driftnet fishery (Northridge 1990). Cheng (2006) noted that leatherbacks were present in China's waters mainly from April to December, and that "…fisheries bycatch is [their] main threat…"; Cheng and Chen (1997) documented a leatherback caught in a coastal setnet fishery in Taiwan "…and released at the scene." In Terengganu, Malaysia, an estimated 77 and 33 leatherbacks were caught incidentally in drift/gillnets in 1984 and 1985, respectively (Chan et al. 1988). In Australian waters, there are no known occurrences of leatherback bycatch in gillnets in recent years; however, historically, the northern Australian barramundi gillnet fishery and the southern Australian tuna driftnet fishery had low and presumed high impact, respectively (Limpus 2006).

In the Indian Ocean, off the coast of South Africa, 8% (1 to 11 turtles per year between 1993–2007) of the sea turtle bycatch in Natal Shark Board gillnets were leatherbacks (Nel 2008).

In a global review of driftnet bycatch, Northridge (1990) concluded that when coastal driftnet fisheries are considered, and the potential impact of the Pacific large mesh fishery and other tropical fisheries, where catch rates have not been studied, are taken into account, driftnet fisheries may be found to contribute significantly to the death of leatherbacks at sea.

Pot fisheries.—Lazell (1976) noted that pot buoys, draped with streamers of brown algae, may resemble, from the turtle's point of view, *Cyanea* jellyfish, a favorite leatherback prey item. He speculated that turtles approach these buoys quickly, reach for a potential meal, and become wrapped in buoy lines instead.

Summarizing a decade (1977–1987) of data, Prescott (1988) implicated entanglement (primarily in lobster pot lines) in 89% ($n = 51$) of adult leatherback strandings in Cape Cod Bay, Massachusetts. Similarly, from 1990–2000, 92 leatherbacks were reported entangled in pot lines from New York through Maine, suggesting that with the "…proliferation of pot gear in Massachusetts shelf waters, where leatherbacks are known to forage, [the] potential for interaction is high…" (Dwyer et al. 2003). In Florida, 8% ($n = 44$) of leatherback strandings between 1980 and 2007 were found entangled in the buoy line of a crab trap or lobster pot (A. Foley, pers. comm.).

Sánchez et al. (2008) reported the incidental capture of three leatherbacks in May 2004 in Uruguay (southwestern Atlantic Ocean), entangled in the mainline of a snail trap fishing vessel in May 2004.

In the Eastern Atlantic, two of six turtles obtained for gut content analyses perished entangled in lobster pot lines in English waters (Hartog and van Nierop 1984).

Limpus (2009) observed that entanglement in buoy lines to rock lobster pots may be the most significant cause of death from human-related activities for the leatherback turtle in Australian continental shelf waters. A Tasmanian study indicated that 75% of leatherbacks entangled in lobster pot lines are released alive, although post-release survival rates are unknown (Department of the Environment, Water, Heritage and the Arts 2008).

Duangsawasdi (2006) reported that a female leatherback "…died after becoming entangled in a crab trap line at Thaimuang Beach, Phanga Province…" in Thailand.

Trawl fisheries.—In the Western Atantic, leatherbacks are rare but regular casualties of shrimp nets, with interview data indicating that 24 were caught 3–5 km from shore during the spring of 1976 in Georgia, United States (Hillestad et al. 1978). Lee and Palmer (1981) provide records of six leatherbacks caught by trawlers in North Carolina, United States waters.

In Canada, in August 1946, an adult leatherback was accidentally captured by a longline trawl in Trinity Bay, Newfoundland (Squires 1954), and in just two months (August and September) in 1986, eight leatherbacks were captured in groundfish gillnets and trawls in Newfoundland waters (J. Lien, pers. comm.). In Venezuela, onboard observers identified leatherbacks to comprise 12.5% of turtles captured between February 1991 and December 1993 (Marcano and Alió 2000). Incidental capture in shrimp trawls is also documented in the Guianas (Tambiah 1994).

In the 1980s, an estimated 400 leatherbacks were caught annually off the coast of Terengganu, Malaysia (Brahim et al. 1987); trawl nets were responsible for some 60% of the total number of turtles caught, with the balance attributed to driftnets (Chan et al. 1988). Pilcher et al. (2006) attributed "…the single, largest confirmed record of leatherback turtles in the Red Sea…" to bycatch records from observers onboard foreign trawlers in Eritrean waters (Red Sea), where 39 leatherback catches were recorded, or about 1.6% of the sea turtle catches between 1996 and 2005. In contrast, Limpus (2006) reported that leatherbacks were rarely caught in trawling activities (< 1 death per year between the 1970s and the 1990s) in Australian waters and, since the introduction of Turtle Excluder Devices (TED) in the Northern Prawn Fishery in 2000, there have been no records of leatherback bycatch (Perdrau and Garvey 2005).

Regional summaries and general notes.—In the Western Atlantic, Bleakney (1965) presented records of leatherback sightings from eastern Canada (1889–1964) and remarked that in 46% ($n = 26$) of cases, the turtle had been entangled, often fatally, in a net or drowned in fishing gear. A later (1976–1985) analysis of leatherback sightings in Newfoundland revealed that 70% ($n = 20$) had been captured by salmon nets, herring nets, gillnets, trawl lines, or crab pot lines (Goff and Lien 1988).

In a detailed survey of hundreds of European Atlantic sea turtle sightings, Brongersma (1972) provided documentation of the untimely death of male and female leatherbacks, typically adults or near adults, in a wide variety of nets and other fishing paraphernalia, including pot lines, buoy ropes, mackerel driftnets, trawl nets, sardine driftnets, shark lines with herring bait, and ropes and wires. The largest leatherback on record drowned after becoming entangled in whelk-fishing lines off the coast of Wales, U.K. (Morgan 1990).

Bycatch is also a problem the full length of West Africa, from the Canary Islands ("…where the bodies of turtles caught accidentally in industrial fishing nets wash up on the shore…" Fretey 2001) to Namibia, where leatherbacks are "…caught incidentally with driftnets, longlines and in trawls…" (Bianchi et al. 1999). Fretey (2001) confirms the presence of *D. coriacea* in 26 West African countries: he reports the killing of gravid females on the nesting beach in 14 of these countries, including all major nesting grounds, and the incidental capture of leatherbacks in fishing nets (and by harpoon in Guinea) in 17 countries. In nearly all cases the meat is consumed as part of traditional practice, in only four countries was it noted that meat was sold in a market setting.

In the Indian Ocean, national reports contributed information that led Humphrey and Salm (1996) and later Hamann et al. (2006) to confirm that bycatch is a serious survival threat to leatherback turtles on the eastern seaboard of Africa.

IUCN (2001) recognizes Sri Lanka and the Andaman and Nicobar Islands of India as the last three areas in South Asia that have nesting populations of leatherback turtles. To quantify the problem of incidental catch in Sri Lanka, the Turtle Conservation Project interviewed 13,760 fishers to ascertain the scope of the bycatch problem. Fishers reported 5241 turtle entanglements during the period from November 1999 to June 2000 between Kalpitiya and Kirinda (Sri Lanka); 20% died and nearly one in 10 turtles caught was a leatherback. The "…fishermen were of the unanimous opinion that the mortality caused by their nets was the major cause for the decline in turtle populations [all species] around the island…" (Kapurusinghe and Saman 2005).

Summarizing non-breeding records of leatherbacks in Australian waters (1940–1975), Limpus and McLachlan (1979) reported on entanglement and/or drowning in shark nets, prawn trawls, buoy lines, shark lines and lobster pot lines.

Noteworthy is that bycatch issues are increasingly receiving attention at the highest levels of government, including at the International Fisheries Forums (2002–2008), the United States National Marine Fisheries Service's International Technical Expert Workshop on Marine Turtle Bycatch in Longline Fisheries (Long and Schroeder 2004) and Technical Workshop on Mitigating Sea Turtle Bycatch in Coastal Net Fisheries (Gilman 2009), the Bellagio Conferences on Sea Turtle Conservation in the Pacific (2003, 2007), the Expert Consultation on Interactions between Sea Turtles and Fisheries within an Ecosystem Context (Food and Agricultural Organization of the United Nations 2004), and the Technical Consultation on Sea Turtle Conservation and Fisheries (Food and Agricultural Organization of the United Nations 2005).

Some (Bache 2005, Eckert and Hemphill 2005) argue that because of their flagship appeal, sea turtles command attention in this arena, focusing science, technology, policy, and media attention on the highly complex issues of bycatch as they relate both to marine ecosystem management and the economics of fishing, and promoting a new regime of mechanisms and processes for handling emergent marine bycatch issues.

Progressive policy responses are evident worldwide. Using the Pacific region as an example, the Inter-American Tropical Tuna Commission (IATTC), which oversees longline fisheries operating in the eastern Pacific Ocean, requires vessels fishing for tuna and tuna-like species to take steps to reduce the frequency and severity of fishing gear interacting with turtles in accordance with Guidelines produced by the Food and Agricultural Organization (FAO) of the United Nations. The Western and Central Pacific Fisheries Commission (WCPFC) requires shallow-set longline fisheries to use either large circle hooks, whole finfish bait, or other mitigation measures proven to reduce interaction with or increase the survivorship of sea turtles.

The Pacific Islands Forum Fisheries Agency (FFA) has an Action Plan for Sea Turtle Bycatch Mitigation that covers a range of collaborative activities to be carried out by members, relevant Pacific Island regional organizations, research agencies and other concerned parties, and assists members in meeting the obligations of the WCPFC Sea Turtle Conservation and Management Measures. Both the IATTC and WCPFC require their members and cooperating non-members to safely handle and release sea turtles they encounter and provide bycatch data to their respective Secretariats.

The Indian Ocean Tuna Commission (IOTC), which includes member countries in the western Pacific Ocean, passed a Resolution in 2009 requiring members fishing for tuna and tuna-like species to implement the FAO Guidelines to reduce sea turtle mortality in fishing operations, as well as to safely handle and release entangled or by-caught sea turtles and to collect data on interactions with gillnets (I.K. Kelly, pers. comm.).

International trade.—The Convention on International Trade in Endangered Species of Wild Fauna and Flora (CITES) was established to protect wild species from the threat of over-exploitation by means of a system of import and export controls. The Convention regulates international trade in animals and plants, whether dead or alive, and any recognizable parts or derivatives thereof.

Dermochelys coriacea is listed (since 1977) in CITES-Appendix I, a designation that effectively bans international trade in specimens or products except by special permit showing that such trade is not detrimental to the survival of the species and that it is not for primarily commercial purposes (Lyster 1985). Only one country, Suriname, maintains a CITES reservation on *Dermochelys*, but "…the exemption is mostly a matter of principle…" (Reichart and Fretey 1993) because there is no international commercial trade in this species. Illegal, informal commerce does persist, however, especially between adjoining countries (Chacón and Eckert 2007, M. Girondot, pers. comm.).

Marine debris and pollution.—Drowning or debilitation resulting from entanglement in persistent marine debris (e.g., fishing line, fishing nets, cargo netting) poses a survival threat to all sea turtle species. Relevant literature is best summarized by Balazs (1985), O'Hara et al. (1986), Witzell and Teas (1994), and Lutcavage et al. (1997).

The ingestion of persistent marine debris, notably plastic bags, presumably mistaken for jellyfish, is a serious and pervasive threat to sea turtles on a global scale (Balazs 1985, Witzell and Teas 1994) and results in an undetermined number of deaths each year. Reviewing data available at the time, Mrosovsky (1981) concluded that "…44% of adult non-breeding leatherbacks have plastic in their stomachs." More recently, Mrosovsky et al. (2009) analyzed autopsy records of 408 leatherback turtles, spanning 123 years (1885–2007), and found that plastic was reported in 34% of these cases; "… blockage of the gut by plastic was mentioned in some accounts."

In the Western Atlantic, an adult stranded in New York in 1980 had ~180 m of heavy duty nylon fishing line in its gastrointestinal tract, with the leading end extending from its mouth (Sadove 1980). Of 15 leatherbacks washed ashore on Long Island (New York) during a 2–3 week period in the summer of 1982, 73% had as many as 15 plastic bags "…totally blocking their stomach openings…" (Luginbuhl 1982). In French Guiana, 51 of 101 leatherbacks necropsied had "floating debris" (mainly plastic bags) in their stomachs (Kelle and Feuillet 2008). Esophagus and stomach contents of two leatherbacks (135 cm, 136 cm CCL) stranded on the coast of Brazil between August 1997 and July 1998 included plastic bags as the main debris ingested, mostly white and colorless pieces (Bugoni et al. 2001).

In the Eastern Atlantic, 87% of leatherbacks examined near La Rochelle, France, had swallowed plastic (Duron and Duron 1980). In another case, the stomach of a leatherback was obstructed with plastic (Duguy et al. 1980) and the extreme emaciation of the animal, combined with its stomach pathology, suggested that plastic was what had killed it. In an assessment of mortality factors near the French coast of the Bay of Biscay, Duguy et al. (1998) concluded that "...the main threat for the species [was] the ingestion of floating waste." In September 1988, an adult male washed ashore at Porthtowan (England); "...death may have been caused by a polyethylene bag and fishing line caught in its throat..." (Penhallurick 1990).

In September 2000, an adult female leatherback died while being hauled aboard a swordfish longline vessel in the Azores; a variety of hard and soft plastic pieces were identified in the stomach and intestine and the authors concluded that "...cases of plastic ingestion are strongly underestimated in the Azores..." (Barreiros and Barcelos 2001). In the Mediterranean, Travaglini et al. (2006) collected and examined the digestive tract contents of four dead adult leatherbacks found between 1995 and 2005 in the mid-southern Tyrrhenian Sea (Italy), documenting ingestion of "...plastic, fishing lines and pieces of nets."

In the Eastern Pacific, 14% ($n = 140$) of leatherbacks captured in an illegal commercial fishery near Lima, Peru, in 1980 showed clear evidence of plastic twisted into elongate forms suggesting peristaltic transport; plastic bags and film were "common" in the intestinal tracts of leatherback carcasses discarded by these fishermen (Fritts 1982).

In the Western Pacific, Starbird and Audel (2000) documented an adult female, encountered during nesting in Papua, Indonesia (formerly Irian Jaya), that had partially ingested a nylon fishing net: "One end of the net was lodged within the digestive tract of the turtle, and the other end trailed out the left side of the turtle's mouth, where it had worn a fibrous groove at the joint of the mandibles. The net had a large cluster of goose-neck barnacles (*Lepas* spp., 0.5–2 cm length) attached. Two strands of the net (~ 1 m) were pulled from the turtle's mouth; the distal ends of the net were covered with blood. Further attempts to extract the net were discontinued as it was obviously damaging the turtle internally."

In the Indian Ocean, Hughes (1974a) reported that an adult female stranded in Natal, South Africa, "...had its duodenal tract completely filled by a sheet of heavy plastic..." and that this had undoubtedly contributed to the death of the animal.

Bacon (1970) opined that some injuries evident on nesting females coming ashore in Trinidad resulted from "...collisions with rocks or with the driftwood which is abundant offshore [the nesting beach]." Laurance et al. (2008) concluded that industrial logging, expanding rapidly in Central African rainforests, posed a direct threat to nesting by leatherback turtles because "...lost logs float out to sea and then often wash ashore, where they accumulate on beaches...," causing 8–14% of all nesting attempts "...to be aborted or disrupted." Similarly, upland deforestation in Costa Rica results in accumulations of "...a wide variety of debris and garbage on the beach..." that can block access to gravid females and fatally trap hatchlings (Chacón and Eckert 2007). The problem has also been documented in the Guianas (Fretey 1981, Pritchard and Trebbau 1984).

Little is known about the effects of other forms of pollution. Metal contaminant (trace metals, arsenic, selenium) analyses on 35 adult and subadult leatherbacks entangled in fishing gear or found stranded around the coast of Britain (1992–1996) indicated "...considerable interindividual variance in the levels of metals investigated...," but general patterns were similar (i.e., liver levels generally exceeding those of muscle) and levels were described as low overall (Godley et al. 1998). Similar results were reported for leatherbacks in French Guiana (Guirlet et al. 2008). Mckenzie et al. (1999) reported concentrations of individual chlorobiphenyls and organochlorine pesticides in sea turtle tissues collected from the Mediterranean (Cyprus, Greece) and European Atlantic waters (Scotland) between 1994 and 1996; results from two adult male leatherbacks showed concentrations were highest in adipose tissue and ranged from 47–178 mg kg^{-1} wet wt.

Deem et al. (2006) reported that organochlorine and polychlorinated biphenyl (PCB) concentrations were below measurable limits in blood from leatherbacks in Gabon; in addition, lead and mercury levels were significantly lower than those typically found in bird and mammal species, suggesting that they were unlikely to have adverse health effects. Davenport et al. (1990) and Davenport and Welch (1990) reported similar findings for concentrations of PCBs and trace metals in an adult male leatherback that stranded in Wales, U.K. (see Storelli and Marcotrigiano 2003).

Stewart et al. (2008) and Guirlet et al. (2008) concluded that contaminant concentrations were conferred from female leatherbacks to their eggs.

Other.—Embryonic mortality resulting from tidal inundation and erosion claims > 50% of nests per annum at some locations (Mrosovsky 1983, Whitmore and Dutton 1985, Eckert 1987). At study sites on the Caribbean coastline of Colombia and adjoining Panama, only 0.12% ($n = 12{,}159$) of clutches were actually laid in the intertidal zone, but erosion and inundation claimed 16–48% of nests at the three largest rookeries (Patino-Martinez et al. 2008).

Adult females in French Guiana are sometimes unable to reach the sea after nesting, having become trapped behind accumulations of dead trees, impaled against a root or branch, or held prisoner between stumps deeply embedded in the sand (Pritchard 1971b; Fretey 1977, 1981). Alternatively, females disoriented by an inland lagoon or swamp may mistake its reflection for that of the sea and orient toward it after nesting. Turtles mired in the soft mud of a mangrove swamp or river delta typically die from dehydration, exertion or asphyxiation (Fretey 1977, but see Goverse and Hilterman 2003).

The degradation and loss of habitat, nesting habitat in particular, from industrialization and urbanization along the coast (including "expansion of villages": Kinch 2006), is a threat to the survival of sea turtles worldwide (Lutcavage et al. 1997, Formia et al. 2003). In areas where shoreline development coincides with leatherback nesting, both gravid females and hatchlings can become disoriented by artificial lights, straying landward after nesting and dying of exposure or exhaustion (e.g., Western Atlantic: Villanueva-Mayor et al. 2003, L'association Kwata 2009; Eastern Atlantic: Sounguet et al. 2004, Deem et al. 2007). The nesting beach at Ma' Daerah (Terengganu, Malaysia) is "very brightly lit" at night by the burning of flue gas at nearby petrochemical plants; solid waste disposal, both on land and at sea, is also a threat (Sharma and Min Min 2002).

The "main threat" to sea turtles in the Andaman and Nicobar Islands (the most important *Dermochelys* rookery in the northern Indian Ocean) is sand mining for construction (Andrews et al. 2006). Coastal armoring is also reported as a serious threat to nesting habitat in India (Shanker and Choudhury 2006); e.g., in Kerala "…seawalls cover a total length of over 420 km, thus rendering over 70% of the coast totally unsuitable for nesting…" (Dileepkumar and Jayakumar 2006).

Strong weather events, including tsunamis (Hamann et al. 2006b) and unusually high "king tides" (Kinch 2006, Hitipeuw et al. 2007, Tapilatu and Tiwari 2007) threaten coastal nesting habitat. The effects of climate change on leatherback turtles are unclear. A recent review (National Marine Fisheries Service and United States Fish and Wildlife Service 2007) noted that while "…global warming is expected to expand foraging habitats into higher latitude waters (James et al. 2006c, McMahon and Hays 2006), and there is some concern that increasing temperatures may increase feminization on some beaches (Mrosovsky et al. 1984, Hawkes et al. 2007)…," spatial nesting strategies may mitigate concerns about feminizing hatchling sex ratios (Kamel and Mrosovsky 2004) and, in general, a broad geographic distribution and relatively weak nesting beach fidelity (Dutton et al. 1999) may contribute to species-level resilience.

Finally, political instability, civil war, social and religious tension, and/or pervasive poverty can hinder conservation and management efforts at national and regional scales (Formia et al. 2003, Weir et al. 2007).

Population Dynamics

Population dynamics models have been published for leatherbacks nesting in the Eastern Pacific (Spotila et al. 1996), the Western Atlantic (Girondot et al. 2007), and the Western Pacific (National Marine Fisheries Service 2008); "…however, the lack of details for specific variables only serves to reduce the confidence of the results of this exercise…" (Girondot et al. 2007). Models evaluating survival rates of nesting females (e.g., Dutton et al. 2005, Santidrián Tomillo et al. 2007) under different nesting population trend regimes are also available. As our understanding of basic life history parameters grows, these models will become more robust and useful. In the meantime, the status of sea turtle populations is studied largely through trend analysis, incorporating current and historical records of the number of nests or females. Long-term nesting beach studies are providing important insights into demographic variables (e.g., fecundity), but more specific age (or size) class survival rates, wild growth rates (including age at maturity and longevity), and a deeper understanding of population units are still needed. Information on population structure, including sex ratios and juvenile-to-adult ratios, will become increasingly available as in-water research progresses.

Chapter 5: Protection and Management

Conservation Status

The IUCN *Red List of Threatened Species* is the most widely accepted method for assessing species conservation status on a global scale (Rodrigues et al. 2006, Hoffmann et al. 2008, Mace et al. 2008). The leatherback sea turtle first appeared on the *Red List* in 1982, when it was classified as Endangered (Groombridge 1982). Primarily owing to rapid and catastrophic declines in the Pacific Ocean (Spotila et al. 2000), it was reclassified in 2000 as Critically Endangered (Baillie et al. 2004).

The aim of the *Red List* is to assess the extinction risk of individual species using the standardized IUCN Red List Categories and Criteria, and therefore identifying species and regions most in need of conservation action. The results of the *Red List* can identify conservation priorities and inform policy makers in order to target species most in need (Hoffmann et al. 2008). *Red List* results are also used to inform the public and to motivate the global community to reduce the risk of species extinctions (Baillie et al. 2004).

Legal Status

Fretey (2001) has argued that it is "…aberrant to effectively protect sea turtles in one part of their range only to see them subjected to uncontrolled slaughter in another." The leatherback exemplifies this challenge, facing many and significant risks during long-distance migrations that cross the jurisdictions of multiple range States, as well as the high seas. Egg-bearing females, for example, may benefit from complete protection on the nesting beach but be subject to take after entering the waters of a different national jurisdiction. Notwithstanding the progress that has been made to introduce legal frameworks at global and regional scales in recent decades, the international regime for sea turtle conservation is inconsistent at best, without due consideration given to overall governance and coherence issues (United Nations Environment Programme-Convention on Migratory Species 2000, Bräutigam and Eckert 2006). Even where adequate legal protection exists at the national level, the effectiveness of implementation is often stifled by weak political institutions, inadequate law enforcement, lack of capacity or funding, and fragile public support in the face of entrenched poverty, restricted dietary choices, and/or traditional cultural practices and beliefs (Navid 1982, Roberts et al. 2004, Bräutigam and Eckert 2006, Seminoff and Dutton 2007).

The leatherback is explicitly protected under a number of legally binding international agreements, as well as other instruments focusing specifically on turtle conservation and management (recently summarized in Frazier 2002).

Globally the species is included (since 1977) in CITES-Appendix I, a designation that effectively bans trade in specimens or products except by special permit confirming that such trade is not detrimental to the survival of the species, and that it is not for primarily commercial purposes (Lyster 1985). The species is also included in CITES-Appendix I of the Convention on the Conservation of Migratory Species of Wild Animals (CMS), which establishes specific protection obligations among contracting Parties, including a requirement to prohibit the hunting, fishing, capturing or harassing of listed species, as well as measures to conserve their habitat. Furthermore, CMS member States are encouraged to conclude even more comprehensive collaborative agreements for species listed in CITES-Appendix II, including the leatherback.

Various instruments provide for the conservation of species and habitats at the regional level. These include the Protocol concerning Specially Protected Areas and Wildlife (SPAW) to the Convention for the Protection and Development of the Marine Environment of the Wider Caribbean Region (Cartagena Convention); the Convention on Nature Protection and Wildlife Preservation in the Western Hemisphere (Washington or Western Hemisphere Convention); the Convention on European Wildlife and Natural Habitats (Bern Convention); the Convention for the Protection, Management and Development of the Marine and Coastal Environment of the Eastern African Region (Nairobi Convention) and its related protocol on Protected Areas and Wild Fauna; and the Convention for the Protection of the Natural Resources and Environment of the South Pacific Region. Given that the coverage of these instruments is necessarily broad, any provisions with respect to leatherback turtles tend to be generic in scope.

Only four multilateral instruments concluded in recent years focus exclusively on the conservation of sea turtles and their habitats. The Inter-American Convention for the Protection and Conservation of Sea Turtles (IAC), containing specific conservation and management measures and detailed coordination arrangements, is legally binding upon its members in the Americas. In addition, non-binding regional agreements concluded under the auspices of CMS encourage unified recovery and management planning among range States and are highly relevant. The Memorandum of Understanding on the Conservation and Management of Marine Turtles and their Habitats of the Indian Ocean and South-East Asia (IOSEA) puts in place a framework through which States of this region can work together to conserve and replenish depleted sea turtle populations for which they share responsibility. This objective is actively pursued through the collective implementation of an associated Conservation and Management Plan (Hykle 2002). Signatories to the complementary CMS Memorandum of Understanding Concerning Conservation Measures for Marine Turtles of the Atlantic Coast of Africa (Abidjan Memorandum) acknowledge "…their shared responsibility for the conservation and wise management of the sea turtle populations frequenting their waters and shores [and] agree to work closely together to improve the conservation status of the sea turtles and the habitats upon which they depend." A non-binding Memorandum of Understanding of a Tri-National Partnership between the Governments of Indonesia, Papua New Guinea, and Solomon Islands on the Conservation and Management of Western Pacific Leatherback Turtles is also germaine.

Treaties that promote the protection of the marine environment also provide important legal underpinnings for conservation action. Persistent marine debris threatens the survival of leatherback sea turtles through both ingestion and entanglement (see Chapter 4, *Mortality, Factors causing or affecting mortality*, above), and a variety of legal regimes exist to address the problem of ocean dumping both regionally and internationally. These include, among others, the Law of the Sea Convention, Convention on the Prevention of Marine Pollution by Dumping of Wastes and Other Matter (London Convention), International Convention for the Prevention of Pollution from Ships (MARPOL), and the Jakarta Mandate to the Convention on Biological Diversity, which relates to the marine environment, as well as a number of regional agreements, such as those sponsored by the United Nations Environment Programme (UNEP) Regional Seas Programme (McPherson 1985, Lentz 1987, Wold 2002).

Regulatory Measures

Regulatory measures typically prohibit or restrict direct take of eggs and/or turtles, indirect take such as through interactions with fisheries, and domestic sale of or international trade in parts or products, in addition to mitigating, through both law and policy, threats to habitat.

As noted above, at the international level the leatherback is protected under a number of negotiated agreements that, ideally, promote a progressive legal framework at the national or provincial level. For example, Parties to the SPAW Protocol (see *Legal status*, above), are obliged to strengthen their regulatory framework to "… ensure total protection and recovery…" to the species, including prohibiting take, possession and killing; commercial trade (including eggs, parts or products); and, to the extent possible, disturbance during periods of breeding, incubation or migration, as well as other periods of biological stress. Similar obligations are explicit in other international treaties, and these can lend strong impetus to regulatory change at the national level (Anderson 2001).

At the national level, the leatherback benefits from varying degrees of legal protection across its range, and in some instances this protection has been in place for decades. To give a few examples: the species is listed on Schedule 1 of the Indian Wildlife (Protection) Act, 1972; as Endangered throughout its range under the United States Endangered Species Act, 1973; as Vulnerable under the Australian Environment Protection and Biodiversity Conservation Act, 1999; and on Schedule 1 of Canada's Species at Risk Act (SARA) 2003. In Papua New Guinea, the leatherback is the only sea turtle on the protected species list of the Flora and Fauna Protection Control Act, 1976. However, unified regulatory regimes across range States—whether with respect to moratoria or synchronized seasonal fishery closures—designed to benefit the species at a population level have not been achieved in any geographic region (Fretey 2001, Kinan 2005, Bräutigam and Eckert 2006, Hamann et al. 2006a).

In addition to controls on exploitation, there are numerous instances where habitats have been protected. In the case of the Western Central Atlantic region, where Eckert and Hemphill (2005) summarized available data, Sandy Point National Wildlife Refuge (St. Croix, USVI) is recognized as the first federal refuge established specifically to protect sea turtles in the United States. Further south, nesting grounds for some of the world's largest known leatherback breeding colonies are protected by national law: Réserve Naturelle de l'Amana in French Guiana and the Prohibited Areas of Fishing Pond, Matura and Grande Riviere in Trinidad. Costa Rica protects the largest nesting colonies in Central America on both its Caribbean

(Gandoca/Manzanillo National Wildlife Refuge) and Pacific (Las Baulas National Park) shores.

Protected areas designed with leatherbacks in mind are normally biased toward terrestrial habitat and ignore or underrate the need for protecting marine areas. The usual case is for the terrestrial component of the reserve to reflect the biological requirements of nesting, whilst the marine extension, if it exists, bears no resemblance to the species' spatial habitat requirements, thereby reducing its effectiveness. For example, Critical Habitat designated off Sandy Point National Wildlife Refuge includes the waters from the 100 fathom isobath shoreward (National Marine Fisheries Service 1979), although gravid leatherbacks spend very little time in this zone, except to access the nesting beach, but rather range widely offshore during their inter-nesting intervals (Eckert 2002b). Similarly, in the case of the Réserve Naturelle de l'Amana, the offshore component extends only 50–500 m seaward of the nesting beach (Journal Officiel de la République Française 1998). The situation is slightly better in South Africa, where primary nesting beaches have been fully protected in Marine Reserves since 1976 and, in 1998, 200 km of nesting habitat to 5 nm offshore were included in the Greater St. Lucia Wetland Park World Heritage Site (G.R. Hughes, pers. comm.).

There are as yet no protected seascapes designed specifically to safeguard leatherback migration corridors, despite the fact that the species is well known to cross ocean basins to reach widely separated foraging and nesting grounds (see Chapter 3, *Behavior, Migrations and local movements,* above). This highlights both an important gap in the international management framework and the need for international cooperation in taking effective conservation action (Eckert 2006, Turtle Expert Working Group 2007, Shillinger et al. 2008).

An example of a management regime designed to respond to operative threats in a migration corridor is available from the United States. In October 1995, federal regulations established all inshore and offshore waters from Cape Canaveral, Florida to the North Carolina/Virginia border as the 'Leatherback Conservation Zone,' providing for short-term closures of areas in that zone when high abundances of leatherbacks were documented (National Marine Fisheries Service 1995). The ruling was instigated because of seasonal pulses of leatherback strandings associated with their winter and spring migrations; during this time, the turtles, too large to be accommodated by the escape openings of most federally approved Turtle Excluder Devices (TED), were more likely to wash ashore dead. A decade later the ruling is moot because the mandatory use of TEDs with openings sufficient to release the half-ton turtles became law in 2003 throughout the Leatherback Conservation Zone (National Marine Fisheries Service 2003).

Following a consultation mandated by section 7 of the United States Endangered Species Act on the issuance of a permit to take endangered and threatened marine mammals in the California-Oregon drift gillnet fishery, NMFS implemented a time/area closure based on where the majority of leatherback takes had been observed (National Marine Fisheries Service 2001c). The Pacific Leatherback Conservation Area (PLCA) was established in 2001 and prohibits (annually between August 15 and November 15) drift gillnet fishing from Point Sur (36°N) on the California coast seaward to 129°W and north to 45°N on the Oregon coast. The PLCA constitutes 200,000 square miles of the United States' west coast Exclusive Economic Zone and is currently under consideration by NMFS as Critical Habitat for the leatherback (National Marine Fisheries Service 2010).

On a grander scale, the decline of the leatherback has provided impetus for the Eastern Tropical Pacific Seascape Initiative, which proposes an expansive international marine protected area delineated by the exclusive economic zones of Panama, Costa Rica, Ecuador, and Colombia, including their offshore islands, such as Cocos, Gorgona, Mal Pelo, and the Galapagos Islands (Shillinger 2005, United Nations Educational, Scientific and Cultural Organization 2006). The boundaries of this seascape encompass feeding zones and migratory corridors determined from satellite tracking of leatherbacks since the mid-1990s (Seminoff et al. 2007a). Related to this is Resolution 4.111 adopted at the 2008 World Conservation Congress (Barcelona, Spain), which "…requests the United Nations to urge states and regional fisheries management organizations to permanently protect the leatherback turtle and hammerhead sharks through the control and management of the fishing effort…" including through gear-specific solutions and "…a network of spatial and temporal closures of those fisheries that interact with sea turtles and pelagic sharks in scientifically documented biological corridors in the Eastern Tropical Pacific and elsewhere…" (International Union for the Conservation of Nature 2009).

Management Strategies

None of the leatherback's major nesting grounds were discovered before the 1950s, and many of them were only found in the 1960s and 1970s (Pritchard 1997). This active management for the most part was initiated by the leatherback's listing under the United States Endangered Species Act, to various other international conventions in the mid-1970s, and to the assessment and listing on the IUCN *Red List of Threatened Species* in the early 1980s.

Management strategies seek to ensure the survival of threatened and endangered sea turtles by implementing the specific mandates of local, national, and international regulatory regimes. Such strategies typically embrace a suite of research, conservation, education and outreach, and policy initiatives designed to document population abundance, distribution, and trends; identify and fill information gaps; mitigate threats (direct, indirect); and promote public awareness of the species' plight.

Species-specific recovery planning processes assemble the most recent data, evaluate contemporary threats, facilitate dialogue, and promote consensus on priority actions, thereby playing an important role in fostering (and sustaining) commitment on the part of governments, NGOs, communities, and industries to a wide range of management strategies. For leatherbacks, these have included significant human and financial investments in nesting beach surveillance, egg relocation programs, beach clean-ups, surveys of habitat use, bycatch reduction, attention to coastal zone management issues (e.g., beachfront lighting mitigation), designation of protected areas, and distribution of educational and outreach materials, among others.

In the United States, for example, species-specific recovery plans (National Marine Fisheries Service and United States Fish and Wildlife Service 1992, 1998) mandated under the federal Endangered Species Act define criteria that must be met in order for the species to be eligible for delisting [no longer classified as Endangered] under the Act. For Atlantic (including Caribbean) leatherback turtles, these criteria include: adult female population increases over a period of 25 years (as evidenced by a significant trend in the number of nests laid at key sites), nesting habitat where at least 75% of the nesting activity is protected in public ownership, and all priority one tasks successfully implemented.

In the Pacific, all regional populations that use United States' waters must be identified to source beaches, each population must average 5000 females ("…or a biologically reasonable estimate based on the goal of maintaining a stable population in perpetuity…") estimated to nest annually, nesting populations at source beaches must be stable or increasing over a 25-year monitoring period, foraging grounds are "healthy environments" and foraging populations show statistically significant increases at key sites, and all priority one tasks are implemented (summarized in National Marine Fisheries Service and United States Fish and Wildlife Service 2007).

Management in any context is most typically directed toward nesting beaches; the literature is replete with accounts of field projects designed to safeguard beaches and to promote the survival of gravid females and eggs. However, marine habitat protection is also an important component of any comprehensive management strategy. Identifying and protecting "…important foraging and other marine habitats…" receives a high priority ranking in recovery plans developed for United States'

populations of leatherback turtles (National Marine Fisheries Service and United States Fish and Wildlife Service 1992, 1998), but adequately protecting important marine habitats is likely to be problematic, given that migratory corridors and many known foraging areas are located beyond national jurisdictions in both the Atlantic (Morreale et al. 1996; Ferraroli et al. 2004; James et al. 2005b, 2005c; Eckert 2006) and Pacific (Benson et al. 2007a, Shillinger et al. 2008) basins.

All major leatherback populations face threats from artisanal and commercial fisheries, and several mitigative measures have been promulgated. In the United States, these actions include: designation of Leatherback Conservation Zones (see *Regulatory Measures,* above), research into large circle hook technology and bait alternatives to reduce bycatch associated with longlines (Watson et al. 2005; Gilman et al. 2006, 2007), requirements for enlarged openings (to accommodate leatherback girth) in TEDs designed to reduce bycatch associated with trawling (National Marine Fisheries Service 2003), and the suspension of commercial fisheries, such as closure of the Hawaii-based longline fishery in 2001 due to bycatch of sea turtle species (National Marine Fisheries Service 2004, Kinan and Dalzell 2005).

Successful long-term solutions are elusive, and closure of commercial fisheries may invite transferred effects. For example, when the Hawaii-based longline fishery closed there was a reported influx into the United States of lower priced, imported swordfish from unregulated foreign fisheries estimated to have an impact on protected species an order of magnitude greater than the Hawaii-based fleet (Bartram and Kaneko 2004, Sarmiento 2006, Rausser et al. 2009).

Developing 'turtle safe' fishing gear technology that is both effective in reducing interactions and mortality while practical for fishery implementation, coupled with measures to address mortality in other life stages, is a widely accepted approach to preventing species extinction (Kaplan 2005, Gilman et al. 2007, Dutton and Squires 2008). By embracing conservation efforts on the nesting beach, as well as fisher-led processes to define alternatives to the use of coastal gillnets that ensnare thousands of gravid leatherbacks every year and compromise fisher income through damaged gear and lost time, Trinidad models a uniquely intergrated approach (Eckert and Eckert 2005, Eckert 2008).

Gaps and Recommendations

That the leatherback sea turtle is a shared marine resource is undisputed. Transoceanic migrations of adults between foraging and breeding grounds are documented, as are the transboundary movements of nesting females within reproductive seasons (resulting in nesting in multiple national jurisdictions). The recovery of the species is clearly dependent upon successful management of threats at the level of Large Marine Ecosystems (LME). An identified challenge is the need for a coordinated, cross-sectoral approach at both diagnostic and operational levels, within and between governments, NGOs, community groups, and other actors to devise solutions to the particularly complex management issues, such as the socio-economics of over-exploitation that these animals currently face.

In the Western Atlantic, a review of sea turtle management and use regimes in 26 nations and territories (Bräutigam and Eckert 2006) suggested the following priorities for immediate action at the national level, and these are broadly applicable to other regions:

- Conduct comprehensive frame surveys (catch and use assessments) to quantify and characterize exploitation, including the landing of turtles at sea or hunting on nesting beaches, the exchange and marketing of turtles and turtle products, the numbers and types of fishers (and gears) involved; processing and marketing patterns, and the importance to livelihoods of the income derived from exploitation of sea turtles;

- Legally establish scientifically-based limits on exploitation, including maximum size limits that protect large juveniles and adult turtles at sea and full protection for nesting turtles;

- Quantify levels of incidental mortality, and implement measures to reduce or eliminate it through time-area closures and/or alternative types of gear or fishing methodology;

- Establish and implement population monitoring programs, especially for the largest colonies, to document population size and trends *in situ*;

- Implement an outreach strategy to increase awareness of and appreciation for the conservation of leatherback turtles, including relationships with broader agendas surrounding land use and development patterns, biodiversity conservation, economic priorities, and cultural norms;

- Design and implement strategies to increase compliance with legal controls on exploitation, trade and other activities impacting on sea turtles; and

- Increase government participation in regional agreements and fora that provide an operational basis for a unified, science-based and multilateral response to species management and recovery.

Recommendations for leatherback turtle conservation in the Eastern Atlantic include an "obvious focus" on Gabon and the Congo, including population monitoring, protection of nest sites, and evaluation of conservation methods; surveys of lesser known nesting areas judged to be "well frequented" in west Africa; measures to reduce direct take ("…except for a few African ethnic groups which do not consume meat, the leatherback turtle is slaughtered everywhere…"); creation of a transborder marine park joining Mayumba and Conkouati (with adequate anti-poaching resources); and an emphasis on basic research (e.g., genetic studies, seasonal movements, biometrics) (Fretey 2001).

The Marine Turtle Conservation Strategy and Action Plan for the Western Indian Ocean (International Union for the Conservation of Nature 1996), although not specific to leatherback turtles, makes generic recommendations focused on communication and information exchange (including training, standardized methodologies for research and management, and a regional database), assessing population size and trend, and monitoring direct take and the impact of fisheries. The Marine Turtle Conservation Action Plan for the Northern Indian Ocean made similar recommendations, lending impetus, in 1999, to the launch of India's "Project Sea Turtle" aimed at identifying and protecting important nesting sites and migratory routes, reducing bycatch, and building capacity for conservation through training, networking, and public awareness (Choudhury et al. 2000, Sharma 2006).

An assessment of the conservation status of the leatherback turtle in more than 40 countries of the Indian Ocean and South-East Asia region (Hamann et al. 2006a) identified gaps in basic biological information, including population genetics and life history attributes of nesting and foraging populations, as well as gaps in management relating to take of eggs, hatchling production and standard monitoring. The report also drew attention to other pertinent issues (direct harvest of turtles, depredation of eggs, incomplete nesting distribution data) and specific research and management needs were identified both geographically and thematically. The report served as an impetus for the Fourth Meeting of IOSEA Signatory States (Muscat, Oman in March 2006) to propose specific recommendations for follow-up action, framed in terms of more than 20 results-oriented projects/activities aimed at leatherback turtles.

In the South Pacific, the Marine Turtle Action Plan 2008–2012 (South Pacific Regional Environment Programme 2007) states that "…marine turtles play an integral ecological role in the functioning of marine habitats [and] an integral part in the traditions of Pacific Island people…" and that information exchange and collaboration at national, regional and international levels is essential "… in order for conservation and management efforts for marine turtles to be effective." To this end, the Action Plan makes recommendations designed to enhance partnerships, reduce threats, build capacity, increase awareness, strengthen policy and legislation (including to promote and protect traditional knowledge and customary practices), support research and monitoring, and achieve sustainable development.

Gaps and priorities for sea turtle research and management in the Western Pacific region were summarized in a 2002 workshop convened by the Western Pacific Regional Fisheries Management Council (Kinan 2002). They include conducting population assessments, identifying nesting and foraging habitats, establishing index monitoring sites (in particular for leatherbacks within the Indo-Malay archipelago of Indonesia, Papua New Guinea, and the Solomon Islands), quantifying directed take and indigenous harvest of eggs and turtles, identifying the source and quantity of bycatch and pelagic mortality in fisheries, and promoting conservation programs to "…increase production of hatchlings at nesting beaches." At the first meeting of the Western Pacific Leatherback Turtle Working Group (Kinan 2005), local and regional experts from Indonesia, Papua New Guinea, Solomon Islands, and Vanuatu catalogued nesting beaches and developed a threat matrix that ranked data deficiencies, directed harvest, and bycatch in coastal fisheries as the most significant threats to leatherback turtles in this region.

To achieve population recovery in the Eastern Pacific, Sarti M. (2002) proposed continuing programs to protect nesting turtles and eggs, to establish regional fisheries programs and agreements to "…minimize or eliminate incidental capture…," to strengthen awareness programs in local communities, to provide economic incentives for the development of alternative economic activities, and to avoid "tourist and urban developments" at important nesting grounds. Other authors have also highlighted the importance of identifying viable livelihood alternatives to killing sea turtles, and providing appropriate community-level assistance through training, financing, market access, and so on (Formia et al. 2003, Kinch 2006, Chacón and Eckert 2007).

Among the alternative economic activities often cited to reduce community reliance on the direct take of sea turtles is ecotourism. According to Troëng and Drews (2004), "…non-consumptive use generates more revenue, has greater economic multiplying effects, has greater potential for economic growth, creates more support for management, and generates proportionally more jobs, social development and employment opportunities for women than consumptive use." Notwithstanding, conservation objectives are unlikely to be met unless residents are directly involved and receiving tangible benefits from the ecotourism venture. In addition, sea turtle ecotourism programs can also generate public support and goodwill toward conservation objectives. In South Africa, engaging with the private sector in using their tourists and presence to give added protection to nesting females "has proved to be an invaluable addition to the protection strategy for sea turtles." (G.R. Hughes, pers. comm.).

Fully addressing the threats to leatherbacks, in particular fisheries bycatch and the degradation of tropical coastlines important for nesting, necessitates greatly expanding and enhancing the effectiveness of conservation and fisheries management efforts at regional and global scales. As noted by Eckert and Hykle (2008), this will rest largely on the ability to fully utilize, and strengthen, when necessary, global and regional treaties, intergovernmental agreements, trade regimes and policy initiatives; international partnerships, facilitated by global information tools and increasing recognition of interdependence; population-level research, facilitated by advanced technologies (e.g., satellites, genetic tools); habitat protection, including ecosystem-level management regimes and transboundary parks; and information-sharing, including training, mentoring, networking, and technology transfer, at grassroots levels.

The importance of taking remedial action cannot be overemphasized. Widespread egg collection, fisheries-related capture and mortality, loss or degradation of habitat to human settlements and industrialization, and, in some cases, uncontrolled take of (typically egg-bearing) adults have been described as management concerns for all major breeding assemblages. With fewer than five "large" nesting colonies (> 5000 nests laid per year; Troëng et al. 2004; also see Chapter 2, *Total area*, above) left on Earth and in light of the near-extirpation in recent years of the two largest colonies (Terengganu, Malaysia: Chan and Liew 1996; Pacific coast of Mexico: Sarti M. et al. 1996, Eckert and Sarti M. 1997, Spotila et al. 2000), it is not unimaginable that further serious declines will occur.

While there is cautious optimism in the Eastern Pacific as remnant nesting colonies rise slightly (Costa Rica: Santidrián Tomillo et al. 2007; Mexico: Sarti M. et al. 2007), the systematic killing of nesting females, widespread collection (or depredation) of eggs, and/or offshore threats, including incidental capture in fishing nets, has been reported at other globally significant sites (Indian Ocean: International Union for the Conservation of Nature 2001, Shanker and Choudhury 2006; Indonesia and Papua New Guinea: Kinch 2006, Benson et al. 2007a, Hitipeuw et al. 2007, Tapilatu and Tiwari 2007; West Africa: Fretey 2001, Fretey et al. 2007a, 2007b; Guianas: Hilterman and Goverse 2007).

Equally important to conservation actions taken at the national level (a modern regulatory regime, consistent monitoring, effective outreach, etc.) is an inclusive mechanism by which species, such as the leatherback, that spend a large proportion of their time in the oceanic commons may be adequately protected. A review of international instruments reveals that the coverage of sea turtles in global and regional treaties, and other intergovernmental agreements and policies, is among the most comprehensive of any species group (see *Legal status*, above). However, by definition these treaties and agreements articulate obligations pertaining to territories under the jurisdiction of States, while few options exist that enable stakeholders to effectively address sea turtle survival issues in international waters and on the high seas (Gjerde and Breide 2003).

The importance of protecting important habitats, including ecosystem-level management regimes and transboundary parks that reflect life history realities, is often overlooked. Future priorities should include the identification of important habitats, including corridors that span multiple national jurisdictions and the high seas, the creation of marine management regimes at ecologically relevant scales and the forging of new governance patterns, and an emphasis on improving management capacity at all levels.

Finally, the importance of creating and maintaining networks and other empowering mechanisms that promote the process of consensus, ensure equitable access to information, and engender a commitment to taking action on behalf of seemingly intractable transboundary environmental issues will only increase as time goes by. This is especially true in regions where poverty and immediate human need (or affluence and apathy), political unrest, and persistent institutional neglect conspire to overrule the need to define patterns of marine resource use that take into account the special needs of species, including the sea turtles, rendered especially vulnerable to over-exploitation by their particular constellation of life cycle and life history traits.

Chapter 6: Mariculture

Facility Considerations

Leatherbacks have proven difficult to maintain in laboratory or aquarium settings. Adults kept in captivity typically die very soon after acquisition (Birkenmeier 1972, Levy et al. 2005); these incidents are rarely published but are generally known among sea turtle biologists. In one of the earliest incidents, an adult male (145 cm SCL) was gaffed in the front right flipper and brought ashore after becoming entangled in a lobster pot line in the Gulf of Maine in 1957. It was placed in captivity in a weakened condition and died a few days later from severe hemorrhaging in both lungs (Ray and Coates 1958). Even hatchlings and young juveniles seem unable to adapt to the constraints of captivity.

Deraniyagala (1939) noted that "…young specimens in captivity…never seem to realize that the sides of their tanks are solid and persistently swim into them, thereby injuring their flippers and snout, which never heal owing to this habit." Spoczynska (1970) described hatchlings in her care as extremely active: "When they tired of swimming from one end of the tank to the other and back again, they tried to get through the glass at one end, repeatedly swimming towards it from a point a few inches away, swimming backwards to this point and then trying again. They would sometimes keep this up for hours, seemingly oblivious to the fact that the glass formed a barrier."

In an attempt to mitigate this persistent and sometimes lethal problem, Birkenmeier (1971) constructed soft-sided enclosures by lining concrete tanks with cloth stretched over wooden frames. Witham (1977) later recommended that tank walls be padded with polyurethane foam or fine mesh suspended near the aquarium sides to reduce the severity of skin abrasions. Foster and Chapman (1975) padded the sides of an indoor tank with foam rubber and Johnson (1989) reported using "an octagonal holding tank with soft vinyl sides." Others have tried to minimize the frenzy activity by keeping water temperatures relatively low and feeding the turtles at night, returning them to a dark aquarium (Phillips 1977). A circular current, which gives the hatchlings something to orient against and lessens their tendency to batter themselves against the tank walls, was innovated by Birkenmeier (1971).

Jones (2009) tethered turtles to PVC™ pipes secured across the tops of oval tanks. Animals < 10 kg were attached to the tether using Velcro™ and cyanoacrylate cement attaching the tether to the posterior portion of their carapace, thus confining them to a section of the tank. Each hatchling could swim or dive in any direction, but was unable to contact other turtles or the tank's bottom and walls. Upon reaching ≥ 10 kg, the juveniles were secured to the tether with a harness made of Tygon™ tubing. The harness circled each shoulder like a backpack and then looped around the caudal peduncle of the animal. Jones (2009), like previous researchers, concluded that preventing turtles from hitting and rubbing the tank walls and bottom was necessary to prevent cuts and abrasions that might lead to infection and an untimely death.

As noted above, unrelenting contact with container walls leads to skin abrasion and subsequent infection. In an early attempt to successfully rear young leatherbacks, Carr and Ogren (1959) were unable to keep them alive for more than 41 days. Two to four weeks after hatching, all 60 turtles developed "yellowish spots" on the carapace; these appeared to be sites of fungus or bacterial infection, the eyes also became discolored. In the three decades since, skin lesions and fungal infections have been among the most commonly cited causes of death.

The appearance of "yellowish spots" was also noted in turtles raised in the United States (Florida), Costa Rica, and Canada (University of British Columbia) (T.T. Jones, pers. comm.). These spots have been treated, with varying degrees of success, with penicillin ointment (Caldwell 1959), gentian violet (Frair 1970), iodine and proflavine (Birkenmeier 1971), and 1% potassium permanganate solution (Foster and Chapman 1975).

Hatchlings with sores and fungal infections were treated by Jones et al. (2000) using povidone iodine (10%) solution and an antifungal topical ointment. Wounds were then debraded with a soft bristled toothbrush to remove damaged skin and promote healing, and the area was coated with a water-resistant anti-fungal ointment before the turtle was returned to its tank. If sores or infections were close to the eyes or mouth, gentamicin gulfate (eye ointment) was administered instead of the iodine solution or anti-fungal gel. Daily treatment only rarely (three cases) resulted in healing. When used alone, antibacterial or anti-fungal creams were ineffective.

Food and Feeding

Feeding behavior in captivity is characterized by somewhat frantic movements of the head, including a rapid opening and closing of the jaws (which open to a remarkable extent) and a sideways twisting or jerking of the head in an attempt to dismember prey. The long clawless front flippers are useless in feeding. Caldwell (1959) observed that the turtles seldom approached food deliberately, but rather it was a "…hit-or-miss proposition." Birkenmeier (1971) later concluded that leatherback hatchlings fed more or less passively, and surmised that a wild hatchling, having chanced upon a swarm of small jellyfish, may simply snap indiscriminately, "…catching more or less automatically what comes into its way."

Jones et al. (2000) noted that hatchlings showed a voracious appetite in captivity; however, when hatchlings lost appetite for several days or more, they were force-fed using fine (1 mm inside diameter) flexible tubes attached to a syringe filled with a liquid rehydrant and an appetite stimulant, but the effort met with limited success. Hatchlings that may have had internal infections or those that exhibited excess buoyancy were tube-fed with antibacterial and anti-gas medications (0.3 cc per 50–75 g of body weight). These efforts also met with limited success. Jones (2009) took a more hands-off approach and only treated turtles showing diminishing appetite and overall lethargy with 5 mg kg^{-1} enrofloxacin or 2.5 mg kg^{-1} amakacin with isotonic, buffered water. Jones (2009) agreed with previous authors that water quality was paramount to maintaining healthy leatherback turtles.

Leatherbacks, including post-hatchlings (Salmon et al. 2004), prefer soft-bodied prey (see Chapter 3, *Nutrition and metabolism, Food,* above); however, providing live jellyfish (or similarly buoyant foodstuffs) to captive animals may be difficult. Tanks drained to about two inches depth resulted in the hatchlings reaching food without having to submerge (Caldwell 1959). Deraniyagala (1939), Birkenmeier (1971), Jones et al. (2000), and Jones (2009) offered food by hand a few inches below the surface.

Although a wide variety of food types appear to be acceptable to captive hatchlings (Table 24), some individuals refuse food entirely. Paradoxically, in one study, turtles that fed well did not grow any more than did non-feeders, and the non-feeders lived longer (all died within 21 days, Spoczynska 1970); however, at 21 days post-hatchling leatherbacks would still have ample yolk reserves, thus explaining the discrepancy (Jones et al. 2007).

Hatchlings housed at the Miami Seaquarium fed well on ground clam and squid, and later chopped fish, but despite their growth they died one after another (Caldwell 1959). Several years later, another Miami Seaquarium hatchling died abruptly at 189 days of age when the diet offered changed from jellyfish to fish; postmortem examination revealed undigested fish blocking the digestive tract (Witham 1977). It may be that while hatchlings will accept fish, they cannot digest or eliminate it properly and death from intestinal obstruction may result (Frair 1970). Nonetheless, Deraniyagala (1939) kept a hatchling alive for 662 days on a diet that included chopped fish.

Jones et al. (2000) fed turtles once daily to satiation with a diet consisting of prescription cat food, bread, vitamins and minerals blended with water and flavorless gelatin. This diet was low in fat (less than 5%), as is typical of natural foods consumed by leatherbacks (Holland et al. 1990, Davenport and Balazs 1991). When available, fresh gelatinous prey (live jellyfish or ctenophores) was substituted for water in the recipe. In a later experiment, Jones (2009) fed turtles three to five times daily to satiation during the first two months, and three times daily to satiation when hatchlings were more than two months of age, on a squid gelatin diet. The diet consisted of squid (Pacific Ocean squid; mantle and tentacles only), vitamins and calcium, blended with flavorless gelatin and hot water. This latter diet adequately maintained turtles for over two years with the largest turtle attaining 42 kg and 72 cm SCL at death (815 days; largest turtle raised in captivity).

Bels et al. (1988) and Jones (2009) have been the most successful to date at keeping leatherbacks alive in captivity. The former incubated 14 eggs (collected in French Guiana) in Paris, France. The resulting hatchlings were kept in filtered, temperature- and light-controlled basins and hand-fed mussels (*Mytilus edulis*). Growth, activity periods, and general behavior were recorded for 1200 days, at the end of which time one individual remained alive and healthy at a weight of 28.5 kg. Turtles were fed but once daily and, though they were fed to satiation, this may have accounted for the relatively slow growth observed (Bels et al. 1988).

In comparison, Jones (2009) fed turtles multiple times daily, basing this feeding regime on personal observations of leatherbacks feeding in the wild (Salmon et al. 2004) and personal experience in rearing leatherbacks (Jones et al. 2000, 2007). Furthermore, Jones (2009) found that the length and weight data pairs from their captive-reared turtles matched those of leatherbacks taken from the wild, suggesting that their turtles were properly conditioned and that the turtles raised by Deraniyagala (1939) and Bels et al. (1988) suffered from sub-optimal conditions, notably inadequate nutrition; these factors probably resulted in reduced growth.

Table 24. Diet, maximum longevity, and cause of death of leatherback sea turtles reared in captivity. With the exception of the juvenile stranded in Puerto Rico, all specimens were obtained as eggs or hatchlings.

Location	Diet	Longevity	Cause(s) of Death	Reference
Western Atlantic				
Costa Rica	fish, plants, invertebrates	41 days (max)	bacterial infection	Carr & Ogren (1959)
Trinidad	salami sausage, chicken liver	Released (?)	(unreported)	Bacon (1970)
USA (USVI) [1]	fish, squid, shrimp, clams, scallops	13 days	drowning	Johnson (1989)
USA	fish, roe, squid, algae, clams	ca. 2 months	(unreported)	Caldwell (1959)
USA	fish, squid, shrimp, algae, 'Jello'	79 days (max)	fungal disease	Frair (1970)
USA	chicken liver	249 days	choked on its food [2]	Philips (1977)
USA	jellyfish	642 days (max)	fish blocking GI tract, septicemia	Foster & Chapman (1975), Witham (1977), Witham & Futch (1977)
Eastern Atlantic				
England [3]	shrimp, squid	21 days (max)	unknown	Spoczynska (1970)
France	mussels	1,200+ days	(unreported)	Bels et al. (1988)
Western Pacific				
Malaysia	fish, prawns, buffalo heart		infection, contaminated water, starvation (?)	Birkenmeier (1971)
Eastern Pacific				
Costa Rica (Playa Grande)	cat food-gelatin	5 weeks	[released alive]	Jones et al. (2007)
USA (Florida) [4]	cat food-gelatin	7 weeks	systemic fungal and bacterial infections (n=26); [released alive, n=9]	Jones et al. (2000)
Canada (British Columbia) [5]	squid-gelatin	815 days (max)	bacterial pneumonia	Jones (2009)
Mexico	'turtle chow,' fish, crab meat	5 months	unknown	López et al. (1990)
Indian Ocean				
South Africa	chicken liver, *Physalia*, pelagic molluscs	3 months	mostly accidental	Hughes et al. (1967)
Ceylon [= Sri Lanka]	fish, eggs, bread, algae, live octopus	662 days (max)	contaminated water	Deraniyagala (1936b, 1939)

[1] a juvenile (29 cm CCL) stranded in Puerto Rico was flown to Coral World, St. Thomas, U.S. Virgin Islands
[2] three (of the original four) were still alive at the time of publication
[3] four hatchlings were air-mailed from Suriname
[4] origin: Palm Beach County, Florida, USA
[5] origin: British Virgin Islands

Literature Cited

Ackerman, R.A. 1997. The nest environment and the embryonic development of sea turtles. Pages 83-106 *in* P. Lutz and J. Musick, editors. The biology of sea turtles. CRC Press, Boca Raton, Florida.

Ackman, R.G., and R.D. Burgher. 1965. Cod liver oil fatty acids as secondary reference standards in the GLC of polyunsaturated fatty acids of animal origin: analysis of a dermal oil of the Atlantic leatherback turtle. Journal of the American Oil Chemists' Society 42:38-42.

Ackman, R.G., S.N. Hooper, and W. Frair. 1971. Comparison of the fatty acid compositions of depot fats from freshwater and marine turtles. Comparative Biochemistry and Physiology 40B:931-944.

Ackman, R.G., S.N. Hooper, and J.C. Sipos. 1972. Distribution of *trans*-6-hexadecenoic and other fatty acids in tissues and organs of the Atlantic leatherback turtle *Dermochelys coriacea coriacea* L. International Journal of Biochemistry 3:171-179.

Adame R., A., and D.A. Salim P. 1985. Estudio preliminar sobre la biología de las tortugas marinas *Lepidochelys olivacea* (Eschscholtz) y *Dermochelys coriacea* (Garman), como contribución al proyecto de conservación e investigación de tortugas marinas de la Universidad Autónoma Benito Juárez de Oaxaca. Thesis, Universidad Autónoma Metrópolitana—Xochimilco, México.

Adams, W.E. 1962. The carotid sinus—carotid body problem in the *Chelonia* (with a note on a Foramen of Panizza in *Dermochelys*). Archives Internationales de Pharmacodynamie et de Thérapie 139:28-37.

Adnyana, W. 2006. Status of leatherback turtles in Indonesia. Pages 51-63 *in* M. Hamann, C. Limpus, G. Hughes, J. Mortimer, and N. Pilcher, compilers. Assessment of the conservation status of the leatherback turtle in the Indian Ocean and SouthEast Asia. Indian Ocean and SouthEast Asia (IOSEA) Species Assessment: Volume I. IOSEA Marine Turtle Memorandum of Understanding Secretariat, Bangkok, Thailand.

Aguirre, A. 2006. Health issues of sea turtles: a conservation medicine approach. Pages 71-76 *in* I. Kinan, editor. Proceedings of the second western Pacific sea turtle cooperative research and management workshop. Volume II: North Pacific loggerhead sea turtles. Western Pacific Regional Fishery Management Council, Honolulu, Hawaii.

Albrecht, P.W. 1976. The cranial arteries of turtles and their evolutionary significance. Journal of Morphology 14:159-182.

Alfaro-Shigueto, J., P.H. Dutton, M.-F. van Bressem, and J. Mangel. 2007. Interactions between leatherback turtles and Peruvian artisanal fisheries. Chelonian Conservation and Biology 6:129-135.

Alvarado, J., and A. Figueroa. 1987. The ecological recovery of sea turtles of Michoacán, México. Special Attention: black turtle. Unpublished final report to the U.S. Deptment of Interior, Fish and Wildlife Service and World Wildlife Fund-U.S. Washington, D.C.

Alvarado, J., A. Figueroa, and H. Gallardo. 1985. The ecological recovery of sea turtles of Michoacán, México. Special Attention: black turtle. Final Report to the U.S. Fish and Wildlife Service and World Wildlife Fund-U.S. Albuquerque, New Mexico.

Amorocho, D., H. Rubio, and W. Diaz. 1992. Observaciones sobre el estado actual de conservación de las tortugas marinas en el Pacífico Colombiano. Pages 155-178 *in* J.V. Rodriguez and H. Sánchez, editors. Contribución al conocimiento de las tortugas marinas en Colombia. INDERENA, Biblioteca Andrés Posada Arango. Libro 4. Bogotá, Colombia.

Anderson, W. 2001. Implementing MEAs in the Caribbean: hard lessons from seafood and Ting. RECIEL [Review of European Community and International Environmental Law] 10:227-233.

Andrews, C.W. 1919. A description of new species of zeuglodont and of leathery turtle from the Eocene of southern Nigeria. Proceedings of the Zoological Society of London 1919:309-318.

Andrews, H.V. 2000. Current marine turtle situation in the Andaman and Nicobar islands—an urgent need for conservation action. Kachhapa 3:19-23.

Andrews, H.V., S. Krishnan, and P. Biswas. 2002. Leatherback nesting in the Andaman and Nicobar islands. Kachhapa 6:15-17.

Andrews, H.V., S. Krishnan, and P. Biswas. 2006. Distribution and status of marine turtles in the Andaman and Nicobar islands. Pages 33-57 *in* K. Shanker and B.C. Choudhury, editors. Marine turtles of India. Universities Press. Hyderabad, India.

Anonymous. 1988. Action alert: leatherback turtle shooting! Sea Turtle Center Newsletter "Keeping it Wild" 2:2-3. Nevada City, California.

Anvene, R.E. 2003. Local exploitation of marine turtles in Equatorial Guinea: market studies. Page 260 *in* J.A. Seminoff, compiler. Proceedings of the 22nd annual symposium on sea turtle biology and conservation. U.S. Department of Commerce, National Oceanic and Atmospheric Administration Technical Memorandum NMFS-SEFSC-503. Miami, Florida.

Ascenzi, P., S.G. Condo, A. Bellelli, D. Barra, W.H. Bannister, B. Giardina, and M. Brunori. 1984. Molecular and functional properties of myoglobin from a marine turtle (*Dermochelys coriacea*). Biochimica et Biophysica Acta 788:281-189.

Atkins, L.S. 1960. The leathery turtle, or luth, *Dermochelys coriacea* (L.), in Co. Cork. Irish Naturalists' Journal 13:189.

Audubon, J.J. 1834. Ornithological biography, or an account of the habits of the birds of the United States of America; accompanied by descriptions of the objects represented in the work entitled The Birds of America, and interspersed with delineations of American scenery and manners, Volume 2. A. & C. Black, Edinburgh, Scotland.

Autar, L. 1994. Sea turtles attacked and killed by jaguars in Suriname. Marine Turtle Newsletter 67:11-12.

Avens, L., and L.R. Goshe. 2008. Skeletochronological analysis of age and growth for leatherback sea turtles in the western north Atlantic. Page 201 *in* A.F. Rees, M. Frick, A. Panagopoulou, and K. Williams, compilers. Proceedings of the 27th annual symposium on sea turtle biology and conservation. U.S. Department of Commerce, National Oceanic and Atmospheric Administration Technical Memorandum NMFS-SEFSC-569. Miami, Florida.

Avens, L., J.C. Taylor, L.R. Goshe, T.T. Jones, and M. Hastings. 2009. Use of skeletochronological analysis to estimate age of leatherback sea turtles *Dermochelys coriacea* in the western north Atlantic. Endangered Species Research 8:165-177.

Babcock, H.L. 1939. Records of the leatherback turtle from Maine waters. Copeia 1939:50.

Bache, S.J. 2005. Marine policy development: the impact of a flagship species. Special Issue: marine turtles as flagships. Maritime Studies 3(2) and 4(1):241-271.

Bacon, P.R. 1970. Studies on the leatherback turtle, *Dermochelys coriacea* (L.), in Trinidad, West Indies. Biological Conservation 2:213-217.

Bacon, P.R. 1971. Sea turtles in Trinidad and Tobago. International Union for the Conservation of Nature (IUCN) Publications New Series, Suppl. 31:1-109.

Bacon, P.R. 1973. The orientation circle in the beach ascent crawl of the leatherback turtle, *Dermochelys coriacea*, in Trinidad. Herpetologica 29:343-348.

Bacon, P.R., and G.K. Maliphant. 1971. Further studies on sea turtles in Trinidad and Tobago. Trinidad Field Naturalists' Club Journal 1971:2-17.

Bacon, P., F. Berry, K. Bjorndal, H. Hirth, L. Ogren, and M. Weber, editors. 1984. Proceedings of the western Atlantic turtle symposium, 17-22 July 1983, San José, Costa Rica. Volume 3: National Reports. RSMAS Printing, Miami, Florida.

Bailey, H., G. Shillinger, D. Palacios, S. Bograd, J. Spotila, F. Paladino, and B. Block. 2008. Identifying and comparing phases of movement by leatherback turtles using state-space models. Journal of Experimental Marine Biology and Ecology 356:128-135.

Baillie, J.E.M., C. Hilton-Taylor, and S.N. Stuart, editors. 2004. IUCN Red List of Threatened Species. International Union for the Conservation of Nature (IUCN). Gland, Switzerland.

Bal, G., N. Breheret, and H. Vanleeuwe. 2007. An update on sea turtle conservation activities in the Republic of Congo. Marine Turtle Newsletter 116:9-10.

Balasingam, E. 1967. The ecology and conservation of the leathery turtle *Dermochelys coriacea* (Linn.) in Malaya. Micronesica 3:37-43.

Balazs, G.H. 1982. Driftnets catch leatherback turtles. Oryx 16:428-430.

Balazs, G.H. 1985. Impact of ocean debris on marine turtles: entanglement and ingestion. Pages 387-429 *in* R.S. Shomura and H.O. Yoshida, editors. Proceedings of the workshop on the fate and impact of marine debris. U.S. Department of Commerce, National Oceanic and Atmospheric Administration Technical Memorandum NMFS-SWFC-54. Honolulu, Hawaii.

Bannikov, A.G., I.S. Darevsky, and A.K. Rustamov. 1971. Zemnovodnykh i Presmykayushchikhsya USSR [*Amphibians and Reptiles of the USSR*]. Izdatelistvo "Mysl," Moscow, Russia.

Bannikov, A.G., I.S. Darevsky, V.G. Ishchenko, A.K. Rustamov, and N.N. Szczerbak. 1977. Opredelitel Zemnovodnykh i Presmykayushchikhsya Fauny USSR [*Guide to Amphibians and Reptiles of the USSR Fauna*]. Prosveshchenie, Moscow, Russia.

Barata, P.C.R., B.M.G. Gallo, S. Santos, V.G. Azevedo, and J.E. Kotas. 1998. Captura incidental da tartartuga marinha *Caretta caretta* (Linnaeus, 1758) na pesca de espinhel de superfície na ZEE brasileira e em águas internacionais. Pages 579-581 *in* Fundação Universidade Federal do Rio Grande, editor. Proceedings of the 11th Semana Nacional de Oceanografia. Rio Grande, Brazil.

Barnard, D.E., J.A. Keinath, and J.A. Musick. 1989. Distribution of ridley, green, and leatherback turtles in Chesapeake Bay and adjacent waters. Pages 201-203 *in* S.A. Eckert, K.L. Eckert, and T.H. Richardson, compilers. Proceedings of the 9th annual workshop on sea turtle conservation and biology. U.S. Department of Commerce, National Oceanic and Atmospheric Administration Technical Memorandum NMFS-SEFC-232. Miami, Florida.

Barreiros, J.P., and J. Barcelos. 2001. Plastic ingestión by a leatherback turtle *Dermochelys coriacea* from the Azores (NE Atlantic). Marine Pollution Bulletin 42:1196-1197.

Bartol, S., and J.A. Musick. 2003. Sensory biology of sea turtles. Pages 79-102 *in* P.L. Lutz, J.A. Musick, and J. Wyneken, editors. The biology of sea turtles, Volume 2. CRC Press, Boca Raton, Florida.

Bartol, S.M., J.A. Musick, and M.L. Lenhardt. 1999. Auditory evoked potentials of the loggerhead sea turtle (*Caretta caretta*). Copeia 1999:836-840.

Bartram, P., and J.J. Kaneko. 2004. Catch to bycatch ratios: comparing Hawaii's pelagic longline fisheries with others. Cooperative Agreement No. NA17RJ1230. Pacific Fishery Research Program and Joint Institute for Marine and Atmospheric Research, University of Hawaii, Manoa.

Baur, G. 1886. Osteologische Notizen uber Reptilien. Zoologischer Anzeiger 9:238:685-690.

Baur, G. 1888. *Dermochelys, Dermatochelys* oder *Sphargis*. Zoologischer Anzeiger 11:270:44-45.

Baur, G. 1889. Die systematische Stellung von *Dermochelys* Blainv. Biologische Centralblatt 9:149-153, 181-191.

Baur, G. 1890. On the classification of the Testudinata. American Naturalist 24:530-536.

Baur, G. 1891. The pelvis of the Testudianta, with notes on the evolution of the pelvis in general. Journal of Morphology 4:354-359.

Baur, G. 1893. Notes on the classification of the Cryptodira. American Naturalist 27:672-674.

Behler, J.L., P.C.H. Pritchard, and A.G.J. Rhodin, editors. 1996. Special focus issue: the leatherback turtle, *Dermochelys coriacea*. Chelonian Conservation and Biology 2:139-319.

Bels, V., F. Rimblot-Baly, and J. Lescure. 1988. Croissance et maintien en captivité de la Tortue Luth, *Dermochelys coriacea* (Vandelli, 1761). Revue Française d'Aquariologie 15:59-64.

Bell, B.A., J.R. Spotila, F.V. Paladino, and R.D. Reina. 2003. Low reproductive success of leatherback turtles, *Dermochelys coriacea*, is due to high embryonic mortality. Biological Conservation 115:131-138.

Bellail, R., and C. Dintheer. 1992. La pêche maritime en Guyane française. Flottilles et engins de pêche. IFREMER, Cayenne, French Guiana.

Benabib N., M. 1983. Algunos aspectos de la biología de *Dermochelys coriacea* en el Pacifico Mexicano. Thesis, Universidad Nacional Autónoma de México (UNAM). México, D.F., México.

Benson, S.R., P.H. Dutton, C. Hitipeuw, B. Samber, J. Bakarbessy, and D. Parker. 2007a. Post-nesting migrations of leatherback turtles (*Dermochelys coriacea*) from Jamursba-Medi, Bird's Head Peninsula, Indonesia. Chelonian Conservation and Biology 6:150-154.

Benson, S.R., K.M. Kisokau, L. Ambio, V. Rei, P.H. Dutton, and D. Parker. 2007b. Beach use, internesting movement, and migration of leatherback turtles, *Dermochelys coriacea*, nesting on the north coast of Papua New Guinea. Chelonian Conservation and Biology 6:7-14.

Benson, S.R., K.A. Forney, J.T. Harvey, J.V. Carretta, and P.H. Dutton. 2007c. Abundance, distribution, and habitat of leatherback turtles (*Dermochelys coriacea*) off California, 1990-2003. Fishery Bulletin 105:337-347.

Bentley, P.J. 1976. Osmoregulation. Pages 365-412 *in* C. Gans, editor. Biology of the Reptilia, Volume 5A. Academic Press, London, United Kingdom.

Berkson, H. 1967. Physiological adjustments to deep diving in the Pacific green turtle (*Chelonia mydas agassizii*). Comparative Biochemistry and Physiology 21:507-524.

Betz, W., and M. Welch. 1992. Once thriving colony of leatherback sea turtles declining at Irian Jaya, Indonesia. Marine Turtle Newsletter 56:8-9.

Beverly, S., and L. Chapman. 2007. Interactions between sea turtles and pelagic longline fisheries. WCPFC-SC3-EB SWG/IP-01. Western and Central Pacific Fisheries Commission. Kolonia, Pohnpei State, Federated States of Micronesia.

Bhaskar, S. 1981. Preliminary report on the status and distribution of sea turtles in Indian waters. Indian Forester, November 1981:707-711.

Bhaskar, S. 1985. Mass nesting by leatherbacks in Irian Jaya. World Wildlife Fund (WWF) Monthly Report, January 1985:15-16.

Bhaskar, S. 1987. Management and research of marine turtle nesting sites on the North Vogelkop coast of Irian Jaya, Indonesia. Unpublished report to World Wildlife Fund (WWF) Indonesia.

Bhaskar, S. 1993. The status and ecology of sea turtles in the Andaman and Nicobar Islands. ST 1/93. Centre for Herpetology, MCBT. Madras, India.

Bianchi, G., K.E. Carpenter, J.-P. Roux, F.J. Molloy, D. Boyer, and H.J. Boyer. 1999. Field guide to the living marine resources of Namibia. Food and Agricultural Organization (FAO) species identification guide for fishery purposes. Food and Agricultural Organization of the United Nations, Rome, Italy.

Bickham, J.W. 1981. Two-hundred-million-year-old chromosomes: deceleration of the rate of karyotypic evolution in turtles. Science 212:1291-1293.

Bickham, J.W. 1984. Patterns and modes of chromosomal evolution in reptiles. Pages 13-40 *in* A.K. Sharma and A. Sharma, editors. Chromosomes in evolution of eukaryotic groups, Volume 2. CRC Press, Boca Raton, Florida.

Bickham J.W., and J.L. Carr. 1983. Taxonomy and phylogeny of the higher categories of cryptodiran turtles based on a cladistic analysis of chromosomal data. Copeia 1983:918-932.

Bilinski, J.J., R.D. Reina, J.R. Spotila, and F.V. Paladino. 2001. The effects of nest environment on calcium mobilization by leatherback turtle embryos (*Dermochelys coriacea*) during development. Comparative Biochemistry and Physiology 130:151-162.

Billes, A., and J. Fretey. 2001. Nest morphology in the leatherback turtle. Marine Turtle Newsletter 92:7-9.

Billes, A., J. Fretey, and J.-B. Moundemba. 2003. Monitoring of leatherbacks in Gabon. Pages 131-132 *in* J.A. Seminoff, compiler. Proceedings of the 22nd annual symposium on sea turtle biology and conservation. U.S. Department of Commerce, National Oceanic and Atmospheric Administration Technical Memorandum NMFS-SEFSC-503. Miami, Florida.

Billes, A., J. Fretey, B. Verhage, B. Huijbregts, B. Giffoni, L. Prosdocimi, D.A. Albareda, J.-Y. Georges, and M. Tiwari. 2006. First evidence of leatherback movement from Africa to South America. Marine Turtle Newsletter 111:13-14.

Binckley, C.A., J.R. Spotila, K.S. Wilson, and F.V. Paladino. 1998. Sex determination and sex ratios of Pacific leatherback turtles, *Dermochelys coriacea*. Copeia 1988:291-300.

Birkenmeier, E. 1971. Juvenile leathery turtles, *Dermochelys coriacea* (Linnaeus), in captivity. Brunei Museum Journal 2:160-172.

Birkenmeier, E. 1972. Rearing a leathery turtle, *Dermochelys coriacea*. International Zoo Yearbook 12:204-207.

Bjorndal, K.A. 1980. Demography of the breeding population of the green turtle, *Chelonia mydas*, at Tortuguero, Costa Rica. Copeia 1980:525-530.

Bjorndal, K.A. 1997. Foraging ecology of sea turtles. Pages 199-232 *in* P.L. Lutz and J.A. Musick, editors. The biology of sea turtles. CRC Press, Boca Raton, Florida.

Blainville, M.H. de. 1816. Prodrome d'une nouvelle distribution systématique du règne animal. Bulletin des Sciences par la Société Philomathique de Paris (3)3: P. "111."

Blanck, C.E., and R.H. Sawyer. 1981. Hatchery practices in relation to early embryology of the loggerhead sea turtle, *Caretta caretta* (Linné). Journal of Experimental Marine Biology and Ecology 49:163-177.

Bleakney, J.S. 1965. Reports of marine turtles from New England and eastern Canada. Canadian Field-Naturalist 79:120-128.

Bogert, C.M., and J.A. Oliver. 1945. A preliminary analysis of the herpetofauna of Sonora. Bulletin of the American Museum of Natural History 83:301-425.

Borlase, W. 1758. The natural history of Cornwall. The air, climate, water, rivers, lakes, sea and tides, vegetables, rare birds, fishes, shells, reptiles, and quadrupeds. Oxford, United Kingdom.

Bostrom, B.L., and D.R. Jones. 2007. Exercise warms adult leatherback turtles. Comparative Biochemistry and Physiology 147:323-331.

Bouillon, J., and G. Coppois. 1977. Comparative study of the mesoglea of some cnidarians [Étude comparative de la mésoglée des cnidaires]. Cahiers Biologique Marine 18:339-368.

Boulenger, G. 1889. Catalogue of the chelonians, rhyncocephalians and crocodiles in the British Museum (Natural History). London, United Kingdom.

Boulon, R.H. 1989. Virgin Islands turtle recoveries outside of the U.S. Virgin Islands. Pages 207-209 *in* S.A. Eckert, K.L. Eckert and T.H. Richardson, compilers. Proceedings of the 9th annual workshop on sea turtle conservation and biology. U.S. Department of Commerce, National Oceanic and Atmospheric Administration Technical Memorandum NMFS-SEFC-232. Miami, Florida.

Boulon, R.H., K.L. Eckert, and S.A. Eckert. 1988. Migration: *Dermochelys coriacea*. Herpetological Review 19:88.

Boulon, R.H., P.H. Dutton, and D.L. McDonald. 1996. Leatherback turtles (*Dermochelys coriacea*) on St. Croix, U.S. Virgin Islands: fifteen years of conservation. Chelonian Conservation and Biology 2:141-147.

Bouxin, H., and R. Legendre. 1947. Tortue luth, *Dermochelys coriacea* (L.), observée à concarneau. Comptes Rendus de l'Académie des Sciences, Paris 225:464-466.

Bowen, B.W., and S.A. Karl. 1996. Population structure, phylogeography, and molecular evolution. Pages 29-50 *in* P. Lutz and J.A. Musick, editors. The biology of sea turtles. CRC Press, Boca Raton, Florida.

Bowen, B.W., and S.A. Karl. 2007. Population genetics and phylogeography of sea turtles. Molecular Ecology 16:4886-4907.

Bradshaw, C.J.A., C.R. McMahon, and G.C. Hays. 2007. Behavioral inference of diving metabolic rate in free-ranging leatherback turtles. Physiological and Biochemical Zoology 80:209-219.

Brahim, S., E.H. Chan, and A.K. Rahman. 1987. An update on the population status and conservation of the leatherback turtle of Terengganu. Pages 69-77 *in* A. Sasekumar, S.M. Phang, and E.L. Chong, editors. Proceedings of the 10th annual seminar towards conserving Malaysia's marine heritage. Department of Zoology, University of Malaysia. Kuala Lumpur, Malaysia.

Brandner, R.L., S.J. Basford, and R.H. Boulon. 1990. Tagging and nesting research on leatherback sea turtles (*Dermochelys coriacea*) on Sandy Point, St. Croix, U.S. Virgin Islands, 1989. Annual Report to USVI Division of Fish and Wildlife, contract PC-P&NR-215-89. Frederiksted, St. Croix, USVI.

Bräutigam, A., and K.L. Eckert. 2006. Turning the tide: exploitation, trade and management of marine turtles in the Lesser Antilles, Central America, Colombia and Venezuela. TRAFFIC International. Cambridge, United Kingdom.

Briane, J.-P., P. Rivalan, and M. Girondot. 2007. The inverse problem applied to the observed clutch frequency of leatherback turtles from Ya:lima:po Beach, French Guiana. Chelonian Conservation and Biology 6:63-70.

Broin, F. de, and B. Pironon. 1980. Découverte d'une tortue dermochélyidée dans le Miocène d'Italie centro-méridionale (*Matese oriental*), Province de Benevento. Rivista Italiana di Paleontologia e Stratigrafia 86:589-604.

Brongersma, L.D. 1967. British turtles, guide for the identification of stranded turtles on British coasts. British Museum (Natural History), London, United Kingdom.

Brongersma, L.D. 1968. The Soay beast. Beaufortia 15:33-46.

Brongersma, L.D. 1969. Miscellaneous notes on turtles. IIA-B. Proceedings of the Koninklijke Nederlandse Akademie Van Wetenschappen Series C-Biological and Medical Sciences 72:76-102.

Brongersma, L.D. 1970. Miscellaneous notes on turtles. III. Proceedings of the Koninklijke Nederlandse Akademie Van Wetenschappen Series C-Biological and Medical Sciences 73:323-335.

Brongersma, L.D. 1972. European Atlantic turtles. Zoologische Verhandelingen 121:1-318.

Brudenall, D.K., I.R. Schwab, and K.A. Fritsches. 2008. Ocular morphology of the leatherback sea turtle (*Dermochelys coriacea*). Veterinary Ophthalmology 11:99-110.

Brueggeman, J.J. 1992. Oregon and Washington marine mammal and seabird surveys. Final report by Ebasco Environmental (Bellevue, WA) and Ecological Consulting (Portland, OR) for the Minerals Management Service, Pacific OCS Region. OCS Study MMNS 91-0093. Seattle, Washington.

Bugoni, L., L. Krause, and M.V. Petry. 2001. Marine debris and human impacts on sea turtles in southern Brazil. Marine Pollution Bulletin 42:1330-1334.

Burne, R.H. 1905. Notes on the muscular and visceral anatomy of the leathery turtle (*Dermochelys coriacea*). Proceedings of the Zoological Society of London 1905:291-324.

Bustard, H.R. 1972. Sea turtles: natural history and conservation. Collins, London, United Kingdom.

Bustard, H.R., K. Simkiss, N.K. Jenkins, and J.H. Taylor. 1969. Some analyses of artificially incubated eggs and hatchlings of green and loggerhead turtles. Journal of Zoology, London 158:311-315.

Butynski, T.M. 1996. Marine turtles on Bioko Island, Equatorial Guinea. Oryx 39:143-149.

Byrne, R., and S.A. Eckert. 2006. Small leatherback found in Dominica. Marine Turtle Newsletter 111:18.

Caldwell, D.K. 1959. On the status of the Atlantic leatherback turtle, *Dermochelys coriacea coriacea*, as a visitant to Florida nesting beaches, with natural history notes. Quarterly Journal of the Florida Academy of Sciences 21:285-291.

Caldwell, D.K. 1962. Sea turtles in Baja Californian waters (with special reference to those of the Gulf of California), and the description of a new subspecies of north-eastern Pacific green turtle. Los Angeles County Museum Contributions to Science 1:1-31.

Caldwell, D.K., and M.C. Caldwell. 1969. Addition of the leatherback sea turtle to the known prey of the killer whale, *Orcinus orca*. Journal of Mammalogy 50:636.

Cambers, G., and H. Lima. 1990. Leatherback turtles disappearing from the BVI. Marine Turtle Newsletter 49:4-7.

Cameron, T.H. 1923. Notes on turtles. Journal of the Bombay Natural History Society 29:299-300.

Campbell, C.L., C.J. Lagueux, and J.A. Mortimer. 1996. Leatherback turtle, *Dermochelys coriacea*, nesting at Tortuguero, Costa Rica, in 1995. Chelonian Conservation and Biology 2:169-172.

Capra, F. 1949. La *Dermochelys coriacea* (L.) nel Golfo di Genova e nel Mediterraneo (Testud. Sphargidae). Annali del Museo Civico di Storia Naturale di Genova 63:270-282.

Carr, A.F. 1952. Handbook of turtles: the turtles of the United States, Canada and Baja California. Cornell University Press, Ithaca, New York.

Carr, A. 1987. New perspectives on the pelagic stage of sea turtle development. Conservation Biology 1:103-121.

Carr, A., and A. Meylan. 1984. *Dermochelys coriacea* (leatherback sea turtle) migration. Herpetological Review 15:113.

Carr, A., and L. Ogren. 1959. The ecology and migrations of sea turtles, 3, *Dermochelys* in Costa Rica. American Museum Novitates 1958:1-29.

Carr, A.F., Jr., A. Meylan, J. Mortimer, K. Bjorndal, and T. Carr. 1982. Surveys of sea turtle populations and habitats in the Western Atlantic. U.S. Department of Commerce, National Oceanic and Atmospheric Administration Technical Memorandum NMFS-SEFC-91. Miami, Florida.

Carr, T., and N. Carr. 1986. *Dermochelys coriacea* (leatherback sea turtle) copulation. Herpetological Review 17:24-25.

Carr, T., and N. Carr. 1991. Surveys of the sea turtles of Angola. Biological Conservation 58:19-29.

Carriol, R.P., and W. Vader. 2002. Occurrence of *Stomatolepas elegans* (Cirripedia: Balanomorpha) on a leatherback turtle from Finnmark, northern Norway. Journal of the Marine Biological Association of the United Kingdom 82:1033-1034.

Casale, P., P. Nicolosi, D. Freggi, M. Turchetto, and R. Argano. 2003. Leatherback turtles (*Dermochelys coriacea*) in Italy and in the Medeterranean basin. Herpetological Journal 13:135-139.

Castellanos-Michel, R., C. Martínez-Tovar, I. EncisoPadilla, and J. Jacobo-Pérez. 2006. Low presence of the leatherback turtle *Dermochelys coriacea* and hawksbill turtle *Eretmochelys imbricata* in the Jalisco coast, Mexican Pacific (2000-2002). Pages 31-34 *in* N. Pilcher, compiler. Proceedings of the 23rd annual symposium on sea turtle biology and conservation. U.S. Department of Commerce, National Oceanic and Atmospheric Administration Technical Memorandum NMFS-SEFSC-536. Miami, Florida.

Caut, S., E. Guirlet, P. Jouquet, and M. Girondot. 2006a. Influence of nest location and yolkless eggs on the hatching success of leatherback turtle clutches in French Guiana. Canadian Journal of Zoology 84:908-915.

Caut, S., V. Hulin, and M. Girondot. 2006b. Impact of density-dependent nest destruction on emergence success of Guianan leatherback turtles (*Dermochelys coriacea*). Animal Conservation 9:189-197.

Caut, S., E. Guirlet, E. Angulo, K. Das, and M. Girondot. 2008. Isotope analysis reveals foraging area dichotomy for Atlantic leatherback turtles. PLoS ONE 3(3): e1845.doi:10.1371/journal.pone.0001845

Chacón, D., W. McLarney, C. Ampie, and B. Venegas. 1996. Reproduction and conservation of the leatherback turtle *Dermochelys coriacea* (Testudines: Dermochelyidae) in Gandoca, Costa Rica. Revista de Biología Tropical 44:853-860.

Chacón, D., and K.L. Eckert. 2007. Leatherback sea turtle nesting at Gandoca Beach in Caribbean Costa Rica: management recommendations from 15 years of conservation. Chelonian Conservation and Biology 6:101-111.

Chacón, D., N. Valerín, M.V. Cajiao, H. Gamboa, and G. Marín. 2001. Manual para mejores prácticas de conservación de las tortugas marinas en Centroamérica. San José, Costa Rica.

Chaloupka, M., P.H. Dutton, and H. Nakano. 2004. Status of sea turtle stocks in the Pacific. Pages 135-164 *in* Report of the expert consultation on interactions between sea turtles and fisheries within an ecosystem context. FAO Fisheries Report 738. Food and Agricultural Organization of the United Nations, Rome, Italy.

Chan, E.H. 1985. Twin embryos in unhatched egg of *Dermochelys coriacea*. Marine Turtle Newsletter 32:2-3.

Chan, E.H. 1989. White spot development, incubation and hatching success of leatherback turtle (*Dermochelys coriacea*) eggs from Rantau Abang, Malaysia. Copeia 1989:42-47.

Chan, E.H. 1993. The conservation-related biology and ecology of the leatherback turtle, *Dermochelys coriacea*, in Rantau Abang, Terengganu, Malaysia. Ph.D. dissertation, Kagoshima University, Japan.

Chan, E.H., and H.C. Liew. 1989. The leatherback turtle: a Malaysian heritage. Tropical Press Sdn. Bhd. Kuala Kumpur, Malayasia.

Chan, E.H., and H.C. Liew. 1995. Incubation temperatures and sex-ratios in the Malaysian leatherback sea turtle *Dermochelys coriacea*. Biological Conservation 74:169-174.

Chan, E.H., and H.C. Liew. 1996. Decline of the leatherback population in Terengganu, Malaysia, 1956-1995. Chelonian Conservation and Biology 2:196-203.

Chan, E.H., and S.E. Solomon. 1989. The structure and function of the egg shell of the leatherback turtle (*Dermochelys coriacea*) from Malaysia, with notes on attached fungal forms. Animal Technology 40:91-102.

Chan, E.H., H.C. Liew, and A.G. Mazlan. 1988. The incidental capture of sea turtles in fishing gear in Terengganu, Malaysia. Biological Conservation 43:1-7.

Chan, E.H., H.U. Salleh, and H.C. Liew. 1985. Effects of handling on hatchability of eggs of the leatherback turtle, *Dermochelys coriacea*, (L.). Pertanika 8:265-271.

Chan, E.H., S.A. Eckert, H.C. Liew, and K.L. Eckert. 1991. Locating inter-nesting habitats of Malaysian leatherback turtles *(Dermochelys coriacea)* using radiotelemetry. Pages 133-138 *in* A. Uchiyama and C.J. Amlaner Jr., editors. Proceedings of the 11th international symposium on biotelemetry. Waseda University Press, Tokyo, Japan.

Chaves, A., G. Serrano, G. Martin, E. Arguedas, A. Jimenez, and J.R. Spotila. 1996. Conservation biology of leatherback turtles, *Dermochelys coriacea*, at Playa Langosta, Costa Rica. Chelonian Conservation and Biology 2:184-189.

Chebez, J.C., and C.F. Balboa. 1987. Un nuevo registro de *Dermochelys coriacea* (Linné) (Reptilia—Chelonia—Dermochelidae) en la costa Bonaerense (República Argentina). Amphibia and Reptilia 1:54-56.

Chen, B.-Y., and S.-H. Mao. 1981. Hemoglobin finger-print correspondence and relationships of turtles. Comparative Biochemistry and Physiology 68B:497-503.

Cheng, I.J. 2006. Status of leatherback turtles in China. Pages 32-36 *in* M. Hamann, C. Limpus, G. Hughes, J. Mortimer, and N. Pilcher, compilers. Assessment of the conservation status of the leatherback turtle in the Indian Ocean and SouthEast Asia. Indian Ocean and SouthEast Asia (IOSEA) Species Assessment: Volume I. IOSEA Marine Turtle Memorandum of Understanding Secretariat, Bangkok, Thailand.

Cheng, I.-J., and T.-H. Chen. 1997. The incidental capture of five species of sea turtles by coastal setnet fisheries in the eastern waters of Taiwan. Biological Conservation 82:235-239.

Chevalier, A., and E.A. Duchesne. 1851. Mémoire sur les empoisonnements par les huitres, les moules, les crabes, et par certains poissons de mer et de rivière. Annales D'hygiène Publique et de Médecine Légale 46:108-147.

Chevalier, J., and M. Girondot. 1998. Dynamique de pontes des tortues luths en Guyane francaise durant la saison 1997. Bulletin de la Société Herpétologique de France 85-86:5-19.

Chevalier, J., M.H. Godfrey, and M. Girondot. 1999. Significant difference of temperature-dependent sex determination between French Guiana (Atlantic) and Playa Grande (Costa Rica, Pacific) leatherbacks (*Dermochelys coriacea*). Annales des Sciences Naturelles 20:147-152.

Choudhury, B.C. 2006. Status of leatherback turtles in India. Pages 45-50 *in* M. Hamann, C. Limpus, G. Hughes, J. Mortimer, and N. Pilcher, compilers. Assessment of the conservation status of the leatherback turtle in the Indian Ocean and SouthEast Asia. Indian Ocean and SouthEast Asia (IOSEA) Species Assessment: Volume I. IOSEA Marine Turtle Memorandum of Understanding Secretariat, Bangkok, Thailand.

Choudhury, B.C., S.C. Sharma, and S.K. Mukherjee. 2000. The sea turtle conservation agenda of India. Pages 100-106 *in* N. Pilcher and G. Ismail, editors. Sea turtles of the Indo-Pacific: research, management and conservation. ASEAN Academic Press Ltd, United Kingdom.

Chu Cheong, L. 1990. Observations on the nesting population of leatherback turtles, *Dermochelys coriacea*, in Trinidad. Caribbean Marine Studies 1:48-53.

Chua, T.H. 1988a. Nesting population and frequency of visits in *Dermochelys coriacea* in Malaysia. Journal of Herpetology 22:192-207.

Chua, T.H. 1988b. On the road to local extinction: the leatherback turtle (*Dermochelys coriacea*) in Terengganu, Malaysia. Pages 153-158 *in* A. Sasekumar, R. D'Cruz, and S. Lim Lee Hong, editors. Proceedings of the 11th annual seminar of the Malaysian Society of Marine Sciences. University of Malaya, Kuala Lumpur, Malaysia.

Chua, T.H., and J.I. Furtado. 1988. Nesting frequency and clutch size in *Dermochelys coriacea* in Malaysia. Journal of Herpetology 22:208-218.

Cohen, E., and G.B. Stickler. 1958. Absence of albumin-like serum proteins in turtles. Science 127:1392.

Collard, S.B. 1990. Leatherback turtles feeding near a watermass boundary in the Eastern Gulf of México. Marine Turtle Newsletter 50:12-14.

Congdon, J.D., A.E. Dunham, and R.C. van Loben Sels. 1993. Delayed sexual maturity and demographics of Blanding's turtles (*Emydoidea blandingii*): implications for conservation and management of long-lived organisms. Conservation Biology 7:826-833.

Congdon, J.D., A.E. Dunham, and R.C. van Loben Sels. 1994. Demographics of common snapping turtles (*Chelydra serpentine*): implications for conservation and management of long-lived organisms. American Zoologist 34:397-408.

Constantino, M.A., and M. Salmon. 2003. Role of chemical and visual cues in food recognition by leatherback posthatchlings (*Dermochelys coriacea* L). Zoology 106:173-181.

Cope, E.D. 1871. On the homologies of some of the cranial bones of the Reptilia, and on the systematic arrangement of the Class. Proceedings of the American Association for the Advancement of Science 19:194-246.

Cornelius, S.E. 1976. Marine turtle nesting activity at Playa Naranjo, Costa Rica. Brenesia 8:1-27.

Crim, J.L., L.D. Spotila, J.R. Spotila, M.P. O'Connor, R.D. Reina, C.J. Williams, and F.V. Paladino. 2002. The leatherback turtle, *Dermochelys coriacea*, exhibits both polyandry and polygyny. Molecular Ecology 11:2097-2106.

Crognale, M.A., S.A. Eckert, D.H. Levenson, and C.A. Harms. 2008. Leatherback sea turtle *Dermochelys coriacea* visual capacities and potential reduction of bycatch by pelagic longline fisheries. Endangered Species Research 5:249-256.

Crossland, S.L. 2003. Factors disturbing leatherback turtles (*Dermochelys coriacea*) on two nesting beaches within Suriname's Galibi Nature Preserve. Pages 137-138 *in* J.A. Seminoff, compiler. Proceedings of the 22nd annual symposium on sea turtle biology and conservation. U.S. Department of Commerce, National Oceanic and Atmospheric Administration Technical Memorandum NMFS-SEFSC-503. Miami, Florida.

Cruz W., L.E., and G. Ruiz. 1984. La preservacíon de la tortuga marina. Ciencia y Desarrollo 56:66-79.

Cruz W., L.E., A.L. Sarti M., A.E. Villaseñeor G., B. Jimenez A., M. Robles D., and T. de Jesus Ruiz M. 1986. Informe de trabajo de investigación y conservación de la tortuga Laud (*Dermochelys coriacea*) en Mexiquillo, Michoacán. Temporada de anidación 1984-1985. Michoacán, México.

Davenport, J. 1987. Locomotion in hatchling leatherback turtles, *Dermochelys coriacea*. Journal of Zoology, London 212:85-101.

Davenport, J. 1988. Do diving leatherbacks pursue glowing jelly? Bulletin of the British Herpetological Society 24:20-21.

Davenport, J., and G.H. Balazs. 1991. 'Fiery bodies'—are pyrosomas important items in the diet of leatherback turtles? Bulletin of the British Herpetological Society 37:33-38.

Davenport, J., and J. Welch. 1990. Metal levels in a leatherback turtle. Marine Pollution Bulletin 21:40-41.

Davenport, J., D.L. Holland, and J. East. 1990. Thermal and biochemical characteristics of the lipids of the leatherback turtle *Dermochelys coriacea*: evidence of endothermy. Journal of the Marine Biological Association of the United Kingdom 70:33-41.

Davenport, J., G.H. Balazs, J.V. Faithfull, and D.A. Williamson. 1993. A struvite faecolith in the leatherback turtle *Dermochelys coriacea* Vandelli: a means of packing garbage? Herpetological Journal 3:81-83.

Davenport, J., J. Wrench, J. McEvoy, and V. Camacho-Ibar. 1990. Metal and PCB concentrations in the "Harlech" leatherback. Marine Turtle Newsletter 48:1.

Deem, S.L., E.S. Dierenfeld, G.-P. Sounguet, A.R. Alleman, C. Cray, R.H. Popenga, T.M. Norton, and W.B. Karesh. 2006. Blood values in free-ranging nesting leatherback turtles (*Dermochelys coriacea*) on the coast of the Republic of Gabon. Journal of Zoo and Wildlife Medicine 37:464-471.

Deem, S.L., F. Boussamba, A.Z. Nguema, G.-P. Sounguet, S. Bourgeois, J. Cianciolo, and A. Formia. 2007. Artificial lights as a significant cause of morbidity of leatherback sea turtles in Pongara National Park, Gabon. Marine Turtle Newsletter 116:15-17.

Delaugerre, M. 1987. Statut des tortues marines de la Corse (et de la Mediterranee). Vie Milieu 37:243-264.

Demetropoulos, A., and M. Hadjichristophorou. 1995. Manual on marine turtle conservation in the

Mediterranean. UNEP(MAP)SPA, IUCN, Cyprus Wildlife Society, Fisheries Department in Cyprus. Manre, Cyprus.

Department of the Environment, Water, Heritage and the Arts (DEWHA). 2008. *Dermochelys coriacea*. Species profile and threats database. Department of the Environment, Water, Heritage and the Arts, Canberra, Australia.

Deraniyagala, P.E.P. 1930. The Testudinata of Ceylon. Ceylon Journal of Science (B) 16:43-88.

Deraniyagala, P.E.P. 1932. Notes on the development of the leathery turtle, *Dermochelys coriacea*. Ceylon Journal of Science (B) 17:73-102.

Deraniyagala, P.E.P. 1934. Some phylogenetic features in the leathery turtle *Dermochelys coriacea*. Ceylon Journal of Science (B) 18:200-206.

Deraniyagala, P.E.P. 1936a. The nesting habit of the leathery turtle, *Dermochelys coriacea*. Ceylon Journal of Science (B) 19:331-336.

Deraniyagala, P.E.P. 1936b. Some post-natal changes in the leathery turtle, *Dermochelys coriacea*. Ceylon Journal of Science (B) 19:225-239.

Deraniyagala, P.E.P. 1939. The tetrapod reptiles of Ceylon. Volume 1: Testudinates and Crocodilians. Colombo Museum Natural History Series. Colombo.

Deraniyagala, P.E.P. 1941. The nesting of the leathery turtle, *Dermochelys coriacea* (Linné). Proceedings of the Linnean Society, London 153:121-123.

Deraniyagala, P.E.P. 1952. A colored atlas of some vertebrates from Ceylon. Volume 1: Fishes. Ceylon National Museums Publication, The Ceylon Government Press, Ceylon [now Sri Lanka].

Deraniyagala, P.E.P. 1953. A coloured atlas of some vertebrates from Ceylon. Volume 2: Tetrapod Reptilia. Colombo Government Press, Colombo, Ceylon [now Sri Lanka].

Desjardin, N.A. 2005. Spatial, temporal, and dietary overlap of leatherback sea turtles (*Dermochelys coriacea*) and ocean sunfishes (family Molidae). M.S. thesis, Florida Atlantic University, Boca Raton.

Desvages, G., and C. Pieau. 1992. Aromatase activity in the gonads of turtle embryos as a function of the incubation temperature of the egg. Journal of Steroid Biochemistry and Molecular Biology 41:851-853.

Desvages, G., M. Girondot, and C. Pieau. 1993. Sensitive stages for the effects of temperature on gonadal aromatase activity in embryos of the marine turtle *Dermochelys coriacea*. General and Comparative Endocrinology 92:54-61.

Dileepkumar, N., and C. Jayakumar. 2006. Sea turtles of Kerala. Pages 137-140 *in* K. Shanker and B.C. Choudhury, editors. Marine turtles of India. Universities Press, Hyderabad, India.

Dohl, T.P., M.L. Bonnell, R.C. Guess, and K.T. Briggs. 1983. Marine mammals and seabirds of central and northern California, 1980-1983: Synthesis of Findings. Unpublished report to the U.S. Department of Interior, Minerals Management Service, Los Angeles, California.

Dollo, L. 1901. Sur l'origine de la tortue luth (*Dermochelys coriacea*). Bulletin de la Societe Royale Des Sciences Medicales et Naturelles De Bruxelles 1-26.

Dollo, L. 1903. *Eochelone brabantica*, tortue marine nouvelle du Bruxellien (Eocène moyen) de la Belgique (sur l'évolution des Chéloniens marines). Bulletins de l'Académie Royale de Belgique 1903:792-850.

Donoso-Barros, R. 1966. Reptiles de Chile. Universidad de Chile, Santiago, Chile.

Dossa, J.S., B.A. Sinsin, and G.A. Mensah. 2007. Conflicts and social dilemmas associated with the incidental capture of marine turtles by artisanal fishers in Benin. Marine Turtle Newsletter 116:10-12.

Dow, W., K. Eckert, M. Palmer, and P. Kramer. 2007. An atlas of sea turtle nesting habitat for the Wider Caribbean Region. The Wider Caribbean Sea Turtle Conservation Network and The Nature Conservancy. Wider Caribbean Sea Turtle Conservation Network (WIDECAST) Technical Report No. 6. Beaufort, North Carolina.

Downie, R., and M. Reilly, editors. 1992. Report on the University of Glasgow Conservation Expedition to Trinidad and Tobago, 1991. Department of Zoology, University of Glasgow, Scotland.

Doyle, T.K., J.D.R. Houghton, R. McDevitt, J. Davenport, and G.C. Hays. 2007. The energy density of jellyfish: estimates from bomb-calorimetry and proximate-composition. Journal of Experimental Marine Biology and Ecology 343:239-252.

Doyle, T.K., J.D.R. Houghton, P.F. O'Súilleabháin, V.J. Hobson, F. Marnell, J. Davenport, and G.C. Hays. 2008. Leatherback turtles satellite-tagged in European waters. Endangered Species Research 4:23-31.

Drake, D.L., and J.R. Spotila. 2002. Thermal tolerances and the timing of sea turtle hatchling emergences. Journal of Thermal Biology 27:71-81.

Duangsawasdi, M. 2006. Status of leatherback turtles in Thailand. Pages 143-148 *in* M. Hamann, C. Limpus, G. Hughes, J. Mortimer, and N. Pilcher, compilers. Assessment of the conservation status of the leatherback turtle in the Indian Ocean and SouthEast Asia. Indian Ocean and SouthEast Asia (IOSEA) Species Assessment: Volume I. IOSEA Marine Turtle Memorandum of Understanding Secretariat, Bangkok, Thailand.

Duguy, R. 1968. Note sur la fréquence de la tortue luth (*Dermochelys coriacea* L.) près des côtes de la Charente-Maritime. Annales de la Société des Sciences Naturelles de Charente-Maritime 4:8-16.

Duguy, R., M. Duron, and C. Alzieu. 1980. Observations de tortues luth (*Dermochelys coriacea*) dans les pertuis charentais en 1979. Annales de la Société des Sciences Naturelles de Charente-Maritime 6:681-691.

Duguy, R., P. Moriniere, and C. Le Milinaire. 1998. Facteurs de mortalité observés chez les tortues marines dans le golfe de Gascogne. Oceanologica Acta 21:383-388.

Duguy, R., P. Moriniere, and A. Meunier. 1999. Observations de tortues marines en 1998 (Atlantique). Annales de la Société des Sciences Naturelles de Charente-Maritime 8:911-924.

Duguy, R., P. Moriniere, and A. Meunier. 2000. Observations de tortues marines en 1999 (Atlantique et Manche). Annales de la Société des Sciences Naturelles de Charente-Maritime 8:1025-1034.

Duguy, R., P. Moriniere, and A. Meunier. 2001. Observations de tortues marines en 2000 (Atlantique et Manche). Annales de la Société des Sciences Naturelles de Charente-Maritime 9:17-25.

Duguy, R., P. Moriniere, and A. Meunier. 2002. Observations de tortues marines en 2001 (Atlantique et Manche). Annales de la Société des Sciences Naturelles de Charente-Maritime 9:161-172.

Duguy, R., P. Moriniere, and A. Meunier. 2003. Observations de tortues en 2002 (Atlantique et Manche). Annales de la Société des Sciences Naturelles de Charente-Maritime 9:265-273.

Duguy, R., P. Moriniere, and A. Meunier. 2004. Observations de tortues marines en 2003 (Côtes Atlantiques). Annales de la Société des Sciences Naturelles de Charente-Maritime 9:361-366.

Duguy, R., P. Moriniere, and A. Meunier. 2005. Observations de tortues marines en 2004 (Côtes Atlantiques Annales de la Société des Sciences Naturelles de Charente-Maritime 9:461-466.

Duguy, R., P. Moriniere, and A. Meunier. 2006. Observations de tortues marines en 2005 (Côtes Atlantiques). Annales de la Société des Sciences Naturelles de Charente-Maritime 9:607-611.

Duguy, R., P. Moriniere, and A. Meunier. 2007. Observations de tortues marines en 2006 (Côtes Atlantiques). Annales de la Société des Sciences Naturelles de Charente-Maritime 9:695-698.

Duméril, A.M.C., and G. Bibron. 1835. Erpétologie générale ou histoire naturelle complète des reptiles. Tome 2. Librarie Encyclopédique de Roret, Paris, France.

Dung, P.H. 2006. Status of leatherback turtles in Viet Nam. Pages 156-163 *in* M. Hamann, C. Limpus, G. Hughes, J. Mortimer, and N. Pilcher, compilers. Assessment of the conservation status of the leatherback turtle in the Indian Ocean and SouthEast Asia. Indian Ocean and SouthEast Asia (IOSEA) Species Assessment: Volume I. IOSEA Marine Turtle Memorandum of Understanding Secretariat, Bangkok, Thailand.

Dunlap, C.E. 1955. Notes on the visceral anatomy of the giant leatherback turtle (*Dermochelys coriacea* Linnaeus). The Bulletin of the Tulane Medical Faculty 14:55-69.

Dupuy, A.R. 1986. The status of marine turtles in Senegal. Marine Turtle Newsletter 39:4-7.

Duron-Dufrenne, M. 1978. Contribution à l'étude de la biologie de *Dermochelys coriacea* (Linné) dans les pertuis charentais. Thèse de 3ème cycle de l'Université de Bordeaux, France.

Duron-Dufrenne, M. 1987. Premier suivi par satellite en Atlantique d'une tortue luth, *Dermochelys coriacea*. Compte-Rendu de l'Académie des Sciences de Paris, Série III, 304:399-402.

Duron, M., and P. Duron. 1980. Des tortues luths dans le pertuis charentais. Le Courrier de la Nature 69:37-41.

Dutton, D.L., P.H. Dutton, M. Chaloupka, and R.H. Boulon. 2005. Increase of a Caribbean leatherback turtle *Dermochelys coriacea* nesting population linked to long-term nest protection. Biological Conservation 126:186-194.

Dutton, P.H. 1996. Use of molecular markers for stock identification, fingerprinting, and the study of mating behavior in leatherback turtles. Pages 79-86 *in* B.W. Bowen and W.N. Witzell, editors. Proceedings of the international symposium on sea turtle conservation genetics. U.S. Department of Commerce, National Oceanic and Atmospheric Administration Technical Memorandum NMFS-SEFSC-396. Miami, Florida.

Dutton, P.H., and S.K. Davis. 1998. Use of molecular genetics to identify individuals and inter mating behavior in leatherbacks. Page 42 *in* R. Byles and Y. Fernandez, compilers. Proceedings of the 16th annual symposium on sea turtle conservation and biology. U.S. Department of Commerce, National Oceanic and Atmospheric Administration Technical Memorandum NMFS-SEFC-412. Miami, Florida.

Dutton, P., and D. Squires. 2008. Reconciling biodiversity with fishing: a holistic strategy for Pacific sea turtle recovery. Ocean Development and International Law 39:200-222.

Dutton, P.H., E. Bixby, and S.K. Davis. 2000. Tendency toward single paternity in leatherbacks detected with microsatellites. Page 39 *in* F.A. Abreu-Grobois, R. Briseño-Dueñas, R. Márquez-Millán, and L. Sarti-Martínez, compilers. Proceedings of the 18th international sea turtle symposium. U.S. Department of Commerce, National Oceanic and Atmospheric Administration Technical Memorandum NMFS-SEFSC-436. Miami, Florida.

Dutton, P.H., C.P. Whitmore, and N. Mrosovsky. 1985. Masculinisation of leatherback turtle, *Dermochelys coriacea*, hatchlings from eggs incubated in Styrofoam boxes. Biological Conservation 31:249-264.

Dutton, P.H., S.K. Davis, T. Guerra, and D. Owens. 1996. Molecular phylogeny for marine turtles based on sequences of the ND4-leucine tRNA and control regions of mitochondrial DNA. Molecular Phylogenetics and Evolution 5:511-521.

Dutton, P.H., B.W. Bowen, D.W. Owens, A. Barragan, and S.K. Davis. 1999. Global phylogeography of the leatherback turtle (*Dermochelys coriacea*). Journal of Zoology, London 248:397-409.

Dutton, P.H., S. Roden, L.M. Galver, and G. Hughes. 2003. Genetic population structure of leatherbacks in the Atlantic elucidated by microsatellite markers. Pages 44-45 *in* J.A. Seminoff, compiler. Proceedings of the 22nd annual symposium on sea turtle biology and conservation. U.S. Department of Commerce, National Oceanic and Atmospheric Administration Technical Memorandum NMFS-SEFSC-503. Miami, Florida.

Dutton, P.H., C. Hitipeuw, M. Zein, S.R. Benson, G. Petro, J. Pita, V. Rei, L. Ambio, and J. Bakarbessy. 2007. Status and genetic structure of nesting populations of leatherback turtles (*Dermochelys coriacea*) in the western Pacific. Chelonian Conservation and Biology 6:47-53.

Dwyer, K.L., C.E. Ryder, and R. Prescott. 2003. Anthropogenic mortality of leatherback turtles in Massachusetts waters. Page 260 *in* J.A. Seminoff, compiler. Proceedings of the 22nd annual symposium on sea turtle biology and conservation. U.S. Department of Commerce, National Oceanic and Atmospheric Administration Technical Memorandum NMFS-SEFSC-503. Miami, Florida.

Dyer, W.G., E.H. Williams, Jr., and L. Bunkley-Williams. 1995. Digenea of the green turtle (*Chelonia mydas*) and the leatherback turtle (*Dermochelys coriacea*) from Puerto Rico. Caribbean Journal of Science 31:269-273.

Eckert, K.L. 1987. Environmental unpredictability and leatherback sea turtle (*Dermochelys coriacea*) nest loss. Herpetologica 43:315-323.

Eckert, K.L. 1990. Twinning in leatherback sea turtle (*Dermochelys coriacea*) embryos. Journal of Herpetology 24:317-320.

Eckert, K.L. 1993. The biology and population status of marine turtles in the North Pacific Ocean. U.S. Department of Commerce, National Oceanic and Atmospheric Administration Technical Memorandum NMFS-SWFSC-186. Honolulu, Hawaii.

Eckert, K.L., and J. Beggs. 2006. Marine turtle tagging: a manual of recommended practices. Wider Caribbean Sea Turtle Conservation Network (WIDECAST) Technical Report No. 2. Revised Edition. Beaufort, North Carolina.

Eckert, K.L., and R.K. Bjorkland. 2005. Distribution and status of the leatherback sea turtle, *Dermochelys coriacea*, in the insular Caribbean region. Pages 8-10 *in* M.S. Coyne and R.D. Clark, compilers. Proceedings of the 21st annual symposium on sea turtle biology and conservation. U.S. Department of Commerce, National Oceanic and Atmospheric Administration Technical Memorandum NMFS-SEFSC-528. Miami, Florida.

Eckert, K.L., and S.A. Eckert. 1983. Tagging and nesting research of leatherback sea turtles (*Dermochelys coriacea*) on Sandy Point, St. Croix, U.S. Virgin Islands, 1983. Annual report to the Department of Interior, U.S. Fish and Wildlife Service. USFWS Ref. MIN 54-8480119. Washington, D.C.

Eckert, K.L., and S.A. Eckert. 1985. Tagging and nesting research of leatherback sea turtles (*Dermochelys coriacea*) on Sandy Point, St. Croix, U.S. Virgin Islands, 1985. Annual report to the Department of Interior, U.S. Fish and Wildlife Service, USFWS Ref. MIN 54-8680431. Washington, D.C.

Eckert, K.L., and S.A. Eckert. 1988. Pre-reproductive movements of leatherback sea turtles (*Dermochelys coriacea*) nesting in the Caribbean. Copeia 1988:400-406.

Eckert, K.L., and S.A. Eckert. 1990a. Embryo mortality and hatch success in *in situ* and translocated leatherback sea turtle, *Dermochelys coriacea*, eggs. Biological Conservation 53:37-46.

Eckert, K.L., and S.A. Eckert. 1990b. Tagging hatchling leatherback sea turtles. Marine Turtle Newsletter 51:17-19.

Eckert, K.L., and S.A. Eckert. 1990c. Leatherback sea turtles in Grenada, West Indies: a survey of nesting beaches and socio-economic status. Unpublished report to the Fisheries Department,

Ministry of Agriculture, Lands, Forestry and Fisheries. St. George's, Grenada.

Eckert, K.L., and A.H. Hemphill. 2005. Sea turtles as flagships for protection of the Wider Caribbean Region. Special Issue: Marine Turtles as Flagships. Maritime Studies 3(2) and 4(1):119-143.

Eckert, K.L., and D.J. Hykle. 2008. The future of global and regional sea turtle research and conservation. Pages 4-7 *in* R.B. Mast, B.J. Hutchinson, and A.H. Hutchinson, compilers. Proceedings of the 24th annual symposium on sea turtle biology and conservation. U.S. Department of Commerce, National Oceanic and Atmospheric Administration Technical Memorandum NMFS-SEFSC-567. Miami, Florida.

Eckert, K.L., S.A. Eckert, and D.W. Nellis. 1984. Tagging and nesting research of leatherback sea turtles (*Dermochelys coriacea*) on Sandy Point, St. Croix, U.S. Virgin Islands, 1984, with management recommendations for the population. Annual Report to the U.S. Fish and Wildlife Service, USFWS Ref. #MIN 54-8580175. Washington, D.C.

Eckert, K.L., J.A. Overing, and B.B. Lettsome. 1992. Wider Caribbean Sea Turtle Conservation Network (WIDECAST) sea turtle recovery action plan for the British Virgin Islands. UNEP Caribbean Environment Programme (CEP) Technical Report No. 15. Kingston, Jamaica.

Eckert, K.L., K.A. Bjorndal, F.A. Abreu G., and M.A. Donnelly, editors. 1999. Research and management techniques for the conservation of sea turtles. IUCN/SSC Marine Turtle Specialist Group Publication No. 4. Washington, D.C.

Eckert, K.L., S.A. Eckert, T.W. Adams, and A.D. Tucker. 1989a. Inter-nesting migrations by leatherback sea turtles, *Dermochelys coriacea*, in the West Indies. Herpetologica 45:190-194.

Eckert, S.A. 1989. Diving and foraging behavior of the leatherback sea turtle, *Dermochelys coriacea*. Ph.D. dissertation, University of Georgia, Athens.

Eckert, S.A. 1999. Habitats and migratory pathways of the Pacific leatherback sea turtle, *Dermochelys coriacea*. Final Report to the National Marine Fisheries Service, Office of Protected Resources. Hubbs SeaWorld Research Institute Technical Report 99-190. San Diego, California.

Eckert, S.A. 2002a. Distribution of juvenile leatherback sea turtle *Dermochelys coriacea* sightings. Marine Ecology Progress Series 230:289-293.

Eckert, S.A. 2002b. Swim speed and movement patterns of gravid leatherback sea turtle (*Dermochelys coriacea*) at St. Croix, U.S. Virgin Islands. Journal of Experimental Biology 205:3689-3697.

Eckert, S.A. 2006. High-use oceanic areas for Atlantic leatherback sea turtles (*Dermochelys coriacea*) as identified using satellite telemetered location and dive information. Marine Biology 149:1257-1267.

Eckert, S.A. 2008. Promoting the survival of leatherback turtles in the greater Atlantic Ocean by eliminating capture and mortality associated with coastal gillnets in Trinidad. Unpublished report to the Ministry of Agriculture, Land and Marine Resources, Government of Trinidad and Tobago. Port of Spain, Trinidad.

Eckert, S.A., and K.L. Eckert. 2005. Strategic plan for eliminating the incidental capture and mortality of leatherback turtles in the coastal gillnet fisheries of Trinidad and Tobago: proceedings of a national consultation. Wider Caribbean Sea Turtle Conservation Network (WIDECAST) Technical Report No. 5. Beaufort, North Carolina.

Eckert, S.A., and L. Sarti M. 1997. Distant fisheries implicated in the loss of the world's largest leatherback nesting population. Marine Turtle Newsletter 78:2-7.

Eckert, S.A., M.A. Crognale, and D.H. Levenson. 2006b. The sensory biology of sea turtles: what can they see, and how can this help them avoid fishing gear? Pages 8-17 *in* Y. Swimmer and R. Brill, editors. Sea turtle and pelagic fish sensory biology: developing techniques to reduce sea turtle bycatch in longline fisheries. U.S. Department of Commerce, National Oceanic and Atmospheric Administration Technical Memorandum NMFS-PIFSC-7. Honolulu, Hawaii.

Eckert, S.A., K.L. Eckert, and R.H. Boulon. 1982. Tagging and nesting research of leatherback sea turtles (*Dermochelys coriacea*). Sandy Point, St. Croix, U.S. Virgin Islands, 1981/82. Final report to the U.S. Department of Interior, Fish and Wildlife Service. USFWS Ref. MIN 54-8480019. Washington, D.C.

Eckert, S.A., D. McDonald, and P. Dutton. 1994. *Dermochelys coriacea* (leatherback turtle): billfish interaction. Herpetological Review 25:63-64.

Eckert, S.A., E.H. Chan, H.C. Liew, and K.L. Eckert. 1996. Shallow water diving by leatherback turtles in the South China Sea. Chelonian Conservation and Biology 2:237-243.

Eckert, S.A., K.L. Eckert, P. Ponganis, and G.L. Kooyman. 1989b. Diving and foraging behavior of leatherback sea turtles (*Dermochelys coriacea*). Canadian Journal of Zoology 67:2834-2840.

Eckert, S.A., D.W. Nellis, K.L. Eckert, and G.L. Kooyman. 1986. Diving patterns of two leatherback sea turtles (*Dermochelys coriacea*) during internesting intervals at Sandy Point, St. Croix, U.S. Virgin Islands. Herpetolgica 42:381-388.

Eckert, S.A., D. Bagley, S. Kubis, L. Ehrhart, C. Johnson, K. Stewart, and D. DeFreese. 2006a. Internesting and postnesting movements and foraging habitats of leatherback sea turtles, *Dermochelys coriacea*, nesting in Florida. Chelonian Conservation and Biology 2:239-248.

Eggleston, D. 1971. Leathery turtle (Reptilia: Chelonia) in Foveaux Strait (Note). New Zealand Journal of Marine and Freshwater Research 5:522-523.

Eisenberg, J.F., and J. Frazier. 1983. A leatherback turtle, *Dermochelys coriacea*, feeding in the wild. Journal of Herpetology 17:81-82.

Ekanayake, E.M.L., and K.B. Ranawana. 2001. The average egg count for nesting sea turtles on Rekawa Beach in Sri Lanka. Pages 29-30 *in* A. de Silva, editor. Book of abstracts: 4th world congress of herpetology, 3-9 December 2001. Bentota, Sri Lanka.

Engbring, J., N. Idechong, C. Cook, G. Wiles, and R. Bauer. 1992. Observations on the defensive and aggressive behavior of the leatherback sea turtle (*Dermochelys coriacea*) at sea. Herpetological Review 23:70-71.

Engeman, R.M., R.E. Martin, B. Constantin, R. Noel, and J. Woolard. 2003. Monitoring predators to optimize their management for marine turtle nest protection. Biological Conservation 113:171-178.

Epperly, S.P., J. Braun, and A. Veishlow. 1995. Sea turtles in North Carolina waters. Conservation Biology 9:384-394.

Ernst, C.H., and R.W. Barbour. 1972. Turtles of the United States. The University Press of Kentucky, Lexington, Kentucky.

Ernst, E.M., and C.H. Ernst. 1977. Synopsis of helminths endoparasitic in native turtles of the United States. Bulletin of the Maryland Herpetological Society 13:1-75.

Fallabrino, A., C. Lezama, and P. Miller. 2006. Incidental capture of a leatherback turtle (*Dermochelys coriacea*) by artisanal fishermen off Valizas, Uruguay. Pages 212-214 *in* N. Pilcher, compiler. Proceedings of the 23rd annual symposium on sea turtle biology and conservation. U.S. Department of Commerce, National Oceanic and Atmospheric Administration Technical Memorandum NMFS-SEFSC-536. Miami, Florida.

Ferraroli, S., J.-Y. Georges, P. Gaspar, and Y. La Maho. 2004. Where leatherback turtles meet fisheries. Nature 429:521-522.

Firdous, F. 1989. Male leatherback strands in Karachi. Marine Turtle Newsletter 47:14-15.

Fitter, R.S.R. 1961. The leathery turtle or luth. Oryx 6:116-125.

FitzSimmons, N.N. 1998. Single paternity of clutches and sperm storage in the promiscuous green turtle (*Chelonia mydas*). Molecular Ecology 7:575-584.

Fleming, E. 2001. Swimming against the tide: recent surveys of exploitation, trade, and management of marine turtles in the northern Caribbean. TRAFFIC North America. Washington, D.C.

Fletemeyer, J. 1978. Underwater tracking evidence of neonate loggerhead sea turtles seeking shelter in drifting sargassum. Copeia 1978:148-149.

Fletemeyer, J. 1980. The leatherback: turtle without a shell. Sea Frontiers 26:302-305.

Food and Agricultural Organization of the United Nations (FAO). 2004. Report of the expert consultation on interactions between sea turtles and fisheries within an ecosystem context. FAO Fisheries Report No. 738. Rome, Italy.

Food and Agricultural Organization of the United Nations (FAO). 2005. Report of the technical consultation on sea turtle conservation and fisheries. FAO Fisheries Report No. 765. Rome, Italy.

Formia, A., M. Tiwari, J. Fretey, and A. Billes. 2003. Sea turtle conservation along the Atlantic coast of Africa. Marine Turtle Newsletter 100:33-37.

Formia, A., J. Tomas, and R.C. Alvarez. 2000. Nidification des tortues marines au sud de Bioko. Canopée 18:I-IV.

Fossette, S. 2008. Dive and beak movement patterns in leatherback turtles *Dermochelys coriacea* during internesting intervals in French Guiana. Journal of Animal Ecology 77:236-246.

Fossette, S., H. Corbel, P. Gaspar, Y. Le Maho, and J.-Y. Georges. 2008a. An alternative technique for the long-term satellite tracking of leatherback turtles. Endangered Species Research 4:33-41.

Fossette, S., L. Kelle, M. Girondot, E. Goverse, M.L. Hiltermann, B. Verhage, B. de Thoisy, and J.-Y. Georges. 2008b. The world's largest leatherback rookeries: A review of conservation-oriented research in French Guiana/Suriname and Gabon. Journal of Experimental Marine Biology and Ecology 356:69-82.

Fossette, S., S. Ferraroli, T. Tanaka, Y. Ropert-Coudert, N. Arai, K. Sato, Y. Naito, Y. Le Maho, and J.-Y. Georges. 2007. Dispersal and dive patterns in gravid leatherback turtles during the nesting season in French Guiana. Marine Ecology Progress Series 338:233-247.

Foster, P., and C. Chapman. 1975. The care and maintenance of young leatherback turtles, *Dermochelys coriacea*, at the Miami Seaquarium. International Zoo Yearbook 15:170-171.

Fox, H. 1977. The urinogenital system of reptiles. Pages 1-157 *in* C. Gans and T.S. Parsons, editors. Biology of the Reptilia, Volume 6. Academic Press, New York City, New York.

Frair, W. 1964. Turtle family relationships as determined by serological tests. Pages 535-544 *in* C.A. Leone, editor. Taxonomic biochemistry and serology. Ronald Press Company, New York City, New York.

Frair, W. 1969. Aging of serum proteins and serology of marine turtles. Serological Museum Bulletin 42:1-3.

Frair, W. 1970. The world's largest living turtle. Salt Water Aquarium 5:235-241.

Frair, W. 1977a. Turtle red blood cell packed volumes, sizes, and numbers. Herpetologica 33:167-190.

Frair, W. 1977b. Sea turtle red blood cell parameters correlated with carapace lengths. Comparative Biochemistry and Physiology 56A:467-472.

Frair, W. 1979. Taxonomic relations among sea turtles elucidated by serological tests. Herpetologica 35:239-244.

Frair, W. 1982. Serum electrophoresis and sea turtle classification. Comparative Biochemistry and Physiology 72B:1-4.

Frair, W., R.G. Ackman, and N. Mrosovsky. 1972. Body temperature of *Dermochelys coriacea:* warm turtle from cold water. Science 177:791-793.

Fraser, E.A. 1950. The development of the vertebrate excretory system. Biological Review 25:150-187.

Frazer, N.B. 1983a. Demography and life history evolution of the Atlantic loggerhead sea turtle, *Caretta caretta*. Ph.D. dissertation, University of Georgia, Athens.

Frazer, N.B. 1983b. Survivorship of adult female loggerhead sea turtles, *Caretta caretta*, nesting on Little Cumberland Island, Georgia, USA. Herpetologica 39:436-447.

Frazer, N.B., and J.I. Richardson. 1985. Annual variation in clutch size and frequency for loggerhead turtles, *Caretta caretta*, nesting at Little Cumberland Island, Georgia, USA. Herpetologica 41:246-251.

Frazier, J. 1984. Las tortugas marinas en el Océano Atlántico Sur-Occidental. Boletín de la Asociación Herpetológica Argentina. Serie Divulgación 2:1-22.

Frazier, J. 1987. Semantics and the leathery turtle, *Dermochelys coriacea*. Journal of Herpetology 21:240-242.

Frazier, J. 1998. Measurement error: the great chelonian taboo. Pages 47-49 *in* R. Byles and Y. Fernandez, compilers. Proceedings of the 16th annual symposium on sea turtle biology and conservation. U.S. Department of Commerce, National Oceanic and Atmospheric Administration Technical Memorandum NMFS-SEFC-412. Miami, Florida.

Frazier, J., editor. 2002. Special issue: international instruments and marine turtle conservation. Journal of International Wildlife Law and Policy 5:1-207.

Frazier, J.G., and J.L. Brito Montero. 1990. Incidental capture of marine turtles by the swordfish fishery at San Antonio, Chile. Marine Turtle Newsletter 49:8-13.

Frazier, J., and S. Salas. 1984a. The status of marine turtles in the Egyptian Red Sea. Biological Conservation 30:41-67.

Frazier, J., and S. Salas. 1984b. Tortugas marinas en Chile. Boletin del Museo Nacional de Historia Natural de Santiago, Chile 39:63-73.

Frazier, J., D. Gramentz, and U. Fritz. 2005. *Dermochelys* Blainville, 1816—Lederschildkröten. Pages 249-328 *in* B. von Wolfgang Böhme, editor. Handbuch der Reptilien und Amphibien Europas. Band 3/IIIB: Schildkröten (Testudines) II (Cheloniidae, Dermochelyidae, Fossile Schildkröten Europas). AULA-Verlag, Wiebelsheim, Germany.

Frazier, J., M.D. Meneghel, and F. Achaval. 1985. A clarification on the feeding habits of *Dermochelys coriacea*. Journal of Herpetology 19:159-160.

Frazier, J.G., H.L. Fierstine, S.C. Beavers, F. Achaval, H. Suganuma, R.L. Pitman, Y. Yamaguchi, and C. Ma. Prigioni. 1994. Impalement of marine turtles (Reptilia, Chelonia: Cheloniidae and Dermochelyidae) by billfishes (Osteichthyes, Perciformes: Istiophoridae and Xiphiidae). Environmental Biology of Fishes 39:85-96.

Freiberg, M.A. 1945. Observaciones sobre las tortugas de mar que se encuentran frente a las costas argentinas. Physis 20:50-53.

Fretey, J. 1977. Causes de mortalité des tortues luth adults (*Dermochelys coriacea*) sur le littoral guyanais. Courrier de la Nature 52:257-266.

Fretey, J. 1978. Mensurations de tortues luth femelles adultes, *Dermochelys coriacea* (Linné), en Guyane francaise. Bulletin de la Société Zoologique de France 103(4):518-523.

Fretey, J. 1981. Tortues marines de Guyane. Collection nature vraie, Éditions du Léopard d'Or, Paris, France.

Fretey, J. 1982. Note sur les traumas observés chez des tortues luths adultes *Dermochelys coriacea*

(Vandelli) (Testudines, Dermochelyidae). Revue Française d'Aquariologie 8(1981) 4:119-128.

Fretey, J. 2001. Biogeography and conservation of marine turtles of the Atlantic coast of Africa. UNEP Convention on Migratory Species (CMS) Technical Series Publication No. 6. Bonn, Germany.

Fretey, J., and R. Bour. 1980. Redécouverte du type de *Dermochelys coriacea* (Vandelli) (Testudinata, Dermochelyidae). Bolletin di Zoologia 47:193-205.

Fretey, J., and D. Frenay. 1980. Prédation des nids de tortues luth (*Dermochelys coriacea*) par les chiens des villages indiens Galibi en Guyane française. Revue de Médecine Vétérinaire 131:861-867.

Fretey, J., and M. Girondot. 1987. Recensement des pontes de tortue luth, *Dermochelys coriacea* (Vandelli, 1761), sur les plages de Yalimapo-Les Hattes à Awara (Guyane Française) pendant la saison 1986. Bulletin de la Société Herpétologique de France 43:1-8.

Fretey, J., and M. Girondot. 1988. Nidification de la tortue luth (*Dermochelys coriacea*) sur le littoral de Guyane Française pendant la saison 1987. Annales de la Societe des Sciences Naturelles de la Charente-Maritime 7:729-737.

Fretey, J., and M. Girondot. 1989a. L'activité de ponte de la tortue luth, *Dermochelys coriacea* (Vandelli, 1761), pendant la saison 1988 en Guayane française. Revue Ecologie (Terre Vie) 44:261-274.

Fretey, J., and M. Girondot. 1989b. Hydrodynamic factors involved in choice of nesting site and time of arrivals of leatherback in French Guiana. Pages 227-229 *in* S.A. Eckert, K.L. Eckert, and T.H. Richardson, compilers. Proceedings of the 9th annual workshop on sea turtle biology and conservation. U.S. Department of Commerce, National Oceanic and Atmospheric Administration Technical Memorandum NMFS-SEFC-232. Miami, Florida.

Fretey, J., and J. Lescure. 1979. Rapport sur l'étude de la protection des tortues marines en Guyane française. Notes sur le project de réserve naturelle de Basse Mana. Ministère de la Culture et de l'Environnement. Direction de la Nature et des Paysages, Paris, France.

Fretey, J., and J. Lescure. 1981. Prédation des tortues marines par les oiseaux en Guyane française. L'Oiseau (Revue Française d'Ornithologie) 51:139-145.

Fretey, J., A. Billes, and M. Tiwari. 2002. Report from the West African meeting at the 22nd annual symposium on the biology and conservation of sea turtles, Miami. Marine Turtle Newsletter 98:15-17.

Fretey, J., A. Billes, and M. Tiwari. 2007a. Leatherback, *Dermochelys coriacea*, nesting along the Atlantic coast of Africa. Chelonian Conservation and Biology 6:126-129.

Fretey, J., G.H. Segniagbeto, and M. Soumah. 2007c. Presence of sea turtles in traditional pharmacopoeia and beliefs of West Africa. Marine Turtle Newsletter 116:23-25.

Fretey, J., A. Billes, B. Baxter, and C. Hughes. 2007b. Discovery of a Gabonese leatherback in South Africa. Marine Turtle Newsletter 116:25.

Fritts, T. 1982. Plastic bags in the intestinal tracks of leatherback marine turtles. Herpetological Review 13:72-73.

Fuchs, H. 1910. Uber das Pterygoid, Palatinum and Parasphenoid der Quadrupeden, insbesondere der Reptilien and Saugetiere, nebst einigen Betrachtungen uber die Beziehungen Zwischen Nerven and Skeletteilen. Anatomischer Anzeiger 36:33-95.

Fuller, J.E., K.E. Eckert, and J.I. Richardson. 1992. WIDECAST sea turtle recovery action plan for Antigua and Barbuda. UNEP Caribbean Environment Programme (CEP) Technical Report No. 16. Kingston, Jamaica.

Fürbringer, M. 1874. Zur vergleichenden Anatomie der Schultermuskeln. Jenaische Zeitschrift für Naturwissenschaft 8, 221.

Gaffney, E. 1975. A phylogeny and classification of the higher categories of turtles. Bulletin of the American Museum of Natural History 155:378-436.

Gaffney, E. 1979. Comparative cranial morphology of recent and fossil turtles. Bulletin of the American Museum of Natural History 164:365-376.

García-Muñoz, D. 2000. Estudio de la filopatria y tamaño poblacional de hembras anidadoras de tortuga laúd, *Dermochelys coriacea*, así como parámetros relacionados con su biología reproductiva en el Playón de Mexiquillo, Michoacán. Tesis de Licenciatura (Biología). Facultad de Estudios Superiores Zaragoza. UNAM, México D.F.

Garman, S. 1884a. The North American reptiles and batrachians. A list of the species occurring north of the Isthmus of Tehuantepec, with references. Bulletin of the Essex Institute, Salem 16:3-46.

Garman, S. 1884b. The reptiles of Bermuda. Contributions to the natural history of the Bermudas 1(VI): Bulletin of the United States National Museum 25:285-303.

Gaspar, P., J.-Y. Georges, S. Fossette, A. Lenoble, S. Ferraroli, and Y. Le Maho. 2006. Marine animal behaviour: neglecting ocean currents can lead us up the wrong track. Proceedings of the Royal Society (B) 273:2697-2702.

Georges, J.-Y., and S. Fossette. 2006. Estimating body mass in leatherback turtles *Dermochelys coriacea*. Marine Ecology Progress Series 318:255-262.

Georges, J.-Y., S. Fossette, A. Billes, S. Ferraroli, J. Fretey, D. Grémillet, Y. Le Maho, A.E. Myers, H. Tanaka, and G.C. Hays. 2007. Meta-analysis of movements in Atlantic leatherback turtles during the nesting season: conservation implications. Marine Ecology Progress Series 338:225-232.

Gerrior, P. 1996. Incidental take of sea turtles in northeast U.S. waters. Pages 14-31 *in* P. Williams, compiler. Pelagic longline fishery-sea turtle interactions: Proceedings of an industry, academic and government experts, and stakeholders workshop. U.S. Department of Commerce, National Oceanic and Atmospheric Administration Technical Memorandum NMFS-OPR-7. Silver Spring, Maryland.

Gibbons, J.W., and D.H. Nelson. 1978. The evolutionary significance of delayed emergence from the nest by hatchling turtles. Evolution 32:297-303.

Gilman, E., editor. 2009. Proceedings of the technical workshop on mitigating sea turtle bycatch in coastal net fisheries, 20-22 January 2009, Honolulu. Western Pacific Regional Fishery Management Council, Honolulu, Hawaii.

Gilman, E., D. Kobayashi, T. Swenarton, N. Brothers, P. Dalzell, and I. Kinan-Kelly. 2007. Reducing sea turtle interactions in the Hawaii-based longline swordfish fishery. Biological Conservation 139:19-28.

Gilman, E., E. Zollett, S. Beverly, H. Nakano, K. Davis, D. Shiode, P. Dalzell, and I. Kinan. 2006. Reducing sea turtle bycatch in pelagic longline fisheries. Fish and Fisheries 7:2-23.

Girondot, M., and J. Fretey. 1996. Leatherback turtles, *Dermochelys coriacea*, nesting in French Guiana, 1978-1995. Chelonian Conservation and Biology 2:204-208.

Girondot, M., M.H. Godfrey, L. Ponge, and P. Rivalan. 2007. Modeling approaches to quantify leatherback nesting trends in French Guiana and Suriname. Chelonian Conservation and Biology 6:37-47.

Girondot, M., A.D. Tucker, P. Rivalan, M.H. Godfrey, and J. Chevalier. 2002. Density-dependent nest destruction and population fluctuations of Guianan leatherback turtles. Animal Conservation 5:75-84.

Girondot, M., P. Rivalan, R. Wongsopawiro, J.-P. Briane, V. Hulin, S. Caut, E. Guirlet, and M.H. Godfrey. 2006. Phenology of marine turtle nesting revealed by statistical model of the nesting season. BMC Ecology 6:11.

Gjerde, K.M., and C. Breide, editors. 2003. Towards a strategy for high seas marine protected areas: proceedings of the IUCN, WCPA and WWF experts workshop on high seas marine protected areas, 15-17 January 2003, Malaga, Spain. International Union for the Conservation of Nature (IUCN). Gland, Switzerland.

Gless, J.M., M. Salmon, and J. Wyneken. 2008. Behavioral responses of juvenile leatherbacks *Dermochelys coriacea* to lights used in the longline fishery. Endangered Species Research 5:239-247.

Glüsing, G. 1967. Aufzucht-Versuch junger Lederschilkroten (*Dermochelys coriacea*). Aguarien-und Terrarien Zeitschrift 20:61-63.

Glüsing, G. 1973. Zum Mageninhalt zweier Lederschildkröten, *Dermochelys coriacea*. Salamandra 9:77-80.

Godfrey, M.H., and R. Barreto. 1995. Beach vegetation and seafinding orientation of turtle hatchlings. Biological Conservation 74:29-32.

Godfrey, M.H., and R. Barreto. 1998. *Dermochelys coriacea* (leatherback sea turtle). Copulation. Herpetological Review 29:40-41.

Godfrey, M.H., R. Barreto, and N. Mrosovsky. 1996. Estimating past and present sex ratios of sea turtles in Suriname. Canadian Journal of Zoology 74:267-277.

Godfrey, M.H., R. Barreto, and N. Mrosovsky. 1997. Metabolically-generated heat of developing eggs and its potential effect on sex ratio of sea turtle hatchlings. Journal of Herpetology 31:616-619.

Godfrey, M.H., O. Drif, and M. Girondot. 2001. Two alternative approaches to measuring carapace length in leatherback sea turtles. Pages 177-178 *in* M.S. Coyne and R.D. Clark, compilers. Proceedings of the 21st annual symposium on sea turtle biology and conservation. U.S. Department of Commerce, National Oceanic and Atmospheric Administration Technical Memorandum NMFS-SEFSC-528. Miami, Florida.

Godgenger, M.-C., N. Bréheret, G. Bal, K. N'damité, A. Girard, and M. Girondot. 2009. Nesting estimation and analysis of threats for Critically Endangered leatherback *Dermochelys coriacea* and Endangered olive ridley *Lepidochelys olivacea* marine turtles nesting in Congo. Oryx 43:556-563.

Godgenger, M.-C., A. Gibudi, and M. Girondot. 2008. Activités de ponte des tortues marines sur l'Ouest africain. Rapport d'étude pour Protomac, Gabon. Université Paris Sud, AgroParisTech, CNRS et Protomac, Orsay, France.

Godley, B.J., D.R. Thompson, S. Waldron, and R.W. Furness. 1998. The trophic status of marine turtles as determined by stable isotopes analysis. Marine Ecology Progress Series 166:277-284.

Godley, B.J., A.C. Broderick, L.M. Campbell, S. Ranger, and P.B. Richardson. 2004. An assessment of the status and exploitation of marine turtles in the U.K. Overseas Territories in the Wider Caribbean. Final project report for the Department of Environment, Food and Rural Affairs and the Commonwealth Office, United Kingdom.

Godley, B.J., M.J. Gaywood, R.J. Law, C.J. McCarthy, C. McKenzie, I.A.P. Patterson, R.S. Penrose, R.J. Reid, and H.M. Ross. 1998. Patterns of marine turtle mortality in British Waters (1992-1996) with reference to tissue contaminant levels. Journal of the Marine Biological Association of the United Kingdom 78:973-984.

Goff, G.P., and J. Lien. 1988. Atlantic leatherback turtles, *Dermochelys coriacea*, in cold water off Newfoundland and Labrador. Canadian Field-Naturalist 102:1-5.

Goff, G.P., and G.B. Stenson. 1988. Brown adipose tissue in leatherback sea turtles: a thermogenic organ in an endothermic reptile? Copeia 1988:1071-1074.

Gosse, P.H. 1851. A naturalist's sojourn in Jamaica. Longman, London, United Kingdom.

Goverse, E., and M. Hilterman. 2003. Leatherback stuck in the mud: a matter of life or death? Page 45 *in* J.A. Seminoff, compiler. Proceedings of the 22nd annual symposium on sea turtle biology and conservation. U.S. Department of Commerce, National Oceanic and Atmospheric Administration Technical Memorandum NMFS-SEFSC-503. Miami, Florida.

Goverse, E., M. Hilterman, and M. Godfrey. 2006. Sand temperature profiles of three major leatherback (*Dermochelys coriacea*) nesting beaches in Suriname. Pages 11-13 *in* N. Pilcher, compiler. Proceedings of the 23rd annual symposium on sea turtle biology and conservation. U.S. Department of Commerce, National Oceanic and Atmospheric Administration Technical Memorandum NMFS-SEFSC-536. Miami, Florida.

Grant, G.S., and D. Ferrell. 1993. Leatherback turtle, *Dermochelys coriacea* (Reptilia: Dermochelidae): notes on nearshore feeding behavior and association with Cobia. Brimleyana 19:77-81.

Grant, G.S., H. Malpass, and J. Beasley. 1996. Correlation of leatherback turtle and jellyfish occurrence. Herpetological Review 27:123-125.

Gratiot, N., G. Gratiot, L. Kelle, and B. de Thoisy. 2006. Estimation of the nesting season of marine turtles from incomplete data: statistical adjustment of a sinusoidal function. Animal Conservation 9:95-102.

Gray, J.E. 1825. A synopsis of the genera of Reptiles and Amphibia, with a description of some new species. Annals of Philosophy, Series 2:193-217. [reprinted 1966, Society for the Study of Amphibians and Reptiles]

Greer, A.E., J.D. Lazell, and R.M. Wright. 1973. Anatomical evidence for counter-current heat exchanger in the leatherback turtle, *Dermochelys coriacea*. Nature 244:181.

Groombridge, B. (compiler). 1982. Red Data Book, Amphibia-Reptilia, Part 1: Testudines, Crocodylia, Rhynchocephalia. International Union for the Conservation of Nature (IUCN). Gland, Switzerland.

Gudynas, E. 1980. Notes on the sea turtles of Uruguay. Association for the Study of Reptilia and Amphibia Journal 1:69-76.

Guirlet, E., K. Das, and M. Girondot. 2008. Maternal transfer of trace elements in leatherback turtles (*Dermochelys coriacea*) of French Guiana. Aquatic Toxicology 88:267-276.

Hall, K.V. 1987. Behavior and orientation of hatchling hawksbill and leatherback sea turtles in nearshore waters. Paper presented at the 7th annual workshop on sea turtle conservation and biology. Unpublished "Agenda and Abstracts." Wekiwa Springs State Park, Orlando, Florida.

Halstead, B.W. 1956. Animal phyla known to contain poisonous marine animals. Pages 9-27 *in* E.E. Buckley and N. Porges, editors. Venoms. Publication No. 44, American Association for the Advancement of Science, Washington, D.C.

Hamann, M., C. Limpus, G. Hughes, J. Mortimer, and N. Pilcher. 2006a. Assessment of the conservation status of the leatherback turtle in the Indian Ocean and SouthEast Asia. Indian Ocean and SouthEast Asia (IOSEA) Species Assessment: Volume I. IOSEA Marine Turtle Memorandum of Understanding Secretariat, Bangkok, Thailand.

Hamann, M., C. Limpus, G. Hughes, J. Mortimer, and N. Pilcher. 2006b. Assessment of the impact of the December 2004 tsunami on marine turtles and their habitats in the Indian Ocean and SouthEast Asia. IOSEA Marine Turtle Memorandum of Understanding Secretariat, Bangkok, Thailand.

Harant, H. 1949. Sur la capture d'une tortue luth. Feuille des Naturalistes, n.s. 4 (51e annee), 7-8:77.

Harms, C.A., S.A. Eckert, S.A. Kubis, M. Campbell, D.H. Levenson, and M.A. Crognale. 2007. Field anaesthesia of leatherback sea turtles (*Dermochelys coriacea*). Veterinary Record 161:15-21.

Harrison, E., and S. Troëng. 2002. 2002 leatherback program at Tortuguero, Costa Rica. Unpublished report to the Caribbean Conservation Corporation. San Pedro, Costa Rica.

Hartog, J.C. 1980. Notes on the food of sea turtles: *Eretmochelys imbricata* (L.) and *Dermochelys coriacea* (L.). Netherlands Journal of Zoology 39:595-610.

Hartog, J.C., and M.M. van Nierop. 1984. A study of the gut contents of six leathery turtles *Dermochelys coriacea* (Linnaeus) (Reptilia: Testudines: Dermochelyidae) from British waters and from the Netherlands. Zoologische Verhandelingen 209:1-36.

Hastings, M. 2003. A conservation success: leatherback turtles in the British Virgin Islands. Marine Turtle Newsletter 9:5-7.

Hawkes, L.A., A.C. Broderick, M.H. Godfrey, and B.J. Godley. 2007. Investigating the potential impacts of climate change on a marine turtle population. Global Change Biology 13:923-932.

Hay, O.P. 1898. On *Protostega*, the systematic position of *Dermochelys* and the morphogeny of the chelonian carapace and plastron. American Naturalist 32:929-948.

Hay, O.P. 1908. The fossil turtles of North America. Carnegie Institution 75:1-568.

Hay, O.P. 1922. On the phylogeny of the shell of the Testudinata and the relationships of *Dermochelys*. Journal of Morphology 36:421-445.

Hays, G.C. 2000. The implications of variable remigration intervals for the assessment of population size in marine turtles. Journal of Theoretical Biology 206:221-227.

Hays, G.C., J.D.R. Houghton, and A.E. Myers. 2004b. Pan-Atlantic leatherback turtle movements. Nature 429:522.

Hays, G.C., M.R. Farquhar, P. Luschi, S.L.H. Teo, and T.M. Thys. 2009. Vertical niche overlap by two ocean giants with similar diets: ocean sunfish and leatherback turtles. Journal of Experimental Marine Biology and Ecology 370:134-143.

Hays, G.C., V.J. Hobson, J.D. Metcalfe, D. Righton, and D.W. Sims. 2006. Flexible foraging movements of leatherback turtles across the North Atlantic Ocean. Ecology 87:2647-2656.

Hays, G.C., J.D.R. Houghton, C. Isaacs, R.S. King, C. Lloyd, and P. Lovell. 2004a. First records of oceanic dive profiles for leatherback turtles, *Dermochelys coriacea*, indicate behavioural plasticity associated with long-distance migration. Animal Behaviour 67:733-743.

Heldt, H. 1933. La tortue luth (*Sphargis coriacea* L.). Captures faites sur les cotes tunisiennes (1930-1933). Contribution à l'étude anatomique et biologique de l'espèce. Annales de al Station Océanographique de Salammbo (Tunis) 8:1-40.

Hendrickson, J.R. 1958. The green sea turtle, *Chelonia mydas* (Linn.) in Malaya and Sarawak. Proceedings of the Zoological Society of London 130:455-535.

Hendrickson, J.R. 1980. The ecological strategies of sea turtles. American Zoologist 20:597-608.

Hendrickson, J.R., and E. Balasingam. 1966. Nesting beach preferences of Malayan sea turtles. Bulletin of the National Museum of Singapore No. 33, pt.10:69-76.

Hernández, R., J. Buitrago, H. Guada, H. Hernández-Hamón, and M. Llano. 2007. Nesting distribution and hatching success of the leatherback, *Dermochelys coriacea*, in relation to human pressures at Playa Parguito, Margarita Island, Venezuela. Chelonian Conservation and Biology 6:79-87.

Hildebrand, H. 1987. A reconnaissance of beaches and coastal waters from the border of Belize to the Mississippi River as habitats for marine turtles. Unpublished final report to the U.S. Department of Commerce, National Marine Fisheries Service. P.O. NA-84-CF-A-134. Panama City, Florida.

Hillestad, H.O., J.I. Richardson, and G.K. Williamson. 1978. Incidental capture of sea turtles by shrimp trawlermen in Georgia. Proceedings of the annual conference of the Southeastern Association of Fish and Wildllife Agencies 32:167-178.

Hilterman, M.L., and E. Goverse. 2007. Nesting and nest success of the leatherback turtle (*Dermochelys coriacea*) in Suriname, 1999-2005. Chelonian Conservation and Biology 6:87-100.

Hirayama, R., and T. Chitoku. 1996. Family Dermochelyidae (Superfamily Chelonioidea) from the Upper Cretaceous of North Japan. Transactions and Proceedings of the Palaeontological Society of Japan 184:597-622.

Hirth, H.F. 1982. Weight and length relationships of some adult marine turtles. Bulletin of Marine Science 32:336-341.

Hirth, H.F., and L.H. Ogren. 1987. Some aspects of the ecology of the leatherback turtle *Dermochelys coriacea* at Laguna Jalova, Costa Rica. U.S. Department of Commerce, National Oceanic and Atmospheric Administration Technical Report NMFS 56:1-14. Panama City, Florida.

Hirth, H.F., and W.M. Schaffer. 1974. Survival rate of the green turtle, *Chelonia mydas*, necessary to maintain stable populations. Copeia 1974:544-546.

Hirth, H.F., J. Kasu, and T. Mala. 1993. Observations on a leatherback turtle *Dermochelys coriacea* nesting population near Piguwa, Papua New Guinea. Biological Conservation 65:77-82.

Hitipeuw, C., F. Moga, P. Dutton, S. Benson, M. Tiwari, R. Tapilatu, and H. Gjertsen. 2006. Update on population status and development of multi-stakeholder management of leatherbacks in Papua, Indonesia. Pages 138-139 in M. Frick, A. Panagopoulou, A.F. Rees, and K. Williams, compilers. Book of abstracts for the 26th annual symposium on sea turtle biology and conservation. Island of Crete, Greece.

Hitipeuw, C., P.H. Dutton, S.R. Benson, J. Thebu, and J. Bakarbessy. 2007. Population status and internesting movement of leatherback turtles, *Dermochelys coriacea*, nesting on the northwest coast of Papua, Indonesia. Chelonian Conservation and Biology 6:28-37.

Hodge, R.P. 1979. Geographic distribution: *Dermochelys coriacea schlegeli*. Herpetological Review 10:102.

Hoffmann, M., T.M. Brooks, G.A.B. da Fonseca, C. Gascon, A.F.A. Hawkins, R.E. James, P. Langhammer, R.A. Mittermeier, J.D. Pilgrim, A.S.L. Rodrigues, and J.M.C. Silva. 2008. The IUCN *Red List* and conservation planning. Endangered Species Research 6:113-125.

Hoffman, W., and T.H. Fritts. 1982. Sea turtle distribution along the boundary of the Gulf Stream current off eastern Florida. Herpetologica 38:405-409.

Holland, D.L., J. Davenport, and J. East. 1990. The fatty acid composition of the leatherback turtle, *Dermochelys coriacea*, and its jellyfish prey. Journal of the Marine Biological Association of the United Kingdom 70:761-770.

Hooper, S.N., and R.G. Ackman. 1970. *Trans*-6-hexadecenoic acid in the Atlantic leatherback *Dermochelys coriacea coriacea*, L. and other marine turtles. Lipids 5:288-292.

Hooper, S.N., and R.G. Ackman. 1972. Presence of *trans*-6-hexadecenoic acid in the white jellyfish *Aurelia aurita* Lamark and in a Caribbean gorgonian. Lipids 7:624-626.

Horrocks, J.A. 1987. Leatherbacks in Barbados. Marine Turtle Newsletter 41:7.

Horrocks, J.A. 1989. Leatherback injured off Barbados, West Indies. Marine Turtle Newsletter 46:9-10.

Horrocks, J.A. 1992. WIDECAST sea turtle recovery action plan for Barbados. *In* K.L. Eckert, editor. UNEP Caribbean Environment Programme (CEP) Technical Report No. 12. Kingston, Jamaica.

Houghton, J.D.R., T.K. Doyle, M.W. Wilson, J. Davenport, and G.C. Hays. 2006. Jellyfish aggregations and leatherback turtle foraging patterns in a temperate coastal environment. Ecology 87:1967-1972.

Houghton, J.D.R., T.K. Doyle, J. Davenport, R.P. Wilson, and G.C. Hays. 2008. The role of infrequent and extraordinary deep dives in leatherback turtles (*Dermochelys coriacea*). Journal of Experimental Biology 211:2566-2575.

Houghton, J.D.R., A.E. Myers, C. Lloyd, R.S. King, C. Isaacs, and G.C. Hays. 2007. Protracted rainfall decreases temperature within leatherback (*Dermochelys coriacea*) clutches in Grenada, West Indies: ecological implications for a species displaying temperature dependent sex determination. Journal of Experimental Marine Biology and Ecology 345:71-77.

Hubbs, C.L., and G.I. Roden. 1964. Oceanography and marine life along the Pacific coast of middle America. Pages 143-186 *in* R.C. West, volume editor. Natural Environments and Early Cultures, Volume I of Handbook of Middle American Indians. University of Texas Press, Austin, Texas.

Hudson, D.M., and P.L. Lutz. 1986. Salt gland function in the leatherback sea turtle, *Dermochelys coriacea*. Copeia 1986:247-249.

Huerta, P., H. Pineda, A. Aguirre, T. Spraker, L. Sarti M., and A. Barragan. 2002. First confirmed case of fibropapilloma in a leatherback turtle (*Dermochelys coriacea*). Page 193 *in* A. Mosier, A. Foley, and B. Brost, compilers. Proceedings of the 20th annual symposium on sea turtle biology and conservation. U.S. Department of Commerce, National Oceanic and Atmospheric Administration Technical Memorandum NMFS-SEFSC-477. Miami, Florida.

Hughes, G.R. 1971a. The marine turtles of Tongaland, V. Lammergeyer 13:7-24.

Hughes, G.R. 1971b. Sea turtle research and conservation in South East Africa. Pages 57-67 *in* Marine Turtles. International Union for the Conservation of Nature (IUCN) Publications New Series, Suppl. Paper No. 31. Morges, Switzerland.

Hughes, G.R. 1974a. The sea turtles of south-east Africa, I. Status, morphology and distributions. South African Association for Marine Biological Research, Oceanographic Research Institute. Investigational Report No. 35:1-114. Durban, South Africa.

Hughes, G.R. 1974b. The sea turtles of south-east Africa, II. The biology of the Tongaland loggerhead turtle *Caretta caretta* L. with comments on the leatherback turtle *Dermochelys coriacea* L. in the study region. South African Association for Marine Biological Research, Oceanographic Research

Institute. Investigational Report No. 36:1-96. Durban, South Africa.

Hughes, G.R. 1982. Conservation of sea turtles in the southern African region. Pages 397-404 *in* K.A. Bjorndal, editor. Biology and conservation of sea turtles. Smithsonian Institution Press. Washington, D.C.

Hughes, G.R. 1996. Nesting of leatherback turtle (*Dermochelys coriacea*) in Tongaland, KwaZulu-Natal, South Africa, 1963-1995. Chelonian Conservation and Biology 2:153-158.

Hughes, G.R., and M.T. Mentis. 1967. Further studies on marine turtles in Tongaland, II. Lammergeyer 7:55-72.

Hughes, G.R., A.J. Bass, and M.T. Mentis. 1967. Further studies on marine turtles in Tongaland. Lammergeyer 7:5-54.

Hughes, G.R., B. Huntley, and D. Wearne. 1973. Sea turtles in Angola. Biological Conservation 5:58.

Hughes, G.R., P. Luschi, R. Mencacci, and F. Papi. 1998. The 7000-km oceanic journey of a leatherback turtle tracked by satellite. Journal of Experimental Marine Biology and Ecology 229:209-217.

Hughes, R.C., J.R. Baker, and C.B. Dawson. 1941a. The tapeworms of reptiles, part II, Host Catalogue. The Wasmann Collector 4:97-104.

Hughes, R.C., J.W. Higginbotham, and J.W. Clary. 1941b. The trematodes of reptiles, part II, host catalogue. Proceedings of the Oklahoma Academy of Science for 1940, 21:35-43.

Hughes, R.C., J.W. Higginbotham, and J.W. Clary. 1942. The trematodes of reptiles. Part I: systematic section. American Midland Naturalist 27:109-134.

Hulin, V., V. Delmas, M. Girondot, M.H. Godfrey, and J.-M. Guillon. 2009. Temperature-dependent sex determination and global change: are some species at greater risk? Oecologia 160:493-506.

Humphrey, S.L., and R.V. Salm. 1996. Status of sea turtle conservation in the western Indian Ocean. Proceedings of the western Indian Ocean training workshop and strategic planning session on sea turtles. 12-18 November 1995, Sodwana Bay, South Africa. UNEP Regional Seas Reports and Studies No. 165:1-161. Nairobi, Kenya.

Huntley, B.J. 1974. Outlines of wildlife conservation in Angola. Journal of the Southern Africa Wildlife Management Association 4:157-166.

Huntley, B.J. 1978. Ecosystem conservation in southern Africa. Pages 1333-1384 *in* M.J.A. Werger and A.C. van Bruggen, editors. Biogeography and Ecology of Southern Africa, Monographiae Biologicae 31. W. Junk, Hague, The Netherlands.

Hykle, D. 2002. The Convention on Migratory Species and other international instruments relevant to marine turtle conservation: pros and cons. Journal of International Wildlife Law and Policy 5:105-119.

Ikaran, M., Y. Braet, J. Fretey, L.F. López-Jurado, and D. Roumet. 2008. Dramatic impact of army ants on *Dermochelys coriacea* nests at Pongara National Park (Gabon, Central Africa). Pages 237-238 *in* A.F. Rees, M. Frick, A. Panagopoulou, and K. Williams, compilers. Proceedings of the 27th annual symposium on sea turtle biology and conservation. U.S. Department of Commerce, National Oceanic and Atmospheric Administration Technical Memorandum NMFS-SEFSC-569. Miami, Florida.

Ingle, R.M., and F.G.W. Smith. 1949. Sea turtles and the turtle industry of the West Indies, Florida and the Gulf of México, with annotated bibliography. Special Publication of the Marine Laboratory, University of Miami, Florida.

International Union for the Conservation of Nature (IUCN). 1996. A marine turtle conservation strategy and action plan for the Western Indian Ocean. Prepared by the Marine Turtle Specialist Group for the Species Survival Commission of IUCN. Arlington, Virginia.

International Union for the Conservation of Nature (IUCN). 2001. A marine turtle conservation strategy and action plan for the Northern Indian Ocean. Prepared by the Marine Turtle Specialist Group (MTSG) for the Species Survival Commission (SSC) of IUCN. IUCN/SSC/MTSG Publication No. 3. Washington, D.C.

International Union for the Conservation of Nature (IUCN). 2009. Resolutions and recommendations from the World Conservation Congress, Barcelona, 5-14 October 2008. Gland, Switzerland.

Iverson, E.S., and H.O. Yoshida. 1956. Longline fishing for tuna in the Central Equatorial Pacific, 1954. U.S. Fish and Wildlife Service, Special Scientific Report Fisheries No. 184:1-33.

Jackson, D.C., and H.D. Prange. 1979. Ventilation and gas exchange during rest and exercise in adult green turtles. Journal of Comparative Physiology 134:315-319.

James, M.C. 2004. *Dermochelys coriacea* (leatherback sea turtle) penis display. Herpetological Review 35:264-265.

James, M.C., and T.B. Herman. 2001. Feeding of *Dermochelys coriacea* on medusae in the Northwest Atlantic. Chelonian Conservation and Biology 4:202-205.

James, M.C., and N. Mrosovsky. 2004. Body temperatures of leatherback turtles (*Dermochelys coriacea*) in temperate waters off Nova Scotia. Canadian Journal of Zoology 82:1302-1306.

James, M.C., C.A. Ottensmeyer, and R.A. Myers. 2005a. Identification of high-use habitat and threats to leatherback sea turtles in northern waters: new directions for conservation. Ecology Letters 8:195-201.

James, M.C., S.A. Eckert, and R.A. Myers. 2005b. Migratory and reproductive movements of male leatherback turtles (*Dermochelys coriacea*). Marine Biology 147:845-853.

James, M.C., R.A. Myers, and C.A. Ottensmeyer. 2005c. Behaviour of leatherback sea turtles, *Dermochelys coriacea*, during the migratory cycle. Proceedings of the Royal Society B 272:1547-1555.

James, M.C., C.A. Ottensmeyer, S.A. Eckert, and R.A. Myers. 2006a. Changes in diel diving patterns accompany shifts between northern foraging and south-ward migration in leatherback turtles. Canadian Journal of Zoology 84:754-765.

James, M.C., S.A. Sherril-Mix, K. Martin, and R.A. Myers. 2006b. Canadian waters provide critical foraging habitat for leatherback sea turtles. Biological Conservation 133:347-357.

James, M.C., J. Davenport, and G.C. Hays. 2006c. Expanded thermal niche for a diving vertebrate: a leatherback turtle diving into near-freezing water. Journal of Experimental Marine Biology and Ecology 335:221-226.

James, M.C., S.A. Sherrill-Mix, and R.A. Myers. 2007. Population characteristics and seasonal migrations of leatherback sea turtles at high latitudes. Marine Ecology Progress Series 337:245-254.

Johnson, M.L. 1989. Juvenile leatherback cared for in captivity. Marine Turtle Newsletter 47:13-14.

Jolly, G.M. 1965. Explicit estimates from capture-recapture data with both death and immigration—stochastic model. Biometrika 52:225-247.

Jones, E.C., and R.S. Shomura. 1970. Narrative report *Townsend Cromwell*, Cruise 44. Unpublished report to the Bureau of Commercial Fisheries, Biological Laboratory, Honolulu, Hawaii.

Jones, S. 1959. A leathery turtle *Dermochelys coriacea* (Linnaeus) coming ashore to lay eggs during the day. Journal of the Bombay Natural History Society 56:137-139.

Jones, T.T. 2009. Energetics of the leatherback turtle, *Dermochelys coriacea*. Ph.D. dissertation, University of British Columbia, Vancouver, Canada.

Jones, T.T., R.D. Reina, C.-A. Darveau, and P.L. Lutz. 2007. Ontogeny of energetics in leatherback (*Dermochelys coriacea*) and olive ridley (*Lepidochelys olivacea*) sea turtle hatchlings. Comparative Biochemistry and Physiology 147:313-322.

Jones, T.T., M. Salmon, J. Wyneken, and C. Johnson. 2000. Rearing leatherback hatchlings: protocols, growth, and survival. Marine Turtle Newsletter 90:3-6.

Jonsen, I.D., R.A. Myers, and M.C. James. 2006. Robust hierarchical state-space models reveal diel variation in travel rates of migrating leatherback turtles. Journal of Animal Ecology 75:1046-1057.

Jonsen, I.D., R.A. Myers, and M.C. James. 2007. Identifying leatherback turtle foraging behaviour from satellite telemetry using a switching state-space model. Marine Ecology Progress Series 337:255-264.

Joseph, J.D., R.G. Ackman, and G.T. Seaborn. 1985. Effect of diet on depot fatty acid composition in the green turtle, *Chelonia mydas*. Comparative Biochemistry and Physiology 80B:15-22.

Journal Officiel de la République Française (JORF). 1998. Décrêt N°98-165 portant création de la Réserve Naturelle de l'Amana (Guyane), 14 mars 1998: 3835-3837.

Kamel, S.J., and N. Mrosovsky. 2004. Nest site selection in leatherbacks, *Dermochelys coriacea*: individual patterns and their consequences. Animal Behaviour 68:357-366.

Kaplan, I.C. 2005. A risk assessment for Pacific leatherback turtles (*Dermochelys coriacea*). Canadian Journal of Fisheries and Aquatic Sciences 62:1710-1719.

Kappler, A. 1887. Surinam, rein Land, seine Natur, Bevölkerung und seine Kultur-verhältnisse mit Bezug auf Kolonisation. Stuttgart, J.C. Cotta. Germany.

Kapurusinghe, T. 2006. Status and conservation of marine turtles in Sri Lanka. Pages 173-187 *in* K. Shanker and B.C. Choudhury, editors. Marine turtles of India. Universities Press. Hyderabad, India.

Kapurusinghe, T., and L. Ekanayake. 2002. The nesting frequencies of marine turtles in Rekawa, Southern Sri Lanka. Pages 61-65 *in* A. Mosier, A. Foley, and B. Brost, compilers. Proceedings of the 20th annual symposium on sea turtle biology and conservation. U.S. Department of Commerce, National Oceanic and Atmospheric Administration Technical Memorandum NMFS-SEFSC-477. Miami, Florida.

Kapurusinghe, T., and M.M. Saman. 2005. Marine turtle bycatch in Sri Lanka. Pages 45-46 *in* M.S. Coyne and R.D. Clark, compilers. Proceedings of the 21st annual symposium on sea turtle biology and conservation. U.S. Department of Commerce,

National Oceanic and Atmospheric Administration Technical Memorandum NMFS-SEFSC-528. Miami, Florida.

Kar, C.S., and S. Bhaskar. 1982. Status of sea turtles in the eastern Indian Ocean. Pages 365-372 *in* K.A. Bjorndal, editor. Biology and conservation of sea turtles. Smithsonian Institution Press. Washington, D.C.

Kaufmann, R. 1973. Biología de las tortugas marinas *Caretta caretta* y *Dermochelys coriacea* de la costa Atlántica Colombiana. Revista de la Academía Colombiana de Ciencias Exactas, Físicas y Naturales 14:67-80.

Keinath, J.A. 1986. A telemetric study of the surface and submersion activities of *Dermochelys coriacea* and *Caretta caretta*. Unpublished report to the University of Rhode Island, Kingston, Rhode Island.

Keinath, J.A., and J.A. Musick. 1993. Atlantic leatherback turtle, *Dermochelys coriacea*. Pages 453-455 *in* K. Terwilliger, editor. Virginia's endangered species. McDonald Woodward Publishing Company, Blacksburg, Virginia.

Keinath, J.A., J.A. Musick, and R.A. Byles. 1987. Aspects of the biology of Virginia's sea turtles: 1979-1986. Virginia Journal of Science 38:329-336.

Kelle, L., and G. Feuillet. 2008. La tortue luth. Collection Nature Guyanaise. Cayenne, French Guiana.

Kelle, L., N. Gratiot, I. Nolibos, J. Thérèse, R. Wongsopawiro, and B. deThoisy. 2007. Monitoring of nesting leatherback turtles (*Dermochelys coriacea*): contribution of remote sensing for real-time assessment of beach coverage in French Guiana. Chelonia Conservation and Biology 6:142-147.

Kendall, W.L., and R. Bjorkland. 2001. Using open robust design models to estimate temporary emigration from capture-recapture data. Biometrics 57:1113-1122.

Kinan, I., editor. 2002. Proceedings of the western Pacific sea turtle cooperative research and management workshop. Western Pacific Regional Fishery Management Council, Honolulu, Hawaii.

Kinan, I., editor. 2005. Proceedings of the second western Pacific sea turtle cooperative research and management workshop. Volume 1: West Pacific leatherback and southwest Pacific hawksbill sea turtles. Western Pacific Regional Fishery Management Council, Honolulu, Hawaii.

Kinan, I., and P. Danzell. 2005. Sea turtles as flagship species: different perspectives create conflicts in the Pacific Islands. Special Issue: Marine Turtles as Flagships. MAST/ Maritime Studies 3(2) and 4(1):195-212.

Kinch, J. 2006. Socio-economic assessment study for the Huon Coast. Final technical report to the Western Pacific Regional Fisheries Management Council. Honolulu, Hawaii.

King, F.W., and R.L. Burke. 1997. Crocodilian, Tuatara, and turtle species of the world: online taxonomic and geographic reference. Association of Systematics Collections, Washington, D.C.

Kinunen, W., and P. Walczak. 1971. Persian Gulf sea turtle nesting surveys. Report to Iran Game and Fish Department, Tehran, Iran.

Kirschvink, J. 1980. Magnetic material in turtles: a preliminary report and a request. Marine Turtle Newsletter 15:7-9.

Kisokao, K. 2005. Community-based conservation and monitoring of leatherback turtles at Kamiali Wildlife Management Area performed by Kamiali Integrated Conservation Development Group. Final Report submitted to Western Pacific Regional Fishery Management Council—Contract No. 04-wpc-025. Honolulu, Hawaii.

Kisokau, K.M., and L. Ambio. 2005. The community-based conservation and monitoring of leatherback turtles (*Dermochelys coriacea*) at Kamiali Wildlife Management Area, Morobe Province, Papua New Guinea. Pages 51-58 *in* I. Kinan, editor. Proceedings of the second western Pacific sea turtle cooperative research and management workshop. Volume 1: West Pacific leatherback and southwest Pacific hawksbill sea turtles. Western Pacific Regional Fishery Management Council, Honolulu, Hawaii.

Koch, W. 1934. Lungengefasse und Kreislauf der Schildkroten. Biologia Generalis, Vienna 10:359-382.

Kooyman, G.L. 1989. Diverse divers: physiology and behavior. Zoophysiology Volume 23. Springer-Verlag, Berlin, Germany.

Kooyman, G.L., E.A. Wahrenbrock, M.A. Castellini, R.W. Davis, and E.E. Sinnett. 1980. Aerobic and anaerobic metabolism during voluntary diving in Weddell seals: evidence of preferred pathways from blood chemsitry and behavior. Journal of Comparative Physiology B: Biochemical, Systemic, and Environmental Physiology 138:335-346.

Kotas, J.E., D. dos Santos, V.G. de Azevedo, B.M.G. Gallo, and P.C.R. Barata. 2004. Incidental capture of loggerhead *Caretta caretta* and leatherback *Dermochelys coriacea* sea turtles by the pelagic longline fishery off southern Brazil. Fishery Bulletin 102:393-399.

Krenz, J.G., G.J.P. Naylor, H.B. Shaffer, and F.J. Janzen. 2005. Molecular phylogenetics and evolution of turtles. Molecular Phylogenetics and Evolution 37:178-191.

Kuzmin, S.L. 2002. The turtles of Russia and other ex-Soviet republics (former Soviet Union). Edition Chimaira, Frankfurt, Germany.

L'association Kwata. 2009. Evaluation des impacts de la pollution lumineuse sur les sites de ponte de tortues marines de Rémire-Montjoly. Université des Antilles et de la Guyane, Cayenne, French Guiana.

LaCasella, E., and P.H. Dutton. 2008. Longer mtDNA sequences resolve leatherback (*Dermochelys coriacea*) stock structure. Pages 128-129 *in* A.F. Rees, M. Frick, A. Panagopoulou, and K. Williams, compilers. Proceedings of the 27th annual symposium on sea turtle biology and conservation. U.S. Department of Commerce, National Oceanic and Atmospheric Administration Technical Memorandum NMFS-SEFSC-569. Miami, Florida.

Lambardi, P., J.R.E. Lutjeharms, R. Mencacci, G.C. Hays, and P. Luschi. 2008. Influence of ocean currents on long-distance movement of leatherback sea turtles in the Southwest Indian Ocean. Marine Ecology Progress Series 353:289-301.

Lambie, I. 1983. Two tagging records from Trinidad. Marine Turtle Newsletter 24:17.

Laporta, M., P. Miller, S. Horta, and G. Riestra. 2006. First report of leatherback turtle entanglement in trap lines in the Uruguayan continental shelf. Marine Turtle Newsletter 112:9-11.

Laurance, W.F., J.M. Fay, R.J. Parnell, G.-P. Counguet, A. Formia, and M.E. Lee. 2008. Does rainforest logging threaten marine turtles? Oryx 42:246-251.

Lawalata, J., C. Hitipeuw, N. Ratnawati, D. Utra, I. Ukru, W. Maturbongs, and G. Saija. 2005. Community based management of leatherback turtles residing in Kei Islands: reducing mortality due to traditional hunting practices. Pages 25-36 *in* I. Kinan, editor. Proceedings of the 2nd western Pacific sea turtle cooperative research and management workshop. Volume 1: West Pacific leatherback and southwest Pacific hawksbill sea turtles. Western Pacific Regional Fishery Management Council, Honolulu, Hawaii.

Lazar, B., L. Lipej, D. Holcer, V. Onofri, V. Žiža, P. Tutman, E. Marčelja, and N. Tvrtković. 2008. New data on the occurrence of leatherback turtles *Dermochelys coriacea* in the Eastern Adriatic Sea. Vie et milieu—life and environment 58:237-241.

Lazell, J.D., Jr. 1976. This Broken Archipelago: Cape Cod and the Islands, Amphibians and Reptiles. The New York Times Book Company, New York City, New York.

Lazell, J.D., Jr. 1980. New England waters: critical habitat for marine turtles. Copeia 1980:290-295.

Leary, T.R. 1957. A schooling of leatherback turtles, *Dermochelys coriacea coriacea*, on the Texas coast. Copeia 1957:232.

Lee, D.S., and W.M. Palmer. 1981. Records of leatherback turtles, *Dermochelys coriacea* (Linnaeus), and other marine turtles in North Carolina waters. Brimleyana 5:95-106.

Lee, D.W., C.J. Brown, and T.L. Jordan. 1995. SEFSC pelagic observer program data summary for 1992-1994. U.S. Department of Commerce, National Oceanic and Atmospheric Administration Technical Memorandum NMFS-SEFSC-373. Miami, Florida.

Lee Lum, L. 2006. Assessment of incidental sea turtle catch in the artisanal gillnet fishery in Trinidad and Tobago, West Indies. Applied Herpetology 3:357-368.

Leidy, J. 1856. A synopsis of entozoa and some of the other ectocongeners observed by the author. Proceedings of the Academy of Natural Sciences, Philadelphia 8:42-58.

Lentz, S.A. 1987. Plastics in the marine environment: legal approaches for international action. Marine Pollution Bulletin 18:361-365.

Lescure, J., F. Rimblot, J. Fretey, S. Renous, and C. Pieau. 1985. Influence de la température d'incubation des œufs sur la sex-ratio des nouveaux-nés de la tortue luth, *Dermochelys coriacea*. Bulletin de la Société Zoologique de France 100:355-359.

Leslie, A.J., D.N. Penick, J.R. Spotila, and F.V. Paladino. 1996. Leatherback turtle, *Dermochelys coriacea*, nesting and nest success at Tortuguero, Costa Rica, in 1990-1991. Chelonian Conservation and Biology 2:159-168.

Levenson, D.H., S.A. Eckert, M.A. Crognale, J.F. Deegan, and G.H. Jacobs. 2004. Photopic spectral sensitivity of green and loggerhead sea turtles. Copeia 2004:908-914.

Levy, Y., R. King, and I. Aizenberg. 2005. Holding a live leatherback turtle in Israel: lessons learned. Marine Turtle Newsletter 107:7-8.

Lewison, R.L., S.A. Freeman, and L.B. Crowder. 2004. Quantifying the effects of fisheries on threatened species: the impact of pelagic longlines on loggerhead and leatherback sea turtles. Ecology Letters 7:221-231.

Limpus, C.J. 1984. A benthic feeding record from neritic waters for the leathery turtle (*Dermochelys coriacea*). Copeia 1984:552-553.

Limpus, C.J. 2006. Status of leatherback turtles in Australia. Pages 15-21 *in* M. Hamann, C. Limpus, G. Hughes, J. Mortimer, and N. Pilcher, compilers. Assessment of the conservation status of the leatherback turtle in the Indian Ocean and

SouthEast Asia. Indian Ocean and SouthEast Asia (IOSEA) Species Assessment: Volume I. IOSEA Marine Turtle Memorandum of Understanding Secretariat, Bangkok, Thailand.

Limpus, C.J. 2009. A biological review of Australian marine turtle species. 6. Leatherback turtle, *Dermochelys coriacea* (Vandelli). Unpublished report to the Queensland Environmental Protection Agency. Brisbane, Australia.

Limpus, C.J., and N.C. McLachlan. 1979. Observations on the leatherback turtle, *Dermochelys coriacea* (L.), in Australia. Australian Wildlife Research 1979:105-116.

Limpus, C.J., and N. McLachlan. 1994. The conservation status of the leatherback turtle, *Dermochelys coriacea*, in Australia. Pages 63-67 *in* R. James, editor. Proceedings of the Australian marine turtle conservation workshop, Gold Coast 14-17 November 1990. Queensland Department of Environment and Heritage. Canberra: ANCA. Australia.

Limpus, C.J., V. Baker, and J.D. Miller. 1979. Movement induced mortality of loggerhead eggs. Herpetologica 35:335-338.

Limpus, C.J., N.C. McLachlan, and J.D. Miller. 1984. Further observations on breeding of *Dermochelys coriacea* in Australia. Australian Wildlife Research 11:567-571.

Lindholm, W.A. 1929. Revidiertes verzeichnis der Gattungen der rezenten Schildkröten nebst Notizen zur Nomenklatur einiger Arten. Zoologische Anzeiger 81:275-295.

Linnaeus, C. 1766. Systema Naturae. Editio duodecima, reformata. Tomus I, pars I. Salvii, Holmiae. Stockholm, Sweden.

Livingstone, S.R. 2007. Threats to leatherback and olive ridley nests in the Gamba Complex of Protected Areas, Gabon, with a focus on crab predation. Testudo 6:25-42.

Livingstone, S.R., and S.B. Verhage. 2006. Leatherback nest ecology in the Gamba Complex, Gabon: improving hatchery output. Pages 143-144 *in* M. Frick, A. Panagopoulou, A.F. Rees, and K. Williams, compilers. Book of abstracts for the 26th annual symposium on sea turtle biology and conservation. Island of Crete, Greece.

Lockhart, R. 1989. Marine turtles of Papua New Guinea. Papua New Guinea University of Technology, Department of Math and Statistics Report 1-89.

Lohmann, K.J., and C.M.F. Lohmann. 1993. A light-independent magnetic compass in the leatherback sea turtle. Biological Bulletin 185:149-151.

Lohmann, K.J., M. Salmon, and J. Wyneken. 1990. Functional autonomy of land and sea orientation systems in sea turtle hatchlings. Biological Bulletin 179:214-218.

Lohmann, K.J., C.M.F. Lohmann, L.M. Ehrhart, D.A. Bagley, and T. Swing. 2004. Geomagnetic map used in sea-turtle navigation. Nature 428:909-910.

Lohmann, K.J., B.E. Witherington, C.M.F. Lohmann, and M. Salmon. 1997. Orientation, navigation, and natal beach homing in sea turtles. Pages 107-136 *in* P. Lutz and J.A. Musick, editors. The biology of sea turtles. CRC Press, Boca Raton, Florida.

Lohoefener, R.R., W. Hoggard, C.L. Roden, K. Mullin, and C.M. Rogers. 1989. Distribution and relative abundance of surfaced sea turtles in the north-central Gulf of México: spring and fall 1987. Pages 47-50 *in* B.A. Schroeder, compiler. Proceedings of the 8th annual workshop on sea turtle conservation and biology. U.S. Department of Commerce, National Oceanic and Atmospheric Administration Technical Memorandum NMFS-SEFC-214. Miami, Florida.

Long, K.J., and B.A. Schroeder, editors. 2004. Proceedings of the international technical expert workshop on marine turtle bycatch in longline fisheries. U.S. Department of Commerce, National Oceanic and Atmospheric Administration Technical Memorandum NMFS-F/OPR-26. Miami, Florida.

López S., C., and L. Sarti M. 1988. Programa de investigación y de conservación en el área protegida para tortugas marinas en la zona sur del Estado de Michoacán. Temporada 1987-1988. Informe final de Biología de Campo. Facultad de Ciencias, UNAM. Michoacán, México.

López S., C., L. Sarti M., and N. García T. 1990. Situación actual de las pesquerías de las poblaciones de tortuga golfina *Lepidochelys olivacea* y tortuga laúd *Dermochelys coriacea* en la zona sur del Estado de Michoacán. Temporada 1989-1990. Informe inal de Biología de Campo. Facultad de Ciencias, UNAM. Michoacán, México.

López-Mendilaharsu, M., G. Sales, B. Giffoni, P. Millar, F. Niemeyer Fiedler, and A. Domingo. 2007. Distribución y composición de tallas de las tortugas marinas (*Caretta caretta* y *Dermochelys coriacea*) que interactúan con el palangre pelágico en el Atlántico Sur. Col. Vol. Sci. Pap. ICCAT 60:2094-2109.

López-Mendilaharsu, M., F.D. Rocha, A. Domingo, B.P. Wallace, and P. Miller. 2008. Prolonged, deep dives by the leatherback turtle *Dermochelys coriacea*: pushing their aerobic dive limits. Journal of the Marine Biological Association of the United Kingdom—Biodiversity Records 6274:1-3.

Louro, C.M.M. 2006. Status of leatherback turtles in Mozambique. Pages 87-93 *in* M. Hamann, C. Limpus, G. Hughes, J. Mortimer, and N. Pilcher, compilers. Assessment of the conservation status of the leatherback turtle in the Indian Ocean and SouthEast Asia. Indian Ocean and SouthEast Asia (IOSEA) Species Assessment: Volume I. IOSEA Marine Turtle Memorandum of Understanding Secretariat, Bangkok, Thailand.

Louro, C.M.M., M.A.M. Pereira, and A.C.D. Costa. 2006. Report on the conservation status of marine turtles in Mozambique. Ministério para a Coordenação da Acção Ambiental, República de Mozambique.

Loveridge, A., and E.E. Williams. 1957. Revision of the African tortoises and turtles of the suborder Cryptodira. Bulletin of the Museum of Comparative Zoology 115:163-557.

Lowe, C.H., Jr., and K.S. Norris. 1955. Measurements and weight of a Pacific leatherback turtle, *Dermochelys coriacea schlegeli*, captured off San Diego, California. Copeia 1955:256.

Luginbuhl, C. 1982. Plastic materials harming sea creatures. Press Release, Luginbuhl International Center for Endangered Species, Ellington, Connecticut.

Luschi, P., G.C. Hays, and F. Papi. 2003. A review of long-distance movements by marine turtles, and the possible role of ocean currents. Oikos 103:293-302.

Luschi, P., S. Benhamou, C. Girard, S. Ciccione, D. Roos, J. Sudre, and S. Benvenuti. 2006a. Marine turtles use geomagnetic cues during open-sea homing. Current Biology 17:126-133.

Luschi, P., J.R. Lutjeharms, P. Lambardi, R. Mencacci, G.R. Hughes, and G.C. Hays. 2006b. A review of migratory behaviour of sea turtles off southeastern Africa. South African Journal of Science 102:51-58.

Lutcavage, M., and P.L. Lutz. 1986. Metabolic rate and food energy requirements of the leatherback sea turtle, *Dermochelys coriacea*. Copeia 1986:796-798.

Lutcavage, M.E., P.G. Bushnell, and D.R. Jones. 1990. Oxygen transport in the leatherback sea turtle, *Dermochelys coriacea*. Physiological Zoology 63:1012-1024.

Lutcavage, M.E., P.G. Bushnell, and D.R. Jones. 1992. Oxygen stores and aerobic metabolism in the leatherback turtle. Canadian Journal of Zoology 70:348-351.

Lutcavage, M., A.G.J. Rhodin, S.S. Sadove, and C.R. Conroy. 1999. Direct carapacial attachment of satellite tags using orthopedic bioabsorbable mini-anchor screws on leatherback turtles in Culebra, Puerto Rico. Marine Turtle Newsletter 95:9-12.

Lutcavage, M.E., P. Plotkin, B. Witherington, and P.L. Lutz. 1997. Human impacts on sea turtle survival. Pages 387-409 *in* P.L. Lutz and J.A. Musick, editors. The biology of sea turtles. CRC Press, Boca Raton, Florida.

Lutz, P.L. 1988. Comparison between diving adaptations of marine mammals and sea turtles. Pages 55-58 *in* B.A. Schroeder, compiler. Proceedings of the 8th annual workshop on sea turtle conservation and biology. U.S. Department of Commerce, National Oceanic and Atmospheric Administration Technical Memorandum NMFS-SEFC-214. Miami, Florida.

Lutz, P.L. 1997. Salt, water, and pH balance in sea turtles. Pages 343-362 *in* P.L. Lutz and J.A. Musick, editors. The biology of sea turtles. CRC Press, Boca Raton, Florida.

Lutz, P.L., and T.B. Bentley. 1985. Respiratory physiology of diving in the sea turtle. Copeia 1985:671-679.

Lux, J., R.D. Reina, and L. Stokes. 2003. Nesting activity of leatherback turtles (*Dermochelys coriacea*) in relation to tidal and lunar cycles at Playa Grande, Costa Rica. Pages 215-216 *in* J.A. Seminoff, compiler. Proceedings of the 22nd annual symposium on sea turtle biology and conservation. U.S. Department of Commerce, National Oceanic and Atmospheric Administration Technical Memorandum NMFS-SEFSC-503. Miami, Florida.

Lydekker, R. 1889. On remains of Eocene and Mesozoic Chelonia and a tooth of Ornothopsis. Quarterly Journal of the Geological Society of London 45:227-246.

Lyster, S. 1985. International wildlife law: an analysis of international treaties concerned with the conservation of wildlife. The Research Centre for International Law, University of Cambridge. Grotius Publ. Ltd., Cambridge, United Kingdom.

MacAskie, I.B., and C.R. Forrester. 1962. Pacific leatherback turtles (*Dermochelys*) off the coast of British Columbia. Copeia 1962:646.

Mace, G.M., N.J. Collar, K.J. Gaston, C. Hilton-Taylor, H.R. Akçakaya, N. Leader-Williams, E.J. Milner-Gulland, and S.N. Stuart. 2008. Quantification of extinction risk: IUCN's system for classifying threatened species. Conservation Biology 22:1424-1442.

Magane, S., and J. João. 2003. Local community development in monitoring and protection of sea turtles: loggerhead (*Caretta caretta*) and leatherback (*Dermochelys coriacea*) in Maputo Special Reserve, Mozambique. Pages 100-101 *in* J.A. Seminoff, compiler. Proceedings of the 22nd annual symposium on sea turtle biology and conservation. U.S. Department of Commerce, National Oceanic and Atmospheric Administration Technical Memorandum NMFS-SEFSC-503. Miami, Florida.

Maharaj, A.M. 2004. A comparative study of the nesting ecology of the leatherback turtle *Dermochelys coriacea* in Florida and in Trinidad. M.S. thesis, University of Central Florida, Orlando, Florida.

Maigret, J. 1980. Une tortue luth dans la baie du Levrier. Club des Amis de la Nature en Mauritanie Bulletin 15:12-14.

Maigret, J. 1983. Répartition des tortues de mer sur les côtes Ouest africaines. Bulletin de la Société Herpétologique de France 28:22-34.

Manfredi, M.T., G. Piccolo, F. Prato, and G.R. Loria. 1996. Parasites in Italian sea turtles. I. The leatherback turtles *Dermochelys coriacea* (Linnaeus, 1766). Parasitologia 38:581-583.

Mansueti, R. 1963. Symbiotic behavior between small fishes and jellyfishes, with new data on that between the stromateid, *Peprilus alepidotus*, and the scyphomedusa, *Chrysaora quinquecirrha*. Copeia 1963:40-80.

Mao, S.H. 1971. Turtles of Taiwan. The Commercial Press, Ltd. Taipei, Taiwan.

Marcano, L.A., and J.J. Alió M. 2000. Incidental capture of sea turtles by the industrial shrimping fleet off northeastern Venezuela. Page 107 *in* F.A. Abreu-Grobois, R. Briseño-Dueñas, R. Márquez-Millán, and L. Sarti-Martínez, compilers. Proceedings of the 18th international sea turtle symposium. U.S. Department of Commerce, National Oceanic and Atmospheric Administration Technical Memorandum NMFS-SEFSC-436. Miami, Florida.

Marcovaldi, M.A., G. Sales, J.C.A. Thomé, A.C.C. Dias da Silva, B.M.G. Gallo, E.H.S.M. Lima, E.P. Lima, and C. Bellini. 2006. Sea turtles and fishery interactions in Brazil: identifying and mitigating potential conflicts. Marine Turtle Newsletter 112:4-8.

Maros, A., A. Louveaux, M.H. Godfrey, and M. Girondot. 2003. *Scapteriscus didactylus* (Orthoptera, Gryllotalpidae), predator of leatherback turtle eggs in French Guiana. Marine Ecology Progress Series 249:289-296.

Maros, A., A. Louveaux, C. Lelarge, and M. Girondot. 2006. Evidence of the exploitation of marine resources by the terrestrial insect *Scapteriscus didactylus* through stable isotope analyses of its cuticle. BMC Ecology 6:1-8.

Márquez M., R., A. Villanueva, and C. Peñaflores. 1981. Anidacion de la tortuga laud (*Dermochelys coriacea schlegelii*) en el Pacífico Mexicano. Ciencia Pesquera, Instituto Nacional de Pesca, México 1:45-52.

Márquez M., R. 1990. Sea turtles of the world: an annotated and illustrated catalogue of sea turtle species known to date. FAO Species Catalogue, Fisheries Synopsis 125:1-81.

Matos, R. 1986. Sea turtle hatchery project with specific reference to the leatherback turtle (*Dermochelys coriacea*), Humacao, Puerto Rico, 1986. Unpublished annual report to the Natural Reserves and Refuges Division, Puerto Rico Department of Natural Resources. San Juan, Puerto Rico.

Matos, R. 1987. Sea turtle hatchery project with specific reference to the leatherback (*Dermochelys coriacea*) and hawksbill (*Eretmochelys imbricata*) sea turtles, Humacao, Puerto Rico, 1987. Unpublished annual report to the Natural Reserves and Refuges Division, Puerto Rico Department of Natural Resources. San Juan, Puerto Rico.

Maurer-Spurej, E. 2007. Circulating serotonin in vertebrates. Cellular and Molecular Life Sciences 62:1881-1889.

McCann, C. 1969. First southern hemisphere record of the Platylepadine barnacle *Stomatolepas elegans* (Costa) and notes on the host *Dermochelys coriacea* (Linné). New Zealand Journal of Marine and Freshwater Research 3:152-158.

McDonald, D.L., and P.H. Dutton. 1996. Use of PIT tags and photoidentification to revise remigration estimates of leatherback turtles (*Dermochelys coriacea*) nesting in St. Croix, U.S. Virgin Islands, 1979-1995. Chelonian Conservation and Biology 2:148-152.

McDonald, D., P. Dutton, R. Brandner, and S. Basford. 1996. Use of pineal spot ("pink spot") photographs to identify leatherback turtles. Herpetological Review 27:11-12.

McDonald Dutton, D., A. Barragan, P.A. Mayor, V. Villanueva-Mayor, and R. Boulon. 2000. Tagging and nesting research on leatherback turtles (*Dermochelys coriacea*) on Sandy Point, St. Croix, U.S. Virgin Islands. Unpublished annual report prepared for the U.S. Department of Interior, Fish and Wildlife Service, Pc-PNR-091-2000. Christiansted, St. Croix, U.S. Virgin Islands.

McGowan, A., A.C. Broderick, G. Frett, S. Gore, M. Hastings, A. Pickering, D. Wheatley, J. White, M.J. Witt, and B.J. Godley. 2008. Down but not out: marine turtles of the British Virgin Islands. Animal Conservation 11:92-103.

Mckenzie, C., B.J. Godley, R.W. Furness, and D.E. Wells. 1999. Concentrations and patterns of organochlorine contaminants in marine turtles from Mediterranean and Atlantic waters. Marine Environmental Research 47:117-135.

McMahon, C.R., and G.C. Hays. 2006. Thermal niche, large-scale movements and implications of climate change for a critically endangered marine vertebrate. Global Change Biology 12:1330-1338.

McPherson, M. 1985. Evolution and effectivesness of treaties: marine pollution control. Pages 143-172 *in* R.L. Grundy and R.T. Ford, editors. Year of the Oceans: Science of Information Handling: Proceedings of the 10th annual conference of the International Association of Aquatic and Marine Science Libraries and Information Centers (IAMSLIC). Woods Hole, Massachusetts.

Medrano, L., M. Dorizzi, F. Rimblot, and C. Pieau. 1987. Karyotype of the sea-turtle, *Dermochelys coriacea* (Vandelli, 1761). Amphibia-Reptilia 8:171-178.

Merrem, B. 1820. Versuch eines Systems der Amphibien. Marburg, Gemany.

Mertens, R., and H. Wermuth. 1955. Die rezenten Schildkröten, Krokodile und Brückenechsen. Eine kritische Liste der heute lebenden Arten und Rassen. Zool. Jahrb., Syst, Okologie und Geographie der Tiere, Jena, Gustav Fischer Verlag 83:323-440.

Meylan, A.B. 1982. Sea turtle migration: evidence from tag returns. Pages 91-100 *in* K.A. Bjorndal, editor. Biology and conservation of sea turtles. Smithsonian Institution Press, Washington, D.C.

Meylan, A.B. 1983. Marine turtles of the Leeward Islands, Lesser Antilles. Atoll Research Bulletin No. 278. Smithsonian Institution Press, Washington, D.C.

Meylan, A., P. Meylan, and A. Ruiz. 1985. Nesting of *Dermochelys coriacea* in Caribbean Panama. Journal of Herpetology 19:293-297.

Michel, H.B., and F. Foyo. 1976. Caribbean zooplankton, part I. Navy Department, Office of Naval Research, Department of Defense, Washington, D.C.

Miller, J.D. 1982. Development of marine turtles. Ph.D. dissertation, University of New England, Armidale, New South Wales, Australia.

Miller, J.D. 1985. Embryology of marine turtles. Pages 269-328 *in* C. Gans, F. Billett, and P.F.A. Maderson, editors. Biology of the Reptilia. Volume 14: Development. A. John Wiley and Sons, New York City, New York.

Miller, J.D. 1997. Reproduction in sea turtles. Pages 51-82 *in* P.L. Lutz and J.A. Musick, editors. The biology of sea turtles. CRC Press, Boca Raton, Florida.

Milton, S.L., and P.L. Lutz. 2003. Physiological and genetic responses to environmental stress. Pages 163-198 *in* P.L. Lutz, J.A. Musick, and J. Wyneken, editors. The biology of sea turtles, Volume 2. CRC Press, Boca Raton, Florida.

Mittermeier, R.A., F. Medem, and A.G.J. Rhodin. 1980. Vernacular names of South American turtles. Society for the Study of Amphibians and Reptiles, Herpetology Circular 9:1-44.

Mohan, R.S.L. 1971. Occurrence of the digenetic trematode *Astrorchis renicapite* (Leidy) (Family: Pronocephalidea) in the leathery turtle *Dermochelys coriacea* (Linné) from the Indian Ocean. Journal of the Bombay Natural History Society 68:489-490.

Molony, B. 2005. Estimates of the mortality of non-target species with an initial focus on seabirds, turtles and sharks [EB WP-1]. Kolonia, Pohnpei State, Federated States of Micronesia. Meeting of the Scientific Committee of the Western and Central Pacific Fisheries Commission (WCPFC-SC1). 8-19 August 2005, New Caledonia.

Monroe, R., and C.J. Limpus. 1979. Barnacles on turtles in Queensland waters with descriptions of three new species. Memoirs of the Queensland Museum 19:197-223.

Montiel-Villalobos, M.G., H. Barrios-Garrido, K. Rodríguez-Clark, and R. Lazo. 2006. Towards the identification of key areas for sea turtle conservation in the Gulf of Venezuela. Page 147 *in* M. Frick, A. Panagopoulou, A.F. Rees, and K. Williams, compilers. Book of abstracts for the 26th annual symposium on sea turtle biology and conservation. Island of Crete, Greece.

Montilla F., A.J., J.L. Hernández R., and H.J. Guada M. 2008. Hematological values in leatherback sea turtles (*Dermochelys coriacea*) in Querepare beach, Paria Peninsula, Sucre State, Venezuela. Pages 15-16 *in* A.F. Rees, M. Frick, A. Panagopoulou, and K. Williams, compilers. Proceedings of the 27th annual symposium on sea turtle biology and conservation. U.S. Department of Commerce, National Oceanic and Atmospheric Administration Technical Memorandum NMFS-SEFSC-569. Miami, Florida.

Morgan, P.J. 1990. The leatherback turtle. Cardiff: National Museum of Wales. Wales, United Kingdom.

Morreale, S.J. 1999. Oceanic migrations of sea turtles. Ph.D. dissertation, Cornell University, Ithaca, New York.

Morreale, S.J., G.J. Ruiz, J.R. Spotila, and E.A. Standora. 1982. Temperature-dependent sex determination: current practices threaten conservation of sea turtles. Science 216:1245-1247.

Morreale S.J., E.A. Standora, J.R. Spotila, and F.V. Paladino. 1996. Migration corridor for sea turtles. Nature 384:319-320.

Moulton, J.M. 1963. The recapture of a marked leatherback turtle in Casco Bay, Maine. Copeia 1963:434-435.

Mrosovsky, N. 1968. Nocturnal emergence of hatchling sea turtles: control by thermal inhibition of activity. Nature 220:1338-1339.

Mrosovsky, N. 1971. Black vultures attack live turtle hatchlings. Auk 88:672-673.

Mrosovsky, N. 1972a. The water-finding ability of sea turtles. Behavioural studies and physiological speculations. Brain, Behavior and Evolution 5:202-225.

Mrosovsky, N. 1972b. Spectrographs of the sounds of leatherback turtles. Herpetologica 28:256-258.

Mrosovsky, N. 1977. Individual differences in the sea-finding mechanism of hatchling leatherback turtles. Brain, Behavior and Evolution 14:261-273.

Mrosovsky, N. 1978. Orientation mechanisms of marine turtles. Pages 413-419 in K. Schmidt-Koenig and W.T. Keeton, editors. Animal Migration, Navigation, and Homing. Springer-Verlag, Berlin, Germany.

Mrosovsky, N. 1980. Thermal biology of sea turtles. American Zoologist 20:531-547.

Mrosovsky, N. 1981. Plastic jellyfish. Marine Turtle Newsletter 17:5-6.

Mrosovsky, N. 1983. Ecology and nest-site selection of leatherback turtles, *Dermochelys coriacea*. Biological Conservation 26:47-56.

Mrosovsky, N. 1994. Sex ratios of sea turtles. The Journal of Experimental Zoology 270:16-27.

Mrosovsky, N. 2006. Distorting gene pools by conservation: assessing the case of doomed turtle eggs. Environmental Management 38:523-531.

Mrosovsky, N., and S.F. Kingsmill. 1985. How turtles find the sea. Zeitschrift fur Tierpsychologie 67:237-256.

Mrosovsky, N., and P.C.H. Pritchard. 1971. Body temperatures of *Dermochelys coriacea* and other sea turtles. Copeia 1971:624-631.

Mrosovsky, N., and S.J. Shettleworth. 1975. On the orientation circle of the leatherback turtle, *Dermochelys coriacea*. Animal Behaviour 23:568-591.

Mrosovsky, N., and C.L. Yntema. 1980. Temperature dependence of sexual differentiation in sea turtles: implications for conservation practices. Biological Conservation 18:271-280.

Mrosovsky, N., P.H. Dutton, and C.P. Whitmore. 1984. Sex ratios of two species of sea turtles nesting in Suriname. Canadian Journal of Zoology 62:2227-2239.

Mrosovsky, N., A.M. Granda, and T. Hay. 1979. Sea-ward orientation of hatchling turtles: turning systems in the optic tectum. Brain, Behavior and Evolution 16:203-221.

Mrosovsky, N., G.D. Ryan, and M.C. James. 2009. Leatherback turtles: the menace of plastic. Marine Pollution Bulletin 58:287-289.

Murphy, T.M., S.R. Murphy, D.B. Griffin, and C.P. Hope. 2006. Recent occurrence, spatial distribution, and temporal variability of leatherback turtles (*Dermochelys coriacea*) in nearshore waters of South Carolina, U.S.A. Chelonian Conservation and Biology 5:216-224.

Musick, J.A. 1988. The sea turtles of Virginia with notes on identification and natural history. Virginia Sea Grant Program, Virginia Institute of Marine Science (VIMS). Gloucester Point, Virginia.

Musick, J.A., editor. 1999. Life in the slow lane: ecology and conservation of long-lived marine animals. American Fisheries Society Symposium 23. American Fisheries Society. Bethesda, Maryland.

Myers, G.S. 1933. Two records of the leatherback turtle on the California coast. Copeia 1933:44.

Myers, A.E., and G.C. Hays. 2006. Do leatherback turtles *Dermochelys coriacea* forage during the breeding season? A combination of data-logging devices provide new insights. Marine Ecology Progress Series 322:259-267.

Myers, A.E., P. Lovell, and G.C. Hays. 2006. Tools for studying animal behaviour: validation of dive profile relayed via the Argos satellite system. Animal Behaviour 71:989-993.

Nabhan, G.P. 2003. Singing the turtles to sea. University of California Press, Berkeley, California.

Naro-Maciel, E., M. Le, N.N. FitzSimmons, and G. Amato. 2008. Evolutionary relationships of marine turtles: a molecular phylogeny based on nuclear and mitochondrial genes. Molecular Phylogenetics and Evolution 49:659-662.

National Marine Fisheries Service (NMFS). 1979. Critical habitat for leatherback turtle. Federal Register 44:17711, March 23, 1979. Redesignated and amended at Federal Register 64:14067, March 23, 1999. U.S. Department of Commerce, Silver Spring, Maryland.

National Marine Fisheries Service (NMFS). 1995. Final rule: leatherback conservation zone. Federal Register 60(178):47713-47715, September 14, 1995.

U.S. Department of Commerce, Silver Spring, Maryland.

National Marine Fisheries Service (NMFS). 2001a. Stock assessments of loggerhead and leatherback sea turtles and an assessment of the impact of the pelagic longline fishery on loggerhead and leatherback sea turtles of the Western North Atlantic. U.S. Department of Commerce, National Oceanic and Atmospheric Administration Technical Memorandum NMFS-SEFSC-455. Miami, Florida.

National Marine Fisheries Service (NMFS). 2001b. Endangered Species Act section 7 biological opinion: authorization of pelagic fisheries under the Fishery Management Plan for the Pelagic Fisheries of the Western Pacific Region. U.S. Department of Commerce, NMFS Pacific Islands Regional Office, Honolulu, Hawaii.

National Marine Fisheries Service (NMFS). 2001c. Endangered and threatened wildlife; sea turtle conservation requirements; taking of threatened or endangered species incidental to commercial fishing operations. Federal Register 66:44549-44552, August 24, 2001. U.S. Department of Commerce, Silver Spring, Maryland.

National Marine Fisheries Service (NMFS). 2003. Final rule: endangered and threatened wildlife; sea turtle conservation requirements. Federal Register 68(35):8456-8471, February 21, 2003. U.S. Department of Commerce, Silver Spring, Maryland.

National Marine Fisheries Service (NMFS). 2004. Management measures to implement new technologies for the western Pacific longline fisheries, including a final supplemental Environmental Impact Statement. U.S. Department of Commerce, NMFS Pacific Islands Regional Office, Honolulu, Hawaii.

National Marine Fisheries Service (NMFS). 2008. Biological opinion on proposed regulatory amendments to the fisheries management plan for the pelagic fisheries of the Western Pacific Region. U.S. Department of Commerce, NMFS Pacific Islands Regional Office, Honolulu, Hawaii.

National Marine Fisheries Service (NMFS). 2010. Endangered and threatened species: proposed rule to revise the critical habitat designation for the endangered leatherback sea turtle. Federal Register 75(2):319-335, January 5, 2010. U.S. Department of Commerce, Silver Spring, Maryland.

National Marine Fisheries Service (NMFS) and United States Fish and Wildlife Service (USFWS). 1992. Recovery plan for leatherback turtles, *Dermochelys coriacea*, in the U.S. Caribbean, Atlantic, and Gulf of México. National Marine Fisheries Service, Washington, D.C.

National Marine Fisheries Service (NMFS) and United States Fish and Wildlife Service (USFWS). 1998. Recovery plan for U.S. Pacific populations of the leatherback turtle (*Dermochelys coriacea*). National Marine Fisheries Service, Silver Spring, Maryland.

National Marine Fisheries Service (NMFS) and United States Fish and Wildlife Service (USFWS). 2007. Leatherback sea turtle (*Dermochelys coriacea*): five-year review, summary and evaluation. National Marine Fisheries Service, Silver Spring, Maryland.

National Research Council (NRC). 1990. Decline of the sea turtles: causes and prevention. National Academy Press, Washington, D.C.

Navaz, J.M., and J.G. de Llarena. 1951. Nota acerca de una tortuga de cuero *Dermochelys coriacea* (L.), capturada en aguas de Guipuzcoa. Publicaciones de la Sociedad Oceanográfica de Guipuzcoa 9:1-13.

Navid, D. 1982. Conservation and management of sea turtles: a legal overview. Pages 523-535 *in* K.A. Bjorndal, editor. Biology and conservation of sea turtles. Smithsonian Institution Press, Washington, D.C.

Near, T.J., P.A. Meylan, and H.B. Shaffer. 2005. Assessing concordance of fossil calibration points in molecular clock studies: an example using turtles. The American Naturalist 165:137-146.

Neill, W.H., and E.D. Stevens. 1974. Thermal inertia versus thermoregulation in "warm" tunas and turtles. Science 184:1008-1010.

Neill, W.T. 1958. The occurrence of amphibians and reptiles in saltwater areas, and a bibliography. Bulletin of Marine Science of the Gulf and Caribbean 8:1-97.

Nel, R. 2006. Status of leatherback turtles in South Africa. Pages 125-130 *in* M. Hamann, C. Limpus, G. Hughes, J. Mortimer, and N. Pilcher, compilers. Assessment of the conservation status of the leatherback turtle in the Indian Ocean and SouthEast Asia. Indian Ocean and SouthEast Asia (IOSEA) Species Assessment: Volume I. IOSEA Marine Turtle Memorandum of Understanding Secretariat, Bangkok, Thailand.

Nel, R. 2008. Sea turtles of KwaZulu-Natal: data report for 2007/8 season. Unpublished report prepared for Ezemvelo KwaZulu-Natal Wildlife. Nelson Mandela Metropolitan University, South Africa.

Nellis, D.W. 2000. Predation on leatherback turtle (*Dermochelys coriacea*) hatchlings at Sandy Point National Wildlife Refuge, St. Croix, U.S. Virgin Islands. M.S. thesis, Texas A&M University, College Station.

Nellis, D.W., and S.E. Henke. 2000. Predation of leatherback turtle hatchlings by nearshore aquatic predators. Page 168 *in* H. Kalb and T. Wibbels, compilers. Proceedings of the 19th annual symposium on sea turtle biology and conservation. U.S. Department of Commerce, National Oceanic and Atmospheric Administration Technical Memorandum NMFS-SEFSC-443. Miami, Florida.

Nick, L. 1912. Das Kopfskelet von *Dermochelys coriacea*. L. Zoologische Jahrbücher, Abteilung Fur Anatomie und Ontogenie der Tiere 33:1-238.

Nielsen, E. 1959. Eocene turtles from Denmark. Meddelelser fra Dansk Geologisk Forening 14:96-114.

Nishimura, S. 1964a. Records of occurrence of the leatherback turtle in adjacent waters to Japan. Physiological Ecology Kyoto 12:286-290.

Nishimura, S. 1964b. Considerations on the migration of the Leatherback turtle, *Dermochelys coriacea* (L.), in the Japanese and adjacent waters. Publications of the Seto Marine Biological Laboratory 12:61-73.

Nöel-Hume, I., and A. Nöel-Hume. 1954. Tortoises, terrapins, and turtles. Foyle's Handbooks, London, W. & G. Foyle. London, United Kingdom.

Nordmoe, E.D., A.E. Sieg, P.R. Sotherland, J.R. Spotila, F.V. Paladino, and R.D. Reina. 2004. Nest site fidelity of leatherback turtles at Playa Grande, Costa Rica. Animal Behaviour 68:387-94.

Northridge, S. 1990 (Draft). Driftnet fisheries and their impact on non target species: a worldwide review. Marine Resources Assessment Group, London, United Kingdom.

Nuitja, I.N.S., and J.D. Lazell. 1982. Marine turtle nesting in Indonesia. Copeia 1982:708-710.

Ogden, J.A., A.G.J. Rhodin, G.J. Conlogue, and T.R. Light. 1981. Pathobiology of septic arthritis and contiguous osteomyelitis in a leatherback turtle (*Dermochelys coriacea*). Journal of Wildlife Diseases 17:277-287.

Ogren, L., editor. 1989. Proceedings of the second western Atlantic turtle symposium (WATS). U.S. Department of Commerce, National Oceanic and Atmospheric Administration Technical Memorandum NMFS-SEFC-226. Miami, Florida.

O'Hara, K., N. Atkins, and S. Iudicello. 1986. Marine wildlife entanglement in North America. Center for Environmental Education, Washington, D.C.

Oliver, L.J., M. Salmon, J. Wyneken, R. Hueter, and T.W. Cronin. 2000. Retinal anatomy of hatchling sea turtles: anatomical specializations and behavioral correlates. Marine and Freshwater Behaviour and Physiology 33:233-248.

Ordoñez, C., S. Troëng, A. Meylan, P. Meylan, and A. Ruíz. 2007. Chiriqui Beach, Panama, the most important leatherback nesting beach in Central America. Chelonian Conservation and Biology 6:122-126.

Owens, D.W. 1980. The comparative reproductive physiology of sea turtles. American Zoologist 20:549-563.

Owens, D.W., M.A. Grassman, and J.R. Hendrickson. 1982. The imprinting hypothesis and sea turtle reproduction. Herpetologica 38:124-135.

Paddock, S.N., J.A. Seminoff, S.R. Benson, and P.H. Dutton. 2007. Characterizing the foraging ecology of leatherback turtles (*Dermochelys coriacea*) using stable carbon and nitrogen isotope analysis of egg shells. Pages 312-133 *in* A.F. Rees, M. Frick, A. Panagopoulou, and K. Williams, compilers. Proceedings of the 27th annual symposium on sea turtle biology and conservation. U.S. Department of Commerce, National Oceanic and Atmospheric Administration Technical Memorandum NMFS-SEFSC-569. Miami, Florida.

Paladino, F.V., M.P. O'Connor, and J.R. Spotila. 1990. Metabolism of leatherback turtles, gigantothermy, and thermoregulation of dinosaurs. Nature 344:858-860.

Paladino, F.V., J.R. Spotila, M.P. O'Connor, and R.E. Gatten, Jr. 1996. Respiratory physiology of adult leatherback turtles (*Dermochelys coriacea*) while nesting on land. Chelonian Conservation and Biology 2:223-229.

Parker, W.K. 1868. A monograph on the structure and development of the shoulder-girdle and sternum in the Vertebrata. R. Harwicke, London, United Kingdom.

Parnell, R., B. Verhage, S.L. Deem, H. Van Leeuwe, T. Nishihara, C. Moukoula, and A. Gibudi. 2007. Marine turtle mortality in southern Gabon and northern Congo. Marine Turtle Newsletter 116:12-14.

Parsons, T.S. 1968. Variation in the choanal structure of recent turtles. Canadian Journal of Zoology 46:1235-1263.

Parsons, T.S. 1970. The nose and Jacobson's organ. Pages 99-191 *in* C. Gans and T.S. Parsons, editors. Biology of the Reptilia, Volume 2. Academic Press, New York City, New York.

Patino-Martinez, J., A. Marco, L. Quiñones, and B. Godley. 2008. Globally significant nesting of the leatherback turtle (*Dermochelys coriacea*) on the Caribbean coast of Colombia and Panama. Biological Conservation 141:1982-1988.

Pehrson, T. 1945. Some problems concerning the development of the skull of turtles. Acta Zoologica 26:157-184.

Peñate, J.G., M. Karamoko, S. Bamba, and G. Djadji. 2007. An update on marine turtles in Côte d'Ivoire, West Africa. Marine Turtle Newsletter 116:7-8.

Penhallurick, R.D. 1990. Turtles off Cornwall, The Isles of Scilly and Devonshire. Dyllansow Pengwella, Great Britain.

Penhallurick, R.D. 1991. Observations of leatherback turtles off the Cornish coast. Marine Turtle Newsletter 52:12-14.

Penick, D.N. 1996. Thermoregulatory physiology of leatherback (*Dermochelys coriacea*) and green sea turtles (*Chelonia mydas*). Ph.D. dissertation, Drexel University, Philadelphia, Pennsylvania.

Penick, D.N., J.R. Spotila, M.P. O'Conner, A.C. Steyermark, R.H. George, C.J. Salice, and F.V. Paladino. 1998. Thermal independence of muscle tissue metabolism in the leatherback turtle, *Dermochelys coriacea*. Comparative Biochemistry and Physiology A 120:399-403.

Perdrau, M., and J. Garvey. 2005. Northern prawn fishery data summary 2004. Logbook Program, Australian Fisheries Management Authority, Canberra, Australia.

Perry, A. 1982. Magnetite in the green turtle. Pacific Science 36:514.

Petit, G. 1951. Capture d'unet luth à La Nouvelle (Aude). Vie et Millieu 2:154-155.

Petro, G., F.R. Hickey, and K. Mackay. 2007. Leatherback turtles in Vanuatu. Chelonian Conservation and Biology 6:135-137.

Philip, M. 2002. Marine turtle conservation in Papua New Guinea. Pages 143-146 *in* I. Kinan, editor. Proceedings of the western Pacific sea turtle cooperative research and management workshop. Western Pacific Regional Fishery Management Council, Honolulu, Hawaii.

Phillips, E.J. 1977. Raising hatchlings of the leatherback turtle, *Dermochelys coriacea*. British Journal of Herpetology 5:677-678.

Piedra, R., E. Vélez, P. Dutton, E. Possardt, and C. Padilla. 2007. Nesting of the leatherback turtle (*Dermochelys coriacea*) from 1999-2000 through 2003-2004 at Playa Langosta, Parque Nacional Las Baulas de Guanacaste, Costa Rica. Chelonian Conservation and Biology 6:111-117.

Pilcher, N. 2006. Final report: the 2005-2006 leatherback nesting season, Huon Coast, Papua New Guinea. Unpublished report prepared for the Western Pacific Regional Fishery Management Council, Honolulu, Hawaii.

Pilcher, N., S. Mahmud, and J. Tecklemariam. 2006. Status of leatherback turtles in Eritrea. Pages 40-42 *in* M. Hamann, C. Limpus, G. Hughes, J. Mortimer, and N. Pilcher, compilers. Assessment of the conservation status of the leatherback turtle in the Indian Ocean and SouthEast Asia. Indian Ocean and SouthEast Asia (IOSEA) species assessment: Volume I. IOSEA Marine Turtle Memorandum of Understanding Secretariat, Bangkok, Thailand.

Pineda, H., L. Cuellar, and L. Sarti M. 2004. The influence of the moon and tides in the nesting of the leatherback sea turtle (*Dermochelys coriacea*). Pages 273-274 *in* M.S. Coyne and R.D. Clark, compilers. Proceedings of the 21st annual symposium on sea turtle biology and conservation. U.S. Department of Commerce, National Oceanic and Atmospheric Administration Technical Memorandum NMFS-SEFSC-528. Miami, Florida.

Pitman, R.L., and P.H. Dutton. 2004. Killer whale predation on a leatherback turtle in the Northeast Pacific. Pacific Science 58:497-498.

Poglayen-Neuwall, I. 1953. Untersuchungen der Kiefermuskulatur und deren Innervation bei Schildkroten. Acta Zoologica 34:241-292.

Polunin, N.V.C. 1975. Sea turtles: reports on Thailand, West Malaysia and Indonesia, with a synopsis of data on the 'conservation status' of sea turtles in the Indo-West Region. International Union for the Conservation of Nature (IUCN). Morges, Switzerland.

Polunin, N.V.C. 1977. Wildlife Thailand. Conservation News 1977:6-10.

Potts, W.T.W. 1968. Osmotic and ionic regulation. Annual Review of Physiology 30:70-104.

Prange, H.D., and D.C. Jackson. 1976. Ventilation, gas exchange and metabolic scaling of a sea turtle. Respiratory Physiology 27:369-377.

Prange, H.D., and R.A. Ackerman. 1974. Oxygen consumption and mechanisms of gas exchange of green turtle (*Chelonia mydas*) eggs and hatchlings. Copeia 1974:758-763.

Prescott, R.L. 1988. Leatherbacks in Cape Cod Bay, Massachusetts, 1977-1987. Pages 83-84 *in* B.A. Schroeder, compiler. Proceedings of the 8th annual workshop on sea turtle conservation and biology. U.S. Department of Commerce, National Oceanic and Atmospheric Administration Technical Memorandum NMFS-SEFC-214. Miami, Florida.

Price, E.R., B.P. Wallace, R.D. Reina, J.R. Spotila, F.V. Paladino, R. Piedra, and E. Vélez. 2004. Size, growth, and reproductive output of adult female leatherback turtles *Dermochelys coriacea*. Endangered Species Research 5:1-8.

Price, E.R., F.V. Paladino, K.P. Strohl, P. Santidrián-Tomillo, K. Klann, and J.R. Spotila. 2007. Respiration in neonate sea turtles. Comparative Biochemistry and Physiology 146:422-428.

Prince, R.I.T. 1994. Status of the Western Australian marine turtle populations: the Western Australian Marine Turtle Project 1986-1990. Pages 1-14 *in* J. Russell, editor. Proceedings of the Australian marine turtle conservation workshop, Gold Coast 14-17 November 1990. Queensland Department of Environment and Heritage. Canberra, ANCA. Australia.

Prince, R.I.T. 2004. Stranding of small juvenile leatherback turtle in Western Australia. Marine Turtle Newsletter 104:3-4.

Pritchard, P.C.H. 1964. Turtles of British Guiana. Journal of the British Guyana Museum and Zoo 39:19-32.

Pritchard, P.C.H. 1967. Living turtles of the world. T.F.H. Publications, Inc. Jersey City, New Jersey.

Pritchard, P.C.H. 1969. Sea turtles of the Guianas. Bulletin of the Florida State Museum, Biological Sciences 13:85-140.

Pritchard, P.C.H. 1971a. The leatherback or leathery turtle, *Dermochelys coriacea*. International Union for the Conservation of Nature (IUCN) Monograph 1:1-39. Morges, Switzerland.

Pritchard, P.C.H. 1971b. Sea turtles in French Guiana. Pages 38-40 *in* Marine Turtles. International Union for the Conservation of Nature (IUCN) Publication New Series, Suppl. Paper No. 31. Morges, Switzerland.

Pritchard, P.C.H. 1972. Sea turtle research and conservation in French Guiana, 1972. Unpublished report submitted to the Florida Audubon Society. Orlando, Florida.

Pritchard, P.C.H. 1973. International migrations of South American sea turtles (Cheloniidae and Dermochelidae). Animal Behaviour 21:18-27.

Pritchard, P.C.H. 1976. Post-nesting movements of marine turtles (Cheloniidae and Dermochelyidae) tagged in the Guianas. Copeia 1976:749-754.

Pritchard, P.C.H. 1979a. Encyclopedia of turtles. T.F.H. Publications, Inc., Neptune City, New Jersey.

Pritchard, P.C.H. 1979b. Marine turtles of Papua New Guinea: research findings, management recommendations, and directions for future research. Report to the Department of Lands and Environment. Konedobu, Papua New Guinea.

Pritchard, P.C.H. 1980. *Dermochelys coriacea*. Catalogue of American Amphibians and Reptiles 238:1-4.

Pritchard, P.C.H. 1981. Marine turtles: a review of their status and management in the Solomon Islands. Prepared for the Ministry of Natural Resources, Honiara, Solomon Islands.

Pritchard, P.C.H. 1982. Nesting of leatherback turtle *Dermochelys coriacea* in Pacific México, with a new estimate of the world population status. Copeia 1982:741-747.

Pritchard, P.C.H. 1985. Recovery of a tagged leatherback. Marine Turtle Newsletter 32:8.

Pritchard, P.C.H. 1987. Synopsis of biological data on the leatherback sea turtle, *Dermochelys coriacea*. Partial draft submitted to the second western Atlantic turtle symposium (WATS II), 12-16 October 1987, Mayagüez, Puerto Rico.

Pritchard, P.C.H. 1996. Are leatherbacks really threatened with extinction? Chelonian Conservation and Biology 2:303-305.

Pritchard, P.C.H. 1997. Evolution, phylogeny, and current status. Pages 1-28 *in* P.L. Lutz and J.A. Musick, editors. The biology of sea turtles. CRC Press, Boca Raton, Florida.

Pritchard, P.C.H., and P. Trebbau. 1984. The turtles of Venezuela. Society for the Study of Amphibians and Reptiles. Ithaca, New York.

Pritchard, P., P. Bacon, F. Berry, A. Carr, J. Fletemeyer, R. Gallagher, S. Hopkins, R. Lankford, R. Márquez M., L. Ogren, W. Pringle Jr., H. Reichart, and R. Witham. 1983. Manual of sea turtle research and conservation techniques. Second edition. Center for Environmental Education, Washington, D.C.

Quinn, N.J., and B.L. Kojis. 1985. Leatherback turtles under threat in Morobe Province, Papua New Guinea. PLES (An Environmental Education Magazine for the South Pacific Region) 1:79-99.

Quinn, N.J., B. Anguru, K. Chee, O. Keon, and P. Muller. 1983. Preliminary surveys of leatherback rookeries in Morobe Province, with notes on their biology. Fisheries Research Report Series No. 83. University of Technology, Lae, Papua New Guinea.

Rabon, D.R., Jr., S.A. Johnson, R. Boettcher, M. Dodd, M. Lyons, S. Murphy, S. Ramsey, S. Roff, and K. Stewart. 2003. Confirmed leatherback turtle (*Dermochelys coriacea*) nests from North Carolina, with a summary of leatherback nesting activities north of Florida. Marine Turtle Newsletter 101:4-8.

Rader, H., M.A. Ela Mba, W. Morra, and G. Hearn. 2006. Marine turtles of the southern coast of Bioko

Island (Gulf of Guinea, Africa), 2001-2005. Marine Turtle Newsletter 111:8-10.

Rainey, W.E. 1981. Guide to sea turtle visceral anatomy. U.S. Department of Commerce, National Oceanic and Atmospheric Administration Technical Memorandum NMFS-SEFC-82. Panama City, Florida.

Rainey, W.E., and P.C.H. Pritchard. 1972. Distribution and management of Caribbean sea turtles. Contribution No. 105, Virgin Islands Ecology Research Station, Caribbean Research Institute, College of the Virgin Islands, St. Thomas, U.S. Virgin Islands.

Ralph, C.R., R.D. Reina, B.P. Wallace, P.R. Sotherland, J.R. Spotila, and F.V. Paladino. 2005. Effect of egg location and respiratory gas concentrations on developmental success in nests of the leatherback turtle, *Dermochelys coriacea*. Australian Journal of Zoology 53:289-294.

Ramírez, P.A.U., and L.V. Gonzáles A. 2000. Incidence of marine turtles in the Mexican longline tuna fishery in the Gulf of México. Page 110 *in* F.A. Abreu-Grobois, R. Briseño-Dueñas, R. Márquez-Millán, and L. Sarti-Martínez, compilers. Proceedings of the 18th International sea turtle symposium. U.S. Department of Commerce, National Oceanic and Atmospheric Administration Technical Memorandum NMFS-SEFSC-436. Miami, Florida.

Ranzani, C. 1832. Camilli Ranzani de Testudine coriacea marina. Bononiae 3-11 tab iv.

Rathbun, G.B., T. Carr, N. Carr, and C.A. Woods. 1985. The distribution of manatees and sea turtles in Puerto Rico, with emphasis on Roosevelt Roads Naval Station. Report to Naval Facilities Engineering Command. San Juan, Puerto Rico.

Rathke, M.H. 1846. Ueber die Luftröhre, die speiseröhre und den Magen der *Spargis coriacea*. Archiv für Anatomie und Physiologie. Germany.

Rathke, M.H. 1848. Über die Entwicklung der Schildkröten. Friederich Vieweg und Sohn, Braunschweig.

Rausser, G., S. Hamilton, M. Kovach, and R. Sifter. 2009. Unintended consequences: the spillover effects of common property regulations. Marine Policy 33:24-39.

Ray, C., and C.W. Coates. 1958. Record and measurements of a leatherback turtle from the Gulf of Maine. Copeia 1958:220-221.

Raymond, P.W. 1984. Sea turtle hatchling disorientation and artificial beach front lighting. Center for Environmental Education, Washington, D.C.

Raynaud, A., J. Fretey, and M. Clergue-Gazeau. 1980. Epithelial structures of temporary existence appended on branchial arches in the embryos of the leathery turtle (*Dermochelys coriacea*). Bulletin Biologique de la France et de la Belgique 1980:72-99.

Raynaud, A., J. Fretey, J. Brabet, and M. Clergue-Gazeau. 1983. Animal morphogenesis—a scanning electron microscopic study of the epithelial structures appended to visceral arches of the embryos of the leathery turtle (*Dermochelys coriacea*). Comptes Rendus Hebdomadaires des Séances de l'Académie des Sciences, Paris 296:297-302.

Read, A.J. 2007. Do circle hooks reduce the mortality of sea turtles in pelagic longlines? A review of recent experiments. Biological Conservation 135:155-169.

Rebel, T.P. 1974. Sea turtles and the turtle industry of the West Indies, Florida, and the Gulf of México, revised edition. University of Miami Press. Coral Cables, Florida.

Rees, A.F., A. Saad, and M. Jony. 2004. First record of a leatherback turtle in Syria. Marine Turtle Newsletter 106:13.

Reichart, H.A., and J. Fretey. 1993. WIDECAST sea turtle recovery action plan for Suriname. *In* K.L. Eckert, editor. UNEP Caribbean Environment Programme (CEP) Technical Report No. 24. Kingston, Jamaica.

Reina, R.D., T.T. Jones, and J.R. Spotila. 2002b. Salt and water regulation by the leatherback sea turtle *Dermochelys coriacea*. Journal of Experimental Biology 205:1853-1860.

Reina, R.D., J.R. Spotila, F.V. Paladino, and A.E. Durham. 2009. Changed reproductive schedule of eastern Pacific leatherback turtles *Dermochelys coriacea* following the 1997-98 El Niño to La Niña transition. Endangered Species Research 7:155-161.

Reina, R.D., P.A. Mayor, J.R. Spotila, R. Piedra, and F.V. Paladino. 2002a. Nesting ecology of the leatherback turtle, *Dermochelys coriacea*, at Parque Nacional Marino Las Baulas, Costa Rica: 1988-1989 to 1999-2000. Copeia 2002:653-664.

Reina, R.D., K.J. Abernathy, G.J. Marshall, and J.R. Spotila. 2005. Respiratory frequency, dive behaviour and social interactions of leatherback turtles, *Dermochelys coriacea* during the inter-nesting interval. Journal of Experimental Biology and Ecology 316:1-16.

Remane, A. 1936. Wirbelsäule und ihre Abkömmlinge *in* L. Bolk et al., editors. Handbuch der vergleichenden Anatomie der Wirbeltiere. Urban und Schwarzenberg, Berlin (Germany) and Vienna (Austria).

Renous, S., F. Rimblot-Baly, J. Fretey, and C. Pieau. 1989. Caractéristiques du développement embryonnaire de la tortue luth, *Dermochelys coriacea* (Vandelli, 1761). Annales des sciences naturelles. Zoologie et Biologie Animale 10:197-229.

Reyes, C., and S. Troëng. 2001. 2001 leatherback program at Tortuguero, Costa Rica. San Pedro, Costa Rica. Unpublished report to the Caribbean Conservation Corporation. Gainesville, Florida.

Reynolds, D.P. 2000. Emergence success and nest environment of natural and hatchery nests of the leatherback turtle (*Dermochelys coriacea*) at Playa Grande, Costa Rica, 1998-1999. M.S. thesis, Drexel University, Philadelphia, Pennsylvania.

Rhodin, A.G.J. 1985. Comparative chondro-osseous development and growth of marine turtles. Copeia 1985:752-771.

Rhodin, A.G.J., and R.C. Schoelkopf. 1982. Reproductive data on a female leatherback turtle, *Dermochelys coriacea*, stranded in New Jersey. Copeia 1982:181-183.

Rhodin, A.G.J., J.A. Ogden, and G.J. Conlogue. 1981. Chondro-osseous morphology of *Dermochelys coriacea*, a marine reptile with mammalian skeletal features. Nature 290:244-246.

Rhodin, J.A.G., A.G.J. Rhodin, and J.R. Spotila. 1996. Electron microscopic analysis of vascular cartilage canals in the humeral epiphysis of hatchling leatherback turtles, *Dermochelys coriacea*. Chelonian Conservation and Biology 2:250-260.

Richardson, J.I. 1982. A population model for adult female loggerhead sea turtles (*Caretta caretta*) nesting in Georgia. Ph.D. dissertation, University of Georgia, Athens.

Ridgeway, S.H., E.G. Wever, J.G. McCormick, J. Palin, and J.H. Anderson. 1969. Hearing in the giant sea turtle, *Chelonia mydas*. Proceedings of the National Academy of Sciences 64:884-890.

Rieder, J.P., P.G. Parker, J.R. Spotila, and M.E. Irwin. 1998. The mating system of the leatherback turtle: a molecular approach. Bulletin of the Ecological Society of America 77 (Suppl. 3, Part 2):375.

Rimblot, F., J. Fretey, N. Mrosovsky, J. Lescure, and C. Pieau. 1985. Sexual differentiation as a function of the incubation temperature of eggs in the sea turtle, *Dermochelys coriacea* (Vandelli, 1761). Amphibia-Reptilia 6:83-92.

Rimblot-Baly, F., J. Lescure, J. Fretey, and C. Pieau. 1986-1987. Sensibilité à la température de la différenciation sexuelle chez la tortue luth, *Dermochelys coriacea* (Vandelli, 1761); application des données de l'incubation artificielle à l'étude de la sex-ratio dans la nature. Annales des Sciences Naturelles, Zoologie, Paris 13e Série, 1986-1987:277-290.

Rivalan, P. 2003. La dynamique des populations de tortues luths de Guyane française : recherche des facteurs impliqués et application à la mise en place de stratégies de conservation. Université Paris Sud, Orsay, France.

Rivalan, P., A.-C. Prévot-Julliard, R. Choquet, R. Pradel, B. Jacquemin, and M. Girondot. 2005a. Trade-off between current reproductive effort and delay to next reproduction in the leatherback sea turtle. Oecologia 145:564-574.

Rivalan, R., M.H. Godfrey, A.-C. Prévot-Julliard, and M. Girondot. 2005b. Maximum likelihood estimates of tag loss in leatherback sea turtles. Journal of Wildlife Management 69:540-548.

Rivalan, P., R. Pradel, R. Choquet, M. Girondot, and A.-C. Prévot-Julliard. 2006. Estimating clutch frequency in the sea turtle *Dermochelys coriacea* using stop-over duration. Marine Ecology Progress Series 317:285-295.

Roberts, J.T., B.C. Parks, and A.A. Vásquez. 2004. Who ratifies environmental treaties and why? Institutionalism, structuralism and participation by 192 nations in 22 treaties. Global Environmental Politics 4:22-64.

Robins, C.M., S.J. Bache, and S.R. Kalish. 2002. Bycatch of sea turtles in longline fisheries – Australia. Bureau of Rural Sciences Final Report to the Fisheries Resources Research Fund, Agriculture, Fisheries and Forestry – Australia, Canberra.

Rodrigues, A.S.L., J.D. Pilgrim, J.F. Lamoreux, M. Hoffmann, and T.M. Brooks. 2006. The value of the IUCN Red List for conservation. Trends in Ecology and Evolution 21:71-76.

Roithmayr, C., and T. Henwood. 1982. Incidental catch and mortality report. Unpublished final report submitted to the U.S. Department of Commerce, National Marine Fisheries Service. Pascagoula, Mississippi.

Romer, A.S. 1956. The osteology of the reptiles. University of Chicago Press, Chicago, Illinois.

Ross, J.P. 1982. Historical decline of loggerhead, ridley and leatherback sea turtles. Pages 189-195 *in* K.A. Bjorndal, editor. Biology and conservation of sea turtles. Smithsonian Institution Press, Washington, D.C.

Ross, J.P., and J.A. Ottenwalder. 1983. The leatherback sea turtle, *Dermochelys coriacea*, nesting in the Dominican Republic. Pages 706-713 *in* A.G.J. Rhodin and K. Miyata, editors. Advances in herpetology and evolutionary biology. Museum of Comparative Zoology, Cambridge, Massachusetts.

Rostal, D.C., F.V. Paladino, R.M. Patterson, and J.R. Spotila. 1996. Reproductive physiology of nesting leatherback turtles (*Dermochelys coriacea*) at Las Baulas National Park, Costa Rica. Chelonian Conservation and Biology 2:230-236.

Rothschild, B.M. 1987. Decompression syndrome in fossil marine turtles. Annals of the Carnegie Museum 56:253-258.

Saba, V.S., P. Santidrián-Tomillo, R.D. Reina, J.R. Spotila, J.A. Musick, D.A. Evans, and F.V. Paladino. 2007. The effect of the El Niño and the Southern Oscillation on the reproductive frequency of eastern Pacific leatherback turtles. Journal of Applied Ecology 44:395-404.

Saba, V.S., G.L. Shillinger, A.M. Swithenbank, B.A. Block, J.R. Spotila, J.A. Musick, and F.V. Paladino. 2008a. An oceanographic context for the foraging ecology of eastern Pacific leatherback turtles: consequences of ENSO. Deep-Sea Research 1:646-660.

Saba, V.S., J.R. Spotila, F.P. Chavez, and J.A. Musick. 2008b. Bottom-up and climatic forcing on the worldwide population of leatherback turtles. Ecology 89:1414-1427.

Sadove, S. 1980. Marine turtles. SEAN Bulletin 5:15.

Sale, A., P. Luschi, R. Mencacci, P. Lambardi, G.R. Hughes, G.C. Hays, S. Benvenuti, and F. Papi. 2006. Long-term monitoring of leatherback turtle diving behaviour during oceanic movements. Journal of Experimental Marine Biology and Ecology 328:197-210.

Salmon, M., T.T. Jones, and K.W. Horch. 2004. Ontogeny of diving and feeding behavior in juvenile sea turtles: leatherback sea turtles (*Dermochelys coriacea* L.) and green sea turtles (*Chelonia mydas* L.) in the Florida Current. Journal of Herpetology 38:36-43.

Sánchez, P., M. Laporta, P. Miller, S. Horta, and G. Riestra. 2008. First report of leatherback (*Dermochelys coriacea*) entanglement in trap lines in the Uruguayan continental shelf, southwestern Atlantic Ocean. Page 108 *in* H. Kalb, A.S. Rohde, K. Gayheart, and K. Shanker, compilers. Proceedings of the 25th annual symposium on sea turtle biology and conservation. U.S. Department of Commerce, National Oceanic and Atmospheric Administration Technical Memorandum NMFS-SEFSC-582. Miami, Florida.

Santidrián Tomillo, P., V.S. Saba, R. Piedra, F.V. Paladino, and J.R. Spotila. 2008. Effects of illegal harvest of eggs on the population decline of leatherback turtles in Parque Nacional Marino Las Baulas, Costa Rica. Conservation Biology 22:1216-1224.

Santidrián Tomillo, P., E. Vélez, R.D. Reina, R. Piedra, F.V. Paladino, and J.R. Spotila. 2007. Reassesment of the leatherback turtle (*Dermochelys coriacea*) nesting population at Parque Nacional Marino Las Baulas, Costa Rica: effects of conservation efforts. Chelonian Conservation and Biology 6:54-62.

Santidrián Tomillo, P., J.S. Suss, B.P. Wallace, K.D. Magrini, G. Blanco, F.V. Paladino, and J.R. Spotila. 2009. Influence of emergence success on the annual reproductive output of leatherback turtles. Marine Biology 156:2021-2031.

Sapsford, C.W. 1978. Anatomical evidence for intra-cardiac blood shunting in marine turtles. Zoologica Africana 13:57-62.

Sapsford, C.W., and G.R. Hughes. 1978. Body temperature of the loggerhead sea turtle *Caretta caretta* and the leatherback sea turtle *Dermochelys coriacea* during nesting. Zoologica Africana 13:63-69.

Sapsford, C.W., and M. Van der Riet. 1979. Uptake of solar radiation by the sea turtle (*Caretta caretta*) during voluntary surface basking. Comparative Biochemistry and Physiology 63A:471-474.

Sarmiento, C. 2006. Transfer function estimation of trade leakages generated by court rulings in the Hawaii longline fishery. Applied Economics 38:183-190.

Sarti M., L. 2002. Current population status of *Dermochelys coriacea* in the Mexican Pacific coast. Pages 87-89 *in* I. Kinan, editor. Proceedings of the western Pacific sea turtle cooperative research and management workshop. Western Pacific Regional Fishery Management Council. Honolulu, Hawaii.

Sarti M., L., L. Flores O., and A. Aguayo L. 1991. Una nota sobre la alimentacion de *Orcinus orca*. XVI Reunión Internacional para el estudio de los mamiferos marinos. Nuevo Vallarta y la Cruz de Huanacaxtle, Bahía de Banderas. 2-5 April 1991, Nayarit, México.

Sarti M., L., S.A. Eckert, N. García T., and A.R. Barragán. 1996. Decline of the world's largest nesting assemblage of leatherback turtles. Marine Turtle Newsletter 74:2-5.

Sarti M., L., A. Villaseñor G., B. Jimenez A., M. Robles D., and T. Ruiz M. 1986. II Informe de trabajo "Investigación y conservación de las tortugas laúd *Dermochelys coriacea* y golfina *Lepidochelys olivacea* en Mexiquillo, Michoacán." Temporada de anidación 1985-1986. SEDUE (Subdelegación de Ecología), Michoacán, México.

Sarti M., L., B. Jimenez A., J. Carranza S., A. Villaseñor G., and M. Robles D. 1987. III Informe de trabajo "Investigación y Conservación de las tortugas laúd *Dermochelys coriacea* y golfina *Lepidochelys olivacea* en Mexiquillo, Michoacán." Temporada de anidación 1986-1987. SEDUE (Subdelegación de Ecología), Michoacán, México.

Sarti M., L., A. Villaseñor G., J. Carranza S., and M. Robles D. 1989a. V Informe de trabajo "Investigación y Conservación de las tortugas laúd *Dermochelys coriacea* y golfina *Lepidochelys olivacea* en Mexiquillo, Michoacán." Temporada de anidación 1988-1989. SEDUE (Subdelegación de Ecología), Michoacán, México.

Sarti M., L., A. Villaseñor G., B. Jimenez A., J. Carranza S., and M. Robles D. 1989b. Evaluacion prospectiva de las tecnicas conservacionistas utilizadas en el playon de Mexiquillo, Michoacán, México: *Dermochelys coriacea* y *Lepidochelys olivacea*, temporada de anidación 1986-1987. SEDUE (Subdelegación de Ecología), Michoacán, México.

Sarti M., L., A.R. Barragán, D. García Muñoz, N. García, P. Huerta, and F. Vargas. 2007. Conservation and biology of the leatherback turtle in the Mexican Pacific. Chelonian Conservation and Biology 6:70-78.

Sarti M., L., A. Barragán, F. Vargas, P. Huerta, E. Ocampo, A. Tavera, A. Escudero, D. Vasconcelos, M.A. Angeles, N. Morisson, and P. Dutton. 2006. The decline of the Eastern Pacific leatherback and its relation to changes in nesting behavior and distribution. Pages 133-136 *in* N. Pilcher, compiler. Proceedings of the 23rd annual symposium on sea turtle biology and conservation. U.S. Department of Commerce, National Oceanic and Atmospheric Administration Technical Memorandum NMFS-SEFSC-536. Miami, Florida.

Schaub, M., R. Pradel, L. Jenni, and J.-D. Lebreton. 2001. Migrating birds stop over longer than usually thought: an improved capture-recapture analysis. Ecology 82:852-859.

Schmidt-Nielsen, K. 1985. Animal physiology: adaptation and environment. Third edition. Cambridge University Press, Cambridge, United Kingdom.

Schnars, J.L., and E.A. Standora. 2004. Secondary sea-finding cues in olive ridley (*Lepidochelys olivacea*) and leatherback (*Dermochelys coriacea*) hatchlings. Page 368 *in* M.S. Coyne and R.D. Clark, compilers. Proceedings of the 21st annual symposium on sea turtle biology and conservation. U.S. Department of Commerce, National Oceanic and Atmospheric Administration Technical Memorandum NMFS-SEFSC-528. Miami, Florida.

Schroeder, B.A., and N.B. Thompson. 1987. Distribution of the loggerhead turtle, *Caretta caretta*, and the leatherback turtle, *Dermochelys coriacea*, in the Cape Canaveral Florida area: results of aerial surveys. Pages 45-53 *in* W.N. Witzell, editor. Ecology of east Florida sea turtles. U.S. Department of Commerce, National Oceanic and Atmospheric Administration Technical Report NMFS 53. Miami, Florida.

Schulz, J.P. 1964. Zeeschildpadden, 1, Een Literatuurstudie; 2, Zeeschildpadden in Suriname. Paramaribo, Dienst Landsbosbeheer. Paramaribo, Suriname.

Schulz, J.P. 1971. Situation report on marine turtles nesting in Surinam. Pages 68-74 *in* Marine Turtles. International Union for the Conservation of Nature (IUCN) Publication New Series, Supple. Paper 31. Morges, Switzerland.

Schulz, J.P. 1975. Sea turtles nesting in Surinam. Zoologische Verhandelingen 143:1-143.

Schumacher, G.H. 1973. The head muscles and hyolaryngeal skeleton of turtles and crocodilians. Pages 101-199 *in* C. Gans, editor. Biology of the Reptilia, Volume 4D. Academic Press, London, United Kingdom.

Sears, J.H. 1887. *Dermatochelys coriacea*, trunk back or leathery turtle. Essex Inst. 18, 1886:87-94.

Seminoff, J.A., and P.H. Dutton. 2007. Leatherback turtle (*Dermochelys coriacea*) in the Gulf of California: distribution, demography, and human interactions. Chelonian Conservation and Biology 6:137-142.

Seminoff, J.A., and W.J. Nichols. 2007. Sea turtles and the Alto Golfo: a struggle for survival. Pages 405-424 *in* R.S. Felger and B. Broyles, editors. Dry borders. University of Utah Press, Salt Lake City, Utah.

Seminoff, J.A., F.V. Paladino, and A.G.J. Rhodin. 2007a. Refocusing on leatherbacks: conservation challenges and signs of success. Chelonian Conservation and Biology 6:1-6.

Seminoff, J.A., F.V. Paladino, and A.G.J. Rhodin, editors. 2007b. Special focus issue: the leatherback turtle, *Dermochelys coriacea*, No. 2. Chelonian Conservation and Biology 6:1-160.

Shaffer, H.B., P. Meylan, and M.L. McKnight. 1997. Tests of turtle phylogeny: molecular, morphological, and paleontological approaches. Systematic Biology 46:235-268.

Shanker, K., and B.C. Choudhury, editors. 2006. Marine turtles of the Indian Subcontinent. Universities Press, Hyderabad, India.

Shanker, K., B. Pandav, and H.V. Andres. 2003. Sea turtle conservation research and management techniques. A GOI-UNDP Project Manual. Centre for Herpetology/Madras Crocodile Bank Trust. Mamallapuram, Tamil Nadu, India.

Sharma, D.S.K., and L. Min Min. 2002. Partnerships in turtle conservation: a case study at Ma' Daerah, Terengganu, Peninsular Malaysia. Pages 125-130 *in* I. Kinan, editor. Proceedings of the western Pacific sea turtle cooperative research and management workshop. Western Pacific Regional Fishery Management Council, Honolulu, Hawaii.

Sharma, S.C. 2006. Background and scope of the GOI-UNDP sea turtle project. Pages 22-29 *in* K. Shanker and B.C. Choudhury, editors. Marine turtles of India. Universities Press, Hyderabad, India.

Shaver, D.J. 1990. Hypothermic stunning of sea turtles in Texas. Marine Turtle Newsletter 48:25-27.

Sherrill-Mix, S.A., M.C. James, and R.A. Myers. 2007. Migration cues and timing in leatherback sea turtles. Behavioral Ecology 19:231-236.

Shillinger, G.L. 2005. The Eastern Tropical Pacific Seascape: an innovative model for transboundary marine conservation. Pages 320-331 *in* R. Mittermeier et al., editors. Transboundary conservation—a new vision for protected areas. CEMEX, Conservation International, Agrupacion Sierra Madre. Washington, D.C.

Shillinger, G.L., D.M. Palacios, H. Bailey, S.J. Bograd, A.M. Swithenbank, P. Gaspar, B.P. Wallace, J.R. Spotila, F.V. Paladino, R. Piedra, S.A. Eckert, and B.A. Block. 2008. Persistent leatherback turtle migrations present opportunities for conservation. PLoS Biol 6:1408-1416.

Shoop, C.R., and R.D. Kenney. 1992. Seasonal distributions and abundances of loggerhead and leatherback sea turtles in waters of the northeastern United States. Herpetological Monographs 6:43-67.

Shoop, C.R., T.R. Doty, and N.E. Bray. 1981. Sea turtles in the region between Cape Hatteras and Nova Scotia in 1979. Pages IX-2—IX-85 *in* A characterization of marine mammals and turtles in the mid- and north-Atlantic areas of the U.S. outer continental shelf. Annual Report for 1979: Cetacean and Turtle Assessment Program. University of Rhode Island, Kingston, Rhode Island.

Simkiss, K. 1962. The sources of calcium for the ossification of the embryos of the giant leathery turtle. Comparative Biochemistry and Physiology 7:71-79.

Siow, K.T. 1982. Leathery turtle (*Dermochelys coriacea*) conservation programme in Rantau Abang, Terengganu, Malaysia. Pages 83-90 *in* K.S. Ong and A.A. Jothy, editors. Proceedings of the first marine science conference, Malaysian Society of Marine Science. Penang, Malaysia.

Sipos, J.C., and R.G. Ackman. 1968. Jellyfish (*Cyanea capillata*) lipids: fatty acid composition. Journal of the Fisheries Research Board, Canada 25:1561-1569.

Sivasundar, A., and K.V. Devi Prasad. 1996. Placement and predation of nest in leatherback sea turtles in the Andaman Islands, India. Hamadryad 21:36-42.

Sjögren, S.J. 1945. Über die embryonalentwicklung dees Sauropsiden-magens. Acta Anatomica Supplement 2:1-223.

Smith, A. 1849. Appendix to illustrations of the zoology of South Africa. Reptiles. London: 1-28.

Smith, H.M., and E.H. Taylor. 1950. An annotated checklist and key to the reptiles of México, exclusive of snakes. Bulletin of the United States National Museum 199:1-253.

Smith, H.M., and R.B. Smith. 1980. Synopsis of the herpetofauna of México. Volume VI: Guide to Mexican turtles. Bibliographic addendum 3. John Johnson. North Bennington, Vermont.

Smith, M.A. 1951. The British amphibians and reptiles. The New Naturalist. Collins Publishers, London, United Kingdom.

Sola, C.R., de. 1931. The turtles of the northeastern states. Bulletin of the New York Zoological Society 34:130-159.

Solomon, S.E., and J. Reid. 1983. The effect of the mammillary layer on egg shell formation in reptiles. Animal Technology 34:1-10.

Solomon, S.E., and J.M. Watt. 1985. The structure of the egg shell of the leatherback turtle (*Dermochelys coriacea*). Animal Technology 36:19-27.

Solomon, S.E., and T. Baird. 1979. Aspects of the biology of *Chelonia mydas* L. Pages 17:374-381 *in* M. Barnes, editor. Oceanography and marine biology: an annual review. Aberdeen University Press, Aberdeen, Scotland, United Kingdom.

Soslau, G., B.P. Wallace, C. Vicente, S.J. Goldenberg, T. Tupis, J. Spotila, R. George, F. Paladino, B. Whitaker, G. Violetta, and R. Piedra. 2004. Comparison of functional aspects of the coagulation cascade in human and sea turtle plasmas. Comparative Biochemistry and Physiology 138:399-406.

Sotherland, P.R., B.P. Wallace, J.R. Spotila, C. Ralph, and T. Muir. 2007. Tidal movement of the water table and its effect on oxygen levels in leatherback turtle (*Dermochelys coriacea*) nests at Parque Nacional Las Baulas, Costa Rica. Page 62 *in* R.B. Mast, B.J. Hutchinson, and A.H. Hutchinson, compilers. Proceedings of the 24th annual symposium on sea turtle biology and conservation. U.S. Department of Commerce, National Oceanic and Atmospheric

Administration Technical Memorandum NMFS-SEFSC-567. Miami, Florida.

Soto, J.M.R., R.C.P. Beheregaray, and R.A.R. de P. Rebello. 1997. Range extension: nesting by *Dermochelys* and *Caretta* in southern Brazil. Marine Turtle Newsletter 77:6-7.

Sounguet, G.-P., C. Mbina, and A. Formia. 2004. Sea turtle research and conservation in Gabon by Adventures Sans Frontières: an organizational profile. Marine Turtle Newsletter 105:19-21.

Southwood, A.L., R.D. Andrews, M.E. Lutcavage, F.V. Paladino, N.H. West, R.H. George, and D.R. Jones. 1999. Heart rates and diving behavior of leatherback sea turtles in the eastern Pacific Ocean. Journal of Experimental Biology 202:1115-1125.

Southwood, A.L., R.D. Andrews, F.V. Paladino, and D.R. Jones. 2005. Effects of diving and swimming behavior on body temperatures of Pacific leatherback turtles. Physiological and Biochemical Zoology 78:285-297.

Spoczynska, J.O.I. 1970. Rearing hatchlings of *Dermochelys coriacea* L. British Journal of Herpetology 4:189-192.

Spotila, J.R., and E.A. Standora 1985. Environmental constraints on the thermal energetics of sea turtles. Copeia 1985:694-702.

Spotila, J.R., P.W. Lommen, G.S. Bakken, and D.M. Gates. 1973. A mathematical model for body temperatures of large reptiles: implications for dinosaur ecology. American Naturalist 107:391-404.

Spotila, J.R., M.P. O'Connor, P. Dodson, and F.V. Paladino. 1991. Hot and cold running dinosaurs: body size, metabolism and migration. Modern Geology 16:203-227.

Spotila, J.R., R.D. Reina, A.C. Steyermark, P.T. Plotkin, and F.V. Paladino. 2000. Pacific leatherback turtles face extinction. Nature 405:529-530.

Spotila, J.R., A.E. Dunham, A.J. Leslie, A.C. Steyermark, P.T. Plotkin, and F.V. Paladino. 1996. Worldwide population decline of *Dermochelys coriacea*: are leatherback turtles going extinct? Chelonian Conservation and Biology 2:209-222.

South Pacific Regional Environment Programme (SPREP). 2007. Marine Turtle Action Plan 2008-2012. Pages 19-30 *in* Pacific islands regional marine species programme 2008-2012. Secretariat of the South Pacific Regional Environment Programme. Apia, Samoa.

Squires, H.J. 1954. Records of marine turtles in the Newfoundland area. Copeia 1954:68.

Standora, E.A., and J.R. Spotila. 1985. Temperature dependent sex determination in sea turtles. Copeia 1985:711-722.

Standora, E.A., J.R. Spotila, J.A. Keinath, and C.R. Shoop. 1984. Body temperatures, diving cycles, and movement of a subadult leatherback turtle, *Dermochelys coriacea*. Herpetologica 40:169-176.

Standora, M., K.P. Baker, and F.V. Paladino. 2000. Acoustic orientation and sound discrimination in leatherback (*Dermochelys coriacea*) and olive ridley (*Lepidochelys olivacea*) sea turtle hatchlings. Page 8 *in* H.J. Kalb and T. Wibbels, compilers. Proceedings of the 19th annual symposium on sea turtle biology and conservation. U.S. Department of Commerce, National Oceanic and Atmospheric Administration Technical Memorandum NMFS-SEFSC-443. Miami, Florida.

Starbird, C., and H. Audel. 2000. *Dermochelys coriacea* (leatherback sea turtle): fishing net ingestion. Herpetological Review 31:43.

Starbird, C.H., and M.M. Suarez. 1994. Leatherback sea turtle nesting on the north Vogelkop coast of Irian Jaya and the discovery of a leatherback sea turtle fishery on Kei Kecil Island. Page 143 *in* K.A. Bjorndal, A.B. Bolten, D.A. Johnson, and P.J. Eliazar, compilers. Proceedings of the 14th annual symposium on sea turtle biology and conservation. U.S. Department of Commerce, National Oceanic and Atmospheric Administration Technical Memorandum NMFS-SEFSC-351. Miami, Florida.

Starbird, C.H., A. Baldridge, and J.T. Harvey. 1993. Seasonal occurrence of leatherback sea turtles (*Dermochelys coriacea*) in the Monterey Bay region, with notes on other sea turtles, 1986-1991. California Fish and Game 79:54-62.

Stebbins, R.C. 1966. A field guide to western reptiles and amphibians. Riverside Press, Houghlin Mifflin Co., Boston, Massachusetts.

Stejneger, L. 1907. Herpetology of Japan and adjacent territory. Bulletin of the United States National Museum 58:1-577.

Stejneger, L., and T. Barbour. 1917. Checklist of North American amphibians and reptiles. Harvard University Press, Boston, Massachusetts.

Stephen, A.C. 1961. Scottish turtle records 1954-1960. Scottish Naturalist 70:43-47.

Sternberg, J. 1981. The worldwide distribution of sea turtle nesting neaches. Sea Turtle Rescue Fund, Center for Environmental Education, Washington, D.C.

Stewart, K.R. 2007. Establishment and growth of a sea turtle rookery: the population biology of the leatherback in Florida. Ph.D. dissertation, Duke University, Durham, North Carolina.

Stewart, K., and C. Johnson. 2006. *Dermochelys coriacea*—leatherback sea turtle *in* P.A. Meylan, editor. Biology and conservation of Florida turtles. Chelonian Research Monographs 3:144-157.

Stewart, K., C. Johnson, and M.H. Godfrey. 2007. The minimum size of leatherbacks at reproductive maturity, with a review of sizes for nesting females from the Indian, Atlantic and Pacific Ocean basins. Herpetological Journal 17:123-128.

Stewart, K., J.M. Keller, C. Johnson, and J.R. Kucklick. 2008. Baseline contaminant concentrations in leatherback sea turtles and maternal transfer to eggs confirmed. Page 30 *in* A.F. Rees, M. Frick, A. Panagopoulou, and K. Williams, compilers. Proceedings of the 27th annual symposium on sea turtle biology and conservation. U.S. Department of Commerce, National Oceanic and Atmospheric Administration Technical Memorandum NMFS-SEFSC-569. Miami, Florida.

Steyermark, A.C., K. Williams, J.R. Spotila, F.V. Paladino, D.C. Rostal, S.J. Morreale, M.T. Koberg, and R. Arauz. 1996. Nesting leatherback turtles at Las Baulas National Park, Costa Rica. Chelonian Conservation and Biology 2:173-183.

Stick, K., and L. Hreha. 1989. Summary of the 1988 Washington/Oregon experimental thresher shark gillnet fishery. State of Washington Department of Fisheries Progress Report No. 275. Seattle, Washington.

Stinson, M.L. 1984. Biology of sea turtles in San Diego Bay, California, and in the northeastern Pacific Ocean. M.S. thesis, San Diego State University, San Diego, California.

Storelli, M.M., and G.O. Marcotrigiano. 2003. Heavy metal residues in tissues of marine turtles. Marine Pollution Bulletin 46:397-400.

Suarez, A., and C.H. Starbird. 1996. Subsistence hunting of leatherback turtles, *Dermochelys coriacea*, in the Kai Islands, Indonesia. Chelonian Conservation and Biology 2:190-195.

Swimmer, Y., and R. Brill, editors. 2006. Sea turtle and pelagic fish sensory biology: developing techniques to reduce sea turtle bycatch in longline fisheries. U.S. Department of Commerce, National Oceanic and Atmospheric Administration Technical Memorandum NMFS-PIFSC-7. Honolulu, Hawaii.

Tambiah, C.R. 1994. Saving sea turtles or killing them: the case of U.S. regulated TEDs in Guyana and Suriname. Pages 149-151 *in* K.A. Bjorndal, A.B. Bolten, D.A. Johnson, and P.J. Eliazar, compilers. Proceedings of the 14th annual symposium on sea turtle biology and conservation. U.S. Department of Commerce, National Oceanic and Atmospheric Administration Technical Memorandum NMFS-SEFSC-351. Miami, Florida.

Tapilatu, R.F., and M. Tiwari. 2007. Leatherback turtle, *Dermochelys coriacea*, hatching success at Jamursba-Medi and Warmon Beaches in Papua, Indonesia. Chelonian Conservation and Biology 6:154-159.

Taranetz, A.J. 1938. [*On the new findings of southern elements in the ichthyofauna of the northwestern part of the Japan Sea*]. (Original in Russian). Vestnik Dalnevostochnogo Filiala Akademii Nauk SSSR 28:113-127.

Tarvey, L. 1993. First nesting records for the leatherback turtle *Dermochelys coriacea* in northern New South Wales, Australia, and field management of nest sites. Pages 233-237 *in* D. Lunney and D. Ayers, editors. Herpetology in Australia: a diverse discipline. Royal Zoological Society of New South Wales, Chipping Norton, New South Wales, Austrialia.

Terentjev, P.V., and S.A. Chernov. 1949. Opredelitel presmykayushchikhsya i zemnovodnykh [*Key to Amphibians and Reptiles, Third Edition*]. Moscow. Translated from Russian by L. Kochva, Israel Program for Scientific Translations, Jerusalem (1965).

Thomé, J.C.A., C. Baptistotte, L.M. de P. Moreira, J.T. Scalfoni, A.P. Almeida, D.B. Rieth, and P.C.R. Barata. 2007. Nesting biology and conservation of the leatherback sea turtle (*Dermochelys coriacea*) in the state of Espírito Santo, Brazil. Chelonian Conservation and Biology 6:15-27.

Thompson, M.B. 1993. Oxygen consumption and energetics of development in eggs of the leatherback turtle, *Dermochelys coriacea*. Comparative Biochemistry and Physiology 104:49-453.

Threlfall, W. 1978. First record of the Atlantic leatherback turtle (*Dermochelys coriacea*) from Labrador. Canadian Field-Naturalist 92:287.

Threlfall, W. 1979. Three species of Digenea from the Atlantic leatherback turtle (*Dermochelys coriacea*). Canadian Journal of Zoology 57:1825-1829.

Tickell, S.R. 1862. A rare and little-described species of turtle. Journal of the Asiatic Society of Bengal 31:367-370.

Tobias, W. 1991. Turtles caught in Caribbean swordfish net fishery. Marine Turtle Newsletter 53:10-12.

Travaglini, A., G. Treglia, G. De Martino, and F. Bentivegna. 2006. Preliminary observations on dietary habits of leatherback turtles found in the mid-southern Tyrrhenian Sea, Italy. Page 205 *in* M. Frick, A. Panagopoulou, A.F. Rees, and K. Williams, compilers. Book of abstracts for the 26th annual symposium on sea turtle biology and conservation. Island of Crete, Greece.

Tripathy, B., K. Shanker, and B.C. Choudhury. 2006. Sea turtles and their nesting habitats along the Andhra Pradesh coast. Pages 68-87 *in* K. Shanker and B.C. Choudhury, editors. Marine turtles of India. Universities Press, Hyderabad, India.

Troëng, S. 2000. Predation of green (*Chelonia mydas*) and leatherback (*Dermochelys coriacea*) turtles by jaguars (*Panthera onca*) at Tortuguero National Park, Costa Rica. Chelonian Conservation and Biology 3:751-753.

Troëng, S., and C. Drews. 2004. Money talks: economic aspects of marine turtle use and conservation. World Wildlife Fund (WWF)-International, Gland, Switzerland.

Troëng, S., D. Chacón C., and B. Dick. 2004. Possible decline in leatherback turtle *Dermochelys coriacea* nesting along the coast of Caribbean Central America. Oryx 38:395-403.

Troëng, S., E. Harrison, D. Evans, A. de Haro, and E. Vargas. 2007. Leatherback turtle nesting trends and threats at Tortuguero, Costa Rica. Chelonian Conservation and Biology 6:117-122.

Tucker, A.D. 1988. A summary of leatherback turtle, *Dermochelys coriacea*, nesting at Culebra, Puerto Rico, from 1984-1987 with management recommendations. Unpublished report to the U.S. Department of Interior, Fish and Wildlife Service, Washington, D.C.

Tucker, A.D., and N.B. Frazer. 1991. Reproductive variation in leatherback sea turtles, *Dermochelys coriacea*, at Culebra National Wildlife Refuge, Puerto Rico. Herpetologica 47:115-124.

Tucker, A.D., and K.V. Hall. 1984. Leatherback turtle (*Dermochelys coriacea*) nesting in Culebra, Puerto Rico, 1984. Unpublished annual report to the U.S. Department of Interior, Fish and Wildlife Service, Washington, D.C.

Turtle Expert Working Group (TEWG). 2007. An assessment of the leatherback turtle population in the Atlantic Ocean. U.S. Department of Commerce, National Oceanic and Atmospheric Administration Technical Memorandum NMFS-SEFSC-555. Miami, Florida.

Underwood, G.L. 1970. The eye. Pages 1-97 *in* C. Gans and T.S. Parsons, editors. Biology of the Reptilia, Volume 2. Academic Press, New York City, New York.

United Nations Environment Programme-Convention on Migratory Species (UNEP-CMS). 2000. Conservation measures for marine turtles of the Atlantic coast of Africa. CMS Technical Series No. 5. Bonn, Germany.

United Nations Educational, Scientific and Cultural Organization (UNESCO). 2006. Eastern tropical Pacific seascape project. <http://whc.unesco.org/en/activities/14/> (15 April 2011).

Vaillant, M.L. 1877. Note sur la disposition des vertèbres cervicales chez quelques Chéloniens. Bulletin de la Société Philomáthique, Paris 3. 1:13-15.

Vaillant, M.L. 1896. Remarques sur l'appareil digestif et le mode d'alimentation de la Tortue luth. Comptes rendu Scéanes Académie des sciences (Paris) 123:654-656.

van Buskirk, J., and L.B. Crowder. 1994. Life-history variation in marine turtles. Copeia 1994: 66-81.

van Denburgh, J. 1905. On the occurrence of the leatherback, *Dermochelys*, on the coast of California. Proceedings of the California Academy of Sciences 4:51-61.

van Denburgh, J. 1922. The reptiles of western North America. Pages 623-1028 *in* Occasional papers of the California Academy of Sciences. II: Snakes and Turtles. San Francisco, California.

van Denburgh, J. 1924. A fifth record of the Pacific leatherback turtle on the coast of California. Copeia 1924:53.

Vandelli, D. 1761. Epistola de Holothurio, et *Testudine coriacea* ad celeberrimun Carolum Linnaeum Equitem Naturae Curiosum Dioscoridem II. Consatti, Patavii (Padova). Italy.

Vaz Ferreira Guadalupe, C. 1972. Relaciones de convivencia entre *Libinia spinosa* Milne Edwards (Decapoda, Brachyura) y Discomedusae. Boletin de la Sociedad Zoologica del Uruguay 2:64-66.

Vandelli, D. 1761. Epistola de Holothurio, et *Testudine coriacea* ad celeberrimun Carolum Linnaeum Equitem Naturae Curiosum Dioscoridem II. Consatti, Patavii (Padova). Italy.

Verhage, B., and E.B. Moundjim. 2005. Three years of marine turtle monitoring in the Gamba Complex of Protected Areas, 2002-2005. Unpublished report to World Wildlife Fund (WWF). Libreville, Gabon.

Verhage, B., E.B. Moundjim, and S.R. Livingstone. 2006. Four years of marine turtle monitoring in the Gamba Complex of Protected Areas, Gabon, Africa, 2002-2006. Unpublished report to World Wildlife Fund (WWF). Libreville, Gabon.

Versluys, J. 1907. Een goed ontwikkelt parasphenoid bij *Dermochelys coriacea* Linn. Tijdschrift der Nederlandsche Dierkundige Vereeniging (2)10, 3:18-19.

Versluys, J. 1910. Bemerkungen zum Parasphenoid von *Dermochelys*. Anatomischer Anzeiger 36:487-495.

Versluys, J. 1913. On the phylogeny of the carapace, and on the affinities of the leathery turtle, *Dermochelys coriacea*. Report of the 83rd Meeting of the British Association for Advancement of Science. Reports on the State of Science, Birmingham, U.K. Sect. D. 791-807 (reprint: 1-17).

Versluys, J. 1914. Über die Phylogenie des Panzers der Schildkröten und über die Verwandtschaft der Lederschildkröte *Dermochelys coriacea*. Palaontologische Zeitschrift 1:321-346.

Villanueva-Mayor, V., J. Alfaro, and P. Mayor. 2003. Orientation of leatherback turtle hatchlings, *Dermochelys coriacea*, at Sandy Point National Wildlife Refuge, U.S. Virgin Islands. Pages 235-236 *in* J.A. Seminoff, compiler. Proceedings of the 22nd annual symposium on sea turtle biology and conservation. U.S. Department of Commerce, National Oceanic and Atmospheric Administration Technical Memorandum NMFS-SEFSC-503. Miami, Florida.

Villaseñor G., F. 1988. Aves costeras de Michoacán, México. Tesis Profesional. Biología, Universidad de Michoacán de San Nicolas del Hidalgo. Michoacán, México.

Villiers, A. 1958. Tortues et crocodiles de l'Afrique Noire Francaise. Initiations Africaines 15:1-354.

Völker, H. 1913. Über des Stamm-, Gliedma Ben- und Hautskelet von *Dermochelys coriacea* L. Zoologische Jahrbücher, Abteilung Fur Anatomie und Ontogenie der Tiere 33, 3:431-552. tfl 30-33.

Von Meyer, H. 1847. Mittheilungen an Prof. Bronn. Neues Jahrbuch für Mineralogie, Geologie und Paläontologie Stuttgart: 572-580.

Vose, F.E., and B.V. Shank. 2003. Predation on loggerhead and leatherback post-hatchlings by gray snapper. Marine Turtle Newsletter 99:11-13.

Wallace, B.P., P.R. Sotherland, J.R. Spotila, R.D. Reina, B.F. Franks, and F.V. Paladino. 2004. Biotic and abiotic factors affect the nest environment of embryonic leatherback turtles, *Dermochelys coriacea*. Physiological and Biochemical Zoology 77:423-432.

Wallace, B.P., C.L. Williams, F.V. Paladino, S.J. Morreale, R.T. Lindstron, and J.R. Spotila. 2005. Bioenergetics and diving activity of internesting leatherback turtles *Dermochelys coriacea* at Parque Nacional Marino Las Baulas, Costa Rica. Journal of Experimental Biology 208:3873-3884.

Wallace, B.P., P.R. Sotherland, P.S. Tomillo, S.S. Bouchard, R.D. Reina, J.R. Spotila, and F.V. Paladino. 2006a. Egg components, egg size, and hatchling size in leatherback turtles. Comparative Biochemistry and Physiology 145:524-532.

Wallace, B.P., S.S. Kilham, F.V. Paladino, and J.R. Spotila. 2006b. Energy budget calculations indicate resource limitation in Eastern Pacific leatherback turtles. Marine Ecology Progress Series 318:263-270.

Wallace, B.P., J.A. Seminoff, S.S. Kilham, J.R. Spotila, and P.H. Dutton. 2006c. Leatherback turtles as oceanographic indicators: stable isotope analyses reveal a trophic dichotomy between ocean basins. Marine Biology 149:953-960.

Wallace, B.P., P. Sotherland, P. Santidrián-Tomillo, R. Reina, J. Spotila, and F. Paladino. 2007. Maternal investment in reproduction and its consequences in leatherback turtles. Oecologia 152:37-47.

Wallace, B.P., and T.T. Jones. 2008. What makes marine turtles go: a review of metabolic rates and their consequences. Journal of Experimental Marine Biology and Ecology 356:8-24.

Wallace, B.P., and V.S. Saba. 2009. Environmental and anthropogenic impacts on intra-specific variation in leatherback turtles: opportunities for targeted research and conservation. Endangered Species Research 7:1121.

Watson, J., S. Epperly, A. Shah, and D. Foster. 2005. Fishing methods to reduce sea turtle mortality associated with pelagic longlines. Canadian Journal of Fisheries and Aquatic Sciences 62:965-981.

Wegner, R.N. 1959. Der Schädelbau der Lederschildkröte *Dermochelys coriacea* Linné (1766). Abhandlungen der Deutschen Akademie der Wissenschaften zu Berlin, Klasse fuer Chemie, Geologie und Biologie 4:1-80.

Weir, C.R., T. Ron, M. Morais, and A.D.C. Duarte. 2007. Nesting and at-sea distribution of marine turtles in Angola, West Africa, 2000-2006: occurrence, threats and conservation implications. Oryx 41:224–231.

Wells, K.L. 1960. A note on turtles. Malayan Nature Journal 14:108-120.

Wermuth, H., and R. Mertens. 1977. Testudines, Crocodylia, Rhynchocephalia. Das Tierreich 100:1-174.

Whitmore, C.P., and P.H. Dutton. 1985. Infertility, embryonic mortality and nest-site selection in leatherback and green sea turtles in Suriname. Biological Conservation 34:251-272.

Wibbels, T. 2003. Critical approaches to sex determination in sea turtles. Pages 103-134 *in* P.L. Lutz, J.A. Musick, and J. Wyneken, editors. The biology of sea turtles, Volume 2. CRC Press, Boca Raton, Florida.

Wieland, G.R. 1900. The skull, pelvis and probable relationships of the huge turtles of the genus

Archelon from the Fort Pierre Cretaceous of South Dakota. American Journal of Science, series 4, 9:237-251.

Wieland, G.R. 1902. Notes on the Cretaceous turtles *Toxochelys* and *Archelon*, with a classification of the marine testudinata. American Journal of Science, series 4, 14: 95-108.

Willgohs, J.F. 1956. Nye funn av laerskilpadde i Nordsjoen, og litt. om artens utbredelse og levevis. Naturen 9:532-544.

Willgohs, J.F. 1957. Occurrence of the leathery turtle in the northern North Sea and off western Norway. Nature 179:163-164.

Williams, E.E. 1950. Variation and selection in the cervical central articulations of living turtles. Bulletin of the American Museum of Natural History 94:505-562.

Williams, E.H., L. Bunkley-Williams, R.H. Boulon, Jr., K.L. Eckert, and N.L. Bruce. 1996. *Excorallana acuticauda* (Isopoda, Corallanidae) an associate of leatherback turtles in the northeastern Caribbean, with a summary of isopods recorded from sea turtles. Crustaceana 69:1014-1017.

Wills, J.H., Jr. 1966. Seafood toxins. Pages 147-163 *in* Toxicants occurring naturally in foods. Publication No. 1354, National Academy of Sciences. National Research Council, Washington, D.C.

Witham, R. 1977. *Dermochelys coriacea* in captivity. Marine Turtle Newsletter 3:6.

Witham, R., and C.R. Futch. 1977. Early growth and oceanic survival of pen-reared sea turtles. Herpetologica 33:404-409.

Witherington, B.E., and L.M. Ehrhart. 1989. Hypothermic stunning and mortality of marine turtles in the Indian River Lagoon System, Florida. Copeia 1989:696-703.

Witherington, B.E., and R.E. Martin. 1996. Understanding, assessing, and resolving light pollution problems on sea turtle nesting beaches. Florida Marine Research Institute Technical Report TR-2. Tallahassee, Florida.

Witt, M.J., A.C. Broderick, D.J. Johns, C. Martin, R. Penrose, M.S. Hoogmoed, and B.J. Godley. 2007a. Prey landscapes help identify potential foraging habitats for leatherback turtles in the NE Atlantic. Marine Ecology Progress Series 337:231-243.

Witt, M.J., R. Penrose, and B.J. Godley. 2007b. Spatio-temporal patterns of juvenile marine turtle occurrence in waters of the European continental shelf. Marine Biology 151:873-885.

Witt, M.J., A.C. Broderick, M.S. Coyne, A. Formia, S. Ngouessono, R.J. Parnell, G.-P. Sounguet, and B.J. Godley. 2008. Satellite tracking highlights difficulties in the design of effective protected areas for critically endangered leatherback turtles *Dermochelys coriacea* during the inter-nesting period. Oryx 42:296-300.

Witt, M.J., B. Baert, A.C. Broderick, A. Formia, J. Fretey, A. Gibudi, G.A.M. Mounguengui, C. Moussounda, S. Ngouessono, R.J. Parnell, D. Roumet, G.-P. Sounguet, B. Verhage, A. Zogo, and B.J. Godley. 2009. Aerial surveying of the world's largest leatherback turtle rookery: a more effective methodology for large-scale monitoring. Biological Conservation 142:1719-1727.

Witzell, W.N. 1984. The incidental capture of sea turtles in the Atlantic U.S. Fishery Conservation Zone by the Japanese tuna longline fleet, 1978-1981. Marine Fisheries Review 46:56-58.

Witzell, W.N. 1999. Distribution and relative abundance of sea turtles caught incidentally by the U.S. pelagic longline fleet in the western North Atlantic Ocean, 1992-1995. Fishery Bulletin 97:200-211.

Witzell, W.N., and W.G. Teas. 1994. The impacts of anthropogenic debris on marine turtles in the western North Atlantic Ocean. U.S. Department of Commerce, National Oceanic and Atmospheric Administration Technical Memorandum NMFS-SEFSC-355. Miami, Florida.

Wold, C. 2002. The status of sea turtles under international environmental law and international environmental agreements. Journal of International Wildlife Law and Policy 5:11-48.

Wolke, R.E. 1981. Summary report of sea turtle necropsy research, U.S. Atlantic seaboard, 1980. Report to the National Marine Fisheries Service, Southeast Fisheries Center, Miami, Florida.

Wood, R.C. 1973. Fossil marine turtle remains from the Paleocene of the Congo. Annales du Musee Royal de l'Afrique Centrale, Sciences Zoologiques, Tervuren, Belgique 75:1-28.

Wood, R.C., J. Johnson-Gove, E.S. Gaffney, and K.F. Maley. 1996. Evolution and phylogeny of leatherback turtles (Dermochelyidea), with descriptions of new fossil taxa. Chelonian Conservation and Biology 2:266-286

Worrell, E. 1963. Reptiles of Australia. Angus and Robertson, Sydney, Australia.

Wyneken, J. 1997. Sea turtle locomotion: mechanisms, behavior, and energetics. Pages 165-198 *in* P.L. Lutz and J.A. Musick, editors. The biology of sea turtles. CRC Press, Boca Raton, Florida.

Wyneken, J. 2001. The anatomy of sea turtles. U.S. Department of Commerce, National Oceanic and Atmospheric Administration Technical Memorandum NMFS-SEFSC-470. Miami, Florida.

Wyneken, J., and M. Salmon. 1992. Frenzy and post-frenzy swimming activity in loggerhead, green, and leatherback hatchling turtles. Copeia 1992:478-484.

Wyneken, J., A.G.J. Rhodin, A. Garces, and J.A.G. Rhodin. 2003. Cardiopulmonary structure and function in leatherback and green sea turtles. Page 28 *in* J.A. Seminoff, compiler. Proceedings of the 22nd annual symposium on sea turtle biology and conservation. U.S. Department of Commerce, National Oceanic and Atmospheric Administration Technical Memorandum NMFS-SEFSC-503. Miami, Florida.

Yañez A., P. 1951. Vertebrados marinos chilenos, III Reptiles. Revista de Biología Marina 3:1-19.

Yerger, R.W. 1965. The leatherback turtle on the Gulf coast of Florida. Copeia 1965:365-366.

Yusuf, A., H. Suganuma, A. Wahid, and Y. Bakarbessy. 2006. The leatherback sea turtle conservation system at Jamursba Medi, Indonesia. Page 106 *in* N. Pilcher, compiler. Proceedings of the 23rd annual symposium on sea turtle biology and conservation. U.S. Department of Commerce, National Oceanic and Atmospheric Administration Technical Memorandum NMFS-SEFSC-536. Miami, Florida.

Zangerl, R. 1980. Patterns of phylogenetic differentiation in the Toxochelyid and Chelonid sea turtles. American Zoologist 20:585-596.

Zug, G.R. 1966. The penial morphology and the relationships of the cryptodiran turtles. Occasional Papers of the Museum of Zoology, University of Michigan 647:1-24.

Zug, G.R., and J.F. Parham. 1996. Age and growth in leatherback turtles, *Dermochelys coriacea* (Testudines: Dermochelyidae): a skeletochronological analysis. Chelonian Conservation and Biology 2:244-249.

Zulkifli, T., A. Ahmad, K.Y. Ku-Kassim, and M.I. Mahyam, editors. 2004. Conservation and enhancement of sea turtles in the Southeast Asia region. Marine Fishery Resources Development and Management Department, Southeast Asian Fisheries Development Center. Kuala Terengganu, Malaysia.

Zullo, V.A., and J.S. Bleakney. 1966. The cirriped *Stomatolepas elegans* (Costa) on leatherback turtles from Nova Scotia waters. Canadian Field-Naturalist 80:162-165.

Appendix A

Life stages of the leatherback sea turtle, *Dermochelys coriacea* (photographers in parentheses).

Hatchling pips the egg (Scott A. Eckert); crosses the nesting beach (Jenny Freestone); and swims (Scott A. Eckert)

Very young juvenile strands alive in Dominica, West Indies (Rowan Byrne; Byrne & Eckert 2006)

Yearling raised in captivity at the University of British Columbia, Vancouver, Canada (Robert George, DVM)

An adult female nests in French Guiana (Benoit deThoisy) and dives off the Mexican Pacific coast (Scott A. Eckert)

Appendix B

Leatherback sea turtle cranial skeleton: skull dorsal, ventral views. Source: Wyneken (2001:23, 24).

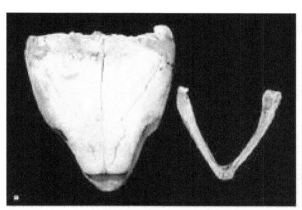
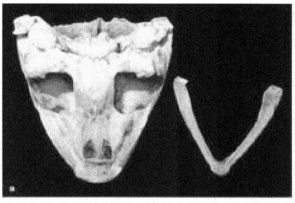
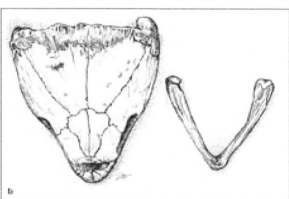
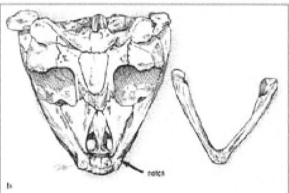

Figs. 43a and 43b. *Dermochelys coriacea*, dorsal skull and lower jaw. The bones fit together more loosely than in other species. The leatherback skull and skeleton has been described as neotenic (having embryonic characteristics) in form because of the lack of bony fusions.

Figs. 44a and 44b. *Dermochelys coriacea*, ventral skull and lower jaw. Note the lack of a secondary palate and the loose articulations of the bones.

Appendix C

Leatherback sea turtle post-cranial skeleton. Sources: Fretey (1981:21) adapted from Deraniyagala (1939), and Pritchard & Trebbau (1984:254) with carapace bones (D) adapted from Remane (1936) and the plastral view of the shell with elimination of remnants of mosaic bones (E) adapted from Deraniyagala (1939).

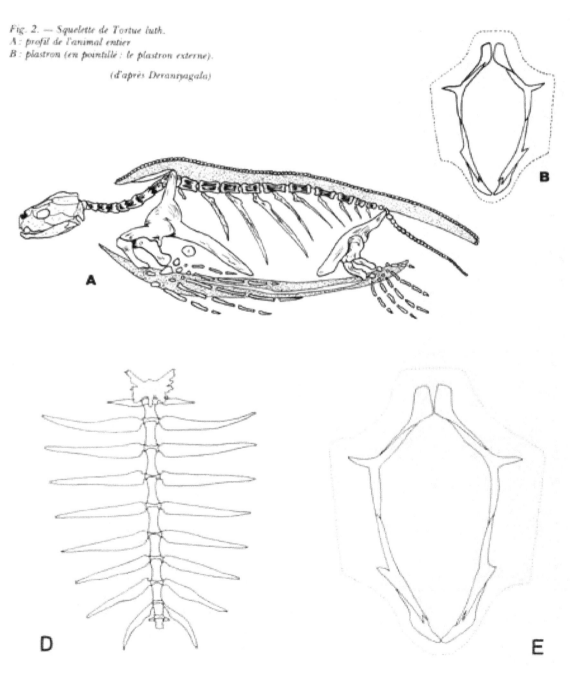

Leatherback sea turtle post-cranial skeleton: front, hind flippers. Source: Wyneken (2001:53, 57).

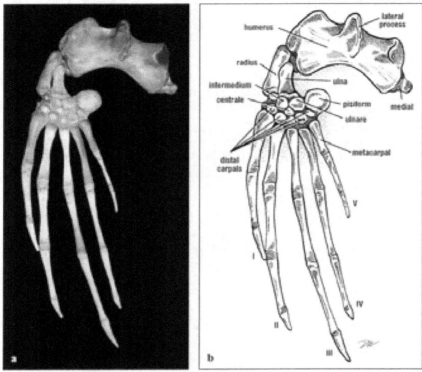

Figs. 102a and 102b. *Dorsal view of a leatherback flipper.*

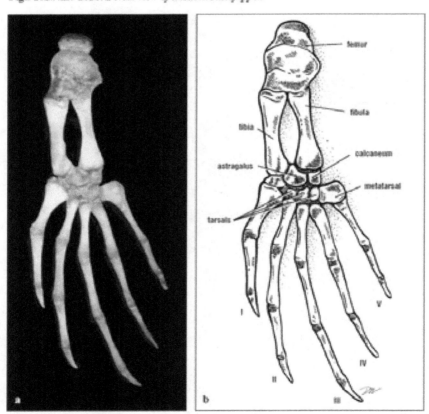

Figs. 109a and 109b. *Dorsal view of a leatherback hind limb. The articulated hind limb shows the extensive cartilages between bones that are typical of the leatherback skeleton. The hind foot is wide and the digits somewhat elongated. Digits are designated by numbers, with I being the digit on the tibial side and V on the fibular side.*

Leatherback sea turtle post-cranial skeleton. Of the usual dermal elements in the carapace, only the nuchal bone is present in *Dermochelys*, leaving the relatively unexpanded ribs free. A complete skeleton on display at the Réserve naturelle de l'Amana in French Guiana illustrates how the "narrow and feeble" ribs remain unfused (but to the vertebrae) in the adult. The slightly flexible keeled carapace owes its form to a mosaic of thousands of small polygonal bones called osteoderms. Photos: (top) Linda Rieu, WWF; (bottom) Scott A. Eckert, WIDECAST.

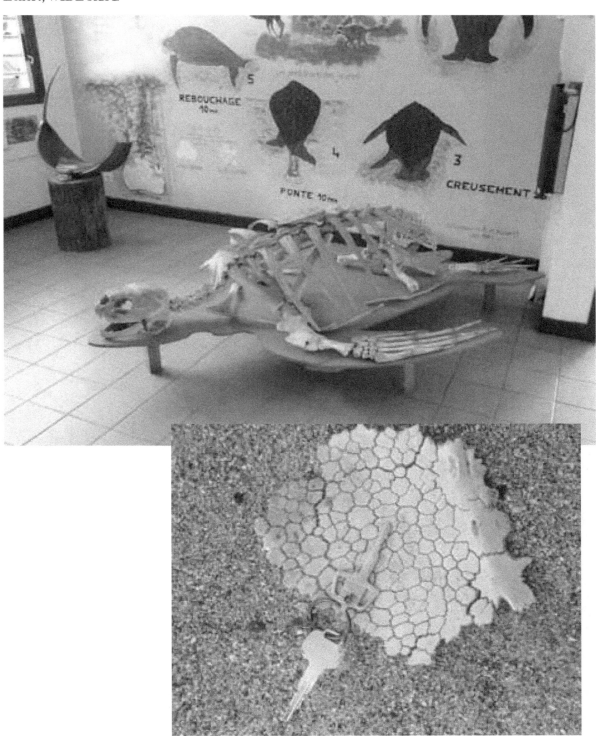

Appendix D

Nesting sequence of the leatherback sea turtle. Approach from the sea (Kimberly Maison), site preparation ("body-pitting") and nest chamber excavation (Scott A. Eckert), egg-laying (Alicia Marin), and nest covering (with measuring) and return to the sea (Carol Guy Stapleton).

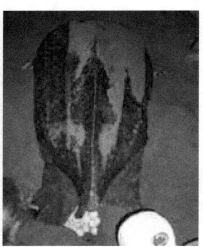

U.S. Department of the Interior
U.S. Fish & Wildlife Service
Route 1, Box 166
Shepherdstown, WV 25443

http://www.fws.gov

January 2012